YANKEE CITY

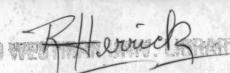

by
W. Lloyd Warner
J. O. Low
Paul S. Lunt
Leo Srole

One volume, abridged edition

Selected and edited by
W. Lloyd Warner

New Haven and London, Yale University Press 1963

To the memory of Edmund E. Day

Preface

THE TEXT of this one-volume edition has been taken from all five volumes of the Yankee City Series. Part ɪ of the present edition derives from Volume ɪ, on the modern community (published 1941), Volume ɪɪ, on the status system (1942), and Volume ᴠ, on symbolic behavior (1959). Part ɪɪ is from the volume on the corporation and the factory (1947); Part ɪɪɪ comes from the volume on ethnic groups (1945). The materials on religion and other sacred symbolic behavior in *The Living and the Dead* were published in paperback form under the title, *The Family of God*, by the Yale University Press (1961). Since they can be found elsewhere, and for the sake of brevity, most tables and charts have been eliminated.

With brief exceptions, including some introductory material, the original text has not been added to or changed; only minor editing has been done to interrelate the several parts of present chapters.

The research on Yankee City was started in 1930 following three years' study of the aborigines of North Australia. The field work on the New England community was pursued by young social scientists, most of them students in social anthropology at Harvard University; most of the analysis was done by graduate students and others at the University of Chicago. All of their names, many of them now well known, are listed in the several volumes of the Yankee City Series. I wish again to thank all of them for their contributions to this research and for the privilege of working with them.

The acknowledgments previously made hold now, including those to our research colleagues and to our financial and professional sponsors. Thanks are given too for brief borrowings from books of mine published elsewhere.

J. O. Low, our friend and colleague, recently died. He was an intimate friend and a highly valued associate. All of us loved him and treasure his memory.

Our association with the Yale University Press has been a long and satisfactory one. I hope the Press and the highly talented people who have helped us and guided our efforts will allow us this opportunity to thank them and to acknowledge publicly our personal and professional indebtedness.

W. LLOYD WARNER

East Lansing, Michigan

September, 1962

Contents

from Vol. 1, 3, 5

Contents   xi

TABLES

FIGURES

Introduction

THE RESEARCH on Yankee City, which this volume reports, studied a contemporary American community to learn about the nature of its social system, to understand how the system and its parts operated, and to identify and interpret the collective symbolic life of the city. The immediate interest was in the community itself; the larger and more important purposes were to use the community as a convenient microcosm for field study, thus to gain new knowledge about the larger American social life, and with similar studies of other societies, to use the results comparatively. The end achieved, it was hoped, might be a more detached view of our own culture.

The major field study was done approximately from 1930 to 1935; later and less intensive work was continued until shortly before the publication of the last volume (1959). The same general approach to the gathering of evidence and its analysis was used as for the earlier field study of the Australian aborigines. A perusal, however, of the five volumes of the series on which the present edition is based quickly reveals that the theories, points of view, and techniques of sociology and social psychology were very much a part of the study. The several intellectual traditions of this study go back immediately and directly to such social scientists as A. R. Radcliffe-Brown, Robert H. Lowie, and Bronislaw Malinowski. The influence of George Mead, Emile Durkheim, George Simmel, and Jean Piaget is strongly felt. The three years' field work on the Australian aborigines established a research model and left its mark on the results of this study of an American community.

Part I of this volume reports on the institutional life of the community and on the social class system. The family, cliques, associations, and other social institutions including the church, school, and politics are examined.

The six social classes are discussed and described. These include the three highest: the old-family aristocracy (upper-upper), the new-family level (lower-upper), and the upper-middle class. These three are sometimes referred to collectively as the Level above the Common Man. The social characteristics of the lower-middle class, one of the largest in the community, exceeded in size only by the upper-lower, are also described. These two levels are sometimes grouped as the Level of the Common Man. Finally, the people of the Level below the Common Man (the lower-lower class), an important one for understanding our feelings about prestige and the operations of power, are studied.

The meanings of status and rank as they relate to the inter-relations of social structure and class values are given detailed treatment. The criteria for the study of rank, in which American social class and other forms can be categorized, are founded on such basic considerations as human adaptations, the effect on the life chances of the individual, and the biological persistence of the species. Two kinds of basic questions about access to each other by the members of the species of any given group help us meet the demands of several tests. First, are the statuses (or status) within a system of rank open to movement to and from them so that those who might seek access or seek to leave them may do so? Is the system of assignment of status such that each individual's position is free so that he can move vertically or horizontally toward others and they to him? Can he and they compete for higher status or strive to maintain their own? Or is the status system closed so that men cannot move from status to status, their own individual positions being so fixed that their careers are confined to one status (or level of rank) and competition for any other status not possible?

The second kind of basic question to be asked is: To what extent are the life of a society and the activities of each indi-

vidual controlled by any order of rank? Is the order's province
limited to certain activities? Is it limited to particular periods
and times? Is it limited to certain individuals? Does it regulate
part of the lives of some people for part of the time but not all
of it? What and how much does it control? In brief, and to
apply terms, is it a limited hierarchy segmenting the membership and activities of the group, or is it inclusive, generally
comprising everyone and all or most of the activities that make
up the round of life of the group and each individual?

When the two polar types of status control—the closed form
(not accessible to free competition) and the open (accessible
to movement into it and allowing movement out)—are combined with the two polar types of hierarchy—the general and
all-inclusive one, which covers most or all of the activities of
the individual in the society, and the segmentary or limited
one, whose controls are confined to a limited part of the society
and its behavior—four basic forms of rank are logically recognizable. Each of the four logical types is satisfied by empirical
reality in the United States. The four types are:

1. The inclusive or general system with open statuses
where free competition prevails among individuals and
families for position. Social class in Yankee City and in
the United States is but one variety. Successful competition is expressed in social mobility.

2. The limited or segmentary system within which the
ranked statuses are open to free competition and there is
movement in and out of the available statuses. Some of
the associations studied in Yankee City are examples.

3. The inclusive or general system whose statuses are
closed and not open to competition. The position of the
individual is fixed in the color caste system of America.

4. The limited or segmentary system closed to free competition where, for the purposes of the hierarchy, the position of the individual is fixed and there is no movement
from status to status. (Part II in this volume, which dis-

cusses certain factories, gives illustrations of this type.)

It will be noted that social class, which allows competition for the more prestigeful and powerful positions, is at one extreme and that color caste, which prohibits movement and competition, is at the other extreme of status closure. The position of the individual and his family is not fixed in social class, for his life chances and those of his family can be, by the nature of the system, improved by competing freely for higher position. The position of the individual and his family in a classical caste system is fixed and determined by birth. He is not free to compete for all or some of the prestige and power of the higher caste. His life chances, as far as caste is involved, are limited. The two forms of rank, however, are alike inasmuch as each covers the whole or most of the activities of those who are members of either system.

Social class is not the same as economic class. Social class refers to levels which are recognizable in the general behavior and the social attitudes of the people of the whole community where such levels exist. Although economic factors are of prime importance and are some of the principal determinants of social class, they are insufficient to account for all social-class behavior or for its presence in contemporary America.

In Part II, the emergence of the modern factory and corporation is studied. The rise of big-city capitalism and the great corporation, particularly as they affect the factories and social life of a small city, are interpreted. The meanings of the closure of the factories for self-advancement, a subsequent strike, and the effective rise of modern unionism are analyzed.

The significance of the ethnic group in American life is considered in Part III. The rise of the later generations of the Irish, Jews, Italians, and several other ethnic groups is interpreted. The advance of the ethnic groups up the steps of the occupational and class ladders and the movement from the lower residential areas up to the higher ones are empirically observed, measured, and interpreted. The symbols of political and class conflict are identified and interpreted.

Part I. Social Class and Social Structure in Yankee City

CHAPTER 1

Yankee City: The Community and its People

YANKEE CITY is situated on a harbor at the mouth of a large river in New England. The pilot of an airplane looking down some 10,000 feet might see the harbor as the dark hand of a giant with its five fingers reaching for the sea. So viewed, the river flowing through the brown land toward the white sandy shores is an arm extended straight back from the hand that bends sharply some few miles from the sea. The streets of the town run along the banks of the river for a few miles up from the harbor until they almost reach the bend in the river.

In shape the town is a long thin rectangle which bends at each end. Near the center of the rectangle at the bank of the river is a square around which the business district is located. The residential area covers the two ends of the rectangle as they extend up and down the river. From the two ends of the town square a highway extends along the water front for the full length of the town. This river street is paralleled, on the other long side of the rectangle, by another broad street which runs along a ridge of high ground from one end of the city to the other. In the center of the city the residential area projects beyond the outline of the rectangle for a few blocks, and a number of dwellings are found outside the rectangle at either end, but, generally speaking, the population is concentrated within the few blocks of streets between the river and the broad street which parallels it on the ridge. The town sits on high ground with a river on one side and flatlands on the other.

The two long avenues, Hill Street and River Street, are connected by a large number of side streets which cross several short streets as they climb from the river to the summit of the hill. A highway, one of the more important motor roads connecting southern with northern New England, crosses the center of Yankee City and leaves it over a large bridge. A railway line parallels this highway and has a station in the town.

Along the river are a large number of wharves and shipyards which were once employed in the sea trade but which were abandoned when the town turned to manufacturing. Most of the factory sites are in and near the business district, but a few are situated in each arm of the rectangle. The residences tend to be larger and better kept on the Hill Street than on the River Street side of the town. There are six cemeteries in the community and one fairly large park and a few small ones.

Several smaller towns are situated in the surrounding countryside. Yankee City maintains its own economic life and is not a satellite community to a large city. It does, however, look to Boston as its metropolis, and movement to and from Boston by automobile and train is frequent. Some of its citizens look ultimately to New York, but none of them would admit it; a very few of them look to Europe for their social centers, and all of these admit it.

Yankee City has some 17,000 people.[1] There are a few more women in its population than there are men. Slightly over 50 per cent of the population were born in or near Yankee City;

1. The reader will notice as he goes through the pages of this volume that our samples of the population vary according to the subject under investigation. The census reports for Yankee City give 15,000 people, but these reports cover only the incorporated large town of Yankee City and do not include the population of the several areas outside the incorporated community which are a part of the town. In addition to the people who live in nearby areas and who are part of the social system of the community, many people come in from outside communities such as Boston and even New York and are a part of the social system. This volume includes some 16,785 people for its largest sample.

23.50 per cent were foreign-born; and the remainder were born elsewhere in the United States. The first impression one gains of the town is that it has a living tradition inherited from generations of Yankee forebears. Yankee City is "old Yankee" and proud of it.

About one fourth of the employable population are in the shoe industry. The other principal but smaller economic activities are silverware manufacturing, the building trades, transport, and electric shops. The clamming industry, the only remaining economic activity of the town which depends on the sea, employs about 1 per cent of those who work for a living.

The semiskilled workers constitute the largest group (46.19 per cent) in our occupational sample. The workers in the factories compose the great bulk of this group. Only 5.28 per cent are classifiable as unskilled.[2] The professional,[3] proprietary, and managerial group comprise a seventh of those economically occupied; wholesale and retail store managers and similar proprietors, 7.92 per cent; clerks and kindred workers, 14.90 per cent; and skilled workers, 11.37 per cent. When the unemployment study was made in 1933, 50.73 per cent of those who were employable had jobs at which they were working,[4] 30.61 per cent were employed part-time, and 18.66 per cent were without work. A little over 13 per cent of the total population were recipients of relief.

According to ethnic affiliations, the Yankees comprised 53.80 per cent (9,030) of the 16,785 individuals represented

2. This sample is somewhat biased because when we studied occupation we did not get as full a census of the unskilled as we did of those who were semi and fully skilled, since a smaller proportion of the latter were in the factories which we studied. However, Yankee City, being an industrial town where skill, as it is ordinarily defined, is more useful than elsewhere, has a higher percentage of skilled workers than most communities.

3. U. S. Bureau of the Census, Alphabetical Index of Occupations by Industries and Social-Economic Groups, 1937. Prepared by Alba M. Edwards, Ph.D., for use in the National Unemployment Census, Washington, U. S. Government Printing Office, 1937.

4. The total sample for the unemployment study was 5,005.

in our study, and the nine other ethnic groups, 45.55 per cent (7,646).[5] There were 3,943 Irish, 1,466 French Canadians, 397 Jews, 284 Italians, 677 Poles, 412 Greeks, 246 Armenians, and 141 Russians. The Negroes, with 80 individuals, constituted the smallest group in the population. The Irish are the oldest ethnic group in Yankee City, other than the Yankees, and the Jews next in order of age. The Russians, Poles, Greeks, and Armenians are comparatively recent migrants.

Yankee City is one of the oldest Yankee cities in the United States. It was founded early in 1600 and by shipbuilding, fishing, and sea trade grew into one of the most prominent of the colonial New England communities. It quickly became a city of several thousand inhabitants. After certain fluctuations in size it attained approximately its present population and has succeeded in maintaining but not in adding to it. At one time the town was of sufficient commercial importance to compete on equal terms with Boston in its trade activities. The histories of the state in which it is located tell of its importance politically and socially and of the role it played in the life of New England at a period of its greatest prosperity. While still an important shoe and silverware manufacturing center, Yankee City is no longer of the same comparative importance; with the general growth of population and industry throughout the United States, like many other New England communities it has not grown but maintained a stable population in a stable society.

The city's earlier farming and shipping industries have largely gone. They helped employ the early Irish immigrants, but with the appearance of the factory the Irish and new immigrant groups were recruited for less skilled jobs in the shoe, textile, and other industries. The older ethnic groups have moved into varying occupations, and some of them have succeeded in climbing to the top of the occupational ladder.

Economically and socially Yankee City is organized very much like other American industrial towns. Its business district is supported by the residential area which surrounds it, and the residential area is supported, at the base at least, by workers

5. There were 109 whose ethnic affiliations were unknown.

who are largely maintained by the wages and salaries of the factories. The town has a city government with a mayor and council; city officials, boards, and committees direct such activities as the school, police, and fire departments. The mayor, council, and school board are elected by the voters.

There are a number of grade schools, parochial and public, and one public high school. There are a large number of Protestant churches, the principal ones belonging to the Congregational, Presbyterian, Unitarian, Baptist, Methodist, and Episcopalian denominations. The two Catholic churches are staffed primarily by Irish and French-Canadian priests and nuns; the congregation of the largest Catholic church is Irish, and of the other, French-Canadian. The Jews have one synagogue in the community and the Russians and Greeks have remodeled a Protestant church into a Greek Orthodox house of worship. There are thousands of members of lodges, secret societies, and fraternities, and of organizations such as the Rotary, Kiwanis, and Chamber of Commerce.

Yankee City is an American town. Its people live a life whose values are in general as understandable to Middle Westerners as they are to men from the Pacific and Atlantic coasts. Specific differences are present; certain kinds of behavior are more definite and more highly developed than elsewhere in the United States, and other ways of life are not quite so heavily accented in Yankee City as in the South or in the West. But while it is important, for a full understanding of the community, to know these differences, it would be erroneous to emphasize them and forget the fundamental similarity to other American towns.

Space, Time, and Population

Seen from the broad view of the human geographer or ethnologist, the history of the United States, its several regions, and its many communities, including Yankee City, is a movement of huge populations from the European land mass westward across a great barrier of water to another part of the earth's land surface. It began in the random efforts of the period of discovery, in the trial and error of exploration. The first phase of the mass migration was from the extreme limits of the Euro-Asian land mass to the coastal periphery of the North American continent. A second phase consisted of at least three aspects, all significant to Yankee City and the historic movement of which she was a part. There was the continuing movement of people across the water to the little coastal cities; and an advance by some of them into the new land, which coincided with the settling of others on the coast. Meanwhile, economic and social interaction was maintained among old and new communities on this and the other side of the Atlantic. Yankee City, from its beginnings, received new settlers from England, some remaining, others leaving for the new frontiers that continually formed with the movement westward. The migrants coming into and going out of this and other settlements of the seaboard carried diverse technical, moral, and spiritual equipment which they modified to adjust to the influences of the new regions. Meanwhile the culture and the general technology differentiated and developed. Greater and greater power for satisfying man's creative needs was exerted over the natural environment.

The history of those who settled on the seaboard involved the establishment and consolidation of new social forms and the remodeling of the older ones brought with them to fit the new physical and human conditions. The history of the migratory peoples who pushed inland beyond the permanent settlements to the new peripheries emphasized random experiment, the need for adaptive responses by each individual and family to immediate conditions for survival, with consequent emphasis on individual autonomy, freedom of choice in action, and the need to share and communicate what was learned.

The moving frontier was a continuous process, a mass advance into a continent, but there were rhythms of comparative quiet and settlement followed by surges of population into and beyond the natural barriers of mountains and deserts and the human ones established by colonizing powers or hostile Indians. As the established order of the older settlements on the seaboard continued to give birth to new western frontiers, the values and beliefs of the new and old conditions influenced each other. From these influences many of the events of history were made, some few of which survive in professional histories and in the memories of the inhabitants, but all *felt* in the mental life of each generation which gives literal embodiment to them.

The conservative and traditional tendencies of the older settlements like Yankee City meant a steady increase in the ordering of the relations of community life, greater control over the human and natural environment, and an increasing appeal to the established order of the past to govern present choices and solve present dilemmas, rather than to the present or future. Political, economic, and moral values and judgments were apt to be conservative in the sense of conserving the past and resisting changes that eliminate it. Furthermore, it meant in fact that those at the top in the community, whose way of life, security, prestige, and power were derived from established forms, were likely to be political, economic, and social conservatives.

When Yankee City began, the local historians all tell us, twenty-two men and their wives and children landed on the Parker River with a general grant in hand to the land, heads of families receiving title in fee simple to a few acres of land and the rights to common pasturage. It may be observed parenthetically that the records show even at this early stage that some men received very small grants and others very large ones. It may be presumed that degree of skill and number of able-bodied persons in the family, as well as status in the group, influenced the distribution.

We shall start with the population figures as a rough measurement of the city's growth. Increase in population is an expression not only in fact—of the developing strength and power of the community—but in American thought and values: of being "bigger and better" and as something positive and good.

Although in the beginning, before Yankee City was founded, Massachusetts as represented by the Separatists at Plymouth grew very slowly, the colony of Massachusetts Bay immediately prospered economically and socially as well as in numbers, partly because of the great Puritan exodus from England. According to reliable local histories, some 2,000 were present by 1630 and by 1640 over 20,000 persons inhabited the small cities, which included such places as Salem, Boston, Ipswich, and the town we have called Yankee City. The twenty-two founding families of Yankee City contributed their bit to this total. By 1760 there were approximately 1,600,000 individuals in the thirteen colonies, one-fourth of them Negro slaves. By 1765 the population of Yankee City, by the computations of the province of Massachusetts Bay, had grown to 2,882. Massachusetts was second only to Virginia in population, and Philadelphia was America's largest city. By the time of the Revolution Yankee City had grown to 3,700, and in 1790, in the first U.S. census, it was 4,800. Ten years later it had grown to almost 6,000. In the census just before the beginning of the War of 1812 it reached a grand total of 7,600, but immediately thereafter dropped considerably, to 6,850 in 1820 and 6,375 in 1830. These increases and decreases, we shall see, are directly related to the economic and social development of the community and to the estimations of it by those who lived and wrote during the times.

After 1830 the population began to rise again, from approximately 7,000 in 1840 to over 13,000 in the 1860's (part of the last ten-year increase was produced by annexation of an urban area). In the seventies it dropped slightly, and thereafter at ten-year intervals increased to reach 14,500 by the turn of the century and 15,000 in 1930.

Since Yankee City has not recently lost population and is still important economically and an autonomous, self-run community, the town in one sense remains the important city she once was. Absolutely speaking, this is true; relatively, it is not. In the difference we find the story of her rise to greatness and the long aftermath when the rapid pace of changing times and the development of a vast continental United States left her behind and the greatness went elsewhere.

The population of the United States in 1790 was almost entirely east of the Alleghenies (95 per cent of the approximate four million total). By 1850 only 55 per cent resided east of these mountains, New England's rate of growth being but 10 per cent, whereas that of the new Northwest had been a 75 per cent increase. At the close of the Revolution there were only five cities with over 8,000 population. Yankee City then, with approximately 4,000 population, ranked as one of the largest in Massachusetts, and in size and economic development an important one in the nation. By 1850, although more than double in population, it was only one of more than a hundred cities of its size or larger; no longer one of the few but far behind the great centers of the eastern seaboard and western prairie. It had come down to a small place in the reckoning of those who count importance in terms of bigness.

The relative shrinkage of Yankee City was not only in numbers but in physical space. At the end of the Revolutionary War the United States extended, politically speaking, to the east bank of the Mississippi. Thomas Jefferson, the agrarian, the Southern equalitarian disciple of Rousseau and a hater of cities, in 1803 purchased the Louisiana Territory and more than doubled the land surface of the United States. Soon after followed the annexation of Texas, the land taken by the Mexican War, and the Oregon Treaty, so that by 1850 more land had been added to the great continental nation than was its total possession at the close of the Revolution. The nation now stretched all the way from the Atlantic to the Pacific and from what is present-day Canada to modern Mexico. By the middle of the twentieth century Yankee City was a small town in one of the smaller states at one extreme corner of a continental nation. Furthermore, it was in a nation that was turning its attention from New England and the Atlantic seaboard toward the great prairies and beginning to look at the far distances of the Pacific.

The great increase in territory and population, as everyone knows, was accompanied by tremendous movements of people across the Alleghenies immediately after the Revolutionary

War, and thence gradually on to the Pacific coast. In 1700 the frontier for Yankee City and the United States was little more than a few miles up "the river" and other coastal rivers. But shortly before the Revolution the early pioneers started across the Alleghenies. Immediately after, some migrants from Yankee City joined the others in the great march into and across the prairies. States soon appeared that became powerful political rivals of Massachusetts and her New England cousins. Kentucky, with 70,000 people, was admitted into the Union in 1792; Tennessee in 1796. Then in rapid succession sovereign prairie states—as sovereign and powerful in Congress as the Bay State herself—were created and rapidly settled, to become heavy competitors in the struggle to settle the economic and political destinies of the United States. While Yankee City after the War of 1812 suffered its first major decline, such rapidly growing states as Indiana, Mississippi, Illinois, and Alabama were sending their senators and congressmen to the national capital. Meanwhile, on the eastern seaboard itself, migration had spread northward into Maine; in 1820 that state left Massachusetts and joined the Union. Some of its coastal cities became competitors for Yankee City's maritime and inland trade.

In brief, although from the beginning the Puritan inhabitants of Yankee City obeyed the Lord's command and were fruitful and multiplied exceedingly, and for nearly two centuries Yankee City grew to become a city of size, prominence, and power, not long thereafter the rapid westward spread of United States territory and the huge increases of the nation's population left her behind, reduced (in these respects) to a community of no more than ordinary importance. Instead of a young city with a great future she had become an old city with a great past.

The Social and Economic Foundations of the City's History

The early settlers of Yankee City were farmers, but not long after their arrival they began the enterprises that in time made them largely a seafaring people. According to local records the first wharf was built in 1655. By 1700 interest in commercial enterprises had grown to such an extent that the land along the river, hitherto held in common, was divided into river lots. "For two hundred years," says Samuel Eliot Morison, "the Bible was the spiritual, the sea the material sustenance of Massachusetts. . . . For two centuries and more, the tidal waters [of the river] . . . midwifed hundreds of noble vessels; and Yankee City was the mart for a goodly portion of interior New England. . . . [As early as] 1660 shipbuilding had become a leading industry in Yankee City." By the time the Constitution was signed, "the lower river from Haverhill to Yankee City was undoubtedly the greatest shipbuilding center of New England, at this period as in colonial days."[6]

Following a brief depression after the Revolution, the people of Yankee City quickly regained the prosperity they had enjoyed before the war. They continued to harvest great oak logs from up the river and turn them into ships, the cordage industries flourished, fishing prospered, the distillation of rum and the rum trade yielded splendid profits. Capitalistic enterprises such as building bridges across the river and canals around the falls, and trade in lumber, farm, and manufactured produce with the populations of the interior, contributed their portions to the renewed prosperity. A class of powerful merchant princes had firmly established their dynasties.

From 1790 to 1812 the mouth of the river harbored the greatest shipbuilding center in New England and the United States. At the same time the sea industry was led by some of the most astute men in the country. Yankee City supplied many—some say most—of the great names among merchant princes of the time. We have noted that the population almost doubled from the Revolutionary War through the period up to the census of 1810. From 1790 to 1806 the duties collected on imports tripled, while the sea-carrying trade in general grew enormously.

A high civilization had been established and a powerful economy founded which poured great wealth into the city and

6. Samuel Eliot Morison, *The Maritime History of Massachusetts, 1783-1860* (Boston, Houghton Mifflin, 1924), pp. 101-02.

the rest of maritime New England. A great war had been won
and a vigorous new nation established. A powerful party, the
Federalists, dominated by the wealthy merchants of New England and the southern planters, through the instrument of the
Constitution, was running the country. Here Yankee City
reached her greatest moment.

Some of the great names associated with the mercantile
empires centered in Yankee City were the Lowells, the Jacksons, and the Tracys, as well as the more lately arrived Bartlets
and Browns. In Yankee City as elsewhere in the harbor towns
of Massachusetts, says Morison, "there was a distinct class of
merchant princes who lived in magnificent style, surrounded
by suggestions of oriental opulence." After the Revolution and
up to the War of 1812, "they clung to the ways and fashions
of colonial days or of 1790 at the latest, unwilling to admit
even by the cut of a waistcoat that Robespierre could change
the world."

With their wealth the great merchants first built elegant
mansions, such as the Dalton and Tracy houses, in the center
of town and established country estates a few miles distant.
Just before the turn of the century they started building along
Hill Street, using the craftsmen whose competence had bested
Europe in the building of ships. They surrounded their homes
with gardens, filled them with furnishings and the other facts
and symbols of European civilization. "Federalist architecture
has here left perhaps her finest permanent trace. Hill Street,"
Morison remarks, "winding along a ridge commanding the
river, rivals Chestnut Street of Salem, despite hideous inter-
polations of the late nineteenth century. The gambrel-roofed
type lasted into the seventeen-nineties, when the Yankee City
merchants began to build square, three-storied, hip-roofed
houses of brick, surrounded with ample grounds, gardens, and
'housins.' "[7]

Within these houses, dressed in the "small clothes" and "tic

7. Ibid., p. 153.

wigs" of court life of the eighteenth century, the great families accumulated the wealth, prestige, and power that ruled Yankee City and soon, with families from similar cities such as Salem and Boston, dominated the life of New England. Speaking of this period, Morison states:

> Yankee City boasted a society inferior to that of no other town on the continent. Most of the leading families were but one generation removed from the plough or the fore-castle; but they had acquired wealth before the Revolution, and conducted social matters with the grace and dignity of an old regime. . . . We read of weekly balls and routs, of wedding coaches drawn by six white horses with liveried footmen, in this town of less than eight thousand inhabitants. When personal property was assessed, several Yankee City merchants reported from one thousand to twelve hundred gallons of wine in their cellars.[8]

From colonial times onward antagonism existed between the wealthy cultured towns and the new farming communities, spread along the western frontiers as they moved to the prairie and then to the Far West. The people of Yankee City shared this feeling of hostility. True, merchants and financiers were economically interested in developing the back country. Moses Titcomb was one of the important men in Yankee City who helped to develop and settle "the wild country in the interior." Many others could be mentioned—for example, Samuel Parsons, son of a Yankee City minister, who led the expeditions and pioneers into Ohio when the Northwest Territory was opened. This, too, was a great land speculation.

But men in the back country were often in debt to those in the cities. Much of their land was owned and controlled by absentee landlords, some in Yankee City. The legislature of Massachusetts clearly reflected the differences between the two areas. Its members from the interior were radical and liberal;

8. Ibid., p. 190.

those from the sea communities, conservative and often reac-
tionary. During the period following the Revolution, at the
time of the Articles of Confederation and later during the de-
liberations which resulted in the new Constitution, men of the
back country were for fiat money; those from the cities stood
for "sound money." Local histories tell us that Yankee City,
like the older cities of the seacoast, enjoyed a larger representation in the state legislative halls in proportion to its popula-
ion than those in the interior.

The dissension between the frontier and the sea towns was
brought to a climax and open conflict in Shays' Rebellion.
Yankee City sent an entire regiment under command of one of
its prominent citizens to put down this insurrection. At the
same time, during the unsettled period between the end of the
war and the establishment of the new government under the
Constitution, the great merchants and other men of property,
as well as those engaged in the scores of industries connected
with shipping and trade, were disturbed by the continuing
spirit of rebellion. Their distress and the similar feelings of
others of their kind in the other twelve colonies undoubtedly
were directly related to the movement which resulted in the
Constitution. Many of the men remembered today—Rufus
King, Theophilus Parsons, Tristram Dalton—are not the small,
valiant Revolutionary heroes we sometimes think of as our
founding fathers; they are the men who prevented the western
revolutionaries from taking power and ruling in a fashion
which, it was feared, would in violence and disorder be similar
to that of revolutionary France.

Once the Constitution was adopted and the strong new central government under Washington and the Federalists established, the city and its merchants prospered enormously. Some
of the leading merchants, along with John Hancock, specu-
lated in Continental money and, through their perspicacity
and Hamilton's Federalist benevolence, accumulated fortunes.
Meanwhile, the Federalist Party policy of neutrality in the wars
between France and England had given most of the carrying
trade and much of the shipbuilding of the time to the sea cities

of Massachusetts—communities near the mouth of this river receiving the largest share. All classes benefited. Despite official neutrality, the Federalists maintained close relations with England and expressed hostility to Republican France. Among other things, they favored the rule of the few; their principles and programs embodied the aristocratic ideals of maritime New England. Their opponents under Jefferson and Madison represented those who advocated expansion into the interior, philosophers of equalitarian agrarianism and political champions of revolutionary France. They were not popular in Yankee City. The economic classes of all levels earned their living, and a good one, from the sea and the older way of life. They were Federalists.

When Tristram Dalton set forth from his Yankee City mansion as one of the two senators who first sat for Massachusetts, he came as a representative not only of the state but of his conservative, aristocratic class. When George Washington made his grand presidential tour of the new nation, recently established by the Constitution, he came not only as the Father of his Country and leader of all his people, but as a visiting Virginia aristocrat, a Federalist, and one of the wealthiest men in the land. When he arrived in Yankee City he was entertained in the great houses of the town by people who knew him as an equal and were ardent members of his party. The requirements of *political* history would make it highly probable that both Dalton and Washington should be honored today; but the values associated with the highly regarded old-family status would make it even more likely. Thus the democratic ideals of the greatest good for the greatest number and the aristocratic ones of recognition of the high worth of the few all combined.

The citizens of the town itself at the time of Washington's visit recognized that its social and economic life was built upon the strong economic foundations of the sea and the power of the new central government under the Federalist Party. They recognized Washington not only as "first in their hearts" as a countryman, but as first among those beyond New England who understood them and were willing and able to help those

who were helping themselves. This recognition of class position
and interests extended beyond the borders of the United States
even to Canada and England. Moreover, they recognized revolutionary France clearly as an enemy and by the same token
found themselves in sympathy with the unhappy French aristocracy.

The great climax of Yankee City's economic and social history came immediately after the Revolutionary War and continued until the War of 1812. Before the Revolution there had
been opulence, beautiful houses, and a gentle way of life; the
merchant princes had already established themselves; but it
was in the period after the war that the city flowered and the
wealth of the sea was turned into a socially recognized superior
status. The great merchants, certain lawyers, clergy, and other
professional men were a confident, powerful prestige group
who dominated the life of the town. Their class sentiments
prompted them to marry into similar families, and they gave
their own women in marriage to men like themselves. Their
sons and daughters inherited the legacies and great houses after
being trained to maintain their economic competence and social graces and the continuation of the family, its name and
status. In short, in this brief euphoric period, well prepared by
two hundred years of economic and social growth, the society
produced as part of its social structure a superior status whose
members, by their political, economic, and social achievements,
validated in their own minds and those of others their superior
position. It was sanctioned by social approval and deference
given to it. Marriage within the group and descent from it as
the generations went by established it as a birth aristocracy,
the superior old-family part of the upper class.

Although later generations strengthened the lineage of the
old families and wove a newer one by marriage and achievement, the classic period, as it were, is the moment of history in
which present-day Yankee City can return to greatness. When
it does so, the city legitimizes the status of the old-family class.
This was the time when Yankee City and New England were
at the zenith of their power and glory. When the city looks

back to this period as the time of greatness, families of the birth elite who can trace their position through a superior lineage to the great men and families of that high period automatically legitimize their superior status, for it was then that the upper-upper-class status itself, as a recognized position, was securely established. Once lineage is given superior place in the status hierarchy, birth into a family with such lineage is sufficient for membership in the superior class. It cannot be a matter for surprise that the custodians of tradition in Yankee City who determine what symbols and periods of history will receive particular attention are members of the old-family class. That they favor the "great" period and their own ancestors more than others and that the town approves is even less surprising. Their lineal ancestors and the town's social ancestors are often the same.

The embargo and catastrophic War of 1812 ended this period. Yankee City did not recover from the destruction of her shipping and commerce, not only by the war itself but by the government policies of the southern and western agrarians, first under the leadership of Jefferson and Madison and later under new men from the western states. Other cities in Massachusetts—though not all—did retrieve the places they once held. Boston rapidly rose to be the great metropolis of New England. Evidence of the decline of Yankee City and the end of the period of power and glory was fully summarized at the time (1825-26) by Caleb Cushing, able son of a prominent local family. After speaking of the embargo and the war he declares: "During that calamitous period, our seamen were thrown out of employment; our traders lost their customers; the farmers, who had looked to us for foreign commodities, and of whom we had purchased lumber, and provisions, left our market,—and our merchants were compelled to sit down idly and see their ships rotting in the docks."

Having summarized the melancholy state of Yankee City's commerce and her decline and noted the development of Boston, he asked himself why Yankee City did not "resume its prosperity, and continue to Rise." His explanation was not the embargo, or the war, or the recent fire that had ravaged the town. While conditions of trade now required ships of larger draft, the sandbar at the mouth of the river impeded navigation and confined it to the smaller vessels. Rapids and falls only a short distance inland prevented river navigation into the rich interior of farms and forest. A canal built by the enterprise of local capitalists in 1792 did not permit transportation of "heavy goods" from and to the market of Yankee City. Meanwhile, at the very falls that had prevented the city's growth as a great river port, the manufacturing community of Lowell had grown up and the Middlesex Canal routed inland trade away from Yankee City into Boston.

The name Lowell, city and family, is connected with the rise and loss of place of Yankee City. The Lowell family is a good example of what happened to it. They had a part in building the city into a maritime and mercantile power. Yet it was Francis Lowell, born to the same great family while it was contributing to the intelligence, energy, and prestige of the local merchant princes, who helped to establish power manufacturing in America. The city of Lowell not only in fact dimmed Yankee City's greatness but is a symbol of the inland movement of glory away from the coast to the great industrial and manufacturing communities of the interior. These in turn were expressions of the change from a technology of the sea to the new industrial technology of the land. They were developments, also, of the new relation of the eastern seaboard to the great populations of the West as contrasted to those along the American and European borders of the Atlantic.

Francis Lowell and other members of the merchant families of Yankee City had been instrumental in establishing the new manufactories that were growing up throughout New England. His uncle, John Lowell (son of the minister whose church had been struck by the bolt of lightning Benjamin Franklin earlier investigated in Yankee City), had preceded him among the earlier emigres to Boston. While visiting in England, Francis had seen the great textile mills and machinery that had led to rapid advances there. He and others copied and improved the English machines and, soon after, started great mills in New England. After his early death, the textile mills at Lowell were established and the city was given his name in recognition of his industrial pioneering.

Within a few years Lowell and other inland metropolitan towns drew the population of the towns of the sea to them. While this was occurring, Boston became the financial center toward which many of the great families of Salem, Yankee City, and elsewhere migrated. There they reinvested their wealth in the industry of Lowell and similar inland cities that were to supply the needs of the agrarian millions who were rapidly settling the prairie and southern states. Southern cotton increasingly filled the New England mills. Yankee manufactured goods, carried westward by Yankee traders, were sold to the pioneers of the great land empire in the West. Meanwhile Yankee money was invested in land and other speculations that were part of the migration and settlement of the West. From these investments great fortunes were developed. It is often thought that this change from the mercantile and marine period to that of manufacturing and land trading meant that the old maritime families lost their controls and their place in the society and the economy, and that new people and new families succeeded them. While some great merchants and shipbuilders were ruined and some new families did rise to power and place, the change from sea to land was not accompanied by an entire change of personnel. Rather— like the Lowells—many if not most of those who once had power re-invested their money, brains, and energy in their new enterprises and maintained their economic dominance and social position.

Caleb Cushing, writing at the time, recognized this change and the meaning of it to investors and families such as his own. He declares in his history of Yankee City:

> The most efficient and comprehensive reason of the decline of the town is, in truth, the immense alteration of the general condition of business during the last fifteen

years. The whole of Europe, with the exception of its extreme eastern regions, is in a state of peace. We are no longer the carriers for its many nations. The sphere of our commercial enterprise is wonderfully narrowed. Our capital is now driven into new channels, and the entire circle of the relations of business and trade has undergone a radical revolution. Foreign commerce now requires a larger capital than formerly, and the profits on it are less. We are beginning to perceive and appreciate the importance of encouraging and protecting domestic industry, for the most substantial reasons; and if we did not, the impossibility of employing all the resources of the country in commerce would force open our eyes to see the necessity of investing a portion of it in manufactures. Here, then, we lose our population whilst other towns gain it.

Morison, commenting on these conditions says,

Just before the war ended, two scions of shipbuilding families, Francis C. Lowell and Patrick Jackson [also from a great house on Hill Street] prepared against peace by setting up power looms at Waltham, in the first complete American factory . . . . On a social pinnacle of their own making [in Boston and New England] were the mercantile emigres from Essex County . . . the Lowells, the Higginsons, and the Jacksons, who (according to Colonel Henry Lee) "came up from Yankee City to Boston, social and kindly people, inclined to make acquaintances and mingle with the world pleasantly, but they got some Cabot wives who shut them up." . . . *Despite the rise of manufacturing, merchants continued to dominate the social life of Boston* [*italics ours*].[9]

The author might have added Yankee City and all the cities and towns of Massachusetts that changed from the sea to the

9. Ibid., p. 129. See also pp. 213-14.

land for their living. Socially as well as economically speaking, his statement means that the old-family status continued and that many if not most of the families of prestige maintained the continuity of a birth elite, even though they had changed the sources of their income. Prestige now came not only from the power of their present economic position but from the great past they had established from the sea, and also socially as part of the high culture of western Europe, by now well founded on the shores of both sides of the Atlantic.

It is small wonder that in 1812, with ruin about them—a disaster of federal policy—many contemplated what the rest of the United States has called treason and plotted among themselves to join Canada and once more become a part of the political union of British peoples; or considered secession, a movement that culminated in the notorious Hartford Convention. During the transition from the sea to the land they saw their respectable and profitable way of life being destroyed by the agrarian South and the West, and by the forces of democracy that came from revolutionary France as well as from the new frontier states which espoused the cause of France against that of Britain. Once the transition had been made, all New England learned what Francis Lowell and others had quickly understood, and they too became integral parts of a continental United States and were able to continue in the great traditions established by their fathers.

Ecological Areas

On the basis of such criteria as the size and condition of the house, the amount and payment of rent, class membership, property values, crime and delinquency, percentage of foreign-born, distribution of ethnic groups, and recognition by the members of the community, we divided Yankee City into twelve ecological areas, as shown in the accompanying map (Fig. 1).

Oldtown (area 11), the original settlement—still having a separate town government, lies at the easternmost extremity of the town; while Newtown (area 10), the most recently de-

Fig. 1. *The Ecological Areas of Yankee City*

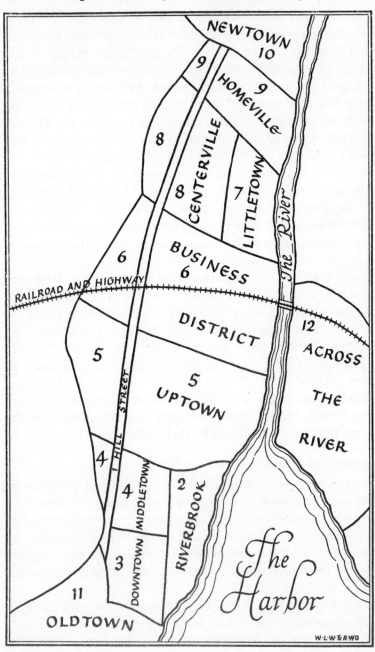

veloped residential area, lies at the westernmost extremity. These two areas are connected by Hill Street (area 1), on the north side of which most of the other areas are located. The Business District (area 6) conveniently divides the residential section into two halves. In this study the area called Across the River (area 12) has also been included, because a large number of its people have sufficient participation with the residents of Yankee City to make them socially a part of the town.

Of the areas most clearly defined by the inhabitants, Hill Street and Riverbrook are outstanding: the former is considered "the best part of town"; the latter, the "lowest part of town." The remaining areas, except Homeville, which is believed to be composed of "good solid Americans," are less distinct. But they vary considerably as we shall see upon further analysis.

There is no significant difference in the sex ratio of any area except Hill Street, which contains a significantly high proportion of women. Inasmuch as there is in this area a heavy concentration of the upper-upper class, in which women are more numerous than men, part of the disparity can be accounted for on the class basis.

An ecological analysis of renters who pay by the month, as against those who pay by the week, indicates that a relatively high proportion (over 60 per cent) of the renters of Riverbrook, Downtown, Middletown, Uptown, Littletown, Centerville, and Oldtown pay rent by the week; a corresponding proportion of the renters of Hill Street and Newtown pay rent by the month.

In this connection the median rentals of the various areas are also important. The median monthly rental for all areas is $18.77. The highest rentals were paid in Hill Street, Homeville, Uptown, and the Business District; the lowest, in Newtown and Oldtown areas. These last two areas tend to be high in social prestige despite the low rentals. Their low rentals are in part due to their peripheral location.

When each area is examined as a cultural unit, certain ethnic living patterns become apparent. Hill Street is an area characterized by a high concentration of Yankees and, with the exception of the peripheral Greeks and Negroes, a low concentration of all other ethnic groups. Riverbrook contains a high percentage of French Canadians and Russians and a low percentage of Greeks, Italians, and Jews. The Downtown district has a high concentration of French Canadians, Poles, and Russians and is avoided by the Irish, Armenians, and Italians. Middletown is significant for the number of French Canadians, Poles, Russians, Greeks, and Jews, and for a low distribution of Yankees, Irish, Armenians, and Italians.

The Uptown area has high concentrations of Irish, Jews, and Greeks, and is avoided by the Yankees and Armenians. In the Business District there is a significant distribution of the Irish, French, Greeks, Armenians, Italians, and Negroes, and a low distribution of Yankees, Poles, and Russians. In Littletown there is a high distribution of Irish, Armenians, and Italians, but this district is avoided by Yankees, Poles, and Russians. In Centerville the Irish, Armenians, and Italians reside in significantly high numbers; the Yankees, Poles, Russians, and Greeks, in significantly low numbers. In the Homeville area the Yankees are concentrated in significantly high numbers; the French, Irish, Poles, Russians, Greeks, Armenians, and Jews are in significantly low numbers.

The Newtown area contains a significantly high number of Yankees, a low distribution of French Canadians, Irish, and Jews, and no Russians, Armenians, or Negroes. Oldtown is comprised of a significantly high number of Yankees, and all the other ethnic groups either are significantly low or are not found here. The Yankees also form a significantly high percentage of the population Across the River, where there is a low concentration of Poles and Irish and where there are no Russians, Greeks, Armenians, Jews, and Negroes.

All classes seek out certain areas to live in and avoid, or are excluded from, others. Hill Street is a region where the two upper classes and no others reside in significantly high numbers. Riverbrook is avoided by the four highest classes but it has a high concentration of upper-lower and lower-lower people. The Downtown region has no upper-upper residents, is avoided by the next three classes, but is significantly high for the lower-lower class. All classes except the lower-lower avoid the Middletown region. The two upper classes stay out of the Uptown area in significant numbers, the next three classes are neither high nor low in it, and the lower-lower class is significantly high there. All four of the highest classes avoid the Business District; the upper-lower class prefers it; and the lower-lower is there in neither high nor low numbers. Littletown has a somewhat similar distribution. Centerville is an area preferred by the upper-lower class. Homeville is the preferred region of the two middle classes and, except for the upper-lower class, is avoided by all others. Newtown's residents are upper-upper and lower-middle. All four of the highest classes live in Oldtown.

The Houses of Yankee City

The dwellings of Yankee City are chiefly one- or two- family houses; the community contains few apartments, almost no one lives in a hotel, and only a small percentage of the population resides in business structures. Naturally the houses vary considerably in size, in condition of repair, and in the economic and social evaluation placed upon them. For purposes of this investigation they were divided into three sizes—large, medium, and small—and each of these types was classified according to three conditions of repair—good, ordinary, and bad. (Social evaluation of the house further depended upon rent, assessor's value, and prestige statements gained through interview.) The distribution of the various types of houses, moreover, varies considerably according to ecological area, class, and ethnic group.

Of the people in the community, 46.69 per cent live in small houses, 43.38 per cent in medium-sized houses, 7.22 per cent in large houses, and 2.71 per cent in structures built primarily for business purposes.[10]

10. This sample includes 12,770 individuals. Across the River is not

Slightly over 3 per cent of the people of Yankee City live in houses which are large and in good repair, 2 per cent are in large houses in ordinary repair, and a little under 2 per cent are in big houses which are in bad condition.

The occupants of medium-sized houses in good repair include 9 per cent of the total population; those in houses of medium repair, 20 per cent; and those in houses in bad repair, 15 per cent.

Only 7 per cent of the people live in small and good houses, whereas 16 and 23 per cent live in small houses in ordinary and bad repair.

The large houses in good condition are assessed at a median value of $3,967, the highest in the community. The large and medium are next ($3,738), and the large houses in bad repair are third ($2,717). The houses of medium size and in good condition are fourth ($2,277), and those which are medium both in size and condition are fifth ($1,982). Houses which are small in size and in good condition ($1,722) outrank houses which are medium in size but in bad condition ($1,572). Small houses in ordinary condition are assessed at $1,537, and small houses in bad condition rank last with a median value of $1,283.

As can readily be seen from the above figures, the large houses, most of which are comparatively old and of Georgian design, are most highly valued despite their condition; but the small houses which are in good condition are given a higher assessed value than those of ordinary size which are in bad condition. The high value of a large house is partly due to the fact that the size of the plot of land it occupies tends to be larger than that occupied by a smaller house.

Furthermore, large houses in good repair command the highest rentals in Yankee City. They have a median monthly rental of $32.67. The large houses in medium repair rent for less ($23.27) than houses of ordinary size and good repair

included, only part of Oldtown is, and none of the houses of people who come to Yankee City from other communities is part of this sample.

($26.19). The large houses in bad repair rank eighth ($18.80). They are topped by small houses in good condition ($22.56), medium-sized houses in ordinary repair ($20.87), small houses in medium repair, and business structures ($18.86). The house rentals of business structures outrank those of medium-sized houses in bad repair ($17.63) and the small houses in bad repair, which are last ($17.16).

The rental value of a house does not always correspond exactly to its assessed evaluation. The renter pays more for a house which is in good repair than for any other type of house. The large, medium, and small houses in good repair are ranked in that order in the highest rental group; the large, medium, and small houses in poor repair are ranked in that order in the lowest rental group; and the houses in medium condition are in the intermediate group. The only exception to this absolute ranking—by condition and by size—is that large houses in medium repair receive higher rentals than small houses in good condition. There is still a tendency for largeness to be given high value. The renter is primarily interested in condition, secondarily in size, while the assessor tends to value large houses (and their surrounding land), regardless of condition, above smaller-sized houses and lots.

Where Good and Bad Houses Are Located

The good and bad houses of Yankee City are unequally distributed through the city. Almost 21 per cent of Hill Street's houses are large and good while less than 2 per cent of those of Riverbrook are of this type; on the other hand, less than 5 per cent of Hill Street's houses are small and bad, but over 30 per cent of those in Riverbrook are of this least-desired type.

Let us briefly review the facts about the house types of each area. Hill Street has more large and good houses than would be expected by chance. It also has more large houses in medium condition and medium-sized houses in good or medium repair. It has fewer people than would be expected who live in houses which are of all three sizes but in bad condition. It has fewer people who live in business structures or in small houses in good repair.

Riverbrook, on the other hand, is an area where there are more houses than would be expected by chance which are small and in bad repair or of ordinary size and in bad repair. It is an area avoided by people who live in large houses in good condition or ordinary-sized houses in good or in medium condition. It is also an area which lacks business structures which serve as dwellings.

In the Downtown area, people do not have houses which are large, no matter what their condition, but show a preference for small houses (which are in need of repair) and for business structures. The Middletown area evinces mixed preferences: it shows high preference for small, medium, or large houses in bad repair, but also for medium-sized houses in ordinary repair.

The Uptown people rent or own business structures and houses in bad repair and of medium size. They avoid in significant numbers medium or small houses which are in ordinary repair.

The Business area likewise demonstrates mixed preferences. Large houses in medium or bad repair and medium-sized houses in ordinary repair are those in which people live in significant numbers. They then favor medium-sized houses which are in good or bad repair or small houses which are in good condition. The Littletown area favors business structures and medium-sized houses in medium or bad repair. These people do not show a preference for large or small houses in medium repair. The people of Centerville live in houses which are medium in size and in good or medium repair, and they stay out of business structures and small houses of medium repair.

The Homeville inhabitants prefer houses medium in size and medium or good in condition or houses which are small and in good or medium repair. They avoid houses which are large no matter what their condition, business structures, and medium or small houses in bad repair.

What Classes Get What Houses

Just as the house types are disproportionately divided among the several areas, so they are unequally distributed among the six classes. Large proportions of the upper-upper and lower-upper houses and almost none of the lower-middle, upper-lower, and lower-lower are big and in good condition. On the other hand, large sections of the lower-lower and upper-lower houses but none of the upper-upper are small and bad.

Statistical measurement gives further support to these conclusions. It shows that houses which are in good or medium repair are of high significance in the three highest classes and of low significance in the three lowest levels. It demonstrates that the intermediate types of houses (M x G, M x M, and S x M) are favored by the two middle classes and by no other stratum; that whereas the upper-middle class is significantly high and the lower-middle significantly low for large and good houses, the reverse is true at the other end of the scale of preferred houses, for the upper-middle class is significantly low and the lower-middle significantly high for the small and medium houses.

Bad housing, whether the place be large, medium, or small, is a characteristic of the lower-lower class but of no other, for the lower-lower group and no other class is significantly high for all three of those types. Moreover, the lower class does live in significantly low numbers in all types of houses which are in good repair. In brief, as one descends in the class order the type of house becomes smaller and less preferrable, and as one ascends the house tends to become larger and better. The upper classes get the better homes; the middle classes, the ordinary houses; and the lower classes, the poor ones.

Houses and History

It would be instructive to examine the history of the objects which received ritual consecration during Yankee City's Tercentenary Celebration and relate them to the present part of our discussion. Over half were dwellings, all occupied. Let us observe these family residences in the light of the discussion concerning the town's periods of affluence and greatness, its relative loss of position, and the creation of an old family class through lineage. We may ask which houses were chosen. What kind of people live in them now? Who built them? What kind of people have lived in them during the interim? And how do the answers to these questions relate to the larger problems of the historic periods and the meaning of the symbols of the Tercentenary.

The official guide of the Tercentenary gave a special section to the "Homes" of Yankee City and the list of houses honored by markers:

> Like other seaport towns of New England [it declared], Yankee City has many excellent homes of 17th, 18th and early 19th Centuries. In the beginning, these buildings were simple farm houses, generally with one huge chimney in the middle of the house, with the stairway in front and rooms on either two or three sides. . . . As time went on, the Colonies grew prosperous and larger houses were necessary. The Short House, No. 6 Hill Street, with a chimney at either end, was built in 1720. It is a fine example of early 18th Century architecture. About the middle of the Century, comes the Dalton House on State Street with its fine panelled rooms and elaborate stair rail with intricate spiral newel post. . . .
>
> Yankee City is especially rich in three-story houses. Two of these were built in 1771—the Lowell-Johnson House, 203 Hill Street, built by John Lowell, and the Dexter House, 201 Hill Street, built by Jonathan Jackson. The former of these is one of the best existing examples of its type and, with its towering and symmetrical chimneys and handsomely detailed porch and windows, is a splendid picture of the dignified and stately life immediately preceding the Revolution.
>
> In the short space of this article, it is impossible to do justice to the great number of interesting houses with

which Yankee City abounds. It was a shipbuilding community and that industry developed splendid craftsmen
whose work may be seen in countless cornices, doorways
and window heads on almost every street of the city.

These brief sketches tell us in a general way about the
houses and some of the interests and values of those who
created them. With notable exceptions, such as the small home
of William Lloyd Garrison, most of the houses listed were
identified and categorized in our study of all the houses in the
community as large and in good or medium condition. Although less than 6 per cent of the people of Yankee City lived
in such houses, two-thirds of the houses marked with signs
within the incorporated city belonged to this superior category.
The present people who occupy them belong largely to the
upper class; most are owned and occupied by the old-family
aristocracy.

There is considerable historical evidence to help us learn
the past meaning of the houses to those who built and later
lived in them and what they meant in the social setting of their
time. Timothy Dwight during his great tour of the New England states visited the city at the turn of the eighteenth century.
Dwight, former president of Yale, conservative Calvinist and
aristocrat whose words were often not commendatory, declared:

Hill Street, which lies . . . almost on the summit of the
acclivity, is remarkably handsome; and commands a
noble prospect. . . . The houses, taken collectively, make
a better appearance than those of any other town in New
England. Many of them are particularly handsome. Their
appendages, also, are unusually neat. Indeed, an air of
wealth, taste and elegance, is spread over this beautiful
spot with a cheerfulness and brilliancy, to which I know
no rival. . . .

The wealth of this town is every where visible in the
buildings and their appurtenances. Several of the inhabitants are possessed of large fortunes. You will remember,

that two of the associate founders of the Theological
seminary at Andover, Moses Brown, and William Bart-
lett, Esqrs. are citizens of Yankee City.

The manners of the inhabitants are, I think, unusually
agreeable. They are easy, unaffected, graceful, yet marked
with simplicity, and on that account peculiarly pleasing.
They are also distinguished for their hospitality; and in
a public, liberal spirit are not exceeded.

Their morals and religion, there is reason to believe,
are on a higher scale, than those of most other towns in
New England, of the same size. Upon the whole, few
places, probably, in the world, furnish more means of a
delightful residence than Yankee City.[11]

We have examined the high period of the past when the
symbolic objects were built. We have ascertained the present
position of the houses in Yankee City. We have not yet attempted to determine what the position of the houses was in
the social status structures of the intervening years. The answer to this question is of considerable theoretical importance
for a number of reasons. It will illuminate our understanding
of the relation of these symbols to the social structure through
time. For those interested in problems of status and social
class it will throw further light on the legitimation of the
aristocracy's social "right" to their high position.

The committee for the Tercentenary Procession and the historical markers utilized several local histories and a number
of more general ones to guide them. One of the local sources
was a book on *Old Yankee City Houses* written by the owner
and occupant of one of them. The book presents a "collection
of views . . . intended to show some specimens of the houses
built in Yankee City during the period when it ranked as one
of the principal shipping and commercial centers of the country—near the time of the American Revolution and during the
early part of the nineteenth century." A picture of each house

11. Timothy Dwight, *Travels in New-England and New-York,* 1
(New Haven, T. Dwight, 1821), pp. 439-40.

is usually given a full page, with the chronology of owners on the facing page. The list of owners is a "lineage" for the house and—for those in Yankee City conversant with the meaning of the times—the claims of the house and its occupants to high status. The vast majority of the houses listed are among those marked for the Tercentenary. Approximately 90 per cent are in the Hill Street area. Of these, two-thirds are on Hill Street itself. Six out of ten were built in the period following the signing of the Constitution through the War of 1812; a few before, and a very few after that time.

A fourth of the houses are now owned and occupied by those who trace family ownership back to the Great Period; some to an earlier period, the seventeenth century. Many have changed hands only once in the last hundred years. The houses not only are symbols of the upper class but in fact gave shelter and grace to generations of families whose parents and children with marriages into similar families transmitted the values and beliefs and other products and symbols of superior status down through the years.

We know enough about the past owners to say that most were in the upper class at all periods of the history of the houses; some were moving hopefully into that class when they purchased or built them; a few occupants, present and past, have not achieved upper-class position. The houses as cultural products and symbols of high position were from the beginning in the custody of high-status people. As such and as symbols they accumulated and held the social power and prestige of that high level. What they are and stand for as a style of life and a social class has been held together by a system whose nuclear structure is the family, and by the interconnected generations who have inherited or acquired positions in the system.

Further examination of the lineage of the great houses shows that very few were built after the War of 1812. The criterion "old" in Yankee City houses means mansions built before the end of the War of 1812—well over half from 1790 to 1815. Not only were great names created in this period and great families founded to which future generations could trace their lineage, but the old-family status itself then became a superior point of reference, so that those who hold high status now feel that they do in fact embody the virtues of a superior class. In brief, the great period was when the highest status in Yankee City and New England was established and in fact and symbol legitimated.

CHAPTER 2

Social Class and Social Structure

Class and Social Structure

WHEN the research of Yankee City began, the director wrote a description of what he believed was fundamental in our social system, in order that the assumptions he held be explicitly stated and not become unconscious biases which would distort the field work, later analysis, and ultimate conclusions. If these assumptions could be stated as hypotheses they were then subject to criticism by the collection of data which would prove, modify, or disprove them. Most of the several hypotheses so stated were subsumed under a general economic interpretation of human behavior in our society. It was believed that the fundamental structure of our society, that which ultimately controls and dominates the thinking and actions of our people, is economic, and that the most vital and far-reaching value systems which motivate Americans are to be ultimately traced to an economic order. Our first interviews tended to sustain this hypothesis. They were filled with references to "the big people with money" and to "the little people who are poor." They assigned people high status by referring to them as bankers, large property owners, people of high salary, and professional men, or they placed people in a low status by calling them laborers, ditchdiggers, and low-wage earners. Other similar economic terms were used, all designating superior and inferior positions.

All our informants agreed that certain groups, of whom we

shall soon speak, were at the bottom of the social order, yet many of the members of these groups were making an income which was considerably more than that made by people whom our informants placed far higher in the social scale. It seemed evident that other factors contributed to their lower positions.

Other evidences began to accumulate which made it difficult to accept a simple economic hypothesis. Several men were doctors; and while some of them enjoyed the highest social status in the community and were so evaluated in the interviews, others were ranked beneath them although some of the latter were often admitted to be better physicians. Such ranking was frequently unconsciously done and for this reason was often more reliable than a conscious estimate of a man's status. We found similar inequalities of status among the ministers, lawyers, and other professional men. When we examined the business and industrial world, we discovered that bankers, large manufacturers, and corporation heads also were not ranked equally but were graded as higher or lower in status. An analysis of comparative wealth and occupational status in relation to all the other factors in the total social participation of the individuals we studied demonstrated that, while occupation and wealth could and did contribute greatly to the rank-status of an individual, they were but two of many factors which decided a man's ranking in the whole community. For example, a banker was never at the bottom of the society, and none in fact fell below the middle class, but he was not always at the top. Great wealth did not guarantee the highest social position. Something more was necessary.

In our efforts to find out what this "something more" was, we finally developed a social-class hypothesis which withstood the later test of a vast collection of data and of subsequent rigorous analysis. By social class is meant two or more orders of people who are believed to be, and are accordingly ranked by the members of the community, in socially superior and inferior positions. Members of a class tend to marry within their own order, but the values of the society permit marriage up and down. A class system also provides that children are born into the same status as their parents. A class society distributes rights and privileges, duties and obligations, unequally among its inferior and superior grades. A system of classes, unlike a system of castes, provides by its own values for movement up and down the social ladder. In common parlance, this is social climbing, or in technical terms, social mobility. The social system of Yankee City, we found, was dominated by a class order.

When we examined the behavior of a person who was said by some to be "the wealthiest man in our town" to find out why he did not have a higher position, we were told that "he and his family do not act right." Their moral behavior was "all right," but they "did not do the right things." Although they were Yankees by tradition and not members of any ethnic group, we were told that "they did not belong to the right families" and that "they did not go around with the right kind of people." Our informants further said that the members of this family "didn't know how to act," and that they were not and could not be members of the "right" groups. The interviews clearly demonstrated, however, that all the members of the family were regarded as "good people," and their name was always a lure when marriage was contemplated for a young woman "of good breeding," even though there was some danger that she would be looked upon as "lowering herself" by such a marriage. Similar analysis of the men in industry and business who occupied lower positions brought forth the same kind of information.

Interviews about, and with, people who were ranked socially high by our informants but had little money or occupational status brought out the opposite kind of information, supplying further confirmatory evidence for our first tentative theory of a class system. These interviews revealed that "you don't need but a little money in Yankee City to do the right thing," or as it was sometimes said, "you have to have a little money but it is the way one uses it which counts." Questions about such people often brought out such statements as: John Smith belongs to the X group," followed by remarks to the effect that

"Henry Taylor and Frank Dixon and other prominent men who are at the top also belong to it." These same people, we were informed, "went around with the Fred Brown clique" or "went with the Country Club crowd," which were small groups of close friends.

In these interviews certain facts became clear which might be summarized by saying a person needed specific characteristics associated with his "station in life" and he needed to go with the "right kind" of people for the informants to be certain of his ranking. If a man's education, occupation, wealth, income, family, intimate friends, clubs and fraternities, as well as his manners, speech, and general outward behavior were known, it was not difficult for his fellow citizens to give a fairly exact estimate of his status. If only his social participation in family, clique, and association were known, he could be placed to the satisfaction of all the better informants by the process of identifying his social place with that of the others who were like him.

While making these observations on the criteria of class and attempting to locate people in the class hierarchy, we made a valuable discovery. In the expressions about wealth and occupation to which higher and lower valuations were attached, we noticed that certain geographical terms were used not only to locate people in the city's geographical space but also to evaluate their comparative place in the rank order. The first generalization of this kind which we noticed people using in interviews was the identification of a small percentage of the population as "Hill-Streeters" or people who "live up on Hill Street," these expressions often being used as equivalent of "Brahmin," the rarer "aristocrat," or the less elegant "high mucky-muck," or "swell," or "snoot." The term Hill-Streeter, we soon learned, was employed by people both within and outside of this classification. Whenever an individual was called a Hill-Streeter, all our evidence showed that he was near or at the top of the hierarchy.

Another geographical term with a strong evaluative class meaning was Riverbrook. When a man was said to be a

"Riverbrooker" or to live in Riverbrook, he was held to be at the bottom of the social hierarchy. Interviews showed this generalization to be true regardless of the informant's place in the social scale. Riverbrookers were contemptuously referred to by all, their sexual morals were considered low, and their behavior was usually looked upon as ludicrous and uncouth. An obscene story concerning the seasonal activities of the Riverbrook fishermen was told scores of times by our male informants, usually with amusement, and one heard much about incestuous relations and homosexual behavior among them. These depreciatory stories were told despite the fact that it was easily verifiable that they were no more true of Riverbrookers than they were of other classes. The Riverbrooker was often a good and highly skilled worker in the shoe factories. He frequently earned a good wage by clamming. Usually a good family man, he was but one of the many variants of what is called the typical Yankee. The "low" behavior was attributed to him (as it usually is in similar social situations) because of his low social position, and these beliefs helped subordinate him when expressed by those who felt themselves above him.

With the acquisition of the terms Hill-Streeter and Riverbrooker as designations for the two extremes of class, our next problems were (1) to find out to whom the expression did and did not refer, (2) to learn what distinctions, if any, were made to differentiate other groups than these two, and (3) to discover who used any or all of these terms.

A descriptive expression which appeared with considerable frequency in our interviews was "the classes and the masses." This expression was seldom used by the people referred to as "the masses" but quite frequently by those who considered themselves "the classes." The lower members of the community sometimes spoke of those in the higher statuses as "the upper classes," and when this expression was used by them it was ordinarily synonymous with Hill-Streeter. We soon found, however, that when "the masses" was used, not all the people who were so designated were Riverbrookers, and that most of them were believed to be higher in status. A distinction was made within the masses between Riverbrookers and people of somewhat higher status.

Another geographical expression which frequently appeared in the interviews was "Side-Streeter," used in contradiction to Hill-Streeter. In some contexts a Side-Streeter was anyone who was not a Hill-Streeter, but more careful interviewing indicated that to a Hill-Streeter a Side-Streeter and a Riverbrooker were different. "People who live in Riverbrook are at the bottom" and "Of course Side-Streeters are better than Riverbrookers" were frequently explicitly stated by the better informants. A Side-Streeter was one who was not on the social heights of Hill Street or in the social depths of Riverbrook. He was somewhere in between. Living along the streets connecting the river area with Hill Street, the Side-Streeters were socially as well as territorially intermediate.

All Side-Streeters were not the same, we discovered. Some were superior and others inferior, the former being commonly called by another geographical term—"Homevillers." The Homevillers were "good people," but few of them were in any way "socially acceptable." Certain informants placed all of them in "the classes." Homeville is a fairly definitely defined area in Yankee City at the northern end of the community. The Homeville people, we roughly estimated at the time, were people in the midsection of the social scale but on the whole nearer the top than the bottom. The term "middle class" or "upper-middle class" was often used as equivalent for Homeviller. The Homevillers and their like, it developed through our later associational analysis, were graded ordinarily into two groups (upper-middle and lower-middle classes) and separated from a lower stratum of Side-Streeters who were too much like the Riverbrookers in many of their characteristics to be classed with the Side-Streeters of high status. The distinctions between the lower group of Homevillers and this lowest group of Side-Streeters were not so clearly marked as the others.

At this point we saw that Hill Street was roughly equivalent to upper class, Homeville to at least a good section of the middle class, and Riverbrook to the lowest class. We perceived, too, that these geographical terms were generalizing expressions by which a large number of people could be given a class designation but which nevertheless did not define class position explicitly. When the people classed as Hill-Streeters were located on a spot map it soon developed that not all of them lived on Hill Street and that not all the people living on Hill Street were Hill-Streeters (upper class). Many of the people who were by class Hill-Streeters lived elsewhere in the city, and some of them were fairly well concentrated in two areas other than Hill Street. We found a similar generalization to be true of the Riverbrookers and Homevillers. This discovery further demonstrated that these designations were terms of rank employed by the members of a "democratic" society to refer obliquely to higher and lower social statuses in the community.

Careful interviewing among people who were called Hill-Streeters showed that the members of this group divided the general upper class into a higher and a lower subdivision. Our informants made frequent references to people of "old family" and to those of "new families." The former were individuals whose families, it was believed, had participated in upper-class behavior for several generations and who could trace this behavior through the father's or mother's line or both for three or more generations. An upper-class genealogy of this kind has been called a lineage for the purposes of this report. Long residence in Yankee City was very important, but length of residence by itself did not establish a family at the apex of the class system since in all of the six classes later established we found families with written and attested genealogies which went back two hundred and in some cases even three hundred years to the founding of the community. Some of the lower members of the upper class could also trace their genealogies well back, but their recent mobility upward if they had "come up from below" was enough to prevent an immediate claim to such a lineage. Their recent ancestors, unlike those of the uppermost members of the upper class, had not participated for a sufficient period of time in the forms of behavior and the social position which were ranked as upper class by the community. With the separation of the upper-upper from the lower-upper class, and the upper-middle from the lower-middle, we had distinguished five classes clearly and a sixth less definitely. We knew at this time that the sixth class fell somewhere in between the middle and the lowest class, but it was still possible that it might be not one but several classes. Eventually, however, we were able to establish the existence of six classes: an upper-lower and a lower-lower class in addition to the upper and lower subdivisions of the middle and upper classes.

The amount of membership in associations is comparatively larger than that in most of the other social structures of Yankee City. Despite their size, associations tend to segment the society into separate groups, and some of them help to maintain higher and lower ranking in the community. With this knowledge, we were able to place with greater exactness than we could by the use of the geographical classification a large sample of the members of Yankee City society.

Certain clubs, our interviews showed, were ranked at such extreme heights by people highly placed in the society that most of the lower classes did not even know of their existence, while middle-class people showed that they regarded them as much too high for their expectations. A very few of them, indeed, were looked upon as so exclusive that some of the Hill-Streeters might be excluded on family grounds. Of other clubs whose members were mainly Hill-Streeters, it was felt that any Hill-Streeter was eligible for membership if he had the other necessary qualifications (such as being a male of a certain age or interested in certain kinds of hobbies). These clubs, however, were considered too high for the vast majority of the people of Yankee City to aspire to, and it was clear that many, if not most, of the lower classes did not know of their existence. It was also felt that others did aspire to them but were not chosen because "they did not belong socially."

Below this last level of clubs were other associations which included Hill-Streeters but also had members "from further down" who were "not acceptable socially." There were still

Fig. 2. *The Class Hierarchy of Yankee City*

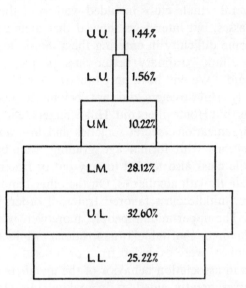

U. U.	1.44%
L. U.	1.56%
U.M.	10.22%
L.M.	28.12%
U. L.	32.60%
L. L.	25.22%

UNKNOWN~ 0.84%

other associations where these same individuals who were not accepted socially were members and were considered to be at the top of the membership, and all other members were felt to be below them. Some associations of this kind were sufficiently high so that there were members of the community who were too low to do more than aspire to membership. There were other associations too low for Hill-Streeters to join and still others which the two middle classes refused to enter. While interviews demonstrated that certain associations or clubs were believed to contain only the "best people," others mostly the "best people" but with additions, and still others only the "lowest people," some associations did not seem to be graded in class; people "of all kinds" were said to belong to them.

From a later understanding of associations, we discovered that members of the three higher classes belonged to associations which we named social clubs. The three lower classes did not. All three of the upper classes belonged to associations organized for charitable purposes. Certain of these clubs had only female members, others only male, and still others were mixed. Several female clubs included women of the three uppermost classes, but interviews showed that their lower members had some difficulty in entering them. Some female clubs refused to admit "ordinary better-class people," and some members said, "We will have only our own kind."

Ordinarily Hill-Streeters did not belong to occupational associations, but Homevillers did. Hill-Streeters tended to avoid fraternal organizations, secret societies and insurance orders, and associations with formal age grading. Members of the upper-middle class also tended to stay out of fraternal orders and associations with auxiliaries. On the other hand, members of the lower-middle class favored fraternal orders and semi-auxiliaries. The upper-middle people, moreover, were allowed into and favored charitable organizations, while the lower-middle members were excluded from or refused to join them. The breaks in association behavior of the members of the two middle classes greatly aided us in making our classification and in separating members of the two groups.

Lower-middle-class people did not participate in female and mixed social clubs, and since women were very conscious of class in Yankee City, the knowledge of this fact greatly aided us in our interviewing. If a person was a member of several charitable organizations, a social club or two, and possibly an occupational association, but not of a fraternal lodge, and he was not considered a member of the new or old families of Hill-Streeters, it was more than likely that he was upper-middle class. A small amount of interviewing soon demonstrated whether this was true or not. Ordinarily he had a family and was a member of a few cliques; usually we possessed information about their members; often some of them had been placed by earlier interviews. With this information it was not too hard to locate this individual in his exact place in the class system.

Associations were of great value in placing large groups of people in a fairly exact status within the class system. But because these people belonged to other social structures, such as the family and clique, which made much finer status discriminations, it was possible to place them with even greater exactness. Our study of family membership demonstrated that the vast majority of families had but one class represented in their membership. Although there were very minor rank differences in family membership, the members of a family ordinarily participated as a unit in their place in the social structure. Ultimately, we estimated that 95.15 per cent of the members of the upper-upper class belonged to families in which there were only upper-upper-class people; that 87.26 per cent of lower-upper persons belonged to families confined to their own class; and that the corresponding percentages for the other classes were 91.36 for upper-middle; 90.17 for lower-middle; 86.33 for upper-lower; and 95.98 for lower-lower.

Cliques tended to include two or even three classes in their membership, but on the whole they, too, drew fairly sharp class lines. Of the upper-upper class, 36.59 per cent belonged to cliques in which there were only upper-uppers; 20.74 per cent of the clique members in the lower-upper class, 20.12 per cent in upper-middle, 14.47 per cent in lower-middle, 15.68 per cent in upper-lower, and 24.64 per cent in the lower-lower class belonged to cliques confined to their own class.

All of the types of social structure and each of the thousands of families, thousands of cliques, and hundreds of associations were, member by member, interrelated in our research. With the use of all structural participation, and with the aid of such additional testimony as the area lived in, the type of house, kind of education, manners, and other symbols of class, it was possible to determine very quickly the approximate place of any individual in the society. In the final analysis, however, individuals were placed by the evaluations of the members of Yankee City itself, e.g., by such explicit statements as "she does not belong" or "they belong to our club." Naturally there were many borderline cases. A class system, unlike a caste or any other clearly and formally marked rank order, is one in which movement up and down is constantly taking place in the lives of many people. At the time of our study, for example, some people were moving into the lower-upper class from the upper-middle. Our interviews showed pressure on these mobile people from those above them and the development of new social behavior and memberships among them. It was a problem in these and similar cases from other classes where such people should be placed. In order to make a complete study, it was necessary to locate all of them in one of the six classes, and this we did to the best of our ability on the basis of the entire range of phenomena covered by our data.

Distinctions between the upper-upper and lower-upper, old family and new family, groups are quite clear. Differences between the upper-middle people who were not new family but who belonged to associations like them, and who were of the "better class" in Homeville and similar areas, are quite easily observed. The separation of the upper-middle from the lower-middle class is clear and distinct, but that between the lower-middle and upper-lower is less clear and, in certain respects, the least distinct of all. The distinction between the lower-lower and upper-lower class is easily made by finding out to whom the expressions "he is a Riverbrooker" or "he is the same as a Riverbrooker" apply.

It must not be thought that all the people in Yankee City are aware of all the minute distinctions made in this book. The terms used to refer to such definitions as are made vary according to the class of the individual and his period of residence. The terms Hill-Streeter, Side-Streeter, Homeviller, and Riverbrooker would be known to all classes. Occasionally such terms are used only in their geographical sense, but far more often they are applied as terms of status and rank.

The Family in the Class System

The maintenance of a family's social position in any hierarchal society through an extended period of time is, in large part, dependent upon the vertically coordinate social positions of the marrying pair. If the society is organized on the principle of caste, the males and females of two uniting families must be members of the same caste; they express by the marriage their social equivalence and help maintain the continuing location of their families' place. All the values and sanctions of a caste help to enforce such equivalent marriages.

In a class system, however, there is an ambivalent situation, for only part of the values and sanctions of class act in this way. A positive sanction is placed on bettering oneself, making a "fine marriage," and a negative sanction on the opposite of "lowering oneself" or "marrying beneath oneself." Those opposing tendencies are normally resolved in a class system in such a way that these people maintain an approximation of their premarital positions by and after marriage. Nevertheless, despite the pressure to marry at one's own level, a certain number of people marry above and below their own social position. Such behavior is a part of the general situation in a class society, the reason being that there are relatively few methods available for imposing either physical or social segregation which might prevent upward or downward marriages.

The Yankee City class which has the best chance to express its social distance is the upper. This class has more mechanisms to express social distance, and often it can and does translate social distance into geographical and spatial distance. The private school, large grounds, nurses for children, large houses, and infrequent use of public conveyances all geographically express and help maintain distance between the members of this group and those who might want to become socially nearer to them.

The problem of marriage in a class system, when social position is to be maintained, is one in which there must be an equivalance of place not only for the marrying pair of one generation but for the many generations which succeed each other. In class, unlike caste, there are three possibilities of marriage instead of the one in caste. A person may marry above, below, or evenly. Thus the maintenance of a given position is much more difficult since the generations of marrying pairs must maintain repeating cycles of equal marriages.

In our interviews certain "old families" were repeatedly referred to as the uppermost group in Yankee City, and among these families a certain few were felt to be higher than all others. Representatives of these topmost families were interviewed not only to discover how they lived and thought but also to determine which families they placed in the old-family or upper-upper group, and which they put in the new-family classification, or lower-upper category. The same was done with the other groups beneath them. From such groupings of families as we obtained by our interviewing, it was possible to work out a continuous vertical extension of members of families from the top to the bottom of the Yankee City society and to place each individual in one of the several classes. Family histories were examined and the behavior of living descendants analyzed in an effort to discover why they occupied the positions they did in the class hierarchy. To indicate the kind of material that was collected and to present the reader with the evidence for the development in our methods for the study of class, summaries of a few cases in the upper-upper group are given below.

Let us look first at the Z family. R. Z, according to the testimony of our informants and of historical documents, was a lawyer who came to Yankee City from Connecticut. First mentioned in the local history around 1800, he was a prominent official of the town—chairman of the selectmen, representative to the Grand Council—and was sufficiently important to make the public welcoming addresses when President Monroe, General Lafayette, and other prominent people came to Yankee City. From our historical vantage point, he seems to have been one of the early New England capitalists. He was interested in building canals and locks in the river and his company became the corporate overlord of a great industrial city of the state. He helped organize the Atlantic Stage Company, one of the important transportation systems of the day, and he was also concerned with the toll bridge across the

river. He had two sons, D. Z and M. Z, the latter an Episcopalian minister and the successor to a famous divine of New
England. D. Z was the largest owner of ships in Yankee City
at a time when shipowning was of paramount importance to
the town and to New England. He was also president of the
oldest and most respected bank as well as of another important bank in the community. He married Miss T, who belonged
also to a leading family. He was called "Lord Z" by his contemporaries in the community and stories are still told which
illustrate his imperious attitude.

D. Z had three sons, D., R., and S., and a daughter, who
later married a member of the local aristocracy. D. married
an "outsider" and had one daughter who married a manufacturer. This union was blessed with two sons and a daughter.
The sons are in the manufacturing business, and the daughter married Dr. K, a surgeon with an upper-class practice in
Boston. D. went into the wholesale lumber business in Boston
and failed. This was his only business venture. He went into
politics and became a high-ranking Federal official in Cleve-
land's administration.

R. Z went into the wholesale drygoods business with two of
his upper-upper friends and failed. He then became a note
broker and "hired money for people who wanted it largely for
cotton mills, and from th're went into the bond business."
S. Z, the third of the three sons, went into the brokerage business with a friend of his father's. He never married. As administrator of the will of his aunt (the wife of M. Z), he gave
$250,000 to a Yankee City hospital; and out of the income
from another $250,000 he distributed one-fifth to a dental
clinic, two-fifths for the treatment of tuberculosis, and two-
fifths for a community-welfare center in Yankee City.

R. Z married the daughter of a local upper-upper who was
a "brilliant" newspaperman and soldier. He had, by this marriage, one son, N., who married a wealthy woman. He is in
business with his father. The "show place" of Yankee City is
now owned by his father, whose present wife is of an aristocratic Philadelphia family. R. Z (the father) is one of the three

wealthiest men in the state and has an estate of over 3,000 acres near Yankee City and a place in Boston. "He is the only native who has made money outside of town [this is believed, but is not true] who has spent it here and he has a great regard for Yankee City."

Let us now turn to the Y family. There were two Y's who were prominent in the Revolution; both were members of the Council of the Colony at Massachusetts Bay and one became its president. B. Y was a brigadier general in the Mexican War, a famous attorney, an early mayor of Yankee City, one of the first ministers to China, attorney general of the United States, represented the United States in regard to the *Alabama* Claims, and almost became chief justice of the Supreme Court. (He was defeated in this—after he had been nominated by the President, so the story goes—by a senator who was a former citizen of Yankee City and who came from a family which lived on the "side streets.") B. Y had two half-brothers, N. and M. They were shipowners in the East India and Calcutta trade. M. married a local aristocrat and had two sons and two daughters. Both he and his brother N. lived in the same house. N. had one son and three daughters. His son C. went into the East India trade with other leading merchants of Yankee City but the firm was broken up shortly after.

C. Y thereupon took over the direction of one of the older banks and became director of the T Fund (an educational foundation created by a Yankee City person) for giving local men training in technical colleges. C. Y was also a director of the leading bank in the community and president of the association owning the cemetery where many of the upper-uppers buried their dead. His unmarried sister A. lived with him. One daughter married L. O, an upper-upper who had a salary of $40,000 a year. This couple had three children: N., who did not marry; G., who died; and S., who married three wives, each of whom was wealthy. The wives were related to a large number of the members of the upper-upper families in Yankee City and in the surrounding communities. C. died while the

Yankee City research was in progress, and left a sizable fortune to his unmarried sister.

The X family. The members of this family have long been famous as silversmiths, there having been an uninterrupted line of craftsmen in the family since the late 1600's. M. X, the founder of the lineage in this country, was born in 1602 and came to Yankee City in the late 1630's. His son was called M. and the son of M. was called H. Since that time there has been an alternation of the names of M. and H. on a generation basis. The present M., last of the line, lives in one half of a house built by his great-grandfather; his married sister lives in the other half. "His father left him some money and M. didn't have to work after that." He has a brother D., who is a jeweler and well-known horticulturist. His brother's daughter lives across the street with a common first cousin. The family of the first cousin is related to a large number of upper-upper families in Yankee City.

The W family. Colonel W of New Hampshire married into one of the well-known upper-class families of Yankee City. His wife's father was a wealthy merchant and president of two prominent and powerful local banks. The W's had three boys and a girl. The first son married the daughter of a wealthy broker, the second became an officer in the Marines, and the third lives in Yankee City with his sister E., who is in charge of the children's guidance society in one of the larger communities in Massachusetts. The W's are related to many families of upper-upper status in Yankee City.

The V family. The Reverend D. V was the minister of the Oldtown Church in Yankee City for about fifty years, from the early 1800's to the middle of the century. Of his four sons, one went to Illinois, one to Vermont, one to New York, and one remained in Yankee City as editor of the local paper. The last son had three sons and two daughters. His wife was H. E, daughter of Squire E. Squire E was first cousin of the father of H. Y. E, who was one of the oldest and most respected members of the topmost class. Their oldest child later became a lawyer in Honolulu; the second son, a genealogist in London; and the third son, also a lawyer in Honolulu. This last son lived in Yankee City until he was about fifty. D. V, a son of the editor, was an important official in one of the investment companies in the community and, with another member of the upper-class group, reorganized one of the large turnpike companies which he later sold for what was said to be a large sum.

The T family. The T family, whose prominence in the community goes back to the seventeenth century, made their fortune in shipping. They are intermarried with a number of the upper-upper-class families in Yankee City. "There has been money in the T family for over one hundred years and they have made many bequests" to the town of Yankee City. The present generations of this family have, according to the testimony of some of their own group, "married beneath themselves." Their father went into the textile business but found that he could make more money speculating in the market. His brother, now dead, was a consulting electrical expert in partnership with another upper-upper. Their first cousin, S. T, is an inventor. "He has never worked very hard at anything. He is the only T who has kept his money."

In these brief family histories there is a wide range in wealth and occupation and in the number of generations that a family has been in the community. The Z's and Y's are the only very wealthy families; the X's are fairly well-to-do; and the others have but a modest income. It is commonly thought in Yankee City that all old families are descendants of sea captains and that social classes as presently constituted are based upon the earlier division into captains, mates, and seamen. Obviously, this simplification will not hold water.

It will be remembered that the X family were silversmiths; their occupation has very high prestige because the S silver, which bears the family name, is now to be found in such famous collections as that of the British Museum. The first Y was a minister; the second, an editor; the first Z was a lawyer.

The significant thing to note in these histories is that for over one hundred years these families have been among the most prominent in Yankee City. Their occupations have always been those of high social value although they have changed in character with the changing technology. A woman of the upper-upper class contrasted the "new people" with a family like that of the Y's. She said of the latter, "They have a fascinating family history." This characterization would be true of all the family histories of those who belonged to the upper-upper group. Whether as sea captains, merchants, bankers, lawyers, capitalists, or intellectuals, they have been the dominant families in the town, a position which they still retain.

From our investigation of the upper-upper families we concluded that a family was in this class if it had participated in *general* upper-class behavior for several generations. Only through time could a family move from lower-upper to upper-upper. The participation by the families' ancestors for several generations in the two upper strata, and ultimately in the upper of the two, gave it a lineage. A lineage we defined as an unbroken line of ancestors who could be traced through the father's or mother's line, or both, and who would be members of the upper class.

An informant who had definitely formulated her ideas of what factors were involved in class behavior declared, "You have got to have family to get anywhere in Yankee City and you have got to have some money. Not very much, but enough to do the right thing." In other words, money is of importance only as it enables one to carry out the behavior which is felt to be inherently appropriate to the upper-class configuration; and this behavior, it is believed, must have been performed by the former members of a family as well as by its present members. It must be emphasized that the present-day families go back before the American Revolution; and some, like the T's and S's, were prominent almost from the beginning of the settlement.

One of the important facts about lineage as we have defined it in American society is that it is usually bilateral; descent is reckoned not necessarily through the male line alone. When lists are compiled by our informants of the names of those families who were included in the upper class, certain names were not included which we definitely knew to be upper class. Of the members of these families it was said that they belonged to the Y family or Z family, that is, that these individuals traced their descent through the mother rather than the father in order to maintain the height of their position. These people were looked upon as upper-upper, but they were thought of in terms of the lineage and connected with a patronym which was upper class. In a generation or two their present names will be absorbed into the group and will become the names of a lineage in their own right. The authoritative informants in the upper-upper group often spoke of the P's as an old family. Actually their patronym was second generation in Yankee City, but further interviewing showed that the first of the P family married the daughter of Captain Jonathan N, a member of the upper-upper, and since the system of descent in a lineage in Yankee City is bilateral, the P's are now a continuation of the older lineage. Apparently it takes at least two generations, and sometimes more, for one name to supersede another. N. E, granddaughter of Y. Y. E, speaks of the S's (a new lineage) as an old family, but in the generation of her grandfather they were spoken of as Z's (an old lineage).

In the upper-upper group there are a number of definitely known lineages which are recognized by members of this group and by the members of the lower-upper group. These lineages are regarded as a single linked group through a belief in their general superiority to the other groups in the community. This belief is expressed in a common behavior pattern which helps maintain the social distance of those who use it. Mrs. O said, "My husband told me when I came here that the one thing you couldn't do in Yankee City was mix social classes." Another upper-upper informant declared that the old families never had accepted the new people into their group. The members of the topmost group frequently use a kinship terminology in ordinary address, even when they are not related as kinsmen; for

example, the term "cousin" is often used when there is no
traceable relationship. This was explained by one informant
in these words: "She is my cousin not because she is an actual
cousin but because my mother and father grew up with her."
There was strong evidence that the upper-upper class in Yankee City behaved as a biological kinship group to express their
mutual feeling of social proximity to each other and, ob-
versely, to express social distance from those with whom they
did not use such terms.

Although this relation of kinship in the upper-upper class
is sometimes a fiction based upon membership in a common
group, it is nevertheless a definite extension of the family. The
class is highly endogamous and practically everyone is related
in some fashion to the other members. As one of the oldest
and best-informed members of this group commented, "I
haven't an ancestor that landed here [Yankee City] after 1650.
The farthest any went for a wife was to X [a suburb of Yankee
City] and only two went there; so you can see what a community you have struck. All marriages are inside the community." Often these relationships are very distant, but each
member of the class endeavors to link himself and his family
with the others on a kinship basis. One of our most trusted
informants, when speaking of his wife, said, "I didn't know
that she 'existed' until I was twenty-one. I then found out that
her great-grandfather and my great-grandmother were brother
and sister." The first thing he and his wife did was to compare
genealogies.

This brief analysis demonstrates the complicated and often
distant kinship ties which link these people together. At times
a distant or fairly close kinsman may be quietly disowned because he does not belong to this group. There is a standing
feud in Yankee City between the members of two families
who have the same patronym because one individual who belongs to a lower class insists that he traces his lineage back to
common ancestors and, to clinch the point, calls his son by the
Christian name of the original ancestor of the upper-class family. There is a relationship between the members of the two

families but through a different line. It was felt by the upper-class family that their vested rights were being used and that the lower-class family was attempting to augment its social prestige by attaching itself to an upper-class lineage. There can be little doubt that this is what was being attempted since the members of each family were thinking within the social context of Yankee City.

In this semi-endogamous group, marriage with a first cousin is quite frequent and there is very little or no taboo upon it. Micajah X married his first cousin and when he died, another cousin, an N, came back to the community and married the widow. Tracing the lineages of many of the upper-upper-class families is extremely complicated since they have been intermarried for generations and there is a definite feeling of pride on the part of the members of the group in the closeness of the marriages. X. Y. Z, a member of this group, said, "My wife is some relation to the T's in the same way I am; my children are descended from the 'original immigrant' of the T's in sixteen different ways, nine on the mother's side and seven on the father's. That is how intermarried we are around here."

Since the class is largely endogamous, and since males are more apt to leave the city, the necessity to marry within the the class has left many females single. Many of our informants spoke of so-and-so's remaining single because she would never marry below her—"she was too high class for that." S. S, upper-middle class, one of the most respected capitalists in the community, was in love with a woman of the upper-upper group when he was a young man, but "of course, she would have none of him." Such marriages occur but rarely, and when they do, it becomes necessary for the person of lower rank to assume the behavior of the upper group.

An examination of the membership of the lower-upper families presents a very different situation from that of the upper-upper. When we examine the lives of the outsiders who have come to Yankee City to live, several things become evident about their family structure. Most of the outsiders consist of single families of parents and children; that is, the adults who come to Yankee City are essentially in families of procreation, because their parents ordinarily remain in their home communities. Associated with leaving the home community is the fact that the primary control of the old superordinate generation is removed, and at the same time, these individuals are ordinarily separated from their siblings and other kin and tend to be isolated as kindred when they arrive in Yankee City. In addition to their kinship isolation, they also tend to have few social relations with the members of the community. For some little time after arrival their direct relations are primarily those associated with the occupation of the husband and father. Ordinarily they have certain people in the community who act as sponsors for them. Failing such sponsors, it is possible for the family to remain in almost permanent isolation, and instances are cited of people leaving the community because they were not accepted. If the "immigrant" family has been properly sponsored, and if it has the other necessary requirements, it is possible, after a few years, for its members to become a part of the lower-upper class.

Not all of the lower-upper individuals are newly arrived persons from outside the geographical limits of Yankee City. Many of them, born in the community, are recently arrived from a lower position in the social scale. Such people, on the whole, occupy a position similar to those who have come in from the outside since, although they are not separated from the parental generation and their larger kinship group physically, they tend to be separated almost as definitely. A similar lack of relations tends to exist between the older generation and the younger one which has augmented its social position.

One of the most characteristic aspects of the lower-upper class is the unstable situation within the family which, as we have said, arises in part from the lack of control of the superordinate generation and the submission to initiated standards taken over from the class into which they have recently entered. The family arrives, by social mobility, in the lower-upper class where the standards that the members of this family have been taught in their youth are looked upon as vulgar, cheap, and demeaning. They have no older generation on whom they can rely for support. The very elaborate and detailed modes of behavior which are considered marks of their new position cannot be learned by growing into them but must be acquired from a group which is in part hostile to these new members. What they learn they feel is from outside them, and to some extent the adopted behavior is always felt by them to be external and strange. The largely hostile class environment makes it difficult for them to participate with ease and to acquire freely the kind of behavior necessary for them to have in order to consolidate their new positions. They are continually on the defensive. By contrast, a member of the upper-upper group offers his opinions easily and freely even though they may be divergent from those held by other members of his group. He can afford to criticize and to be criticized.

In the lower-upper group, however, there is a tendency to perfect a part of the total behavior expected of an upper-class person, and this part of the behavior frequently becomes for them a substitute for the whole. For example, A. N, a young man of the lower-upper class, owned a large plane which became, according to his own view, the very center of his existence. He spent large sums of money on it, displayed it frequently, and devoted a great amount of his time to overseeing its maintenance. It became to him a symbol of his position, and when he sold it, he said "he felt as though he had sold his bride" or as though "someone in the family had died." While he was in possession of the airplane he was often subjected to the ridicule of the members of the upper-upper group.

Although the upper class is divided into these two groups, the children of the same age grades go to the same schools and, on the whole, participate in the same activities when they are together. This creates a skewed situation between the two generations and the two classes. In the upper-upper, the children are definitely subordinate to the older group and their position is one of great subordination to the parental generation in comparison to that of the younger generation within the families of the classes beneath this group. The adults in the lower-upper class are subordinate to the adults of the upper-

upper class and, in relative social place, they are subordinate to the children of the upper-upper class. The lower-upper children, however, are friends of the upper-upper children and frequently assume a higher position than their parents because of their association with the upper-upper children. The continual association between the growing members of the upper-upper class and those of the lower-upper class helps the latter rise in the social scale while, at the same time, it acts to increase the social distance between the parents and children of the lower-upper group.

Marital Status in Yankee City

At first observation the family system of Yankee City appeared to be one and the same in all six classes, but a detailed analysis demonstrated definite differences. The ethnic groups also manifested considerable variation.

The age at marriage is in direct relation to the status of an individual. If upper class he will marry late; if lower class he will marry young. After marriage, if upper class he will have a small family; if lower class, a large family. Class factors thus influence family life in a variety of ways; family, on the other hand, is a potent mechanism for maintaining the class system. Class as it is now organized could not endure without the auspices of the family which maintains its values and organizes the relations of its members.

Approximately one-third of all Yankee City people fifteen years of age and over have never been married. About half of the single people are women and half men. The married group, consisting of both married and divorced persons, constituted about 58 per cent of the total. There were more women in the widowed group than men.

The number of unmarried persons in the native group is significantly low, while in several of the ethnic groups—Irish, French, Poles, Greeks, Jews, and Italians—the number is significantly high. Conversely, the number of married persons is significantly high for the natives and significantly low for the Irish and Poles. The widowed group shows a significantly large number of natives and a significantly small number of French, Greeks, Italians, and Jews.

In contrast to the ethnics, the native group has a smaller proportion of single persons and a larger proportion of married and widowed individuals. The ethnics tend to have a larger number of single people in their population than the natives partly because many of them are recently arrived from their homeland, and ordinarily such immigrants come as single individuals.

Although the ethnics as a whole have a smaller proportion of married persons among their numbers than the natives, three of the ethnic groups show a higher percentage of married individuals. These three groups are the Negroes, the French Canadians, and the Russians. The Greeks also have a very high proportion of married persons, but somewhat smaller than the natives. The smallest proportion of married persons is found among the Irish.

The median age at the time of marriage in Yankee City is 24.40 years. For women the median age is 23.18 years; for men, 25.92 years. One-fourth are less than twenty-one years of age at the time of marriage. The great majority of these are women; less than 200 are men.

The percentages of subadult males at marriage are far smaller than those of subadult females; on the other hand men marry between the ages of thirty and forty much more frequently than women.

In Yankee City 71.67 per cent of the men are married to women younger than themselves, 10.75 per cent have wives of the same age, and 17.58 per cent have wives who are older.

In all classes except the upper-upper more than half the population of fifteen years or over are married. The figure for the upper-upper class is slightly under 50 per cent. The percentage of those widowed in each class decreases with the class scale. When it is remembered that the percentage of old people, mostly female, is highest in the upper classes, part of the high percentage of widowed people in the upper classes is understood. The newer ethnic groups at the bottom of the class hierarchy have relatively few older people. For example, among the Poles less than 1 per cent is sixty-five years or over, while among the natives this age group constitutes 19.25 per cent of the population.

The median age for marriage for all classes, as we have said earlier, is 24.40 years; but it becomes higher as class status increases. The figures for the six classes are as follows: 27.90 years for the upper-upper class, 26.60 years for the lower-upper class, 26.10 years for the upper-middle class, 25.10 years for the lower-middle class, 24.40 years for the upper-lower class, and 23.20 years for the lower-lower class.

CHAPTER 3

The Family and Family Behavior in the Several Classes

The Family in the Home

AN UPPER-CLASS home in Yankee City contains anywhere from eight to twenty or more rooms, all of which play a definite role in the lives of the individuals who occupy and use them. The living room serves as the focal point in organizing the face-to-face relations of all members of the family group. Most living rooms have fireplaces which, possessing more than utilitarian value, serve as symbols of the unity of the family group. Each individual in the household, moreover, has a specific room of his own, and, in many instances, a private dressing room and bath as well. From these private rooms emerge the specific individual personalities to join the other members of the family in their common activities. Children and servants are usually quartered on the top floors; rooms used by the entire family are generally on the ground floor; and the specialized rooms of adults and more important members of the family are located on the second floor.

There are, of course, variations in this general rule; but the two rooms in which the family spends most time as a group are without question the living and dining rooms. Frequently the living room is divided into two rooms, the smaller and more intimate being set aside for family use, and the other, a parlor, used for the entertainment of guests. If outsiders are invited to such a function as tea, for instance, the larger living room is used; but if the guests include only more intimate friends, they are received in the family living room. The larger living room is seldom used by the family alone.

The dining room is usually restricted to the more intimate participation groups and is rarely used for larger functions except for formal dinners. Meals in the home have different values which depend upon the social status of the family. The upper-class family, for instance, spends more time over its breakfasts and endows this meal with more group significance than do families in other classes.

In upper-class families there are generally servants to perform a large part of the secular household ritual through their daily rounds of tasks and duties which keep the house in order. The mistress of the house ordinarily superintends the activities of her servants, but she does not herself do any of the actual work. However, she and other members of the family perform definite ritual acts which top off the work of their paid employees: arranging flowers, carving at table, lighting the fire, and pouring at tea. Maids serve at the table according to a strictly formalized routine, while the food is prepared by a cook hired especially for that work. Maids are outfitted in uniforms of different types according to the time of day and the specific duties in which they are engaged, their dress symbolizing their subordination to and separation from the family whom they serve. The leisure time accruing to the family that can maintain servants allows more frequent performance of ritual acts outside the home, the women participating in various social activities which bring them conspicuously to the attention of the remainder of the community, and the men indulging in a variety of sports, intellectual interests and hobbies, and community activities by means of which they express and constantly reaffirm their social position.

All of the activities which surround the preparation of the table and the serving and eating of the meal are demonstrations of ritual relations between members of the family, the servants, and objects which have esthetic and traditional value in the house. They are also expressions of the meal as a family communion. Nonmembers of the immediate family—such as collateral kin and clique members—who are invited in to eat at the family table may be said to participate in the "private communion" of the family and household, a secular but highly organized ritual. These ritual elements surrounding the daily life within a household tend to increase in number and intensity of function with the height of the stratification of the family. As household ritual becomes more elaborate, larger and larger sums of money are necessary to maintain it. Most families, however, do not have sufficient income to support a large staff and many of them hire servants for the day or on a part-time basis; a few have no servants at all, but so long as the house is maintained properly, the absence of servants in no way reflects on the social position of the family. There is a certain minimum, of course, which must be met, but anything above that is mere elaboration.

People of the lower-upper class, the so-called new families, adopt the more elaborate ritual in order to demonstrate that they know and follow the behavior patterns of the upper-upper-class people. The elaborate ritual of the upper class in general is associated with strong feelings for property and its correct handling. An upper-middle-class person, in speaking about the Christmas season activities of local charitable associations, said, "Hill-Streeters can well afford to give toys because their children are not destructive; they have more intelligence and are made to respect things, and toys are treated just like furniture; there is a definite place for a thing and their children are taught to put it there." In other words, there is a definitely recognized household arrangement which each child is brought up to respect and the parts of which he must treat with almost ritual care. In this pattern, the antiques, heirlooms, and other properties which have been handed down from the past are the important centers around which other house furnishings are arranged. The inheritance of ritual objects from the past and their use by living lineal descendants provide the members of the upper-class group with a symbolic apparatus which ties the sentiments of the living with those of the dead. The house, its furnishings, and the gardens thus become symbolic expressions of the relations not only between household members but also between the living and the dead.

Many of the houses themselves, as previously mentioned, may be said to possess lineages of their own. Those having no lineage have less value, however old or beautiful they may be. A house with a distinguished lineage is concrete evidence of upper-class status. Although the spatial arrangements of the rooms and their specialization of function help to impress an elaborate ritual on the occupants, the spiritual presence of the ancestors, as experienced through the use of ancestral rooms and furniture, is more important in maintaining a disciplined continuity in the minds of the inhabitants. One of the upper-upper-class families was forced to sell its house to a comparatively wealthy upper-middle-class Irish family. A member of the upper-class family, commenting on what had happened to her old home, said:

> When the N's bought the place, we thought it was awfully nice. He had lots of money to take care of it, which we couldn't, but then they tore out everything: all the walls, all the woodwork, and all the fireplaces. The only thing they didn't touch was the third floor. It used to be my brother's room up in that back room there. When I saw the house after the N's came in, it felt like the family had been massacred. It was nothing against them, I suppose; they're nice people and all that. They just don't understand and they can't appreciate good things. You know that wisteria blooming in the front yard? Well, my sister planted that over forty years ago. The N's came in and even chopped that down.

The implicit assumption in this statement was that the house was not simply a habitation, but a place which had a certain character about it that demanded a particular kind of ritual treatment, which treatment (the N's not being in the upper-class tradition) had been neglected.

The possession of "a house" is a prime requisite for social

mobility; after several generations, the "new people" who live in these houses and who have adopted upper-class behavior will become members of old families and enter the upper-upper class. The value of an old house is so high that even an individual who is a member of an old family is open to criticism if he does not possess a house which is deemed a suitable setting for upper-class behavior. Mrs. W, when referring to a new dwelling purchased by the daughter of one of the community's most prominent men, said "It is deadly to buy a house like that in Yankee City." When asked to explain, she answered, "It has no background."

Many of the objects in these houses are definitely connected with specific personalities in the past and therefore have an even greater value to the members of the family and class than those objects which are only generally related to antiquity. The linkage of specific personalities with material objects is particularly well revealed in the case of the house of Miss K, a living member of an old lineage. Associated with nearly every object and part of the house is a whole cycle of stories relating to various members of the family. The objects are associated not only with past and present members of the family, but with future owners as well. In fact, so great is the general and historical value attaching to antiques connected with distinguished lineages that there is a concerted effort made by their members to prevent others from purchasing them. L. Y, for instance, a member of a prosperous lower-upper-class family, was able to buy only a few pieces from one of the upper-upper families who sold its antiques to people outside the community. Mrs. T, an upper-upper who had fallen into straitened circumstances, sold her antiques to a Boston dealer with the proviso that he come to collect them at night. There is a definite feeling that these objects should not pass to the mobile lower-upper group; this attitude, of course, also helps to prevent the downward mobility of the old families. It seems likely, moreover, that selling these objects to an outsider for purely economic reasons lessens the likelihood that the spiritual value of the family heirlooms will be transferred to the purchaser.

The plants, flowers, and ornamental objects in the gardens are also associated with personalities. Many of the valuable flowering shrubs are connected with the dead members of a family. When the gardens of Yankee City were opened for public inspection, the ones chosen were those which had lineage connections. "The garden of Mrs. E. D, once visited by President Monroe and Lafayette"; the garden of the Y's "has an historic and patriotic record and is unique in New England with its air of an Old World manor." In all the gardens, the plants pointed out were very old and hence had been in the lineage a long while, or else they could be traced back to an English original which had been transported to America by the ancestors of the present owners of the garden. Thus the garden, like the house and its furnishings, functions as a lineage symbol.

It was mentioned earlier that one of the characteristics of the lower-upper class is an overelaboration of one particular aspect of upper-class behavior. From the upper-upper point of view, these elaborations are artificial and "not really a part of the person" because they have been acquired late in life. Consequently they are open to criticism. These attitudes help to keep lower-upper-class persons subordinated and allow the upper-upper group more freedom in conforming to a set pattern of behavior.

Before reviewing the statistical evidence let us examine the profiles of families in the upper-upper class (old family), in the lower-upper (new family), and in the lowest social-class level (clam flats). From them we can learn about the actual human beings, the personal behavior in three classes, and catch glimpses of the other three levels.

Old Family

Mr. and Mrs. John Aldington Breckenridge (UU) left the tea earlier than the others. ("Everyone was there"—meaning "most" of the two upper classes and a few upper-middles.) They refused several offers to be driven the short distance home, declaring that they needed the exercise.

John Aldington, elder brother of Henry Adams Breckenridge, was a tall rugged man, and when he walked down Hill
Street people said he looked as "straight as the mast of a sailing ship." His white mustache and beard glistened in the late
afternoon sunlight. When the people of the town saw him they
bowed respectfully and commented among themselves on how
well he kept his age. His detractors said he was "so lofty" that
he was like the Lowells and spoke "only to God." But, to those
who knew him, he was "a directly spoken person who always
said what he believed to be the truth."

Mrs. John Breckenridge was a lady who had reached her
seventh decade. She managed her home and family with great
efficiency and quiet tact. She had not married until after she
was thirty, but had borne her husband three children.

Many generations had lived in their large Hill Street house,
and not a few of the great names from New England's and the
nation's history had known its hospitality. The furnishings of
the house were simple and included the accumulation of the
several generations of Breckenridges who had inhabited the
place. Oliver Wendell Holmes, who had sometimes driven by
to talk about genealogical matters and to discuss the names of
the well-remembered dead, was remembered by his cherished
gift, a silver inkstand.

From his study, Mr. Breckenridge could see up and down
Hill Street. From memory he could recount the names of all
of the families who lived in the houses on each side of the wide
street. Each house "worth remembering" had a name. There
was the "Captain Brown house," built in 1810 by a famous
captain in the China trade; or the Littlefield house—"he was
said to be the best orator the old Presbyterian Church ever
had, even in the days when every pew in the Church harbored
a captain and his family." When he talked about the houses,
those present symbols of the living past, he usually commented
on some of their occupants. For many of the houses he knew
the names of all of the former occupants but not of the present
ones. "It's one of those new Irish families, you know, and I

don't know much about them"; or, "Those people may be the ones who are doing something out at the silverware factory, but I'm not sure."

Mr. Breckenridge was thumbing through a fat genealogical record of his family when his dinner guest arrived—a New York painter who was staying for a few weeks at the Yankee City Inn.

"I was checking a point in the family history," he said to his guest. "I had an argument at tea about it with Caleb Marshall." He put a marker in the book and placed it on the library table.

"My children say I think more of that book than I do of my Bible—and you know I think they're right."

At dinner the conversation continued on the topic of the history of Yankee City. And the history of Yankee City to Mr. and Mrs. Breckenridge was largely the history of the old families.

"There are only a few of the old families left," she informed her guest. "Many people who are now considered by some to be old family were not when I was a young girl. There are all of these new shoe people—who are nice people, but they don't belong with such families as the Leveretts, the Wentworths, and the Breckenridges. They all seem just a little new to me, and while undoubtedly they are very nice, they are not old family. My sister Louisa says that they probably think we're a bit queer, too, just as we think they're somehow a little odd; and probably we're both right."

The visitor observed that everything seemed to be judged by its comparative age in Yankee City.

"You see," Mrs. Breckenridge explained, "we people who have always lived here remember a great deal. We go back a long time. All the things my little grandmother used to tell me are as fresh in my mind as yesterday. I can remember walking in the cemetery with her while she put flowers on her mother's grave. She was always so sensible and told me all about the people who were buried there. I felt as though I knew them all.

She told me about all her own people. And as I grew older I learned some of the untold secrets of our family and, I am afraid, some of the gossip about the other families.

"I got to know those people better than almost anyone living. Sometimes I still go over there, not just because of duty but because it is somehow satisfying.

"Modern people hate graveyards but they seem places of peace to me. When I walk through now, each gravestone reminds me of someone I knew or someone grandmother knew and told me about.

"Yankee City is the home of people scattered all over this world. I know several members of old families who live out in Honolulu. They are very prominent people there. Ever so often they come back and take a place here; 'just to come home again,' they say. Some of the houses of Hill Street are only open in the summer time when their owners return from New York, Philadelphia, and Washington.

"In one sense, our lovely houses aren't our homes. It may seem odd, but for those of us whose people have always lived here, the cemetery is truly our home, for there live all of our people. All of them. The men and women who lived in these same houses. You see how we feel and why people come home. I could name a number of families who have not lived here, except in the summer, for the last generation; but when they die all of them are sent back here to be buried. To be in a permanent home.

"I honestly feel sorry for the new people. They can't feel the same way we do about such things."

Mr. Breckenridge had interrupted her with a few confirmatory remarks while she spoke. When they left the dinner table he took up the burden of the conversation.

"The old families aren't as powerful as they used to be. The sons don't follow in their fathers' footsteps. New people keep coming in. They're the ones who get control. Not we. Old families used to run this town but not any more."

Yet that very day, while walking to and from his office

(where he had spent some four hours saying "yes" and "no" to people who were attempting to translate their decisions into economic reality) Mr. Breckenridge had been stopped by several people, each with a question to submit to his judgment and authority.

What did Mr. Breckenridge think about the new schoolhouse?

"Well, the one we've got is good enough. This is no time to be spending our money on a new building."

That night the questioner advised his lodge brother to work against the building of a new schoolhouse because "this is no time to be spending our money on a new building."

As he was turning into his gate, one of the ushers of his church (UU) stopped Mr. Breckenridge.

"What did you think of Rev. Ainsley's [UM] sermon last Sunday?"

"I thought it was no better and no worse than the first one he gave three years ago. I knew then he was muddleheaded. He doesn't understand this town. James, we made a mistake in him. We should have waited until we could have found someone like Sutterfield [UU]."

They both agreed that the appointment of Rev. Mr. Ainsley had been a mistake. The Rev. Mr. Ainsley's duties as shepherd of his flock became increasingly difficult. As the months passed, he had an uneasy feeling that the bishop did not seem quite so friendly as before. He and his wife discussed the advantages of taking a parish in a poor neighborhood of some large city where they could do more effective work.

New Family

The Phillip Starrs drove home from the tea in an oversized, custom-built limousine. John Alton had once remarked sarcastically that if Phillip ever lost his money he could put his stove in his car and camp out for the winter. And his hearer is reported to have said, "Or install a calliope in it and join the circus."

The Starrs were one of a small group of families who recently had purchased Georgian houses in one of the more handsome sections on Hill Street.

The large, square house is one of the old ones on Hill Street. Two well-known architects have declared it to be "one of the most beautiful surviving examples of Federal architecture." Several members of certain old families admitted that it was a beautiful home, but they said, "She made a museum out of it. It's too perfect. She spent thousands of dollars to remodel it and make it a perfect example of Federal architecture. The trouble with her is she imitates and always overdoes it." Only a few feet of well-clipped grass separate the house from the sidewalk, but in the rear an expansive lawn, flanked by meticulously tended gardens, glistens in the sunlight. Some people feel that the gardens are overcared for, that the gardener has been too scrupulous, and that the house has been so frequently painted that it shines just a little too much.

Mrs. Starr's furniture had been purchased with the aid of an expert on New England antiques. There was nothing in her house that was not called "authentic Adams," or "a perfect example of Queen Anne." And her gardens, one soon learned, had won numerous prizes.

The garden parties, teas, and dinners Mrs. Starr gave were said by the gossiping members of the old families to be "too elaborate," "too perfect," and "done for effect." Her defenders (many of them trying to be equally perfect) said it was lovely that she could do such nice things and loved entertaining because she did it so well.

Mr. and Mrs. Starr went into the library and awaited dinner there before an open fire. Mr. Starr read the editorials of the Boston *Transcript* and re-examined the financial pages of the Boston *Herald*. He found nothing in the editorials but "good sound sense." He said it was "too bad that more people didn't read them." The financial pages of the *Herald* were somewhat upsetting, for Mr. Starr's income from the sale of one of his shoe factories had been invested in the bonds of several large national and international companies.

Mrs. Starr looked over the magazines on the library table. Those of her husband and son were arranged in a neat row on one side. They included *Fortune, Time, National Geographic*, and *Sports Afield*. Mr. Starr kept the *Saturday Evening Post* by his bedside and Mrs. Starr read the *Pictorial Review* in her own room. Such magazines, not considered fitting symbol's of one's social place and intellectual level, were kept away from the view of casual—perhaps critical?—guests.

Mrs. Starr glanced idly through the magazines to which she and her husband subscribed: *Atlantic Monthly, House Beautiful, Harper's*, and *Vogue*.

Their son Johnny, however, bought *Film Fun* at the local store, and their daughter Katherine sometimes read the movie magazines; but they knew better than to subscribe to them and always gave them to the maid later.

After dinner Mr. Starr took his own car and drove down to the Lowell Club (UU to UM). The Lowell Club was called the "House of Lords" in local speech, while the Out-of-Doors Club was known as the "House of Commons." This was one way of saying that the Lowell Club was "more choosy" about its members—"no Catholics, and only the best people" are allowed in; but "the House of Commons takes in more fellows from the side streets."

The clubhouse of the Lowell Club had been the home of one of the old families. When Mr. Starr entered it that evening, he met many of the men whom he had seen at the tea. He talked with a broker, a manufacturer, and a banker about investment problems and found out from them what Jonathan Wentworth (UU) and John Breckenridge, the directors of several large institutions, had said on the subject. Mr. Wentworth and Mr. Breckenridge did not belong to the Lowell Club. Mr. Starr listened to Alexander French who talked about what the "classes and the masses" were going to do in the coming election. He heard Mr. French express surprise that there was social "class consciousness now among the people." French said that "the solid people like the men in the Chamber of Commerce and the Rotary Club and our own club can be depended on, but one can't always tell about some of the fellows in the Antlers [UU to LM] and the Caribou [UM to LL]. And most of those foreigners down on River Street are the ringleaders in the unions, and they'll vote the other way."

Jackman (UM), owner of one of the shoe factories, said that his foreman had told him that even the Riverbrookers were now joining the unions.

French agreed with Jackman and then told about the last election held by the United States Veterans of All Wars. He prefaced these remarks by saying, "Don't misunderstand me now, because I like that organization. It has a good influence on the town, and I think it is a duty of all of us to support it; but, you know, it's got everybody in it from the clam flats to Hill Street, and now and then some of those fellows from down there go too far. They get us into a jam, and some of us have to get back in and straighten them out.

"Most of our crowd hardly ever goes. Tim Pinkham [LM] and people like him and the bunch from the Antlers [largely LM] and the Three Mast [LM to LL] run it. It got so bad that they had some strip tease dancers down from Boston. Brooks Sinclair [UU] got us all together, and we put on a quiet little campaign and elected Paul Foley [LU]. Paul didn't want to run, but he agreed to when we convinced him that the better people in town should clean things up and raise the standards." Everyone spoke approvingly of the outcome and of Sinclair's campaign.

While this conversation was in progress, Mr. Starr looked at his watch and said that he would have to hurry on or he would be late to the meeting of the February Club (UU to LU). When he stood up to go, Jim Whitecotton (LU) and Cyrus Jordan (LU) arose and departed with him. Alec French stayed on. He was quiet for a moment after they left, remembering what Jordan's wife had told his wife in a burst of confidence: that when his, Alec's, name had been put up before the February Club he had been blackballed, and Mrs. Jordan had said it was because everybody thought "Alec was too young." Alec knew that there were men in the club who were younger than he. He had once been indignant when he had heard an Irish doctor, who lived just off Hill Street, declare that the men in the January (UU to LU) and February clubs thought they were "Lowells and Cabots." But on occasions such as tonight he found it difficult to refrain from harboring similar sentiments himself. Mr. French was still trying to get into the club. Jordan had told him after the last country club dinner when they were having a few drinks together that he was working on Starr and Walton (LU).

Alec had said to forget it all, but he said it in such a way that Jordan knew that he should try again.

Mr. Starr and his companions, on leaving the Lowell Club, drove to the home of Mr. Arthur Walton. The Walton residence was located in the same cluster of houses with that of Mr. Starr. Several members of their discussion group were already present when they arrived, including active or retired owners of several factories, bankers, lawyers, doctors, ministers, a professor, and a writer. All graduates of universities, they were known as "the heads of prominent families in the country." Except for two Democrats, all were Republicans; but those two were both old family. One was from one of the oldest and most respected families in the community. He once said, "The trouble with most of those fellows is that they forget that the Roosevelts were aristocrats and had money in the family before the Revolution. Most of the people who talk are about two generations from gatekeepers. They spend the rest of their lives trying to forget it."

The February Club was a discussion group. The paper of the evening, fittingly entitled "The History of a Yankee Ship," told how the author, a member of an old family, had spent a recent three months in the Dutch Indies in Malaya. He had searched through certain records in Singapore and had come across the tale he was about to relate that evening. It was shortly after the beginning of the nineteenth century when the clipper *East Wind,* sailing under Capt. John Breckenridge and owned by the captain's father, had run into a great typhoon. The captain had more than won his right to his title during the struggle to keep his ship afloat. After the storm, the ship's crew picked up three survivors of a wreck. One of these was Lord Nelson Wellington who later became prominent in the Napoleonic campaigns and the English leader who, many authorities declared, had saved the British Empire.

After the paper, the discussion brought out the facts that Captain Breckenridge was the great-grandfather of John and Henry Breckenridge; that the chief mate was Jonathan Marshall, the lineal ancestor of the Edward Marshalls; and that the builder of the boat, Frederick Alton, was an ancestor of both John Alton and the wife of Elliot Nash. All these names were connected with the club or were old family and intimate friends of its members.

Anecdotes which usually began: "My father told me that the *East Wind* . . ." or "My Uncle John knew old man Cartwright . . ." were told by some of the older members. The members of the new families present referred more often to history books or asked questions of the others.

At the last meeting, Mr. Starr had given his paper. He had talked on "Henry Ford's Contribution to American Industry." At the meeting before that, Mr. James Whitecotton's paper had not been too well liked. It was called "The Place of Modern Philanthropy in a Modern World."

When Mr. Starr returned home he found none of the family there. Mrs. Starr, he learned, had gone to pick up Margaret Churchill. Miss Churchill lived in the downstairs of an old mansion sadly in need of repair. Her income (from her dead brother's will) was enough for her to maintain herself in simplicity but not sufficient to allow renovation of her home or more than a modest scale of living. Everyone said, "I don't see how she does it" and "She never says a word but doesn't she always give the nicest little teas?"

Mrs. Starr had dropped by Margaret's to invite her to see some old silverware she had bought in London and to look at her new clothes from Paris. She had not been able to call Miss Churchill on the telephone because Miss Churchill, regarding this new invention as an unnecessary waste, had never had one installed.

Miss Churchill inspected the silverware and clothes and was pleasantly surprised by gifts of expensive underwear, stockings, and gloves. "They're so cheap over there, my dear; I got them for nothing. I'm glad you think they are beautiful. I thought of you as soon as I saw them."

When Miss Churchill said that she must go, Mrs. Starr suggested that they take a short drive down to the sea. While they drove through the sand dunes, Mrs. Starr adroitly turned the subject to the possibility of her daughter's getting into the House and Home Club. She herself had achieved this eminence because her friend, Miss Churchill, had threatened to resign unless the members who opposed Mrs. Starr agreed to allow her in. The members of the club were still bitter about it, but they blamed "that social climber who took advantage of Margaret" rather than Miss Churchill herself.

Miss Churchill told Mrs. Starr it would take time to accomplish this because Mrs. Walton, Mrs. Jordan, and Mrs. Whitecotton (all LU competitors of Mrs. Starr's), were still in the club. Mrs. Starr dropped the subject. (Her daughter has not yet been invited into the club.)

After dinner, Johnny Starr had left immediately and had driven up to see the Travis Uptons (LU). It was a familiar sight to see his new Packard, which he drove at fifty miles an hour, racing up Hill Street. The local police had asked his father to request John to drive more slowly because it was dangerous. Whenever Johnny "got too tight" and the police found him, they always drove him home; but he had yet to be arrested. He and his friends laughed about the night when they were all tight and had to stop down there by one of the wharves on River Street to sober up. "A cop came up and started to bawl us out, and he was getting ready to arrest us; but when he saw it was John Starr he said, 'Oh, I didn't know it was you, Johnny. Now you just move over and keep quiet and I'll drive you home.' " Johnny said if the cops had run him and his friends in every time they'd found them drunk their record would have been longer than that of the town drunk.

Johnny had studied music in Rome after he had flunked out at Princeton. "I spent all of my time in New York—at the Astor and in the speaks in the 50's. And I never cracked a book while I was at Princeton." The three years in Rome had broadened his knowledge of human sexual behavior, increased his interest in modern painting, sculpturing, and architecture, and taught him enough music to make it possible for him to get a job with one of the wholesale music houses in Boston.

Johnny had returned home from Europe very suddenly, immediately after a friend (LU) of his had committed suicide. This friend was a son of a wealthy hat manufacturer in Yankee City who had accompanied Johnny to Rome "to learn how to write." He took his own life when a blackmailer had threatened to expose certain peculiarities of his career. Johnny himself was considered psychologically unstable and had once talked of going to a psychiatrist to "get all these complexes ironed out."

The Travis Uptons were not exciting people to Johnny. The example of Travis was always being thrown in Johnny's face by his father to show him what he might have done had he, Johnny, followed his father's advice. He wanted to see Travis and his wife about the coming Country Club dance. They were all on the arrangements committee.

Travis was the highly respected son of C. I. Upton. People in his own set always said, "Of course, he can't hold a candle to his father, but he's dependable and a hard worker. It's too bad his wife's a climber and mistreats him, but that's not his fault."

Travis belonged to the Rotary, the Lowell, and January discussion group. The last club closely resembled the February Club in its social composition. His wife belonged to the Women's Club, the Garden Club, and the House and Home Club. She was on the board of the library, the Y.W.C.A., and the S.P.C.C. Except for the Country Club, Johnny Starr belonged to no local organizations. Indeed, he professed contempt for those who did.

When Johnny arrived at the Uptons', he found that they had a couple new to Yankee City as dinner guests. They were from New York and "were dear friends of the Cartwrights and the Putnams, you know." By remarks adroitly dropped in the conversation, it soon developed that the husband was Yale '23 and the wife Vassar '26, and that he had come to Yankee City as the manager of one of the large companies.

While drinks were being mixed, Johnny said, "Well, I feel sorry for you because you've come to a funny town." Everyone laughed politely.

"I don't know," the new lady said, "I think it's all so beautiful, so old, and so lovely."

"It's old all right," Johnny said. "The last novelties came into this town when Victoria was alive, and most of the women who still live here are of the same vintage. The people who run this place haven't had a new idea since General Grant died."

The newcomers continued to laugh politely.

"Don't you believe him," said the hostess. "It's not as bad as he says. They are conservative here. You will find it a little hard to get to know people and everyone will tell you the sad story about the very nice couple that stayed here a year, and no one called on them so they moved away."

"We haven't found them that way. So many nice people have called," said the new lady.

"Of course they will with you because everyone knows who you are. But most people are conservative here," Mrs. Upton continued. "I mean particularly the old families. They take pride in it, I guess. My family have been here only a generation, and we still don't really rate being old family. And the older they are the more conservative they are."

"Yes," said Johnny, "the Wentworths don't even have a bathroom. And they still have an outside privy. They won't install a toilet because if the house was good enough the way their ancestors had it, it's good enough for them. Do you know that there are old families here who won't even put in electric lights? They say they're new and not worth having."

Again everyone laughed politely. Mrs. Upton once more took up the conversation. "It takes time, Mrs. Ainsworth [LU], to get used to this place. I agree with you, it is beautiful. Even Salem's Chestnut Street is no more beautiful than our Hill Street. And, Johnny, you're just wrong about it all. You had too good a time in Rome, and I am afraid you met too many ladies there whose morals were not what they should have been."

While Johnny fixed himself another drink, he commented, "Lord, she's always trying to find out what we did in Rome. But let me get back to my favorite theme. What I can't understand about this place is why all these people are so proud of it all. They talk about this one or that one being a descendant of a family that was in the 'Calcutta trade,' you know. That always burns me up. Why, my father is a successful shoe manufacturer. He worked hard, and he made a lot of money; and he acted smart in saving it. Maybe we should act snooty about that. He sent us kids to good schools, and he's given a lot of money to help this town; but when they say I am the son of a shoe manufacturer that means that we Starrs are too new to count. Take my advice, dear lady, and go far far away."

"If that's the way you feel about it, why do you stay?" said the host. He had entered the conversation after a quiet discussion of business matters with his male guest.

"I don't know; I can't help it. But I keep staying on. I swore I could never come back when I went to Rome, but I did. I am always planning to get out. Sometimes I dream of going to Tahiti, but somehow I always come back here. My mother says whenever I used to get pushed around I always clung to her. I guess that's it. I can't leave Mamma, and I can't leave home."

After having two more highballs, Johnny left. He drove down to River Street and stopped near a small shack where he bought a pint of rye from a Pole. He drank a large part of it by upending the bottle. Then he drove to the interstate highway and started for Boston. On the way, he telephoned a girl who danced at a Boston nightclub. He always grinned when he spoke of her and said he liked her because "she's just a little depraved."

After he called the girl he telephoned his mother and said that he had a business call from Boston and wouldn't be home that night. At the nightclub he finished his rye and bought some more. He never finished it, however, for he passed out and was driven in his car by the girl to her apartment. In the morning she said to him: "Johnny, I can't understand why you always want to pass out. It's no fun to get drunk that way."

Johnny replied, "Nuts! That's the only way to drink. A very wise guy once said, 'I consider it the end of all wisdom to be drunken and go to the dogs.'"

Clam Flats

Going home from the bar after he had said goodnight, Jones (LL) crawled in bed beside his wife and the springs sank in the middle. Three small children were asleep on a mattress in the corner of the room. Two adolescent daughters slept on cots next to the wood stove in the kitchen.

By morning, it had suddenly turned bitter cold. Seven persons were crowded around the iron stove in a small kitchen. There was no central heating in the house because it was too expensive and perhaps "unnecessary." The kitchen table was still littered with the remains of the evening meal. Mr. Sam Jones was smoking his pipe. He and his family had eaten a good meal of bread, potatoes, and clams. Mrs. Jones' brother had given them the clams, a part of the results of his hard diggings on the clam flats that morning. They were the last of the season. He had said, "The damn chlorinating plant's taking all the profit out of clamming. There ain't any money in it any more, and it's hardly worth a man's time to go out there and freeze to death on the flats."

The potatoes had come from a supply which Mrs. Jones had bought when they were cheap. The half-empty gunny sack sat in one corner of the room. She had made the bread they had eaten, and her husband had said it was "a damn sight better than that store bread."

Later in the day Sam Jones went out to see about doing a little road work for the city. Maybe if he could get a good steady job he would get "off the relief." He always came home angry every time he went to the relief office anyway.

"Those bastards are nosy. They always ask questions that are none of their business." He wished times were like they used to be. A man was his own boss then. He could clam a little and fish a little and earn a little extra money at the shoe factory, and when he got tired he would go hunting ducks. Why, he remembered the time when little Tim Jones had come into the factory where they were working and told his father the ducks were lighting over on the west pond, and all ten of the cutters from Riverbrook in his room had quit right then and gone hunting. "Now, goddam it, you have to join a union to keep a measly job."

After some inquiries, he heard there were no municipal jobs to be had, nor were there jobs at any of the shoe factories. He came home and lay down on the unmade bed. He took yesterday's copy of the Boston *Record* out of his pocket and glanced at the box scores. He then began a story in an old copy of *Cosmopolitan*. Someone knocked at the door, but he didn't answer. He was afraid it might be the S.P.C.C. girl, or the truant officer, or the relief worker, or someone from the veterans' bureau, or from the church which gave him coal, or just someone who would try to tell him what to do. After a brief period the knocking ceased and the unknown caller went away. His life was filled with people like that. Jones went on with his story; but before he had finished the magazine dropped from his hands. Sam Jones snored.

They lived in a region of the town where two or more families crowded into one small house, where people seldom owned their own homes, but rented a few rooms. The houses were run-down and needed paint. Toilet facilities were limited. A garden was rare, and there was little or no attempt to keep a lawn.

One of the most noticeable characteristics of lower-class housing is the lack of space. Heating usually comes from the coal stove in the kitchen, which in cooler weather turns into the dining and living room as well. Several beds are often found in the one bedroom, and the overflow sleeps on cots in the kitchen-dining room. In rare instances there is a living room with some cheap overstuffed furniture.

The first American ancestors of the Joneses, the Greens, and the Tylers settled around Yankee City and in nearby villages coincidentally with the founding of those communities. Like the ancestors of their fellow citizens on Hill Street, they plowed the rocky soil a very little and fished the shores and sailed their boats to make a living. Legends tell of the ancestors of certain of these Riverbrook families being washed ashore at a nearby town on log rafts when a great storm swept them in from a mysterious southern land; but genealogies and the testimony of gravestones indicate that the Riverbrookers are of good old English stock, that "these degenerate Yankees" are the living descendants of "those who came to America to worship God," to get rich, and "to escape the unpleasant circumstances of their English homeland."

Long before his son was born, the father of Sam Jones had watched his lobster pots in season, helped his brother William when the clamming was profitable, and worked as a stitcher in the P. O. Shoe Factory "when the spirit moved him." Sam's father was the last man, his son said, to take shoes by contract. After him, shoes were no longer made in the home but manufactured in the factory.

The Jones were faced with a problem. That day that very "fresh" girl had called on them again. She had the truant officer (LM) with her. ("One of those goddam Catholics who liked to show his authority.") She had also visited the Frank Tylers. They had both asked Mrs. Jones why her children were not in school. She had wanted to tell "that Mick" it was none of his business but she was afraid he might take her children or do something equally unpleasant in retaliation. The truant officer had said that "unless those kids come more regularly to school,

I am going to have you up in front of Judge Black [UM]." This frightened her because her brother's two boys had been sent to reform school when this same cop had snooped around and caught them and some other boys selling a few things they had taken from a store.

The girl was from the Society for the Prevention of Cruelty to Children (UM). Mrs. Jones smelled cigarette smoke on her, and any woman who would smoke would do anything. What right had she to come around asking questions about a body's own children, a-hintin' that her girls were misbehavin' with some of the boys up at the Smith School? Only yesterday she had beaten the tar out of both of them for this very thing. And she didn't think it did any good. She had tried before and it didn't work. Anyway, the boys weren't foreigners, and if worse came to worst she knew their folks.

Mr. Jones had listened to his wife's account of the incident and said, "Well, Bessie, let's take the kids and get out of this town. Let's go back across the river. This city welfare here is just as nosy. When Johnny broke his leg across the river he had to go to the hospital in an undertaker's wagon, but the doctor over there don't try to tell you how to bring up your kids."

Mr. Jones said he guessed he'd go and talk it over with Frank Tyler.

When the girl from the S.P.C.C. and the truant officer drove away in her shiny new coupe, they rode over to see the principal of the Smith School. The truant officer found Principal Oldfield (UM) out in the schoolyard. He said to him, "The S.P.C.C. gal is in your office. We've just been down to Sam Jones's and the Frank Tylers'. I thought she was going to puke when she went into their kitchens. It did smell pretty terrible."

Oldfield came into his office. He greeted her by saying: "Well, how do you like our Riverbrookers? I hear you've been calling on Mrs. Sam Jones and Mrs. Frank Tyler."

"Why do people have to be so filthy?"

"Because that's the way they like it. Keep them all clean for six months and it would kill them. They cause me more trouble than all the rest of the kids put together. They're dumb and not interested. They don't want to learn anything. But what can you expect when their parents don't want them to either?"

"I suppose delinquency rates must be higher in your school?" she said.

"Delinquency rates! Don't make me laugh! Delinquency rates! Why that little trollop Bessie Jones alone rates about one delinquency a day, and that day they caught her over there behind the old tire factory with those four boys. Well, I'd imagine it was at the rate of every ten minutes. Isn't that right, Fred?"

The truant officer who had taken a subsidiary role and was largely ignored when the principal and the S.P.C.C. girl began their conversation said:

"They keep me busy. Not only on sex crimes. They're easy. But they have no respect for property. They'll steal anything. I've just broken up my third gang this year."

Oldfield looked at the truant officer in a vague way.

"But most of those kids weren't Riverbrookers. Some of them were your own breed of cat."

"Yeah, I know. Some of those shanty Irish are just the same as Riverbrookers. Those new foreigners, some of those Poles and Greeks—give me time and I'll get them all over to the reform school where they'll learn something useful."

"Well, in my small way," said Oldfield, "I keep a lot of them out of trouble. I always advise them to take the commercial and stay out of the Latin and scientific courses in high school. That means they learn a little something useful. I see no use in people like that taking courses that would prepare them for college. Too many people are going to college anyway."

"Are any of them bright?"

"Yes, some are. But they don't last long. They soon peter out."

The minister (UM) of the church attended by most Riverbrookers, his friend and clique mate, the doctor (UM), who had taken a deep interest in these people, and two friends of theirs (LU) were discussing their favorite topic.

"I've known these Riverbrookers—man and boy—well, I guess I've known them all my life," said the doctor. "You've heard people call them 'broken-down Yankees' and accuse them of all the crimes on the calendar. People are always asking me if they all sleep with their daughters. Because there have been one or two cases of homosexuality among them, everyone in Yankee City thinks that all of the Riverbrookers are homosexual. They are always being accused of being lazy and spending all of their time doing nothing. Of course, you've heard the old one about 'their fishing et cetera in the summer but they can't fish in the winter.' This is told you by everyone who uses the little four-letter words.

"Now, as a matter of fact, there's no more incest here than up on Hill Street, and I've heard of very little up there. People up there do get involved in rather strong emotional ties inside their families which sometimes interfere with their marriages. I suspect that aristocrats are more likely to be homosexual than lower-class people."

"One's always hearing that these lower-class kids are said to be more delinquent," said the minister. "I think about all that such a statement means is that the police catch them more often and they get less protection from the police than the people do up on Hill Street."

Philip Alsop (LU) interrupted, "I agree with you. Tim [LU], do you remember the time when we broke into the old Breckenridge house when they were away for the summer and stole their silverware and took all of those things out of their living room? After we had done it, we were all so scared we buried everything out in the pond in the Common."

"I certainly do. I often think of that and all of the other things we did when I hear about these foreign kids and the kids in the clam flats being arrested for stealing."

The minister said, "Why a mother of an adolescent daughter, you all know her—she lives on Hill Street—was complaining to me the other day about the morals of her children and their friends. Some of the children today in Yankee City behave in a way that frightened her. The group her daughter went around with were not acting well at all. She said she knew that some of them were indulging in sexual play. That's not the first time I've heard of our better-class children's morals. Some of the children in the high school, I hear, are doing all sorts of things which they shouldn't be. They are always talking about necking, and I guess a few of them go much further than that. Some of these kids are from good families, too."

Said Phillip Alsop, "I remember when I was playing around before I got married. All my attention to the girls did not come out of pure love. Not by a long shot. We had fun. I don't think these kids today are any worse than we used to be."

"Well, Phil," said the doctor smilingly, "I've heard that you didn't show much interest in the loaf of bread part of Omar's little piece of poetry."

The minister continued, "There are no better Christians in this town than the Riverbrookers. They help each other. They share their food and whatever they have with each other. They don't lose their self-respect and independence because some of them receive charity. I like them. I like them a lot more than some of my parishioners from Hill Street."

—

CHAPTER 4

Economic Life of the Community

Workers in the Various Industries

THE largest and most important industry in Yankee City is shoe manufacturing. The second most important is silverware manufacturing which provides employment for a large group of highly trained workers. At the time of our study most of the workers classed as auto-body and cotton textile employees were unemployed since these industries had left the city and surrounding areas. Farming, moreover, is a negligible pursuit in the economic life of the town, and those who follow the sea have been reduced to a few clammers, insignificant in number, but nevertheless important in the life of the community.

Of the 6,155 workers in Yankee City, 71 per cent are male and 29 per cent female. The male workers are concentrated in significantly high numbers in hat and auto-body factories, in building trades, in transportation, and in clamming, and in significantly low numbers in the shoe industry. The female workers are employed in significantly high numbers in the shoe industry and in electric shops, and in significantly low numbers in silverware factories, auto-body works, building trades, transportation, and clamming.

Over 51 per cent (51.54 per cent) of those employable are Yankees and 47.88 per cent are members of the other ethnic groups.

In half of the major industries there is a higher percentage of ethnics employed than Yankees. These industries are shoe

manufacturing, hat manufacturing, cotton textile manufacturing, retail stores, and transport. The industries in which there
is a higher proportion of Yankees than of the other ethnic
groups combined are silverware, auto-body, electric shops,
building trades, and clamming.

The natives were significantly high in the silverware factories, the building trades, and in clamming. They were significantly low in the shoe factories, hat and cotton textile factories,
and in the retail stores. The Irish were significantly high in
transport, and in "other" economic activities. There was a significantly low number of Irish in the silver factories, the building trades, and in clamming. There was a significantly high
number of French in the shoe and cotton factories and a significantly low number in the silverware factories and in "other"
economic occupations. The Jews were significantly high in the
retail stores and significantly low in the building trades and
transport. There was a significantly high number of Polish
workers in the hat and cotton industries and a significantly low
number in "other" economic activities. The Russians were significantly high in the hat and cotton industries and low in
"other" economic activities. The Greeks were significantly high
in the shoe factories and significantly low in "other" economic
activities. The Armenians were significantly high in the shoe
factories and the retail stores and significantly low in "other"
activities. The Italians were significantly high in the shoe and
hat factories and in the electric shops.

In summary, no ethnic group had a significantly high number of workers in any industry where the natives did except the
Irish in the general economic activity called "others"; and no
ethnic group was significantly low in any activity where the
natives were significantly low. The French, Greeks, Armenians,
and Italians were significantly high in the shoe industry where
the natives were significantly low; and the Poles, Russians and
Italians were significantly high in the hat industry where the
natives were significantly low; the French, Poles, and Russians
were significantly high in the cotton textile factories where the
natives were significantly low, and the Armenians and the Jews

were significantly high in retail stores where the natives were significantly low.

The French and Irish were significantly low in the silverware factories where the natives were high. The Irish and Jews were significantly low in the building trades where the natives were significantly high. The Irish had a low number of workers in the clamming industry where the natives had a significantly high number; and the French, Poles, Russians, Greeks, and Armenians had a significantly low number of workers in "other" economic activities where the natives and Irish had a high number.

Occupations of the Six Classes

There is a high correlation between type of occupation and class position in Yankee City. If a person is a professional man or a proprietor he tends to be upper or middle class; if he is an unskilled worker he tends to be lower class. However, not all professional men are upper class and not all workers are lower class. Although clerks tend to be lower-middle class, some of them are upper class and others are lower class.

Table 1. *Occupation and Class*
(in per cent)

	UU	LU	UM	LM	UL	LL
Professional and proprietary	83.33	85.72	62.16	13.74	2.78	0.73
Wholesale and retail dealers		7.14	15.38	10.87	5.88	2.74
Clerks and kindred workers	16.67	7.14	15.08	28.80	9.19	3.66
Skilled workers			5.23	17.32	12.71	4.57
Semiskilled workers			2.15	27.12	61.53	79.16
Unskilled workers				2.15	7.91	9.14

An analysis of Table 1 shows that professional and proprietary occupations and clerks are found throughout the six classes,
and that there is a sharp drop in the first classification from the
upper-middle to the lower-middle class and from the latter
class to the upper-lower stratum. There is also a break in the
percentage of clerks from the upper-lower to the lower-lower.

There are no skilled or semiskilled workers higher than the
upper-middle group. The day laborer, although ranging from
lower-lower to lower-middle, tends to be lower class.

Most of the lower-lower class is composed of unskilled or
nonskilled workers and the percentage of semiskilled workers
steadily drops away through lower-middle to upper-middle and
disappears in the two upper classes. On the other hand, most
of the upper-upper, lower-upper, and upper-middle occupations are professional and proprietary workers. This occupational group rapidly loses ground to the other categories in the
lower-middle and lower-class strata.

Class and occupation are closely interrelated, but it is a mistake to classify all professional people at the top of the heap
and all workers at the bottom; far too many factors contribute
to a person's social status for such arbitrary ranking to be
exact and accurate.

Property

There were 2,911 persons who owned real estate in Yankee
City. Most of the real estate owned by any individual was less
than $3,000, the median assessed value of all real estate pos-
sessed by each person being $2,391. Slightly over 50 per cent
(50.40 per cent) of the property was owned by males, and
49.60 per cent by females.

The median value of the property of male owners was $2,238
and of females, $2,538. With the exception of males in their
fifties there is a constant increase in the value of real estate
owned by either sex as age increases, but the value of real
estate owned by females at any age level is higher than that of
the males.

Almost 60 per cent of the real property owners of Yankee City were Yankee. The Armenians outranked all other ethnic groups in the percentage of their ownership which was worth more than $20,000. They were followed, in the order named, by the Jews, Irish, Yankees, and French Canadians. No other ethnic groups owned real estate worth this amount. The Jews led the Armenians, Yankees, Poles, Greeks, Irish, and French Canadians for ownership of property above $10,000 and below $20,000. No other groups owned property of this value.

The median value of all real estate increases as the rank of the class increases. For example, 87 per cent of the lower-lower owners held real estate below $3,000; 76 per cent of the upper-lower; 63 per cent of the lower-middle; 38 per cent of the upper-middle; 22 per cent of the lower-upper; and 18 per cent of the upper-upper. More than one half of the three lowest classes of owners fell in this lowest category of ownership. The lower-lower class is last for the proportionate amount of real estate owned at all levels except the lowest where it is first. The upper-upper class leads for the $20,000 classification followed by the lower-upper and upper-middle classes. The lower-upper class ranks first followed by the upper-upper and upper-middle for the $10,000 and $5,000 categories. The upper-middle class is first and the upper-upper and lower-upper next in the $3,000 to $5,000 bracket. Class and property ownership show definite relationship; nevertheless there are property owners of the highest brackets belonging to the lowest classes, and property owners of the lowest brackets belonging to the highest classes.

The value of a person's house (owned and lived in) declines as the rank of his class decreases. The only exception to this rule is that the lower-upper houses have a higher median value than the upper-upper houses. The median value of houses owned and lived in by the upper-upper class was $3,750; for the lower-upper, $4,121; the upper-middle, $2,706; the lower-middle, $1,800; the upper-lower, $1,530; and the lower-lower, $1,202.

How the Six Classes Spent Their Money

When an individual in Yankee City spent money for articles which could be purchased, he was acting in accordance with his system of values and thereby satisfying certain of his desires. The desires of all those who spent money for the things they wanted were basically physical, but the values which dominated the expression of their wants were social. All men and women in Yankee City as physical organisms needed food and shelter, but the values which dictated their choice of a house or food for a meal were socially determined and also expressed the demands, needs, and limitations of their social personalities in a status system.

When a man in the lower-upper class rented a house he paid for physical shelter for his family, but he also paid for the "right kind" of house in the "right" neighborhood which would bring the approval of his friends and his social superiors. In other words, he rented a house which he believed would correspond with and reflect his family's way of life. When his wife gave a dinner party, she bought food that would meet the values of the dinner ritual; and when she dressed that evening, she, her family, and her friends wore clothes proper to the ritual. Many people in classes below the two upper ones earned more money, but the things they purchased were part of a different system of values and were used differently. The average income, however, was greater in the upper classes and consequently they had fewer economic limitations on their social choices; greater economic freedom did not necessarily mean greater social freedom in their selection of the "things they wanted." The etiquette and social rules of the higher classes were more rigid and more restricted; yet choice in action was much more developed than in the lower classes.

The budget of an individual or family is in part a symbol system, or a set of collective representations, that expresses the social values of a person's membership in a group life. This section will analyze the expenditures of the people of Yankee

City to determine the class values in expenditure of money. The comparative proportion of the budgets of the members of each class for twenty-six kinds of items will be presented.

The field study of the budgetary behavior of the classes in Yankee City was done with a forty-page schedule which was used in most cases while a person was interviewed about his expenditures. The total income, twenty-six items of expense, and all the separate expenditures under each item were listed. In this chapter the total income will be treated briefly and we shall confine ourselves almost entirely to an analysis of the several types of expenditure. The problem to which we address ourselves is essentially "social" rather than "economic."[1]

The budgets collected were selected from a cross section— 1,094 individuals represented—of each class. Twenty-one were from the upper-upper class, 28 from the lower-upper class, 319 from the upper-middle class, 397 from the lower-middle class, 209 from the upper-lower class, and 120 from the lower-lower class. The average income of each social class was larger than that of the class beneath it, but the range of income of each class overlapped the range of one or more of the classes below and above it. The lower range of the upper-upper class overlapped the highest end of the range of the lower-lower class.

Let us now define what is meant by each of the twenty-six items of expense. Under rent and shelter, the ordinary rental expenses were included; when a man owned the house in which he lived, the taxes on his house and lot, the interest on mortgages, insurance, water rates, and the upkeep on the physical plant were treated as part of his expenditures for shelter.

All money spent for food at home or at restaurants was classified under the heading of food. Clothes included money spent for ready-made clothes, for the material and making of men's and women's wearing apparel, and for cleaning, pressing, and general upkeep.

Fuel, light, ice, telephone, telegraph, laundry, and house-

1. The percentages of the totals are for total expenditures and not for total income.

hold help expenses were listed under the general heading of house operation.

Money spent on furniture of all kinds, including radio and musical instruments, was included under house equipment. If these articles were bought by installment, only payments made during the year of the budget were included.

Automobile expenses included general upkeep, fines, taxes, and insurance, and that part of the purchase price which was expended for the year of the budget study.

Amusements covered expenditures in theaters, motion pictures, dances, and admission to other entertainments.

A separate item of expense was made for money expended on associations, clubs, and churches (hereafter referred to simply as associations). The expenses listed here were dues and donations, but no moneys spent for charity.

Charitable contributions did not include gifts but such items as community and personal philanthropies to the poor and the needy. Gifts were defined as birthday and holiday presents and those given to friends during such crises as sickness and childbirth. A gift essentially is a symbol given to another who is sufficiently coordinate with the giver to return a similar one, while charity and philanthropy are moneys spent on those who cannot return it. Charities subordinate the receiver and superordinate the giver; presents coordinate a relationship in the Yankee City system of class.

Education was divided into formal and informal categories. The former included all money spent on school tuition, textbooks, music and art lessons, and correspondence courses. Informal education consisted of money spent on home reading, magazines, newspapers, library dues, and book subscriptions and purchases.

Legal expenses were fees paid to lawyers and money spent in the courts.

Medical and health expenditures were for doctors, dentists, oculists, nurses, hospitals, and medicine; and mortuary expenses were for undertakers and cemeteries.

Money spent on personal appearance included payments to

barber and beauty shops and for toothpaste and similar items.

Professional and craft equipments were such things as carpenters' tools, X-ray machines, and other tools and instruments
used by artisans and professional people.

All money spent on photography, including the expense of
amateur photography and of professional services, was classed
under this general heading. Sporting and athletic equipment
was given a separate listing.

State and federal income taxes, poll taxes, and all other
taxes, except those on the house and automobile, were treated
under one general heading.

The other items were postage, tobacco and stationery, moving, travel for pleasure (including vacation expenses), and
travel for business. There was a miscellaneous heading which
included all expenses which the informant could not otherwise
classify.

The highest average income for each individual was in the
lower-upper class. Each person averaged $2,652.61 and the
average income for each family was $6,189.42 in that class.
The individuals in the upper-upper class received the next
highest income: each person averaged $2,133.61, and each
family, $6,400.83. The income of the upper-middle class aver-
aged $832.75 per person or $2,887.48 for each family. The
incomes of the two upper classes were approximately the same,
but that of the upper-middle was considerably smaller than
the two upper classes. However, it was much larger than the
income of the lower-middle class. The income of the lower-
middle class for each person was $449.33 per year and
$1,621.69 for a family. The income of the upper-lower class
was considerably lower than that of the lower-middle. Each
upper-lower person averaged $279.28 per year, and each fam-
ily, $1,216.02 a year. The lower-lower class received the
smallest average income of all classes. Each person in that class
averaged $154.47, and each family, $882.71. (The year was
1933.)

The average expense per year for each person in the lower-
upper class was higher than in any other. The total expenses

of each person in this class averaged $2,279.62. The average expense of the upper-upper class was second: each person in this class spent an average of $2,004.44. The average expense per family was highest in the upper-upper class. Each family spent $6,013.32. Each family in the lower-upper class spent an average of $5,319.12 per year.

Each person in the upper-middle class spent an average of $697.95. Each family spent an average each year of $2,420.07. In the lower-middle class, each person spent an average of $444.24, and each family spent $1,603.29. The members of the upper-lower class spent $284.29 per person, and the families of the upper-lower class averaged $1,237.84 for their total expenses for a year. In the lower-lower class, each person had an average expense of $164.46 a year, and each family spent, on the average, $939.79 a year. All classes except the lower two had a higher income than their total expenses, but the members of each of the lower classes were spending more than they were making. It must be remembered that this budget study was made in 1933, which was one of the "worst years" of the 1930–35 economic depression.

The highest total expense of any family in the upper-upper class was $18,000, and the lowest was $1,485. The highest total expense of any family in the lower-class was $2,725, and the lowest, $340. The highest expense in the lowest class was almost twice that of the lowest expense in the highest class. The expense figures are given rather than the total income figures because at the time of the study the expenses in the several classes were often larger than the income. The total expense, therefore, brings the lowest figures of the lower class up higher than the total income figures do.

The range of expenditures in the lower-upper class was from $12,185 to $851; in the upper-middle class, from $7,800 to $353; in the lower-middle class, from $3,400 to $468; and in the upper-lower class, from $4,425 to $345.

In order that the reader may have the figures for the range of income in each of the classes, we shall present them here. We feel, however, that the total expense figures are of greater significance, inasmuch as they describe what the people got by their spending in Yankee City. The range of income in the upper-upper class was from $20,000 to $1,105; in the lower-upper, from $18,000 to $810; in the upper-middle, from $8,300 to $400; in the lower-middle, from $4,300 to $245; in the upper-lower, from $5,000 to $210; and in the lower-lower class, from $2,800 to $305.

The five categories of expenditure which lead all others for the average amount of money spent yearly by the people of Yankee City are, in the order named, food, house operation, rent, automobiles, and clothing. Each of these five categories is more than 8 per cent and less than 27 per cent of the total amount spent.

The next seven items of largest expense are taxes, formal education, medical care, house equipment, gifts, charity, and associations. All of these items are over 1 per cent and below 4 per cent. The next two items are above 1 per cent and below 2 per cent; they are informal education and travel for vacation purposes. The last categories of expense are 1 per cent or below. They are listed in the order of their size: personal appearance, amusement, travel for business purposes, tobacco, postage and stamps, legal expenses, sporting equipment, professional and technical equipment, mortuary expenses, photographic equipment, and furniture moving.

Food ranks first for the four lowest classes; rent, second; house operations, third; and clothing is fourth for the middle and lower classes. On the other hand, house operation is first for the two upper classes, reflecting the great value placed by them on the house. While food is second in the expenditures of the upper-upper class, it is third for the lower-upper stratum. The automobile ranks second for the lower-upper class, indicating the high selective value placed on conspicuous display by this class. The middle classes give the automobile fifth place and are nearest to the lower-upper class, but they place food, rent, house operation, and clothing before the car in their scale of expenditures. The upper-lower class expends a greater proportion of its budget on the same items as well as medical ex-

penses than on the automobile. The upper-upper people spend
a greater proportion of their money on taxes and formal education than on the automobile. The lower-lower class ranks the
automobile as ninth out of the eighteen categories on which
it spends money. It is noteworthy that whereas all other classes
had few or no categories missing from their lists, almost one-
third were missing from the lower-lower budget.

The problem among the lower classes of paying the doctor
bill ranks on equal terms with that of paying the tax collector
among the two upper classes. Medical expenses ranked fifth for
the two lower classes and sixth for the two middle ones and
eighth and ninth for the upper-upper and lower-upper classes;
on the other hand, taxes ranked fifth and sixth for the upper-
upper and lower-upper classes.

The proportion of the expense money spent for food was
higher in the lower-lower class than in any other. The proportion of the money spent for food by each class decreased as the
rank of the class increased, but the amount of money spent in
each case was more than for the class below (see Table 2).
The lower-lower class spent $74.69 per person a year for its
food, or $426.86 each year for the average family. This repre-
sented 45.42 per cent of its total budget. The upper-lower class
spent $105.21 for each person, or $458.11 for the average
family. This was 37.01 per cent of its total budget.

The lower-middle class spent $139.21, or $502.38 for the
average family. This was 31.35 per cent of its total expense
for a year. Each upper-middle-class person spent an average
of $168.40 a year for food, or a family spent $583.92. This
was 24.12 per cent of all their expenses. Each lower-upper-
class person spent $311.22, and each lower-upper-class family
spent $726.21 a year for its food. This represented 13.64 per
cent of their total expenses. The average member of the upper-
upper class spent $236.09 a year for his food, and each family
spent an average of $708.30 a year for food.

The lower-lower class spent a higher proportion of its money
for rent and shelter than any other class. Again, the position
of a class was in direct relation to the proportion of its budget

Table 2. *Budget of Each Class*
(in per cent)

	UU 4-5	LU 2	UM 3	LM 4-5	UL 1	LL 6
Moving	0.05	0.07	0.06	0.05	0.08	0.04
Photography	2	4	1	3	5	6
	0.08	0.06	0.13	0.07	0.05	0.03
Mortuary	—	—	2	3	1	—
			0.29	0.26	0.67	
Professional equipment	4	—	3	2	1	—
	0.01		0.13	0.26	1.09	
Sporting equipment	4	1	2-3	2-3	5	—
	0.07	0.16	0.09	0.09	0.06	
Legal	3	1	2		4	
	0.12	0.26	0.22	—	0.06	—
Postage	3-4	1	2	3-4	5	6
	0.22	0.57	0.29	0.22	0.18	0.08
Tobacco	6	5	3	4	2	1
	0.27	0.56	1.06	1.05	1.57	1.75
Business-travel	1	4	2	3	5	
	1.34	0.41	0.64	0.47	0.27	—
Amusements	4-5	3	2	1	4-5	6
	0.67	0.89	1.00	1.15	0.67	0.46
Personal appearance	2	6	3-4	1	3-4	5
	1.02	0.81	0.99	1.16	0.99	0.93
Informal education	5	2	3	4	1	6
	0.72	1.32	1.10	1.06	2.44	0.50
Unclassified	1	4	2	3		
	3.71	0.12	0.54	0.13	—	—
Vacation-travel	4	1	3	2	5	6
	1.57	2.25	1.64	1.83	0.32	—
Associations	2	1	4	5	3	6
	1.86	3.34	1.14	1.03	1.69	0.48
Charity	1	3	2	4	5	6
	3.61	2.36	3.22	1.43	1.40	0.54
Gifts	1	4	3	5	6	2
	3.73	2.46	2.59	1.86	1.42	2.60
House equipment	6	1	2	5	3	4
	1.81	4.43	3.04	2.02	2.13	2.10
Medical	1	6	4	3	5	2
	5.21	2.98	3.83	3.96	3.32	4.94
Formal education	1	5	2	3	4	6
	9.79	0.91	2.51	1.66	1.06	0.14
Taxes	1	2	3	6	5	4
	9.83	5.09	0.62	0.28	0.32	0.39
Clothing	1	6	2	3	4	5
	11.25	8.53	10.09	9.88	9.00	8.60
Automobile	4	1	2	3	5	6
	6.04	17.19	8.58	8.21	2.88	1.25
Rent and shelter	6	5	4	3	2	1
	10.38	12.73	16.67	17.31	20.25	20.76
House operation	3	1	2	4	5	6
	14.87	18.86	15.41	13.21	11.07	8.99
Food	6	5	4	3	2	1
	11.77	13.64	24.12	31.35	37.01	45.42

spent for rent. The lower the class, the higher the proportion, and the higher the class, the lower the proportion. The lower-lower class used 20.76 per cent of all the money spent for a year on rent and shelter. The upper-lower class spent 20.25 per cent, and the lower-middle class, 17.31 per cent. The upper-middle class spent 16.67 per cent of its budget for rent; the lower-upper, 12.73 per cent; and the upper-upper spent 10.38 per cent. The two lower classes spent approximately twice as much as the upper-upper, and the two middle classes spent slightly over one-and-one-half times as much as the upper-upper class.

The average rent of the lower-lower-class family was $195.14 a year, or $34.15 for each person. The average rent of the upper-lower class was $250.53, or $57.54 per person. The average rent of the lower-middle-class family was $277.46, or $76.88 for each person. The rent for the upper-middle class was $403.48 for each family, or $116.36 for each person. The average rental for the lower-upper class was $676.87 for each family, or $290.09 per person. The average rental for each upper-upper family was $624.47, or $208.15 for each person. Although the percentage of the expenses is smaller, the amount of money spent for rent, except in the upper-upper class, tends to increase as the rank of the class increases.

The upper-upper class spent a larger percentage of its income on clothes than any other class: 11.25 per cent of its expenses were for clothing. The average person spent $225.59, and the average family in the upper-upper class, $676.75. The upper-middle class spent the next highest proportion of its budget for clothing: 10.09 per cent of its total expenses were for clothing. This amounted to $70.39 for the average person and $244.10 for the average family for the year's expenditure on clothing.

The lower-middle class ranked third for the proportion of its budget spent on clothing: 9.88 per cent of its total expenses were for clothing. The average individual spent $43.91, and the average family spent $158.46. The upper-lower class ranked fourth for the proportion of its budget spent on clothing: 9 per cent of its expenses for a year were for clothing. Each person in that class averaged $25.58 a year for clothing expenses, and each family, $111.40. The lower-upper class ranked fifth: 8.53 per cent of the total expenses of each member of that class were for clothing. This represented $194.54 for each individual, or $453.91 for each family. The lower-lower class ranked last for the percentage of its income spent on clothing. Only 8.60 per cent of its expenses were for clothing. The average lower-lower-class person spent $14.14 a year for clothing, while the average family spent $80.79.

The expenditures for food, shelter, and clothing comprised three-fourths of the lower-lower-class budget, two-thirds of the upper-lower-class budget, approximately three-fifths of the lower-middle-class budget, one-half of the upper-middle-class budget, and about one-third each of the budgets of the two upper classes. For these three items of expense, the lower-lower class used 74.78 per cent of its total yearly expense; the upper-lower class, 66.26 per cent; the lower-middle, 58.54 per cent; the upper-middle, 50.88 per cent; the lower-upper, 34.90 per cent; and the upper-upper, 33.40 per cent. Whereas the lower-lower class had only one-fourth of its small income left to spend for the other things this society offers for money, and the upper-lower class one-third of its budget, the two upper classes had two-thirds of their money left to spend for the other things that money will buy.

The upper-upper class spent a higher percentage of its money on clothing, taxes, formal education, doctors, gifts, charity, and on traveling for business purposes than did any other class. On the other hand, it spent a smaller proportion of its money on food, rent, house equipment, and tobacco than the other five classes. These people also spent a relatively small amount on amusements, informal education, and moving.

The lower-upper class presents a very different picture. They spent more money than any other on automobiles, on providing new equipment for the house and for operating it, than any other social group. They spent a larger percentage of their budget on traveling for pleasure and on their clubs and formal associations than all other classes. They were ahead of the others for legal advice, in their correspondence, and on sporting equipment. They, too, were forced to spend a high proportion of their money on taxes. But unlike the class above them they tended to spend their money on moving and informal education.

They spent less of their money on doctors and personal appearance than all the classes and were next to last on formal education and for such necessities as clothing and rent.

Since the lower-lower class is at the other end of the class order it is enlightening to compare their expenditure order with that of the two upper groups. The lower-lower people led the others for the proportion of their budget spent on food, rent, and tobacco. (There seems clear evidence here that people will eliminate other items from their expenses to spend it on tobacco.) The lower-lower class was sixth and last for most expenditures. These included clothing, automobiles, house operation, charity, formal and informal education, associations, traveling for business or pleasure, amusements, sporting equipment, photography, and moving.

The upper-middle class tends to rank second for a large number of categories and resembles the lower-upper class for the proportion of its money spent on items which are not necessities and the lower-middle for those which are necessities.

The lower-middle class ranks third for a fairly large number of expenditures.

In the budget study one sees the upper-upper class a settled, somewhat sober-minded people spending their money not for automobiles and other items of conspicuous expenditure but on charity, taxes, and traveling for business purposes. The lower-upper class, with money to express its preferences, goes in for conspicuous display, as indicated by expenditures on houses, automobiles, travel for pleasure, and for sports.

The upper-lower class in contrast with the lowest one clearly indicates that their values accent social mobility as much as their pocketbooks will allow. For example, they outranked all others for the proportion of their budget spent on informal

education and on moving (the lower-upper class was second).
Yet they show the pinch of circumstances by ranking second
only to the lower-lower people for the money they spent on
food and shelter. The lower-lower people ordinarily spend their
money on the sheer necessities but the upper-lower extend
themselves to add a few activities to their lives "to improve
their lot."

CHAPTER 5

The Associations of Yankee City

Members of the Associations

THE associational structure of Yankee City extends to virtually every part of the the society—to individuals of both sexes and all ages, to native and ethnic groups, and to all other structures such as the family, the school, the church, and the economic and political organizations. Most associations are themselves interconnected. These affiliations with other groups are so extensive that the individual need only be a member of one of the many associations to be brought more or less intimately into contact with members of these organizations which crosscut the entire community. The association thus acts as one of the foremost mechanisms of integration in Yankee City society.

The formal association is a mechanism which helps place the members of a society in a class hierarchy. It is a type of grouping highly favored in our society, and arranges individuals in an organization which characteristically includes some and excludes others.

The association differs from kinship institutions in that it is a voluntary grouping rather than one into which the individual is born. The behavior of its members, which it helps to regulate, may include almost any kind of activity occurring in the entire society. Again, the association differs primarily from economic structures because ultimate control ordinarily rests with all of the members; decisions on the entrance and exclusion of members are ultimately made by the whole organization rather than by a superordinate group, such as management in the economic structure. Both associations and economic structures have ordinary members and officers. Economic organizations such as the bank, the factory, and the store are divided into two internal groups: that of the owner-manager, where final control is located, and that of the workers, who are subordinate and make no ultimate decisions. When discussions are carried on between workers and management, the workers are frequently represented through workers' associations or labor unions which are separately organized for such purposes. Matters of policy and procedure which ultimately concern the existence of the organization are decided by the managerial group, while the employees have only the smallest part of the control of the internal and external relations of the organization. The labor union only diminishes the absolute position of the owner-managers.

We first analyzed our associational material to determine how the association functioned in the community and developed our first hypothesis on the behavior of this institution. We held the view that one of its basic functions was to integrate the larger structures of the society to the whole community. Such larger structures as the church and economic organizations create antagonisms for their members when they attempt to integrate their behavior to the total community. As an adjunct to such structures, the association helps to resolve these antagonisms; at the same time it may also organize the antagonisms of the members of these structures against the larger community.

All churches and many economic organizations, as well as the school and political structures of Yankee City, surround themselves with associations which act as implements in organizing and resolving their antagonisms toward the larger community. Such associations play a subordinate role to the structure to which they are affiliated. For instance, the Yankee City Second Church has surrounded itself with some twenty

associations whose behavior consists largely of secular activities that cannot be included in the sacred programs to which
the church restricts its behavior, thus partially isolating itself.
One of these connected associations is the Second Church
Men's Club. This group has virtually no connection with the
sacred ritual of the Church but helps to integrate the Church
with the larger society; and, through the participation of its
members in the club's activities, the Church is directly related
to the larger community itself. At meetings of the Men's Club,
a speaker, chosen from the community regardless of his religious affiliation, talks on some topic of current interest, and a
discussion by members and their invited guests follows. At
occasional meetings the members of the Second Church
Ladies' Aid Society prepare and serve supper to the Men's
Club and take part in the recreational program that follows.
The activities of such associations are almost unlimited in
their variation.

We first made a careful analysis of 357 associations in
terms of the 6,874 individuals of Yankee City who composed
their 12,876 memberships.

Small[1] associations were in the preponderance, and over
one-fourth, 28.29 per cent (101), had ten or fewer members
and over a half, 54.34 per cent (194), had twenty or fewer.
There were in all 12,876 members of the 357 associations. Of
the total, 2,021 members (15.70 per cent) belonged to 194
(54.34 per cent) associations whose memberships were 20 or
fewer; and 5,260 to 131 (36.69 per cent) associations whose
memberships ranged between 21 and 80. The remaining 8.96
per cent (32) of the associations had memberships ranging
from 81 to 312; and to them belonged 43.44 per cent (5,595)
of all members we are considering in the Yankee City associational structure.

Thus, somewhat more than two-fifths of the members be-

1. We shall refer to those associations which have 20 members or
fewer as small associations; those with 21 to 80 members as of
medium size; and those with 81 to 312 members as large.

longed to large associations comprising less than one-tenth of the associations, while numerous small and medium-sized groups account for the balance of the members.

Each association was analyzed by class, age, sex, and ethnic and religious affiliation.

The distinction made here between an individual and a member is that an individual is a socio-organic unit while a member is a purely social unit. An individual is counted only once in the population but many times in terms of memberships in organizations like the family, the clique, and the association. One individual, for example, may be a member of six associations while another may belong to only three: the total number of individuals is two; the total number of members, nine.

Individuals of all ages and both sexes are found in the associational structure of Yankee City; memberships of these associations, however, we classified by age and sex. Three age classifications were made: (1) a subadult group of those twenty years of age or younger, (2) an adult group of those over twenty years of age, and (3) a group including both subadults and adults. Behavior patterns of the groups were markedly different for each of these classifications.

Most frequently the association is a structure composed only of adults. A variety of subadult associations exists, but these are usually organized and directed by adults who are members of related groups. An adult member of the Y.W.C.A., for instance, may assume a supervisory position in such subadult associations as the Blue Birds, the Always Ready Club, or the Tri-Hi. Adult sponsorship frequently enrolls the first members, introduces rules of organizations, and later directs the activity of the group.

Subadult associations are frequently short-lived. Often when most of the members of such a group have exceeded certain loosely defined age limits, the association automatically passes out of existence to be replaced by a new one with a different name and membership. Short life, moreover, is not conducive to large membership; so subadult associations frequently do not expand much beyond their original member-ship.

In most subadult associations of mixed sex, a rigid sexual dichotomy is maintained in order to supervise moral behavior. There is no such segregation, however, in groups of very young children who are usually treated more like females. They are customarily supervised by women who play a role similar to that of mother in the family.

Subadult associations which range upward in age toward the twenty-year limit are more likely to be associations of mixed sex. Apparently this is due to the desires of the mem-bers themselves rather than to the wishes of the sponsors. Consequently, conflict frequently results between the interests of the sponsors and members, and many of the older subadult groups are held together only by the efforts of adult sponsors or directors. For example, one girls' club at the Y.W.C.A. has members between the ages of fifteen and eighteen. The direc-tor, a young woman of thirty, commented on this problem as follows: "I can't seem to find any programs that interest the girls. They should be learning to do things such as block print-ing and leather work, and I have tried to interest them. All they want to do on meeting nights is to get away from the Y.W. as early as they can and meet their boy friends who wait outside for them. I guess that their families won't let them out on week nights except for club meetings."

Adult associations of one sex hold many joint meetings with adult associations of the other sex and frequently collab-orate in programs.

Male adult associations are most numerous.

Association structure resembles family structure. The male adult association may be likened to the father and husband, the female adult association to the wife and mother, and sub-adult associations to the sons and daughters. Joint meetings serve to illustrate this point. For example, the men of the American Legion hold a parade on Memorial Day to com-memorate the death of members of the community who fought and died in past wars. The women of the American Legion

Auxiliary prepare and serve lunch. Two troops of the Boy
Scouts, sponsored by the Legion, parade with the men and
assist them in the ceremonial activities of the day.

Associations are found among Yankees and all ethnic
groups: Armenian, French Canadian, Greek, Irish, Italian,
Jewish, Negro, Polish, and Russian. In certain instances the
members are all Yankees or are drawn entirely from a single
ethnic group; in other associational combinations there are
representatives of all ethnic groups.

Those associations whose membership is taken from one
ethnic group concern themselves principally with the maintenance of the solidarity of the group; they keep alive the
members' interest in the homeland, and help to adjust their
relations to the Yankee City community which is new to them.
These "closed" associations are of predominantly immigrant
membership, since newcomers unaccustomed to the ways of
the community protect themselves and their folkways by joining associations comprising members of their own culture.
The closed ethnic association thus supplies them with a focal
point of organization and gives them the necessary feelings
of strength and security.

Subsequent generations of ethnics tend to join associations
which are not closed to all but one ethnic group. This has
proved to be an effective device for moving more quickly into
the social life of the total community. Native members are in
the majority in most associations (other than the closed
variety); and the ethnic is thus brought into contact with other
members, persons who will help him integrate himself to the
behavior of the larger community.

Most people of Yankee City either attend, or claim an
affiliation with, one of the fifteen different churches; some pro-
fess no religious connection. These fifteen churches are of four
different general religious faiths: Roman Catholic (two);
Greek Orthodox (one); Jewish (one); and Protestant
(eleven). Many of the 357 associations are directly connected
with one of these fifteen churches, and their members in most
cases are of the same religion.

The religious faiths of the members of the Yankee City associational system reflect ethnic affiliation and cultural heritage. Most Protestants are Yankees; and most Catholics, Jews, and Orthodox Greeks are ethnics. Negroes and Armenians in Yankee City are the two non-native groups whose members are usually Protestant.

There are also associations open to members of but one religious faith. These associations, however, take on an added significance since, as adjuncts of the church, they carry its influence into the community.

While the church structure restricts behavior to the sacred rituals of its dogma, the associations connected with it may take part in the profane activities of the community at large. Such associations include in their behavior patterns almost every kind of activity indulged in by the entire associational structure. They bowl, play basketball, baseball, and other athletic games; present plays, shows, and specialty acts; hold sales and suppers; and take part in many other activities outside the realm of the sacred.

Usually, but not always, such associations are closed religious groups. Occasionally associations affiliated with some specific church are used as proselytizing mechanisms of this church. This is done by receiving members of other churches and religions, who sometimes become affiliated with the church itself or at least come indirectly under its influence. Certain Boy Scout troops sponsored by the various churches are examples of this practice.

Associations whose members are from more than one religion ordinarily help integrate the members of two or more ethnic groups. In such associations there is a minimum of religious influence and usually little influence from any particular sect. A few associations, however, do have their own religious rites which are designed to be nonsectarian. In this they compete with the church, and because of this competition certain churches refuse to recognize them.

Those associations whose members are entirely from a single religion are ordinarily small in size. As the number of religions represented in the membership of associations increases from two to three and from three to four, the size of the associations changes from medium to large. A marked exception to this rule occurs in those associations whose membership is wholly of the Catholic faith; there large associations are found.

Both Protestants and Catholics are in a far greater number of associations than are people of the Greek Orthodox and Jewish faiths.

Finally, through analysis by class representation of membership, the 357 associations were typed on the basis of the degree to which their membership extended or failed to extend through the six classes. This investigation of the class composition of membership defined nineteen different class types which were combinations of the six classes. These types are:

Type 1: associations whose members are from the upper-upper class only,

Type 2: associations whose members are from the upper-upper and lower-upper classes only,

Type 3: associations whose members are from the upper-upper, lower-upper, and upper-middle classes only,

Type 4: associations whose members are from the upper-upper, lower-upper, upper-middle, and lower-middle classes only,

Type 5: associations whose members are from the upper-upper, lower-upper, upper-middle, lower-middle, and upper-lower classes and no other,

Type 6: associations whose membership extends through all six classes from the upper-upper through the lower-lower class,

Type 7: associations whose members are from the lower-upper and upper-middle classes only,

Type 8: associations with a membership from the lower-upper, upper-middle, and lower-middle classes only,

Type 9: associations which have members from the lower-upper, upper-middle, lower-middle, and upper-lower classes and no other,

U-LL   *Type 10:* associations whose members come from all classes from the lower-upper through the lower-lower,

M   *Type 11:* associations with members from the upper-middle
M and lower-middle classes only,

M-UL *Type 12:* associations whose members are of the upper-middle, lower-middle, and upper-lower classes and no other,

M-LL   *Type 13:* associations with members extending from the upper-middle through all classes to the lower-lower class,

M   *Type 14:* associations with lower-middle-class members only,

M-UL *Type 15:* associations with members from the lower-middle and upper-lower classes and no other,

M-LL *Type 16:* associations whose members are from the lower-middle, upper-lower, and lower-lower classes,

L L   *Type 17:* associations with members from the upper-lower class only,

L   *Type 18:* associations whose members are from the upper-
L lower and lower-lower classes and no other,

L   *Type 19:* associations with members from the lower-lower class only.

In every one of the nineteen class types, it will be seen that members are drawn either from a single class or from a combination of two or more of the six classes in the hierarchy. In no case is there a skip of a single class in any of the combinations. If every possible class combination were present, there would be twenty-one associational class types; however, there are two places in which none of the 357 associations is represented—one with members wholly from the lower-upper class and the other with members entirely from the upper-middle class.

Class Membership of the Associations

The 357 associations comprised members who belonged to from one to six different classes. Those associations with members from three or four different classes accounted for the majority, or almost two-thirds, of the associations and

over three-fifths of all members.[2] About one-tenth of all associations had members from two classes, and another one-
tenth had members from five classes. The associations composed of two classes accounted for only 6.07 per cent of the
associational members, and those of five had about one-sixth.
The associations of two classes were very small, while those
of five classes were of all sizes.

The associations whose members were from six classes were
few in number, and those of one class, still fewer. There is a
tendency for those with six classes to be large associations,
and those with one to be small.

In most cases, the ranking of the associations in the various
types corresponds closely to that for the number of memberships. There were, however, certain marked differences, such
as in Type 6 where the associations ranked sixth and the members second; this indicates that associations whose members
included all classes from the lower-upper down through the
lower-lower tended to be larger in size. Associations ranked
eleventh, and the members, seventh, in Class Type 8. This
means that associations whose members were from the lower-
upper, upper-middle, and lower-middle classes tended to be
large and of medium size. Associations in Class Type 12
ranked third, and the members, ninth; members from the
upper-middle, lower-middle, and upper-lower classes belonged
to smaller associations.

The evidence from male and female membership in associations points to the women's acting more exclusively than the

2. Nine associations (2.52 per cent) had members from only 1 class
and comprised 55 (0.43 per cent) of the 12,876 members of the total
associational structure. Forty-six associations (12.89 per cent) had
members from 2 classes and 783 (6.08 per cent) of all members. One
hundred nineteen (33.33 per cent) had members from 3 classes and
3,750 (29.12 per cent) of the members. Members from 4 classes
belonged to 124 associations (34.74 per cent) and numbered 4,446
(34.53 per cent); from 5 classes, 38 (10.64 per cent) and 2,124
(16.50 per cent) members; and 21 associations (5.88 per cent) had
members from all 6 classes and comprised 1,718 (13.34 per cent of
the total members of all associations.

men. There is only one upper-upper association, a woman's group. There are more women in associations that include only the two upper classes and the upper-middle class; on the other hand, the membership in those associations which extend from the two upper classes into the lower strata of the society are more favored by men. Class Types 4, 5, and 6 for the upper-upper class, 8, 9, and 10 for the lower-upper, 13 for the upper-middle, and 16 for the lower-middle are examples of high male membership in such associations.

Associations in which both sexes are members also tend to be more "democratic" and extend through several classes.

When the upper classes belong to exclusive clubs they do not join those with both men and women, but those with only men or only women. All of the hundred-odd people who belonged to associations which included only the two upper classes were in groups which included only males or only females. On the other hand, over half of the associations in Class Type 3 (upper-upper to upper-middle) included men and women.

The informal association has no explicit entrance and exit rules or membership lists; its members are informally known to each other. The formal association has a name by which its members and others refer to it; the clique has no formal name but depends upon colloquial expressions for its names. The members of a clique refer to themselves as "our gang," "our crowd," "the bunch I go around with," and similar terms; they refer to members of other cliques as the "Jones crowd," or the "Hill Street crowd," or the "Low Street gang."

Despite the apparent fluidity of its structure, the clique has a powerful control over individual behavior. An adolescent member of a boys' or girls' clique will sometimes defy his or her family to maintain the respect of clique mates, should the interests of the two groups run counter to each other; or a mature man or woman may renounce a family of lower status and class to satisfy the claims of his higher status clique.

The clique is one of the structures most favored by social climbers. Once in an association in which there were members of higher classes, a socially ambitious woman often found it possible to gain the "friendship" of certain people of prominence who would sponsor her entrance into their more intimate cliques. Constant identification with clique members of a higher class and possession of the "right" behavior symbols almost guarantee upward mobility. On the other hand, the complete exclusion of a person from the cliques of a class contributes to his downward mobility.

Clique members listed in our study of Yankee City amounted to 22,063. There were 757 upper-upper-class members; 897 lower-upper-class members; 2,744 upper-middle-class members; 7,041 lower-middle-class members; 7,333 upper-lower-class members; and 3,291 lower-lower-class members.

Clique participation tended to be in one or two classes. The upper-upper class led all others for the proportion of its clique members who were in one-class groups (37 per cent). It was followed by the lower-lower class; however, a slightly higher percentage (39 per cent) were in cliques with lower-upper members. The other upper-upper clique combinations were fewer and unimportant.

Structure of the Associational System

The majority of the associations in Yankee City are either formally connected to others in the associational structure or to other structures such as the family, economic organizations, schools, churches, and political structures. These connections are sometimes established in the association's constitution or by-laws, or through the joint work of committees whose membership is drawn from several associations. Through such formal connections, the influence of a single association may reach to other associations and to every other structure of the community. For example, 238 associations are connected with the Y.M.C.A. Connected to these and once removed from the Y.M.C.A. are twenty-five associations, economic organizations, schools, and churches; connected with these are 231 associations twice removed from the Y.M.C.A., and so on until the most distant connections are nine times removed. A total of 650 direct and indirect connections of the Y.M.C.A. relate this association to other associations, economic organizations, schools, churches, and to the political structure. Many other associations present this identical pattern inasmuch as they are a part of the 650 Y.M.C.A. connections, and any one could be similarly used as a focus.

Two different kinds of structural types are found in the associations of Yankee City. These are the simple or single associations and the complex or multiple or integrative. Fig. 3 illustrates the elaboration of both types.

Fig. 3. *Structural Types of Associations*

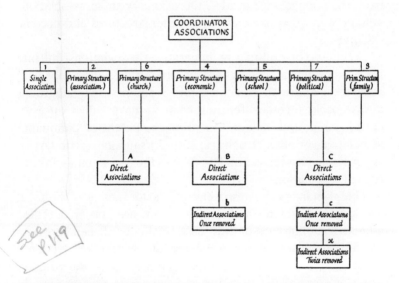

See p. 119

The simple or single associations are separate entities and have no formal affiliations with other associations or other structures. Single associations fall into four generally recognizable subtypes. The first are those associations which are organized around total community interests and crises: hospital associations, charitable societies, and groups which aim to improve the parks and the appearance of the community. The second are certain secret societies which, although not formally affiliated with any other local groups, are usually units of national organizations. In the third category are the closed ethnic associations. A large number of the latter are directly connected with Americanization programs and with benefit and burial functions. The fourth are free-lance associations formed primarily for recreational (athletic) purposes. The birth and mortality rate of these athletic groups is very high as they are loosely organized with a small hierarchy of officers and lacking written rules. Organized on a geographical basis, most of their members live in the lowlands of Riverbrook where much of the ethnic and lower-class population is concentrated. With few exceptions their members were born in this country; and most of them are from the younger age grades. Occasionally these associations affiliate with other associations or other structures and become satellites.

Complex (or multiple or integrative) associations fall into three subgroups according to their structural relationships with each other and with other structures. The first two subgroups always occur together, forming what we have called an associated group, and include (1) primary (parent or dominant) associations or other structures; and (2) satellite (secondary or subordinate) associations. The third is the coordinate (linked) type of association.

The primary association (church, factory, etc.) is the focal point around which satellite associations are clustered. These affiliated satellites are in most cases made up of members who are also members of the dominant association or structure. Frequently committees from the membership of the primary group are appointed to guide and cooperate in programs of activity of the satellites. It is the primary association (or other structure) which rests at the top of the associated group hierarchy and ultimately controls the behavior and policies of the secondary associations. The smallest number of secondary associations connected to a single primary association or other structure of Yankee City is one; the greatest number is 238.

Figure 3 shows that in addition to primary associations other primary structures of the family, economic, school, church, and political organizations may hold the dominant position in the

associated group. Secondary associations may be (1) immediately connected to parent associations or other structures as
in the case of the direct satellite or (2) indirectly affiliated
through other associations. Indirect satellite associations are of
two varieties: (a) once-removed, i.e. immediately subordinate
to those of the direct kind and connected to the primary structure through them; and (b) twice-removed, i.e. satellites which
are in turn inferior to other indirect, once-removed associations
and are affiliated to the parent group through both indirect,
once-removed satellites and direct, secondary associations.

Thus there are three kinds of associated groups, each of
which forms an associational hierarchy with a dominant association or other structure at the top wherein ultimate control is
lodged. These associated groups are (1) the simple associated
group which is composed of a dominant association or other
structure and its direct satellites (A in the chart); (2) the
once-extended associated group with a dominant association
or other structure to which are connected one or more direct
satellites (B) which in turn are connected to one or more once-
removed secondary associations (b) in descending order; and
(3) the twice-extended associated group composed of a dominant association or other structure to which are connected one
or more direct satellites (C) which in turn are superior to one
or more once-removed secondary associations (c) which are
again superior to one or more twice-removed satellites (x).

Associated groups are frequently subdivided into several
separate groups of satellites, all of which are clustered about the
same primary association or other structure. Several of the three
kinds of associated groups—the simple, the once-extended, and
the twice-extended—may be organized around the same dominant association, in which case they become subassociated
groups within the same general associated group.

If an associated group contains any combinations of simple,
once-extended, and twice-extended associated groups, it becomes a subassociated group.

Dominant associations tend to have a much wider range of
activity than do their secondary associations, and in most

instances these satellites confine their activities to a narrow range. Many of them are organized around a single athletic game, such as baseball, basketball, or bowling, because of an interest in these sports on the part of only certain members of the larger parent groups.

The third complex (or integrative) variety of association is the coordinate or link type (at top of Fig. 3). Such associations are neither superordinate nor subordinate to any other association or structure. Their membership is composed of delegates from two or more associations or other structures, and their purpose is the coordination of interests common to these groups. In Yankee City, coordinate associations link together structures of the same order as well as structures of different orders. The groups thus coordinated are as follows: (1) associations, (2) families, (3) economic organizations, (4) churches, (5) schools, (6) associations and churches, (7) associations, churches, and schools, (8) schools and families, and (9) all structures combined. Associations and other structures so linked may be of the single variety with no affiliation or frequently may hold the place of primary associations.

The Masonic Temple Association, for example, is organized to care for the clubhouse or temple in which the five Masonic groups of Yankee City hold their meetings. Its membership comprises several members of the Royal Arch Masons, the Knights Templar, St. John's Lodge, St. Mark's Lodge, and the Eastern Star. This administrative group is not connected with any of these five associations either as a parent or a secondary association but links them by serving their mutual interests in their meeting place.

Likewise, the clergymen of eleven Yankee City Protestant churches have organized into an association called the Federation of Religious Workers. Its purpose is to promote unity of action among the churches and to devise means for bringing nonchurchgoers into regular church attendance. Their program includes an annual outdoor sunrise service attended by the clergy and members of the congregations of the eleven churches, exchange of pulpits by the pastors, and promotion of an annual

Go-to-Church Sunday. At bimonthly business meetings questions pertaining to church affairs are discussed, speeches heard and food served by the women of one of the churches.

The Federation of Religious Workers, as well as other associations which we have defined as units that link other associations or other structures together, acts as an adjunct to the several groups which it connects. The initiative in organizing it and other such associations came from the several separate groups themselves.

Thus it may be said that the single associations are independent of one another in their formal organization and behavior, but linked together through associations which act to coordinate certain of their interests.

Secondary associations were classified according to the origin of their members into two types: first, with members entirely from the groups interlocked, and, second, with members in part or entirely from outside the primary structure.

Secondary associations whose membership completely interlocks with part of that of their parent associations were subdivided into two varieties according to their organization. One of these subtypes is an associated group which is commonly called a league. In the league, two or more small associations form a group for the purpose of competing with each other in some of the following athletic games: baseball, basketball, volleyball, bowling, gymnastics, and minature golf. The combined membership of all the secondary associations of this kind forms the whole membership of their superordinate association. The memberships of the satellites of the same associate group, however, do not overlap. The organization of a league may be said to come from the bottom up, as two or more subordinate associations must be formed before the dominant association is brought into existence at all. In all instances the dominant structure must be an association and not one of the other structures.

In the leagues, the superordinate association acts somewhat as a coordinator inasmuch as its entire membership is gained from other associations. It is, however, in close connection with these groups. It arranges their game schedules and holds occasional meetings which all members are expected to attend. Such meetings are customarily of a recreational nature, and occasional suppers and banquets are held when speeches are heard.

This kind of satellite is perhaps the most impermanent of all; its ephemeral life is probably due to the nature of its athletic behavior patterns, its simple hierarchy of officers which usually includes only a captain and a manager, and its meager rules of organization which are seldom given the more permanent written form. While such associations have a less permanent type of organization than do other satellites, these secondary associations are much more tightly organized than the clique. Unlike the clique, they meet regularly at designated places and govern themselves with a prescribed set of rules.

The second type of secondary associations whose membership completely interlocks with part of that of the dominant groups may be subordinate to primary associations or to other structures. The associated groups in which these secondary associations exist are organized from the top down because the membership of their satellites is derived from the dominant structure. This is the exact reverse of the league where the satellites must first be organized before the dominant association can exist. In further contrast, this second type of satellite assoation with derivative membership may have a membership which in part overlaps that of other satellites of the same associated group.

Satellites whose membership is selected from that of their superordinate groups are connected with associations, families, economic organizations, schools, churches, and the political structure. They alone occur in every possible kind of connection with their dominant associations or other structures. They are the only secondary associations to be represented in every possible place in simple, once-extended, and twice-extended groups, and occur in subassociated groups.

Such secondary associations fall into three distinct patterns as defined by the behavior in which they take part. The first are those satellite associations which play athletic games to the almost complete exclusion of any other activity. The second are similar to the first, but they concentrate their attention on talent display and on the study and discussion of the arts and literature. The third comprise those satellites whose behavior covers a wide variety of activity of all kinds. Frequently their activities play an important role in the everyday life of the community.

Satellites whose membership is derived from that of their dominant associations (or other structures) are more tightly organized than are those whose combined membership forms that of the superordinate association and creates the league. They tend to have an extensive hierarchy of officers, written rules, and a more highly systemized plan of organization. Such secondary associations are as a rule of longer life than the leagues.

An example of the satellite whose membership is derived from that of its primary association is the Forty and Eight. All of its members are also members of the Yankee City American Legion. The Forty and Eight has occasional meetings called "wrecks" which are mostly of a recreational nature; its members carry on drives for members for the parent body and interest themselves in child-welfare work. The Forty and Eight extends the behavior patterns of the American Legion and attracts a select group of members from the dominant body who are desirous of intensifying their activity as Legion members.

There are also satellites whose membership rolls do not coincide with those of the primary associations or other structures with which they are affiliated. When the dominant structure is an association, the members of these secondary associations are usually taken from the immediate and extended families of the members of the dominant groups but differ from them in that they are of the opposite sex or of another age grade. Such satellites may be composed of the female kin of the members of the parent association or of subadult blood relatives of this primary group's members. These kinship qualifications are not always necessary, but they form the underlying pattern.

Most satellites whose membership is drawn from outside the

superordinate associations carry on a wide range of activity at their meetings. Both parents and their satellites are formally organized with an extensive hierarchy of officers and written rules of conduct.

One remaining type of secondary association, classified according to the derivation of its membership, is that in which only a part of the members interlock with those of the primary structure. They are subordinate to the dominant structures which include churches, economic organizations, and the political structure. Satellites of this type have direct connection with primary structures only and function as proselytizing devices for them. In every instance the nuclear members belong also to the dominant structure and interlock the two. Outsiders are added in some cases to increase the prestige in the community of the entire associated group and in others to augment the membership of the secondary association to enable it to function with a large membership in more varied activities.

As with the satellites whose membership is entirely extraneous to that of their dominant structure, associations of this type may have more members than the parent structure.

Examples of secondary associations of this type which were subordinate to churches were eight Boy Scout troops, each of which was affiliated with a church of the Protestant faith. These satellites had subadult males drawn from the members of the several dominant churches as the nucleus of their membership. A great effort was made, however, to bring in boys who belonged to other church organizations and frequently of other religious affiliations.

The second Church of Yankee City dominated a Boy Scout troop which drew a large proportion of its members from other churches and religions. The church membership was predominantly Yankee, but the Boy Scout troop was commonly known as the "League of Nations" because of the great number and variety of ethnics among its members. The minister of the church took a great interest in the group and frequently addressed it. Upon several occasions he emphatically stated that the Scouts was an organization for all boys regardless of race or creed and that it was a great institution for the creation of good will. However, the boys who belonged to other churches were brought directly under the influence of the church which dominated the satellite Boy Scout troop.

Secondary associations with membership drawn partly from the rolls of parent economic organizations and partly from the rest of the community consist almost entirely of satellites whose behavior is centered in a specific athletic game. They compete with other associations whose behavior is similar to their own and attract spectators from the community at large. The attention which these games draw is in some measure reflected upon the dominant economic organization. Approximately one-fourth of the economic structures which had satellite connections brought in members from outside, as well as from within, their own organizations. Those that did so were without exception small organizations which depended upon retail trade for their existence. Such parent groups did not have a sufficiently large membership of their own to form satellite associations whose members competed in athletic games, and it was considered important that the parent group should be identified with satellites which had athletic prestige.

The one association which is subordinate to the library (a part of the political structure of Yankee City) is a group organized for the study and appreciation of music. It is in no way a proselytizing or advertising device as are the satellites of this type which are affiliated with dominant churches and economic organizations. Its membership is both subadult and adult, and of both sexes. It is sponsored and directed by several prominent women of Yankee City.

We were ultimately able to list a total of 899 associations in Yankee City. Most of them were ephemeral and lasted only for a short period of time; many of them which existed when the study began were dead bfore the end of the study. The 357 groups studied included the great majority of the permanent associations of the community. Although not all associations were examined for the names of their members, they were analyzed for structural type to determine how they fitted into the larger social system of Yankee City. Of the grand total, 151 were single or simple associations and were independent of any formal connections with other associations or other structures such as a church or factory; 41 were parent or dominant associations to which satellite associations were attached; 676 were satellites; and 31 were coordinates of other associations.

Figure 4 represents the integration of the associations into the social organization of Yankee City. The six types of structure are listed and the several forms of parent and satellite associations are charted for each type of institution. The number of parent and satellite is found in the appropriate rectangle. The membership of coordinates was composed of certain members selected from the associations and structures which they linked. The Masonic Temple Association, the Veteran Fireman's Association, and the Community Center linked groups of associations. The Community Center, like the Masonic Temple Association, supplied and maintained housing facilities and equipment for use of the groups it linked. The Veteran Fireman's Association linked two associations whose interest was in running their hand-operated fire engines, bowling, and other recreational activities.

All churches joined by the three coordinates were Protestant. The Young People's Interdenominational Council was composed of young people from these churches. Their purpose was to coordinate the programs of activity, both religious and profane, carried on by the Protestant churches of the community. The second coordinate was the Bethel Society, organized to extend charity to sailors and their widows. It was financed largely by contributions collected from the members of Protestant churches. The members of the associations were representatives of the churches in question. The third, the Federation of Religious Workers, has already been described.

Fourteen associations coordinated various economic organizations. Their membership included seven employer-manager groups and seven different groups of employees. They composed such organizations as the trade associations on the one hand

Fig. 4. *The Associational Structure*

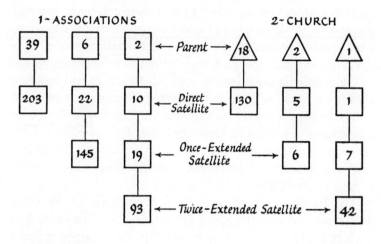

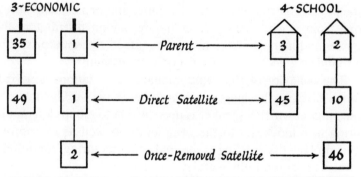

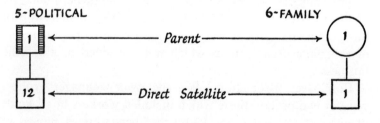

and labor unions on the other. Five of them combined members involved with all varieties of different economic organizations, while nine combined members whose occupations tended to be the same. For the most part, their activities were closely related to the economic organization itself; however, in two instances a wide variety of activity of a recreational nature was included.

The Rotary Club is an example of those owner-manager, coordinator associations which link members of various kinds of economic organizations; and the Hairdressers' Association is an example of those which link economic organizations within a specific occupation.

The Rotary Club had members from many of the retail, wholesale, and manufacturing groups, as well as members from each of the professions. Its membership, for example, included the managers from hardware, clothing, and department stores; one from a wholesale coal company; an oil distributor; the owner and manager from a shoe manufacturing enterprise and a foundry; a doctor; a lawyer; and a clergyman.

The behavior of the owner-manager associations is varied. Some have only business meetings; others have weekly luncheon meetings at which a speaker is present. These groups attempt to bring new industries to the community as well as to improve and protect the existing trade and manufacturing conditions. Others are active only in athletic programs.

The Hairdressers' Association included the owner-managers of local hairdressing and beauty parlors. The membership of this and similar groups was restricted to the owner-managers of economic organizations which were confined to a specific business.

Employees associations, like the owner-manager groups, were of two orders: those which included workers in all kinds of occupations and those whose members were employed in occupations within one economic activity.

Associations which linked employee members from all kinds of occupations confined their activity largely to athletic games. They coordinated the interests of members of the economic organizations whose employees composed their memberships.

An example of link associations whose members are limited to one economic activity is the shoe workers' organizations. There were three organizations of shoe workers, and they were all labor unions. These unions coordinated the workers of the several shoe factories. Another workers' coordinate association is the Yankee City Musicians' Association. It, too, may be called a labor union; it bound the local orchestra organizations together in its common membership of orchestra employees. Such associations were formed principally for the protection and advancement of the workers' interests in relation to their jobs.

Although the behavior of these coordinator associations was not in every instance related to matters directly involving the operations of the economic organizations which they linked together, all of them restricted their membership to a certain defined personnel in the economic structure.

One association coordinated the public schools of Yankee City. This was the Teachers' Association and, as the name implies, its membership was composed of schoolteachers. It closely resembled a labor union in several respects, for salaries, work procedures, and similar topics were discussed at its business meetings. A minimum of recreational activity was connected with it.

There was one association which linked families together. Its membership was restricted to those families which were descended from the persons who first settled Yankee City in the early 1600's. Its principal activity lay in preserving the symbols of ancestry, such as old houses in the community.

Four associations linked associations and churches together. They were made up of members of the churches of the Protestant faith, and in three instances the Y.M.C.A. was linked to them. One of these associations, the Scout Masters, also included the American Legion. This coordinate had a membership of adult sponsors or directors of the Boy Scout troops. Each of these troops was a satellite of one or another of eight different churches of the Protestant faith, of the Y.M.C.A., or of the American Legion. The representatives of these ten structures coordinate churches, the American Legion, and the Y.M.C.A.

The second coordinator association of this kind linked eleven churches and the Y.M.C.A. It was the Interchurch Basketball League, and members of the Protestant churches and of the Y.M.C.A. competed. Each team bore the name of one of the churches or of the Y.M.C.A. The other two associations which linked associations and churches were the Church Baseball League and the Church Bowling League. The first of these two linked six churches of the Protestant faith, the Greek Orthodox Church, and the Y.M.C.A.; the second coordinated six different Protestant churches and the Y.M.C.A.

Two associations linked associations, churches, and schools. They were the Campfire Advisory Committee and the Campfire Guardians Association. Both had as their members the adult sponsors of the Campfire groups. Each of these Campfire groups is a satellite of a church of Protestant faith and of a school, or of the Y.W.C.A. As representative members of these four structures, the members of the Campfire Advisory Committee and of the Campfire Guardians Association coordinated them.

Two Parent-Teacher Associations in Yankee City covered two sections of the community. They coordinated both schools and families and their membership was composed of the schoolteachers and parents of children in the city schools. The members met to discuss their common interests in the orientation of the child in the community.

The last association of the coordinate type was the Citizens Aid Committee; it linked associations, families, schools, churches, and the political structure. This group was organized during the economic emergency in the early days of the depression when the unemployment situation in Yankee City threatened to rend the whole social and economic fabric of the society. At that time the members of all these structures appointed individuals to the membership of the Citizens Aid Committee. This association made plans for furnishing work to the unemployed by encouraging people who were financially able to furnish work to the needy.

Membership status in both the simple and the coordinate associations thus was clearly defined. Members of a simple association did not connect it with other groups, while those of the coordinates were recruited from the groups they linked. Associations and other structures of the primary type were always formally affiliated with one or more satellite associations (as defined in their constitutions or by-laws), but such affiliations were not always organized by interlocking memberships.

The membership of a secondary association may (1) be wholly derived from the superordinate structure with which it affiliates, but in no case does it include the entire membership; or (2) have members who are entirely different from those of the parent organization; or (3) have a membership of which part interlocks with that of the primary association and part does not.

Associations to Which the Members of Each Class Belonged

As the class rank increases, the proportion of its members who belong to associations also increases; and as the position of a class decreases the percentage of those who belong to associations decreases. Forty-one per cent of the total Yankee City population are members of one or more associations. In the upper-upper class, 72 per cent of the people are members of associations; 71 per cent of the lower-upper, 64 of the upper-middle, 49 of the lower-middle, 39 of the upper-lower, and 22 per cent of the lower-lower are associational members. Hence there is a constant decrease in memberships from the upper-upper to lower-lower stratum.

Of all persons belonging to associations, those from the upper-upper class account for 2.55 per cent; the lower-upper, 2.72 per cent; the upper-middle, 16.01 per cent; the lower-middle, 33.63 per cent; the upper-lower, 31.41 per cent; and the lower-lower class, 13.68 per cent.[3]

Persons in the lower-middle and upper-lower classes are the most numerous, each with about the same number of members of associations; together they compose about two-thirds of all individuals in the association structure.

The upper and middle classes are represented in greater numbers than would be expected; the upper-lower class has fewer members; but the most marked drop appears in the lower-lower class. It seems that the association is a far less important structure to lower-lower-class persons than to those of other classes.

If we consider each class separately, we find that of the 357 associations, upper-upper-class members are in 22.96 per cent (82) of them; lower-uppers in 34.72 per cent (124); upper-middles in 72.26 per cent (258); lower-middles in 89.08 per cent (318); upper-lowers in 77.60 per cent (277); and lower-lower members are found in 59.12 per cent (211) of the associations.

Small associations of twenty members or fewer exceeded in number those of larger membership. Small associations constituted the greatest proportion of associations composed of members from the upper-middle, lower-middle, upper-lower, and lower-lower classes; medium associations were the most frequent among those where the upper-middle, lower-middle, and upper-lower classes were represented; and large associations, where members of the lower-upper, upper-middle, and lower-middle classes were present.

Small associations ordinarily had members from three classes, but a fourth class was often represented also. All one-class associations were small. Most associations of medium size,

3. It will be remembered that in Yankee City members of the upper-upper class compose 1.44 per cent of the population; the lower-upper, 1.56 per cent; the upper-middle, 10.22 per cent; the lower-middle, 28.12 per cent; the upper-lower, 32.60 per cent; and the lower-lower class, 25.22 per cent. (Persons of unknown class represent 0.84 per cent.)

with from twenty-one to eighty members, had members from four classes; but some had members from three or five classes. Associations of more than eighty members most frequently had members from three, four, and five classes.

Thus it appears that, as the associations increase in size, the opportunity increases for the members of the lower classes to move upward in the class hierarchy, inasmuch as in the large groups they are in contact with more individuals of the other classes. In like manner, the large association furnishes a device by which members from the upper brackets of the class system may subordinate and control those inferior to them.

Of all classes, the two middle ones have the greatest representation in the medium and large associations. However, the association as a means of gaining status in the community is most popular with persons from the upper-middle and the lower-middle classes. Probably the members of these classes are the most desirous of upward social mobility.

Small associations more frequently have members from one and two classes than do those of large and medium size. Their members are most often from the three lower classes.

Fewer than one-third of the upper-upper-class persons who are association members belong to but one association. This proportion increases as we descend the class hierarchy, and in the lower-lower class reaches its maximum with about three-quarters of the individuals of this class. Conversely, a greater proportion of persons of the upper-upper class (7.43 per cent) belong to ten or more associations than of any of the inferior classes. The amount becomes progressively less as we approach the lower-lower class, where there is none at all. Furthermore, when persons of the upper-upper class belong to a large number of associations the proportion of individuals from other classes in these associations increases, but this pattern tends to shift further down in the class system until it exactly reverses itself in the lower-lower class. Over one-third of all persons with memberships in the associational structure are from the lower-middle and less than one-third from the upper-lower classes. Those from the three largest classes—lower-middle, upper-lower, and upper-middle—compose 81.05 per cent of the total.

More members of the upper-lower than of any other class belong to but one association; and as the rank of the class increases the number of individuals belonging to only one diminishes in each succeeding class. For members who belong to two, three, and four associations, the lower-middle class ranks first. The number of such members grows consecutively smaller in each class as we approach either end of the class structure. The upper-middle class exceeds all others for persons belonging to five, six, eight, and nine associations; and, as we ascend or descend in the class hierarchy, the number of individuals in each class becomes successively smaller. The largest number of persons with seven associational memberships is in the lower-middle class. There are more persons of the upper-upper class who belonged to ten or more associations than in any other class. There is none in the lower-lower class.

Of all classes, persons of the upper-upper and lower-upper who hold association memberships tend to belong to the greatest number of groups, particularly to nine, ten, or more. However, of those who belong to six or fewer, the representation in these two classes is small. These two classes are more active in the associational structure within the limits of their size than are any others. The smallness of their numbers permits persons of the upper classes to make an effort as a group to exert control over the society through this medium. Although the members of these two classes often do not hold offices in the controlling hierarchies of the various groups, they nevertheless effectively exercise certain pressures upon those who do.

Symbolic Life of Associations

The activities of associations provide rich material for symbolic and functional analysis. Much, if not all, of their behavior is directly or indirectly, consciously or unconsciously, symbolic, since what they say and do in a given activity usually stands for something else and thus conforms to our definition of symbolic activity. The full meaning of an associational activity is found not only by treating it in the light of what the members of the association say it is, but by studying the activity and its implications and meanings in terms of the structure itself and the satisfactions which the members receive from what they do. Associational activities are valuable for symbolic analysis because they enter into every part of the American social structure and reflect the variety of sentiments, attitudes, and values of every part of American society.

Before continuing, let us define what an "activity" is to the observer. An activity such as a parade or an installation of officers is a recognized and socially defined public use of symbols in a set of formal or informal social relations. An activity is recognized as such by those who participate in it and by those who study it at the explicit and open level of social behavior (it is not something they do unconsciously). Each activity occurs in a situation which involves the relations of the members alone, or the members of the association in relation to the rest of the community. Each activity includes a symbolic situation in which the members exchange symbols among themselves or with other members of the society, according to the nature of the relationship. For example, the members may belong to a secret society such as the Masons, where they perform rituals known and participated in only by members of their own group. On the other hand, these same members might join in an interfraternity activity where all are involved in a ritual whose successful performance demands that they exchange symbolic objects between them or cooperate in some community activity, such as fund-raising.

To gather representative data from the complex variety and large number of associations involved here, we systematically studied them for a period of two years. We attended meetings, collected records on activities, and carefully followed the detailed reports in the local newspaper. Since most of the news stories were provided by the members themselves, and since we were able to check them by our own observations, we learned to accept what was said as reliable evidence.

Five thousand eight hundred events or activities were recorded during the two-year period, and we were able to classify them into 284 forms (subtypes) and then into 19 types (see Table 3). For example, a boys' club might play a baseball game

Table 3. *Events, Forms, and Types of Activity*

Rank order of events	Type of activity	Number of events	Per cent	Number of forms (sub-types)
1	Drama and talent exhibitions	828	14.28	41
2	Speeches	744	12.83	1
3	Organization	567	9.78	13
4-5	Eating	499	8.60	24
4-5	Fund-raising	499	8.60	22
6	Ritual, secular-external	335	5.78	30
7	Ritual, sacred	333	6.74	23
8	Ritual, secular-internal	306	5.28	21
9	Gifts	291	5.02	14
10	Sedentary games	214	3.69	15
11	Hospitality	198	3.41	8
12	Contests	158	2.72	8
13	Athletic games	157	2.71	23
14	Crafts and skills	126	2.17	8
15	Ritual, secular-sacred	123	2.12	8
16	Socials	119	2.05	2
17	Outings	118	2.03	10
18	Teaching and learning	99	1.71	7
19	Dancing	86	1.48	6
Total		5,800	100.00	284

with another team. The particular game was counted as an event and listed under type of activity as an athletic game, while the form (subtype) of activity was listed under the heading "Baseball."

The activities recorded covered everything from the most sacred to the most profane and secular, from extreme forms of competition and opposition to the most intense cooperative efforts, from the polar extremes of utility and Yankee hard-headedness to the ultimate in philanthropy and good will. They also ranged from the most reasonable and sensible behavior to the ultimate in triviality and nonsense. We shall be concerned here only with their public meanings, and we are interested less in the interpretation of their meaning than in pointing out the multitude and variety of activities of American associations and drawing certain conclusions by using our knowledge of their functional significance.

The social scientist can recognize four types of public ritual among the activities of these associations. The four include only forms that are consciously used by the association for ritualistic purposes. As such, they are pure forms of symbolic behavior. All the other types of activity have varying degrees of ritual, but they are not designed primarily for ritual ends; that is, their ritual significance, when present, is secondary and often not recognized by the participants. The four forms of ritual are: sacred ritual; ritual which combines sacred and secular elements; and secular ritual—this latter being concerned (a) largely with the community beyond the association or (b) wholly or almost completely with its own inner world. As used here the term "ritual" means that the members of the association express in overt symbolic acts the meanings which socially evaluated objects or relationships have for them, and at the same time also state in symbols what their relations are with such objects. The devout Christian, for example, does this in the rite of Communion, as does the patriotic American in some of the exercises customary on Lincoln's Birthday.

Sacred ritual symbolically relates the participants to sacred things—Deity, the spiritual dead, and such things as emblems which represent God and the sacred dead. Secular ritual expresses the values and attitudes of the daily round of life in the community and gives symbolic form to the importance of ordinary things that compose the lives of most people. Certain secular rituals—adopting and maintaining a European War orphan, for instance—symbolize along with other purposes the American alliance with certain European countries and the present feeling of unity with these countries. At the same time, they serve to relate the members of the association to the larger community beyond the association itself. Others, such as celebrating Lincoln's Birthday, flag ceremonies, and similar patriotic rituals, relate the association to the whole community. Still others tie the association symbolically to the families, schools, and the local community. There are thirty forms of these secular rituals.

Twenty-one forms of ritual activity concerned with internal relations are largely composed of symbolic elements which have been created by the members of the associations. Their function is to tie the participants more closely together, emphasize their unity, and indirectly maintain in the feelings of the members their separateness from the larger society.

The several types of ritual, combined, compose about onefifth of all the activities of the associations of Yankee City; the other four-fifths of association activities were divided among fifteen other categories.

Where combinations of ritual are not involved, drama and talent exhibitions are the most popular type of activity. Dramatic exhibitions include everything from classical and contemporary plays to tap dancing and jazz band concerts. Generally they are expressions of the talent of the local people; but what is said and done on the stage is usually pure symbolic communication. Many people in the community, particularly those in the lower classes, use talent to help improve their stations in life and gain social recognition. If they are successful, two developments may follow. They may be recognized economically and advance themselves accordingly, or—and what is more likely—they may be recognized socially by more highly placed persons and participate at a higher level in the social system. Very often, to the observer, the efforts are pathetic, since they accomplish nothing for the participant and even evoke ridicule —the ever-present risk which mobile people must take. The plays vary from classical and modern, which present rigorous and almost scientific representations of modern life and employ the skill and dexterity of first-rate artists, to those which are little more than an opportunity for the participant to exhibit himself in a public place. There were 41 subcategories and 828 events of this sort, composing over one-seventh of the total.

The members of associations of Yankee City and, in fact, those throughout America seem never to tire of listening to speeches. The unfriendly critic or field worker who must attend many of these functions might well say that many of them are dreary, uninformative, and filled with wind. But speeches, even when not listened to by the members, are felt to be necessary and are appreciated as part of what should happen when members meet. Analysis indicates that a considerable proportion of them, when stated in propositional form, are composed of ritual rather than reason. Some of the "best speakers" freely avail themselves of well-tried symbolic and ritual materials and resort to reason only when it is necessary to disguise what they are saying. One-eighth of the many thousands of activities we observed were speeches. Speeches, unlike talent presentations, are usually given by outsiders; the association members merely listen. Like the social set-up for dramatic activities, the amount of participation of most people tends to be minimal. We were unable to classify the speeches into types of subject matter, but our list of subjects indicates clearly that they ranged over every variety of topic.

An activity of associations to which a great amount of time is devoted, ranking third in importance, is organizational work. This includes "reading the minutes," "new business," "making new rules," "voting," etc., and is largely concerned with maintaining the formal organization of the association by expressing the rules in group action and emphasizing the social autonomy of associations, as well as that of the members, by making new rules or rescinding old ones. Usually to the observer, and often to some of us who participate in such organizational forms, what is done seems dull and unimportant; but the prosaic outward forms themselves must be given further examination, for their meaning is of great importance.

For example, long, boring discussions take place over the rules of order, which give opportunities to define the status of members and their officers and, above all, permit the organizational activities of members to express—i.e., symbolize in social form—the democratic character of the association and of the society generally. Criticism of an association's chairman or president, heated reference to "railroading," and declarations about one man's vote being as good as another's are all recognitions of how organizational activity very often voices something more than the "business of the day" or rules of conduct governing the actions of the members. The critical observer, however, leaves with a feeling of futility, for he sees "more time wasted in the discussion of the rules than in action." No doubt this is sometimes true, but more often than not what is being observed and defined as not important is of the utmost significance because of its meaning to those who participate and the emotions which these activities arouse. Ten per cent of the activities were concerned with rules and organization.

Eating, although a biological act, in its social form consists in the sharing of food at a common meal. As Robertson Smith and Ernest Crawley pointed out long ago, it is one of the strongest ways to engender sentiments of oneness among participants while they share group attitudes. Eating is an activity used in the greatest variety of ways to promote solidarity or separate the members of a particular association from all others. Sometimes the participants themselves recognize the unity that the function of "breaking bread together" implies. Their behavior always expresses this significance. A great variety of ways of eating were collected. They range all the way from the utmost formality, etiquette, and prestige, through varying shades of formality to informal basket lunches and suppers. The various forms of eating communal meals comprise about 9 per cent of the activities.

Fund-raising ranks with eating in importance. Twenty-two ways of collecting funds were observed. They included everything from benefit shows and suppers to tag days, auction sales, rummage sales, campaigning, and bazaars. Thus an activity was identified as belonging to the general category of "fund-raising" if one of its immediate explicit purposes was to increase the amount of money in the association's treasury. If another element such as eating—as in the case of a fund-raising supper —was present, this element was also counted under its appropriate category.

The process of fund-raising includes getting money from

both within and outside the membership of the organization. Women's organizations show much more ingenuity and diversity in their fund-raising enterprises than do the men's groups, often disguising or de-emphasizing the purpose. Members and outsiders are invited to play at benefit card parties, eat a benefit lunch, or buy a piece of bric-a-brac at a bazaar and, accordingly, are often doubly rewarded by getting an object of utility and having the moral satisfaction of making a contribution to a worthy cause.

Patterns of mutual obligation are often established between associations, for the members of one organization feel obligated to attend a fund-raising card party or supper of another because their own has just had a similar event. The exchange of services and money, usually in the pleasant context of entertainment, constitutes one of the great contributions of the associations to the social unity of the community, for it knits diverse groups tightly together.

Fund-raising may not be easily viewed as of symbolic significance. There can be no question that part of its ultimate use is purely utilitarian and technical. However, the giving and taking of money in such a context and in the set of relations usually established for such an activity symbolically define what the set of relations is or what it should be. Very frequently it is little more than a gift exchange, sometimes with overtones of competition in it, that looks very much like some of the competitive and cooperative elements of the potlatch of the Northwest Coast Indians. It will be recalled that these Indians made elaborate and very expensive gifts to each other at public ceremonies; the unfortunate recipient, to save face and protect his status, was forced to return an even more elaborate gift or conspicuously to destroy a highly valued object. Thorstein Veblen did not find it difficult to transfer Franz Boas' account of the potlatch among the Indians of the Canadian Pacific coast to his own theory of conspicuous expenditure in contemporary America.

Explicit gift-making and -taking occupy an important part in the life of the associations. The gifts are made between members, or given to, and accepted from, other associations.

Examples are ceremonial presents to a retiring officer and gifts to churches or to worthy philanthropies. There are some fourteen ways listed as proper for giving and receiving gifts. The presents which are supposedly given voluntarily and graciously by one association to another without thought of compensation, like all gifts set up obligations for a return of goods and services in the future or imply repayment for something done in the past. This exchange pattern organizes most of the associations into a system of interaction which emphasizes reciprocity. The goods and services are given as free-will offerings and are returned as such, with no hint of a commercial transaction; yet informal judgments are constantly being made which determine the sequence of such gift-making and the quality of the objects exchanged.

When it is realized that gift-making is one of the many ways of symbolically stating the relations among people and establishing an equilibrium between organizations, its importance to the associations and to the stability of the community can be understood. Such types of activity as fund-raising, various forms of secular and sacred rituals, games, contests, hospitality, outings, dances, as well as most of the other nineteen types, contribute their share to the interactive cooperation and help to organize the competition and subordinate the hostilities that exist between the various social levels, ethnic groups, economic interests, and religious faiths. Although rather obvious, it cannot be too strongly stressed that most of the activities—particularly gift-making—are ways which increase, by act and symbol, the basic integration of the community and help to maintain its present form.

The gifts between two associations may have little value, yet they are visible emblems of social solidarity, and the act of giving evokes latent feelings of solidarity, unity, and interdependence. This cohesiveness is further related to the interconnections established by the interlocking memberships of related associations. This intricate web, when first viewed, is almost overwhelming.

Structural and membership interconnections, our interviews

and observations tell us, organize and express some of the feelings, attitudes, and values of the people who belong to the various associations. The activities among these associations express both the structural connections and the membership interconnections. When two or more associations possess a common core of membership, the members are often brought together for common enterprises which are frequently joint actions or symbolic statements of common membership structure and social values. For example, members of the exclusive dining clubs belong to the less exclusive Rotary Club; their wives, who are members of the Garden Club and other exclusive associations, also belong to the more open Woman's Club. The core of the more highly placed men in Rotary and high-status women in the Woman's Club carry the influence of their other associations into the life of these two clubs. To a lesser extent they take back the effect of some of their experience in Rotary and the Woman's Club to their more highly valued associations. Thus the web of associations functions to draw status distinctions while at the same time pulling the several social levels together.

Symbolic activities favored by men in disproportion to the interest shown by women were: listening to speeches; participating in sacred rituals, particularly those having to do with death (as in the Memorial Day ceremony); and engaging in athletic games and other contests. The ritual participation is partly accounted for by veterans and patriotic organizations. Figure 5 gives the percentages of male and female associations. Women as compared with men show a notable interest in the use and display of skills, in informal social hours, outings, teaching and learning, gift-making and fund-raising. Their disproportionate participation in such events displays a nice balance between informal and formal activities.

Activities of the Social Classes

Although class differences among all types of activity are quite marked and reveal themselves immediately to the observer, they are difficult to demonstrate in quantitative terms. For

Fig. 5. *Male and Female Activities*

MEN		ACTIVITIES	WOMEN	
Per Cent	Rank Order		Rank Order	Per Cent
22	1	Speeches	5	8
12	2	Drama and talent exhibitions	1	13
9	3	Organization	2	10
8	4	Ritual, sacred	9	4
7.5	5	Eating	4	9
6.5	6	Fund-raising	2	10
5	7	Ritual, secular-external	6	7
5	7	Ritual, secular-internal	7	6
4	9	Athletic games	14	2
4	9	Contests	14	2
4	9	Hospitality	12	3
3	12	Gifts	7	6
3	12	Sedentary games	9	4
2	14	Dancing	19	1
2	14	Ritual, sacred-secular	12	3
1	16	Teaching and learning	14	2
1	16	Outings	14	2
1	16	Socials	14	2
0.5	19	Crafts and skills	9	4

example, a comparison of lower- and upper-class associations shows that there is only a small difference in the percentage of total activities devoted to eating (8 per cent for the upper class and 7 for the lower); yet scrutiny of the forms of eating and, of course, actual observation of the style tell quite another story. It was impossible to develop a method which would permit recording of stylistic differences which could be easily counted, but the ordinary procedure previously described of classifying events under their *forms* and *types* did reveal decided differences. Although a comparison of the 284 forms would bring out all the significant differences, we must be content with only an example: a comparison of some of the types of activity of associations composed of members from the three upper (upper-upper to upper-middle) and three lower levels (lower-middle to lower-lower). Certain tendencies, often masked as types by the more general classification, are sufficiently revealed to bring out some of the significant similarities and differences.

Well over a third (38 per cent) of all the activities of the lower group involved purely evocative symbolic behavior—in drama (16 per cent) and ritual (22 per cent)—where symbols are used as symbols of symbols and are designed to evoke emotions rather than refer the attention to objects and things (see Figure 6). Less than a sixth of the activities of upper-level associations were devoted to evocative symbolic behavior (drama, 6 per cent; ritual, 10 per cent). Closer inspection of the two categories tells a significant story. The lower associations were many times more active in sacred rituals than the upper, and two and a half more in those that combined the sacred with the secular. Furthermore, whereas in the lower-class associations there were two and a half times more occurences of secular rituals concerned exclusively with the private world, secular rituals relating to the general community showed no difference in percentage between the two levels.

The statistics made it apparent, and interviewing and field observations verified these conclusions, that organized public activities of the lower classes are concerned far more with religious observance and with the use of sacred collective represen-

Fig. 6. *Activities of Lower- and Upper-Class Associations*

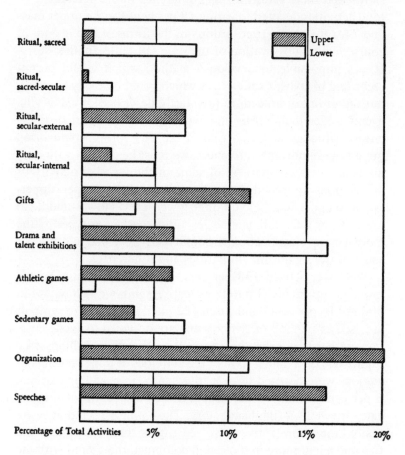

tations which give the feeling of belonging and being related "to the things of the world that matter." Moreover, the use of rituals which relate the associations only to their own members, paradoxically enough, seems to have a similar function; for they, too, encourage the exchange of symbols only among those who belong, and thereby encourage the twin feelings of exclusiveness and belongingness, the mutual regard and respect for the symbols used giving them importance and significance for each participant.

It must not be overlooked that symbols which evoke emotion rather than referring to specific objects and ideas are more easily used by the participants and retain their attention through longer periods. This preference of the lower levels for evocative symbols becomes more sharply significant when the preferences of the higher levels are known. Over a third (37 per cent) of the activities at the higher social level were concerned with speeches and organization business, compared with slightly more than a seventh (15 per cent) at the lower level. Both these activities demand quite different kinds of participation from ritual and drama. Granted that many of the speeches were designed to arouse the emotions and that some of the business had elements of ritual in it, each of these activities tends to be more directly concerned with reality than the other two. The words of speeches have to be placed in propositional and logical form; their meanings are more often concerned with ideas and things than those of drama and ritual. Since members of upper-class associations have had considerable training in school, with a higher education than members of the lower associations, the preference is not surprising. Business activities demand similar interests and, in general, the more precise relating of people to one another. Furthermore, authority and superordination are more easily maintained by their proper exercise.

Twelve of the nineteen types of activity showed considerable difference as between the two groups. Some of these differences are graphically displayed in Figure 6. Those favored by the lower levels are drama, the rituals mentioned above, sedentary games, "social hours," crafts, and teaching and learning. The preferences of the higher levels were for speeches, business and organization, the exchange of gifts, and athletics. There were only minor differences in the occurrence of the other types of activities.

Although many changes are taking place in the associational life of America in preference for certain types of activity, rejection of others, and the relinquishment of older activities to

accept new ones, the basic structure and function of these institutions in the society have fundamentally changed very little.
It seems likely that they will continue important in the lives of
Americans, for they serve their members well and conform to
the way Americans do things. George Babbitt, busy with his
real estate, Martin Arrowsmith in his scientific laboratory, and
Pulham, Esq., in Brahmin Boston, will always pay their dues
and remain "members in good standing."

In the next section we shall present a profile of a large patriotic association to show how the members of the several classes
are interrelated in a large organization.

All Men Are Born Free and Equal

The Patriotic Order of the United States Veterans of All
Wars (UU to LL) was in session. The people of Yankee City
said there were members from all walks of life in the Order.
They ranged from the old families at the top down through the
several layers of Sidestreeters to the veterans from the clam flats
of Riverbrook. It was the night that new officers were to be
elected. The active campaign had been going on for weeks and
everybody was there.

A few weeks earlier a scandal had broken and gossip had
spread through the city. The background of the incident which
had aroused the members and many of the citizens is of considerable interest. Money in the treasury was low. The members
were attending in smaller and smaller numbers. The incumbent
administration was blamed for the lack of interest. It was decided by some of the officers to hold a series of smokers. "Let
the boys tell a few jokes and import a little talent, you know,
a few gals from Boston."

The first smoker was a success. Outsiders were allowed to
come to the other sessions which followed. The small admission
fee they paid helped fill the treasury. The officers were congratulated by some of the members for getting such good turn-outs
and solving the financial problem. "It's all right," they said, "to
have a few evenings with patriotic speakers; but they get dull

after a while, and we need something like these shows to pep the boys up."

No one from Hill Street had come to the smokers, but "those Hill-Streeters never come anyway." They paid their dues and came through for extra assessments. They were always active when called upon to see that the needy members and their families were remembered at Christmas. It was an ever-present hope that some of them, sometime, might help contribute enough money to build a veterans' hall.

People like Mather Blaisdail (UU), Brooks Sinclair, and Travis Upton never came, and people like Alec French and William Camp came very infrequently. When French came some of the brothers said it was because he was trying to rent a house or catch some sucker for an insurance policy. Most of the men who came regularly to the meetings were fellows like Tim Pinkham, who was the president of the Order, some of the fellows from the Antlers and the Caribous (UM to LL), and many of the workers from the shoe and silverware factories, and a few clammers. Men like Tim Pinkham ran things and attended the meetings; and men like the shoe workers and clammers were run by them.

But this meeting was different. There was suppressed excitement. Blaisdail and Travis Upton had entered the large hall and sat down near the center of the room. Even Edward Marshall Jr. was there.

"That's the first time Mr. Marshall's been to one of our meetings since I can remember."

The president got up and went over to where Mr. Marshall was sitting.

"Glad to see you here, Mr. Marshall," he said.

"Glad to be here, Tim. I don't get out to enough of these meetings. I believe all of us should come at least for elections."

Mr. Marshall invited the president to sit beside him. Mr. Pinkham offered Mr. Marshall a cigarette and they both lit their cigarettes from Mr. Marshall's match.

Meanwhile, Mr. Upton, young president of the Booster

Club, Fred Flaherty, and Brooks Sinclair arrived with a group
of the town's prominent businessmen. They waved their hands
to a number of men they knew.

At one side of the hall in the seat across the aisle sat a score
or more of men. Among them were Sam Jones, Tom Green,
and Frank Tyler (LL). Many of them had sweaters on and
were without ties. They smoked, told jokes, and engaged in
horseplay.

After looking at his watch, the president walked to the front
and called the meeting to order. A simple ritual was performed.
It symbolized the "sacrifice" made by the members of this organization in all wars for their flag, their country, and their
homes. It referred to the self-evident fact that all men were born
free and equal and that our democracy guaranteed these things
to all of us. It spoke of the comrades who had fought and died
on foreign fields and assured them that they had not made these
sacrifices in vain; for the Patriotic Order of the United States
Veterans of All Wars was a living expression of those great
ideals for which they had shown this last measure of devotion.

Routine business matters were quickly settled. When it was
announced by the treasurer that he was glad to report a considerable increase in the Order's current funds no one said anything. The nominating speeches began. After a number of them
had been made, Edward Marshall stood up to speak.

"I too seldom meet here with you comrades of former days
and present members of this splendid organization. I came tonight because I believe it my duty to be here to cast my vote for
my good friend, Paul Foley [LU]. I was delighted when your
former president and great leader, William Camp, nominated
him. Paul's a man we all know. He's a living example of what
the Order stands for. He proves that race and creed [Foley was
Catholic] have nothing to do with a man attaining the highest
office our encampment has to offer. He is a good citizen, a good
husband, a splendid businessman, and a loyal member of our
Order. He is a good democrat—democrat with a small 'd.' "

He smiled, and the crowd laughed.

"During this coming year, many grave problems face us. We

must solve them if we are to go forward. Yankee City must solve such questions as getting new industries in order to keep all of our men fully employed. We must have work for our people whether they are employed at the bench or in the business office. We must pull together. There's no organization in this community that better represents the best of our city than our own Order of the United States Veterans of All Wars. There's no man better qualified to lead this order than Paul Foley.

"The other candidates are good men. We can't miss on any of them. Our present president has a good record—one to be proud of. I wouldn't hesitate to vote for any of them. But when the time comes to solve such questions as getting money for a building for our new organization, Paul's the man to do it. I am going to vote for Paul. This is a free country. Our votes are our own. Since each man has only *one* vote, we are all equal. I am going to cast my *one* vote for Paul."

He sat down. After the other speeches were made and the votes taken, it was announced that over half of the members had voted for Paul Foley. On the way out, Edward Marshall took occasion to speak to each of the defeated candidates and their friends. They joked about small matters and some of them called him "Ed," but most of them said "Mr. Marshall," and they were all called by their first names when he spoke to them.

Outside the hall, John Burke (LM) asked Flaherty if he wanted to go with some of the boys down to the Caribous for a bottle of beer. Flaherty said "no," he couldn't because he had another engagement. He started toward his car and was stopped by Mather Blaisdail (UU) who invited him to come up to his house on Hill Street for a highball. Flaherty accepted. He, Foley, Marshall, Blaisdail, and a few others stopped their cars in front of the Blaisdail house.

Patrick Donaghue (UL) and Tim Kelley (UL) drove by shortly afterwards on their way out to Littletown. Kelley said, "These guys up here on Hill Street certainly stick together, don't they?"

Inside Blaisdail's house Scotch highballs were being served. They drank to the new commander and kidded him about how they were going to show him proper respect and asked if he would still speak to them now that he had arrived.

"Don't drink to me," said Foley. "Brooks Sinclair is the man to be congratulated. We all know that he put this thing over. Tell them how you did it, Brooks."

"I didn't do anything," Sinclair replied. Everyone laughed and glanced knowingly at each other.

Flaherty said, "Why, Brooks, I just told somebody the other day that if I wanted to show how this city was run I would draw a lot of lines from all over this town and they would all point to your house."

"Well, to tell the truth," said Sinclair, "I did call up a few people. I wanted to straighten things out and make sure that the Order didn't get into a mess.

"Mather, the last time we were at the February Club the Reverend John Frank Foreman [UU] came to me and said at the last meeting of the ministers' association [UU to UM] they raised hell about those strip tease, hootchy-kootchy gals the boys had at the smoker. I had heard all about it before, but I am ashamed to say I pretended I didn't. I wasn't quite sure how to act. I never had liked the idea of a show like that being run by the Order, but I remember the time when we were in New York, Mather, when we got a little high and went down to Minskey's. I remember all the laughs we got. When I thought of that it made me feel a little like a hypocrite."

Blaisdail replied by commenting on how he had feared he wasn't going to get Paul out of the show because of the blonde on the end.

Sinclair continued: "But I began to see this thing was serious. I heard from all over that people were sore. And several of them said it would hurt the good name of our town if this got around.

"After I talked to a few of you, I got hold of the Reverend and asked him to tell the others to give us a little time because he could trust me to take care of the situation. Well, to make a long story short, I got Flaherty to get ahold of the boys at the Knights of St. Patrick's and swing them into line. He told them Paul was going to run and some of the better citizens were giving him their support. Alec here went down to the Caribous and Fred to the Antlers and got them lined up. Of course, the good word was passed on to the ministers, and Mather here lined up everyone on Hill Street.

"The point about all of this story is our people are sound at heart. Why, I bet even the Riverbrookers voted for Paul after Ed Marshall spoke. Well, you can see I didn't do anything. It was easy."

After Flaherty had refused his invitation, John Burke, in the company of Tim Pinkham, Fred Milkton (LM), and two other fellows, Will Carlton (UL) and Tom Rafferty (UL), drove down to Caribou Hall. They had had their first bottle of beer when John said:

"You know, the thing that happened tonight is what I like about this town. Everybody from top to bottom comes out to vote at a meeting of the Order. Old Ed Marshall was just as interested in the outcome as any of us. There may be differences between our people, but this town is run democratically. It did make me a little sore, though, when Alec French came down here to the hall the other night. It's the first time he's been down at this place since he rode the goat. I knew he was up to something when he came. I'd've been sore if he hadn't told me the whole story about some of those dry balls raising hell about the smokers. He told me enough to let me see that we had to do something. He said that the better elements of this town had to get together and get a new crowd in or the Order was likely to have trouble. I was going to vote for somebody else until he told me that, but he convinced me that we had better have Foley because it would look better."

Somebody said: "Hell, none of those dames had any class. They wouldn't lead nobody astray."

Somebody else made a few anatomical remarks, and another told a story about a traveling salesman and a highly persistent old maid. They had more beer, and the conversation turned to the topic of the layoff at the Neway Factory. Shortly after their second bottle, they left.

After the meeting, Sam Jones, Tom Green, and Frank Tyler stopped at Sam's house. Sam came out with a pint of alcohol. They rode down to the Three Mast Hall [LM to LL] where they found a crowd of shoe workers from the Neway Factory with some clammers and several men on relief. They ordered some near-beer and mixed it with the alcohol. They discussed the Neway layoff and the bad treatment that the workers got over at the P. O. Factory.

Green said: "That goddam Kike they got there now! Why, they say he won't have a girl in the plant that he can't screw. How the hell can a girl keep decent making the wages she gets now with those bastards around? My daddy belonged to the American Order of Mechanics. They hated Kikes."

Jones said: "Well, none of my family ever joined a union but I guess I'm a-goin' to this time. Things are too tough. Maybe they're right. Maybe we should stick together."

The three of them were joined by a Greek who worked in their plant. He had a slight accent. They "didn't like no foreigners but Johnny [LL] was a good guy," and he had taken out his papers. They invited Johnny to have a drink and to catch up with them. He drank one quickly. The talk returned to the layoff.

Johnny said: "See me, I ain't got a goddam cent now. Well, you all remember when I used to have a store. I made a little money, and I had a nice house and a garden for the missus and the kids, and now what have I got? Nothin', that's what I got. I'm back cutting shoes again."

Jones said: "Well, Johnny, cutters don't come no better than you."

"Yeah, I know, but I only been working once a week, and now we are all laid off. I say, there's something wrong, somewhere. Look, I watch those sons-of-bitches drive down from Hill Street. They go along like they're crazy in their big cars. They drive fifty miles a hour. Do they care if they kill one of our kids? Like hell they do. It's those guys who cause this trouble. They got most of the money but they ain't satisfied. They want all of it. Us guys down here ought to do something."

Somebody asked if he had joined the union.

"Well, I wasn't going to tell you 'cause I know how you guys feel about unions, but I have. We got to do something."

Jones, Green, and Tyler agreed that something had to be done. Johnny called out to a man who was better dressed than they were. It turned out that he was a union organizer, and he was invited to sit down at the table. He pulled a bottle of gin out of his pocket. They all had a drink from his bottle. They liked him. He had his veteran's pin on. He said that he belonged to the Order and was proud of it.

Tyler said: "We had an election tonight. Got ourselves a new president. When I seen French and Upton and all of those other bastards lining up for him I wasn't going to vote for him, but when Ez Rodgers said he was okay I changed my mind. I never liked Pinkham anyway. He's always been snooty around here. He never comes down to the Three Mast. He's a member all right, but he just thinks he's too goddam good to 'sociate with guys like us. I could tell election time was around when he came in the other night. He thinks clammers and shoe workers ain't good enough for him."

Johnny interjected: "The goddam rich people up on Hill Street."

Jones snorted and said: "Hill Streeter, hell, he's no Hill-Streeter. Why, he lives over there in Littletown. He ain't got a pot to piss in."

Johnny said, "He don't do no work, does he?"

"Hell, no, he sells insurance. Did you see how he kissed French's ass tonight?"

"Why, it's just like being in the army," said Jones. "The doughboys had to kiss the asses of sergeants like Pinkham, and all of those goddam non-coms stood around just looking for a chance to kiss a shavetail's ass."

The union organizer observed, "Yeah, that's how it is."

They asked him to tell them about the shoe workers' union.

He told them about how bad conditions had been over in New Hampshire and how his union had cleaned things up. They said they guessed they would follow Johnny and join up. Right now it was getting pretty late and they'd better be getting on home. The men parted under the sputtering arc light. Tyler was apparently anxious to prolong the talk, but meeting only the fuddled yawns of his friends he turned down the river road toward the flats and home.

Jones and Green left. They walked down the road along the river toward the flats.

Johnny walked up the road toward the square on River Street. He climbed up several flights of dark stairs. He was a little drunk and stumbled as he went along. As he passed each floor he was cursed in Greek by those he awakened. He opened the door. Two other Greeks were asleep on the bed. He took his shoes off and got in under the army blankets on his cot. He was soon sound asleep.

CHAPTER 6

Status, Role, and Class Position

Status and Role

SOCIAL INSTITUTIONS in all societies, simple or complex, primitive or modern, contain memberships to which their people belong and are assigned by the social system; these institutional memberships are automatically created positions which are basic kinds of status. (In the case of the family, at least some of them seem, in simple outline, to be precultural.) Each membership (or status) is socially defined by what it is and by what the other memberships are which directly or indirectly are related to it. Each membership has its rights and duties, its privileges and obligations, as do the other memberships related to it. As such, status is a socially defined "position located in a social universe." For example, the status *wife* in this and other societies is composed of many obligations and duties as well as rights and privileges, such as those having to do with sexual, economic, and moral behavior. These regulatory rules are orderings of ways of acting for the status; they can be viewed by themselves, but better understood as interrelated to the behavior of the status *husband*, which has its own rights and duties. Both husband and wife are memberships in the family; the latter, as an institution and part of the larger society, helps regulate the conduct of men and women, so that these positions are continuously evaluated and sanctioned.

By studying the culturally evaluated beliefs and values that define the norms of behavior for husband and wife and other

family and social memberships, the social scientist finds the
basic rules that order the world of each. The same general statements hold true for other types of status and institutional memberships, including the church, government, and associations.

Status may be described and identified by its form (what it
is), its functions (what it does), and where it is located in a
given social universe. The functions of a status include what it
does in ordering the social labor of the society, the part it plays
in controlling human biological behavior, and how it acts for
some or all individuals who are socially influenced by it.

Given social differentiation and institutional positions, no
status can exist by itself; its boundaries always include and exclude, for each status there is always an inner world and one
beyond it. Some social activities of some individuals are confined to it; other individuals and behavior take place beyond
its boundaries. Status, here defined, is a term referring to a social rather than to a psychological or individual context.

The term *role* on the other hand emphasizes the person and
individual behavior. Its use here derives from its earlier use for
the stage, individual style, and the way that the actor stylizes
his part and plays his role. Doing so, the individual defines his
personal meanings to others and to himself, while others define
who he is to them as a person and as persons what they mean
to themselves and to him. Many statuses may be implicated
with any particular role. Hamlet, the person, can be the *son*
to his father and mother, *stepson* to the latter's husband, and
brother to his sister. All these statuses are occupied by a given
individual; but the name given Hamlet himself not only refers
to the individual but derives from how he plays his personal
role. Statuses are integral parts of social relations; role derives
from individually and socially defined personal behavior. The
first emphasizes membership in society, the second, the person
in society. Status as here defined is an important unit in the
development of our present analysis of the Yankee City social
system.

We have considered the problem of the relation of an organization like the family, the clique, or the association to the class
hierarchy. These structures we placed in the class system by

counting the number of institutions or individuals appearing in one or more of the strata. This method of analysis gave invaluable insight into how the various institutions were distributed and, by inference, some insight into how they affected, and were affected by, class considerations. We learned, for example, that the family did not tend to spread beyond one class; that the clique, although sometimes confined to only one class, was usually distributed in two; and that the association was seldom confined to one class, a little more frequently comprised two, and most often three or four. A comparison of the spread of these three types of institutions gave us a significant comprehension of how the various classes were interrelated.

A re-examination of the distribution of the various social structures in the class hierarchy, however, yielded much better results for our understanding of institutional and class behavior and ultimately led us to discard these two types of behavior in favor of a system of relations whose ultimate units consisted of relative positions. There were some 357 associations on which we had accurate and approximately complete membership and activity data; the composition of these structures with respect to sex, age, ethnicity, religion, and class had already been determined. But the analysis of the distribution of the associations in class soon demonstrated that the various associations could be typed according to the range of their extension through the six classes. On the basis of the data collected in the field, the associations were typed finally into nineteen varieties called "class types."

In the nineteen class types of associations there were at least nineteen varieties of behavioral relations among the different members of the associational system of Yankee City. Hence the actual behavior of the people in these different types of associations would be expected to vary accordingly. For instance, a man or woman in Type 1 would, in all probability, behave very differently from a man or woman in Type 19. In the case of these two types we already knew this because the individuals in them were upper-upper and lower-lower respectively. However, when we examined the behavior of an upper-upper person who belonged to associations of both Type 1 and Type 6, it immediately became apparent that his relations in the former were quite different from those in the latter. In the Type 1 association all relations are of approximate equivalence since they are all of one class, while the Type 6 relations are not equivalent because the upper-upper members are related to the members of all classes below them. More specifically, an upper-upper individual in Type 6 is related directly to a lower-lower individual and to members of any other interstitial class. The behavior of the same person in an association of Type 1 and an association of Type 6 is obviously quite different. This would also be true of a lower-lower individual belonging to associations of Type 19 and Type 6. In the first he would be with his equals and in the second with representatives of five other classes all superior to his own. A cursory comparison of such types as 11 (UM and LM) and 16 (LM through LL) illustrates the point again. In Type 11 a lower-middle member is subordinate to all other members, whereas in 16 he is superordinate to all the others. In other words, he occupies exactly the opposite position in each of the two types and will in all likelihood behave very differently.

Let us make one other comparison before continuing with more general statements about associational class types. An upper-middle person might belong to a Type 3 association (UU through UM), a Type 6 (UU through LL), and a Type 13 (UM through LL). In the first all his relations would be with people above him and to whom, as a member of a class, he would feel inferior. In the second he would have bilateral relations with people both above and below him. There would be two class positions above him and three below him. In the third type (UM through LL) he would occupy a class position superior to all others and inferior to none; consequently, he would constantly express superordinate class behavior and expect to receive subordinate behavior.

Considerations of this range of behavior exhibited within one class, but based on the relational position in the types of association, led to the formulation of two new hypotheses:

1. Wherever a person's relations with his own class or with other classes varied because of the types of association to which he belonged, there was a lateral extension of social behavior at any one point in the vertical class hierarchy. This extension could be examined by the device of the class types of associations; and for our purposes such an extension at the six levels of the vertical hierarchy constituted a part of the horizontal, or lateral, extension of the society.

2. When the nineteen types of associations were seen as units in the lateral extension of each class, the two dimensions became fifty-four positions. For example, Class Type 2 (UU and LU) now became two positions, one of which consisted of upper-upper people who were in association with lower-upper, and the second of lower-upper people who were in association with upper-upper people. Figure 7 represents the two-dimensional system of positions worked out on the basis of the nineteen class types of associations. A member in any one of the

Fig. 7. *The Associational Positional (Status) System*

1 · 2 · 3 · 4 · 5 · 6 · 7 · 8 · 9 · 10 · 11 · 12 · 13 · 14 · 15 · 16 · 17 · 18 · 19

UU	1	2	3	4	5	6												
LU		7	8	9	10	11	12	13	14	15								
UM			16	17	18	19	20	21	22	23	24	25	26					
LM				27	28	29		30	31	32	33	34	35	36	37	38		
UL					39	40			41	42		43	44		45	46	47	48
LL						49				50			51			52		53	54

fifty-four positions would exhibit a somewhat different type of behavior from that of a member in any other position. A glance back at what has been said about Class Type 1 and Class Type 6 will help to clarify this point.

We have already said that the behavior of an upper-class individual varies in each of these associational types. Because of this difference in behavior, we formulated the positional theory. The upper-middle person belonging to associational Types 3, 6, and 13 is now in Position 16 (formerly called Class Type 3), in Position 19 (Class Type 6), and in Position 26 (Class Type 13). His behavior can now be examined and compared with that of other members of his various positions.

The fifty-four positions of the associational system are seen to extend laterally through nineteen class types. We have earlier examined the distribution of the several structures in class. With the discovery that the associations could be typed for a better understanding of the behavior of individuals in Yankee City, we applied the same conceptual scheme to the other structures of the society.

From the data collected on the several thousand families in Yankee City and their distribution in class, twenty-four class types of families were determined.

These twenty-four types were converted into fifty positions. There are twenty-four lateral positions. Of these, five include the upper-upper class, six the lower class, twelve the upper-middle, eleven the lower-middle, eight the upper-lower, and eight the lower-lower. The lower-lower is more extended laterally in the family structure than it is in the association. There is a greater similarity of behavior among lower-lower people, judged by these measurements, in the associational structure than there is in the family structure, since only six associational positions appear as against eight family positions. This is reversed, however, in the upper-lower where there are ten associational and only eight family positions. In the lower-middle they are approximately equal: eleven family and twelve associational positions. The same is true for the upper-middle, where there are twelve family and eleven associational positions. In the lower-upper there are nine associational against six family positions; in the upper-upper six associational against five family positions.

Of the five upper-upper family positions, none has relations which reach to the upper-lower; only one has relations with lower-middle; two have relations with upper-middle; and two with lower-upper; naturally all five have relations among themselves.

The difference between the relations of an associational position and of a family position is that a man can belong to only one family (as the family has been considered in this study) whereas he may belong to a number of associations. Consequently the associational membership can be interlocked because of the multiple membership of the various individuals in any given class. The family's extension depends on the extended kinship system for its horizontal spread; but membership in the association is characterized by interchangeability from one lateral position to another. The associational system allows the individual to occupy many places—six, for instance, if he is of the upper-upper class—but the family system allows him only one.

The family's usual system of superordinate, subordinate, and coordinate relations, with an ordered scheme of obligations, respect, rights, and duties, is greatly altered in places where the family type spreads over more than one class. Here a priori analysis would lead one to expect that in families where the members are in one class ordinary social relations will be little disturbed by the operation of class principles; but that where the members are distributed through two or more classes, ordinary family relations will be disturbed. In the father-son relation, for instance, the father is ordinarily superordinate and the son subordinate. This follows from the kinship organization. However, if the son's position is superordinate in class, there is a probability either of the son's being superordinate to the father or of a balanced equality because of the opposition of the kinship and class principles. Also, the father may still dominate the son through the strength of the kinship principles. The last possibility, however, is slight. The relation of father-daughter can be similarly deduced, as can those of mother-son and mother-daughter.

Brothers of approximately the same age in this society tend to have equivalent relations; but this relationship is unbalanced through one brother's rising or sinking to a higher or lower position, and one may come to dominate the other. Approximately the same thing is true of sisters and brothers, and among sisters. While an older sibling ordinarily occupies a position of dominance over his juniors, the operation of social mobility may raise one of the younger siblings to a superior class position, with the probability of his dominating his elder. An examination of the positions occupied by any of these kinship personalities in the family positional system will give one a working hypothesis of the kind of behavior one might expect in any specific family under analysis.

The several thousand cliques studied were also put in class types on the basis of the materials gathered in the field. Thirty-one class types of cliques were identified: nine upper-upper, eleven lower-upper, sixteen upper-middle, seventeen lower-middle, twelve upper-lower, and eight lower-lower.

There were seventy-three clique positions and their interrelationships. Other institutions, including such economic organizations as the retail and wholesale stores, factories, and offices of professional men, were also examined and typed. There are twenty-six class types of economic organization, three church class types, two school class types, and one political class type. The political class type, having total class representation, is similar to Class Type 6 in the associational structure, i.e., all six classes are found in the political organizations of Yankee City. The church types include but three: (1) a class type distributed through all six classes; (2) a class type distributed from lower-upper to lower-lower; (3) a class type from upper-middle to lower-lower. The economic class types correspond more closely to the family and clique class types than to the associational class types, since they do not all have positions in sequence as do the associational class types.

The Conversion of Structural Positions into a General System of Positions

When the several internal structures of the community of Yankee City had been analyzed to determine the number and kind of positions and relations, we sought to convert all the relations and positions of the separate structures into one general positional system. If this were possible, we could dispense with the older class and structural analysis and depend entirely on the positional and relational system.

The relations of the family, the clique, and the association, each of which was distributed through one or more classes in the separate class types, were now converted into relations which had no references to the several structures but were seen as general relations or general class types. This was done by breaking down the class types of each of the structures into one general class type. Thus, whenever two or more of the structural types coincided, they were treated as one general class type; whenever only one structure occurred, this also was treated as one general class type. Thirty-four of these general class types were found, and these were converted into eighty-nine positions. However, the problem of actually studying hundreds of thousands of specific social relations which would constitute the general positional system we sought was a difficult one.

Looking at the problem as though we had started from the beginning, our task was to analyze the interview material, which consisted of observations of the acts of our informants and their verbalizations about their own and other people's behavior, into member relations. This we had already done for the relations within the immediate family, the clique, the association, and other structures. Meanwhile we had succeeded in putting each of the several thousand families into class types; and we had done the same for the cliques, associations, economic institutions, and other internal structures of Yankee City. We thus moved through four levels of abstraction: (1) gathering concrete factual interview material (the acts of individuals); (2) looking at all this material as constituting acts which belonged to different kinds of relations of members of the family, the clique, and the association (members in relation); (3) assessing the relations not as specific ones—e.g., husband-wife or father-son relations within the family—but in their *totality* of behavior and class alignments in the community; and (4) formulating the concept of the positional system of each structure and, ultimately, the positional system of the total community. As we progressed from the first to the last stages of the work we constantly reduced the number of items to which we applied our attention.

By means of this latter discipline the millions of social facts collected in our five years of field work were reduced first to several hundred thousand relations, and then to several thousand families, cliques, associations, and other institutions. From the latter we worked out the class types, of which there were thirty-one for the clique, twenty-four for the family, and nineteen for the association; and the class types were in turn reduced to the positional and relational system.

General Description of the Status System

The status system of Yankee City consists of interrelated social structures, differentiated by the class hierarchy in which the individuals of the community are placed. There are six classes and seven different kinds of social structure. Each of the seven types of social structure is composed of one or more separate social structures. For instance, the family type is made up of thousands of single, elementary families, but the church and school types contain comparatively few structures. Each of the six classes and seven types of structure possesses hundreds or thousands of members. The 17,000 individuals who compose the total population of Yankee City are members of both the class and structural systems. An individual can be a member of only one class at a given moment in his life career and at a given moment in the history of Yankee City society. All individuals are treated as occupying but one class in the rank order of Yankee City.

However, a given individual is ordinarily a member of a number of kinds of social structure; and he may participate in all seven kinds of social structure while being a member of but one class. In a few of the seven types of institution he can belong to more than one structure: a man may be a member of two or more associations and several cliques. An individual usually belongs to but one church and school and ordinarily, by reason of his occupation, is a member of but one economic organization. All individuals in Yankee City belong to but one major political organization, the corporate township of Yankee City. For the purposes of this analysis we have placed the individual in but one family. If he is a parent and spouse, he is in his family of procreation (the family he creates by and after marriage). If he is a child or an adult living with his parents, or an adult living with his siblings—but not a parent—he has been placed by this study in his family of orientation (the family into which he was born).

Because an individual belongs to several kinds of separate structures which compose a type, he participates in a number of social situations at the same time. His rank remains unchanged, but his position within that rank is constantly changing. At all times the social statuses which compose the whole field of his participation influence his behavior; they are all interdependent in his life and in the lives of the other individuals who are members of the social system.

Since most of the members of associations, cliques, and families are members of other institutions, and the other members of these additional structures are also members of still other institutions, the whole community of individuals may be viewed as an interrelated, interconnected, and interdependent system of memberships.

We shall hereafter refer to the eighty-nine behavioral situations (or statuses)

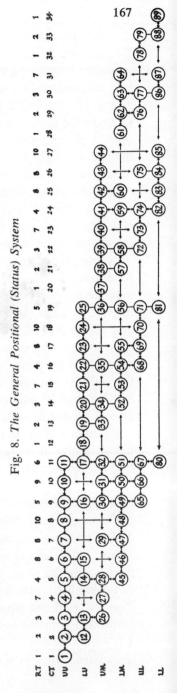

Fig. 8. The General Positional (Status) System

as social positions or statuses, and the total social system of Yankee City as the positional or status system.

Before continuing we shall carefully examine Figure 8. For easy comprehension, a brief description and explanation is necessary. On the left a vertical column of letters (UU to LL) refers to the positions at each level. The eighty-nine class positions beginning with UU at the upper left and ending with LL in the lower right are represented by numbered circles. Double-headed arrows indicate that they are interconnected.

The thirty-four class types (CT) spread from left to right in the second line of the chart. They account for the entire range of relations observed for persons in each class, through membership in the community's institutions.

Above all designations at the left of Figure 8, RT stands for Relational Types. These ten types, running from left to right, indicate the measured amount of connection for the members of each position (in each class) with all other classes. For example, the positions in Relational Type 1 are not directly related to any other class (1, 18, 37, etc.); on the other hand, the relations of positions in RT 6 extend through five other classes, through the society from top to bottom. Other types, such as RT 7, 8, and 10, are composed of positions where all connected classes are not in sequence.

Position 1 in the upper-upper group has no positions directly below it; and the only connections between it and all the positions which are below it are through the other positions found in the upper-upper class, that is, Positions 2 through 11. Position 89, at the other end of the positional system, is the reverse of Position 1 in its relations to the rest of the society. Position 89 has no direct vertical connections with any positions above it, and must depend upon indirect connections through other positions in the same horizontal extension.

Position 11 functions in exactly the opposite manner to Position 1 in the upper-upper group positions. It is directly connected with the lower-lower Position 80 through Positions 17, 32, 51, and 67. This means that a man who belongs to an association such as the American Legion (which extends all

the way through the society) has by virtue of his membership
an internal membership relation with a man who is a member
of the American Legion and who occupies Position 80. As defined here, these two memberships are in direct relation because
they are in the same association and not dependent on some
other group for their interconnections; they have direct, face-
to-face relations within one specific social structure.

Position 80, as the reader may readily infer, is in the same
functional position in the lower-lower group as Position 11 in
the upper-upper group. A man in Position 89 cannot, by virtue
of belonging to that position, be in direct relation with anyone
above. However, this same lower-lower individual, by belonging to Position 80, can and does have direct relations with
members of all five positions directly above. Not only does he
have direct relations internally with the five positions above his
own (i.e., 67, 51, 32, 17, and 11) but at the same time he is
indirectly interconnected with every other position in the whole
of the society. In other words, when a man is born into or joins
Position 1 or 89, he tends to be isolated and only indirectly
connected with the society which is above or below him, whereas an individual who has membership in Position 11 or 80 has
indirect membership relations with all the rest. It might be
further stated that *by indirect relation we mean the relation that
is, first, outside or external to the type of group to which a man
belongs, and second, one of superiority and inferiority.* This
last consideration must be added since a given position in any
one of the six strata can directly combine with all the others at
that level; not only can two positions at a given level be directly
connected by virtue of a member of one being a member of
another, but the same individual could and sometimes does
have a membership in all the positions. A man, for example,
may have a membership in all the positions from 80 through
89. This brings out very clearly a fundamental point in our
method: we are dealing here not with individuals but with
memberships in a positional system.

Although for the purposes of exposition we have confined
our attention to Positions 1 and 11 in the upper-upper group

and Positions 80 and 89 in the lower-lower group, we might just as easily have used Positions 18 and 25 in the lower-upper, 37 and 41 in the upper-middle, 61 and 63 in the lower-middle, and 78 and 79 in the upper-lower. Position 18 in the lower-upper class is almost analogous to Positions 1 and 89 in the upper-upper and lower-lower classes. A person who has membership only in Position 18 would have no direct relations up or down but only direct horizontal relations. The same is true of Positions 37 (UM), 61 (LM), and 78 (UL). There is, however, a difference between these four positions and the other two. Position 1, like all the other ten positions in its general vertical place, cannot be extended upward. Position 89, as well as all the other positions from 80 to 89, cannot be extended downward. However, Positions 18, 37, 61, and 78 are composed of members who are in the same lateral extension with other members in other positions which are capable of being extended up and down.

Positions 25, 41, 63, and 79 are approximately analogous to Position 11; and Positions 81, 82, 86, and 88 are approximately analogous to Position 80. The first series of positions are analogous to Position 11 because they extend their members throughout all the classes which are found between the two end positions. For example, Position 25 extends through 36, 56, 71, to 81, and obviously Position 81 extends internally, directly, and upward through all these positions.

It is possible, by examination of the several types of relational situations of positions, to distinguish ten relational types, as follows: Relational Type 1, positions which have no direct relations outside their own class; Relational Type 2, positions which have direct relations with one adjoining class; Relational Type 3, positions which have vertical relations with two other classes in sequence; Relational Type 4, positions which are in a vertical relation with three other classes in sequence; Relational Type 5, positions which are related to four other classes in sequence; Relational Type 6, positions related to five other classes in sequence; Relational Type 7, two positions not in sequence, that is, skipping one class; Relational Type 8 extends across four classes but contains only three positions, since one is not in sequence; Relational Type 9 extends across five classes, skipping one; Relational Type 10 extends across four classes, skipping two.

It will be noticed that these types are induced from observed relations among the eighty-nine positions. They do not exhaust the logical possibilities of combination.

Until now we have confined our attention almost wholly to the upward and downward extensions of the positional system. Positions 1 through 11 are *in relationship to each other directly and with unlimited interchangeability.* That is, an upper-upper man or woman, by virtue of status, may have direct relations with members of all positions at this level and can belong to all of them; there is no limit to an individual's right to join and participate in all eleven positions.

This is in contrast to the *limited interchangeability in the direct vertical relations.* A man in Position 11 may have direct relations with the members of the five positions below his but he could not join, let us say, Positions 17 or 80 because he is an upper-upper person and those positions are lower-upper and lower-lower respectively. However, as a member of an association which extends through all these positions and has members who have internal and direct relations with each other, he does have limited interchangeability with these other five positions. The rules governing such an institution as an association or a clique commonly declare that all the members are equal. This means that within the associational membership per se there is equality but that class attitudes still operate to differentiate the people who belong to the different positions within this structure. The direct behavior of the individuals in such relations clearly demonstrates this. Part of the behavior shows that the considerations of equality of membership are present. Any member from any stratum is eligible to office, for example. All votes are considered of *equal* value. However, while this is true, class attitudes are still present and feelings of superiority and inferiority differentiate the members into several segments. There is, therefore, *limited* interchangeability in these vertical positions which are in internal relation as compared with the unlimited interchangeability in the direct external relations among the positions which are at the same horizontal level.[1]

Such positions as 13, 32, and 58, to choose three at random, place their members in relations very different from those which we have just discussed. An individual possessing membership in position 13 would have relations both above and below himself. He would have direct relations with Positions 3 and 26. Positions 32 and 58, among others, also have these upward and downward relations. Obviously, the adjustments made by individuals in such memberships are very different from those made by an individual with a membership in Position 1, 11, or 80. A person in Position 13 is constantly adjusting himself in primary relations to persons above him while at the same time making adjustments in direct relation to persons below him. An individual in Position 11 is adjusting his relation only to those below him, while those with whom he has direct relations are adjusting themselves to positions both above and below. An individual in Position 80 adjusts himself only to persons above him whereas the persons above him with whom he has relations are adjusting themselves to positions both above and below their own. In Positions 1, 18, 37, 61, 78, and 89 there is no adjustment up or down, and all relations are those of equivalence.

We have now described and given examples of all the positions which are in sequence vertically and horizontally. There are, however, certain positions which are in direct relationship to each other vertically but are not in vertical sequence. Such positions as 4 and 27, 15 and 46, 8 and 48, 43 and 75, and 44 and 85, to choose several pairs of them, are in direct internal

1. The reader should not be confused by the term "external" as applied to the relations which exist between positions which are horizontally equivalent. It is sometimes confusing to think of one individual as having membership in all of the eleven positions and yet speak of these memberships as external relations. The memberships in the positions are external to each other since each membership is within a group which is within a type. For instance, the memberships of an upper-middle-class person in the Knights of Pythias and the Elks are external to each other, even though they are held by one individual.

relations but are not connected through members from all the intervening classes. Positions 44 and 85 are in direct internal vertical relation, which means that a man or woman in the upper-middle class is in direct relation with a man or woman in the lower-lower because they have membership in the same family or clique. There are greater differences between their positions than between two positions in a sequential relation. Ordinarily the adjustments necessary are much greater than between positions which are next to each other. This does not mean that the adjustments between the members of the two positions will always be more difficult since there are times when the superordinate-subordinate relationship may be sufficiently explicit and well organized to allow the individuals involved in the membership to accept this relation without thought and without a problem of adjustment.

Positions which are in horizontal relations cannot be out of sequence since they are interchangeable and all capable of direct relation.

In summary, the eighty-nine positions, operationally speaking, are a combination of the family, clique, association, school, church, economic, and political structures as they are found in the class system of Yankee City. There are thirty-one types of cliques, twenty-four types of families, nineteen types of associations, twenty-six economic types, three church, two school, and one political. Within each of these types there are a number of individual structures. That is to say, within one general class type there may be twenty or more associations, fifteen or more cliques, and one hundred families, as well as several stores and one or more factories or offices.

There are 71,149 members distributed through the eighty-nine positions. Some positions have only a few; others are large and have hundreds of members.

Status, Structure, and Behavior

The members of Position 1 consciously or unconsciously express the sentiments of the superordinate group in the community. Those who belong to associations and other structures in which only their own class is represented are aware that they are in a so-called "exclusive" group. The members of an upper-upper clique or association, when comparing themselves with other cliques and associations, are usually aware of their exclusiveness and of the fact that they occupy the superior position within the society. Of the several positions in the upper-upper class. Position 1 is viewed as being most satisfactory "socially." The members of a family in this position do not feel the strains present in family groups representing two or more classes. There is no feeling of inferiority about class position on the part of any of the members, and pride is manifested in the family heritage. The members of the upper-upper economic groups, usually office or professional people, are in a position in which the owner or manager is in an economically superior relation but in a coordinate or equal class position. There is a sense of social equality in their relations which is not found where the manager belongs to one class and the employees to another. An office in this position has "prestige."

Position 18 is in the lower-upper class. Its members consciously or unconsciously consider themselves superior to the members of the classes below them; but they feel they belong to the so-called "new people" in the upper class and they recognize the superior position of the members of the class above them. Their relations among themselves in the clique, family, and economic groups are of the same order as described for those same structures in Position 1. The relations of the members of Position 37 in the upper-middle class are all coordinate, and the attitudes expressed among the members of the clique, family, and economic groups are also the same as those found for the structures in Position 1. The members of Position 61 are also in coordinate relations. The fact that they belong to the lower-middle class means that they are aware of their lower status in the social system of Yankee City. The attitudes they express in their associations, clique, family, and economic relations indicate their awareness of being below the other three classes, yet they feel above the other two.

The members of Position 78 are in the upper-lower class.

They enjoy a certain feeling of superiority to those in the bottom group, but they are also aware of their social inferiority to members of the classes above them. They are likely to be "pushy" and ambitious people. The members of Position 89, in the lower-lower group, are coordinate only with the other nine positions in the lower-lower group. The attitudes they express in the association, clique, family, and economic groups are indicative of this fact.

The members of Position 2 have direct and superior internal relations with the lower-upper members of Position 12, and of course the latter have a relation of subordinacy to Position 2. The superiority-inferiority relations are found in the association, clique, and family structures.

The cliques maintain generally friendly relations, but there is sometimes bitter talk by those in Position 12 of not being "fully accepted," and the people in 2 frequently insist that members of 12 "are nice people although they are newcomers." Class claims are made obliquely and with the aid of symbolic references.

The associations frequently include members who are mutually antagonistic on a class basis. Women are accused of being "pushy," of acting like "climbers," or their "faults" are underscored and their virtues ignored. Men are less likely to indicate such feelings, but "kidding" relations express the ambivalent feelings of unity in the club and difference in class. The informal clique relations and associational relations among men and women of Positions 2 and 12 often account for the membership and protection of particular individuals in the lower class.

In Positions 19 and 33 members of two classes are in direct internal relations of superiority and inferiority, and the role of the lower-upper-class member is the reverse of that in Position 12, superior rather than inferior.

The families are those in which children have climbed above their parents, or which include grown siblings who have moved unequally up or down in the class hierarchy. The cliques are intimate but usually with the clear recognition that the members of Position 19 have intimate friends and acquaintances in the upper-upper class (ordinarily through 12) which people in 33 generally lack. The associations are small and ordinarily consist of formal committees which meet infrequently. Social relations in the last-mentioned organizations are not intimate. The lower-upper person, while feeling superior to his upper-middle clique and associational friends, is aware of the fact that he is not implementing his social position by such a relation. Occasionally an adult clique is a survival of an earlier clique when the person in 19 belonged to the class below. Our records show that certain people in a family occupying Position 18, formerly in both a family and a clique of 37, continued the earlier clique relation for a time. Once they had formed strong clique and associational relations of the 12–2 type, however, they began to withdraw from the 19–33 relation. Embarrassment and acrimony often arise from this sort of situation.

In Position 38 the upper-middle-class person is superior with relation to lower-middle-class Position 57, a direct reversal of his relative status in Position 33. The representative economic group here is usually a small store or office. Among the members of all structures there is recognition of the difference in status between the two classes. The members of 38 frequently participate in 33 with lower-upper Hill-Streeters and infrequently with upper-upper Hill-Streeters in 26. This is primarily done in cliques and associations.

The family in these two positions is usually a product of social mobility, the children having climbed to higher statuses than the parents, or having dropped, or siblings having fallen or risen to other social levels. This change of status within families is particularly frequent among ethnic groups.

In Position 62 the lower-middle-class person stands in a superordinate relation to the upper-lower-class person in Position 76; and in Position 79 the upper-lower-class member is superordinate to the lower-lower person in Position 88.

Associations covering this relationship tend to be cliquelike, as for instance subadult cliques which have little more than a name and an informal policy regarding membership. People in associations and cliques in 76 are often men and women with some prized talent or ability. The family members have fallen or risen in the social hierarchy and the usual defenses are present to explain, praise, or condemn the differences among the kindred. The economic groups are typified by small stores and retail establishments.

The family members of Position 79 are apt to be socially mobile ethnic children of parents in 88. The clique members are often courting couples, some of them Yankee Riverbrooker women in 88 who are "going around" with ethnic young men of 79.

We may turn now to the behavioral situations in positions lying in three adjoining classes. Positions 3, 13, and 26 include members in direct internal relation through the association, clique, and family. The upper-upper-class members of Position 3 express attitudes of superiority to the members of the other two positions, but the superiority is manifest with respect to the members of Position 26 more than to those of Position 13. When the members of such an association congregate, they often arrive and leave in cliques, and they frequently group themselves by cliques during the meeting. In these cliques the upper-middle people are often included with the two upper classes. Cliques form in all associations of three or more classes and organize more often than not on class lines.

The members of Positions 3 and 13 feel themselves members of the upper class in relation to the middle class, and a certain unity exists among them; but there is always an associated feeling of difference and opposition between these upper-class members. The members of the three positions, however, have a sense of unity among themselves and superiority to all other members of positions beneath them. This is particularly noticeable in associations where there is a definite recognition on the part of all the members that they are in some way superior to other associations which have members from positions beneath them. One group of men of this sequence is familiarly known as the "House of Lords"; a larger association with members from the lower-middle is called the "House of Commons." The sense of exclusiveness found in Position 1 and Positions 2 and 12 is still maintained in this three-class situation.

This means that while members of Position 26 feel socially inferior to members of the two superior positions, they can maintain feelings of superiority to members of lower positions or to those in their same class who are in lower types of associations.

Family behavior is extremely variant in this position. Many families of this kind are the result of downward mobility of the children, some of whom have dropped lower than others. The resulting strains on the family are severe. Different members participate in higher and lower cliques and find it difficult if not impossible to bring their friends home. The parents maintain a precarious hold on the old family status.

In Positions 20, 34, and 52 the lower-upper-class person's social place is changed and he is now in a position superior to that of members of the other two classes, whereas his status in position 13 in the preceding sequences was one of superiority to the members of Position 26 and inferiority to Position 3. In the sequence of Positions 39, 58, and 72, the upper-middle-class person is in the superior position and the lower-middle and upper-lower people are in an inferior position.

The above positions are treated together because they present the same social situation. All include family, clique, association, and economic groups. The family in each is variant and a product of upward and downward mobility. Most of the cases are due to upward mobility of children and siblings. This is particularly true in the sequence of Positions 63, 77, and 86. The associational and clique behavior is much like that described in 13 and 26.

From this analysis of general behavioral situations it becomes clear that a member of a class is faced with a constantly shifting series of relative positions in the society. At one moment he may participate in relations which are entirely coordinate (see Relational Type 1, Fig. 8). At another time he is in a relation with a class above him, where his position is inferior. And shortly thereafter he may find himself in a superior relation with one class below him (see Relational Type 2, Fig. 8). Still later he may occupy positions in which he is for a time superior to the members of two other classes, inferior to the members of two other classes, or superior to members of a class below him and inferior to the members of a class above him. Such social contexts of behavior, at a given moment in time, may appear in direct face-to-face relations as, for example, in a meeting of an association, in day-by-day family life, or in little clique gatherings for purposes of pleasure; or this behavior may be expressed in the private reveries of the individual. He can feel inferior in his private thoughts and be either aggressive or submissive toward a member of the class above him; or he can feel superior and have reveries of bolstering his own ego by thinking of behavior in which he is always in a superior position. Such behavior in the same status may take forms as variant as snobbishness and openhearted philanthropy.

Let us examine the positions in Relational Type 4. In this sequence of Positions 5, 14, 28, and 45 the members still feel superior to persons in structures which extend to positions below them. The members of these positions are in associations and cliques. There is still conscious exclusion of certain members of the society because they are not considered desirable. The same thing is largely true in the sequence of Positions 22, 35, 54, and 68. Those positions in the sequence 41, 59, 74, and 82, however, belong to a different category; since the vertical extension runs from the lower-lower through the upper-middle classes, there is a feeling of belonging to the "whole" community. This is particularly true of the school and church groups. The very few families which belong to a positional sequence of this kind are highly disrupted by the factor of class, and economic groups ordinarily are strengthened by it. The families are largely ethnic and very mobile.

The schools are ethnic and parochial. The children form cliques which separate them by class, and their teachers recognize "better and poorer" family stock. The churches in this Relational Type (41, 59, 74, and 82) are regarded as inferior to some of those having representatives of the two upper classes in them. Within each church there is clear recognition of the higher and lower statuses of parishioners and clergy.

The positions belonging to Relational Types 5 and 6 tend to have relations which are very much of a kind: the members of the structures involved are either spread throughout the society, as in the case of the six-class type, or lack representation in only one class at the top or the bottom. The attitudes expressed in such associations, schools, and church or political groups in face-to-face relations accent the total-community symbols. There is much talk of "the flag," of "our city," or reference to religious symbols which include everyone in the democratic ideology of equality and fraternity among men and before God. However, differentiation still appears in the attitudes of members of the various positions among themselves. Although an association member of Position 11 in a patriotic organization is believed to be a "comrade" to a "buddy" in Position 80, and equal to him, there is always a clear recognition of their social differences. Each has but one vote in an election of officers, but the man in Position 11 is still a Hill-Streeter and superior, and the man in Position 80 is still a Riverbrooker and believed to be inferior. The subtleties of status allow an expression of deference and inequality, but the demands of democracy insist they are "brothers in fraternity."

The control of churches lies in Positions 11, 17, and 25. The behavior of the ministers shows much more deference to members of these positions than to members in 80 and 81. When crises develop, Positions 11, 17, and 32, in the one sequence, and 25 and 36 in the other are clearly separated from the positions below them. The clique and associational behavior in churches and schools clearly expresses class attitudes.

Most of the economic members of these two sequences are employed in factories.

The political statuses show the same formal recognition of equality and the informal recognition of rank. "That Wop," "those Kikes and Niggers," or "Riverbrookers" become "Mr. This-and-That" in the political meeting or courtroom, but the uncontrolled glance, the inflection of the voice, still say "Wop" and "Kike." When the meeting adjourns, the Riverbrooker in 80 does not go home with the Hill-Streeter in 11.

The positions classified under Relational Types 7–9, where the classes are not in sequence, tend to emphasize differences in class feelings. In Positions 4 and 27 members of cliques and families are in direct relation with each other. Upper-middle-class persons in Position 27, while being pleased with their class relation with members of the upper-upper class, at the same time are aware of the great difference between themselves and the members of Position 4. The same is true of Positions 21 and 53. In Position 40 the place of the upper-middle-class person is the reverse of what it was in Position 27, and he is in a superior place to that of the members of Position 73, two classes below him. In Positions 64 and 87 the lower-middle-class person occupies an analogous place to the upper-lower-member of Position 73.

In Relational Type 8 occurs a certain variation not found in Relational Type 7, since three positions are involved, extending through four classes but skipping one. This means that two positions will be in sequence and one out of sequence. The degree of unity and consciousness of kind will vary, of course, according to which positions are in sequence and which out of sequence within a given structure. In all these situations in Relational Type 8 economic organizations are found. Such a situation tends to strengthen the ordinary superordinate and subordinate relations found in economic organizations. In all these situations the clique is also found. Cliques of this type tend to be less intimate, usually quite large in membership, and frequently of a specialized kind, such as a group of men who hunt or play cards together but whose wives and families are not on intimate terms. Such class situations in a family tend to put special strains on the relations among its members. In the positions of Relational Type 9 the members act much as in the behavioral situations of Type 8.

Of the four positions involved, the three lower ones are in sequence and the top one (Position 10) is in the upper-upper class. Once again the clique and economic groups are found and conform to the rules stated for Relational Type 8 for these two structures.

Relational Type 10, where two classes intervene between the two positions, accentuates the situation found in Relational Type 3, where there is but one intervening class. The clique is found in all six of the positions involved, the economic organization in two of them, and the family in one. What has been said of the clique, economic, and family organizations in Relational Types 7–9 also holds true for Type 10.

The foregoing analysis of behavioral situations found in certain of the eighty-nine positions of the six classes prepares us for variations in the behavior of a member of a given class from moment to moment. It gives, for instance, some foreknowledge of how a specific person will act as he moves from one position to another. Take one example of this. Mr. X and his family are all members of the upper-upper class. In fact, membership in the same class is the normal type of class affiliation for all families. One afternoon at cocktails he was heard discussing the lineages of certain old families with several of his intimate clique friends, also of the upper-upper class. Here all his relations were coordinate, as was obvious from the common attitudes expressed. In the evening he went to the Alpha Club to join some friends for dinner and to read the New York papers. There he was in Position 3. After dinner he attended a meeting of the Beta Club—where he was in Position 2—and discussed with members of his own and the class below him subjects of special interest to that group. On the following day he went to his factory office and conferred with the managerial group and then went out into the shop to consult with some of the men about working conditions. He was at this time in Position 11. That afternoon he went hunting with a few of his old high school friends and was in Position 6; and on Sunday he attended church where he again was in Position 11.

During all these events Mr. X adapted his behavior constantly to fit the position in which he found himself. His behavior as a member of a factory in Position 11 was different from that as a member of a church; but nevertheless certain of his attitudes were common to both cases and certain attitudes expressed to him by the members of other positions were the same. His lower-upper-class minister, when shaking hands on Sunday morning, was just as aware of Mr. X's superior position as was his lower-upper-class manager when he walked into the factory on Monday morning. The constant factor here is the relationship of upper-upper to lower-upper, and the differences involved are primarily those attitudes which are appropriate to the two different kinds of social structure.

Mr. X is an adult male; his behavior in each of these situations is always conditioned by these factors. Were he subadult, or a woman, he would be expected, and expect, to behave differently. Mr. X is a Yankee by birth and tradition and of the Protestant faith; were he Irish and Catholic, he would be expected, and expect, to act differently in each of the positions in which he participates. These social characteristics—age, sex, ethnic affiliation, and religious faith—are also possessed by everyone he meets and modify their behavior. Plainly, in each position these factors in behavior must be accounted for if we are to understand what happens in the events which make up the life of the community.

The Interconnections of Each Class

The foregoing analysis of the status system has been concerned both with the structural and "characteristic" composition of each of the positions and with the comparative place of each structure and characteristic in the total system. The characteristics describe the kinds of people who are being influenced in the eighty-nine positions; the structural memberships give the form of the influence; and the interconnections the amount (by number only) of influence from other positions on a particular one. The influences are from two general sources: those emanating from the same class and those from higher and lower classes.

By counting the number of memberships which individuals hold in each horizontal position, we were able to coordinate the remaining unconnected parts of the system in an interactive whole. To obtain an actual count, we had to use the personality card of each individual to distribute his memberships among the positions. Because of the complexity of the task, only association, clique, and family data (later referred to as ACF) were used, since they are ordinarily the most important in the lives of the individuals. After this, the number of times a member of each of the eighty-nine positions was connected with each of the other positions was counted.

We were now ready to particularize further by asking (1) how many connections in equivalent relations does each position have? and (2) how many connections in superior-inferior relations? The first question needs further refinement if we are

Table 4. *Sample Table of How Interconnections were Counted*

Individuals	Position A memberships	Position B memberships
T	2	2
V	2	5
W	6	4
X	0	8
Y	1	0
Z	0	0
Total memberships	11	19

to get definite answers and develop exact operations to obtain them. It breaks down into a series of questions: (1) What is the total of all the "outward" connections in relations of equivalence that each position has with *all* other positions in its class? (2) How many "outward" connections in relations of equivalence has it with *each* position in its class? (3) What is the total of *all* the "inward" connections in relations of equivalence that other positions have with it? (4) How many "inward" connections in relations of equivalence has *each* of the other positions with it?

The amount of interconnection a position has with another

in its class depends on (1) what proportion of all of a position's connections are with each of the others and (2) what proportion of *its own members* have membership in each of the other positions.

Let us suppose that the community comprises six individuals, T. V. W. X. Y. Z (see Table 4), all belonging to only two positions, A and B, in one class. T has two memberships in A and two in B. Since there are an equal number of memberships in each position, Position A is connected as much with B as B is with A.

Individual V has two memberships in A and five in B. If we disregard all other memberships, from the point of view of A that position would have five "outgoing" connections with B and B would be "inwardly" connected with A only twice. By amount of membership, A would be stimulating more members in B than B would in A.

In the case of individual W, A has more memberships than B. This reverses the membership arrangement of individual V.

Individual X adds another possibility to the membership connections since he is not a member of A but has several memberships in B. Individual Y reverses this situation since he is a member only of A. If only the memberships of these two individuals were considered, Positions A and B would not be connected. Finally, individual Z has no memberships in either, but in other positions not being considered.

There are eleven memberships in A and nineteen in B; but, to reiterate, not all the members of A are connected with B and only some of the members of B are connected with A. To be exact, ten of the eleven members of A are connected with B; eleven of the nineteen members of B are connected with A. Although the larger position, B, has more members connected with the other one, the smaller one, A, has a larger percentage (ten out of eleven) of its total connected with B. This means that the percentage of members of A being influenced by B (inwardly connected) is larger than that of members of B being influenced by A.

It is now necessary to return to the actual positions.

Position 1 has a total of 1,077 outward connections and 1,439 inward connections. This total was found by counting all its outward connections with the other positions of the upper-upper class.[2] By dividing the total of all the outward and inward connections of Position 1 by its connections with each position, the proportion of its connections of equivalence is obtained. For example, 32.87 per cent of its outward connections and 23.84 per cent of its inward connections were with Position 2.

These answers offer a measurement of the total amount of interaction Position 1 has with each of the other upper-upper positions. We know Positions 2 and 3 have, both inwardly and outwardly, more connections with Position 1 than with any other position, and that Positions 6 and 7 have the least connection. Such knowledge indicates that the members of Position 1 are likely to be more influenced by the status behavior in the first two connected positions than with the latter two.

Such an analysis of mutual influencing (social interaction) within a class is very helpful in obtaining an estimate of the probable amount of pressure given and taken by members of a position. There are limitations, however, in the use of this system in determining social interaction, for it must be remembered that the positions have unequal membership. Position 1 has 516 members; Position 2 has 361; and Position 7 has only 9 members. To discover how much each of these positions is connected with Position 1, other operations are necessary. Since Position 2 has 361 members, 354 of whom are also members of Position 1, this means that 98.06 per cent of the members in Position 2 are members of Position 1. On the other hand 343 members of Position 1 are members of Position 2, which means that 66.47 per cent of the members in Position 1 are also in Position 2. Position 1 has 31.59 per cent more members of Position 2 than Position 2 has of the members of Position 1. The number of members of 2 directly influenced by the status

2. It had 354 with Position 2, 392 with 3, 68 with 4, 138 with 5, 1 with 6, 7 with 7, 13 with 8, 46 with 9, 10 with 10, and 48 with 11.

position of 1 is appreciably larger than the number of members of 1 who are influenced by 2.

Let us examine the connections with Position 6, the smallest of the upper-upper positions. Position 1 is connected but once with the one member of Position 6, constituting only 0.09 per cent of the total outward connections of Position 1. The one member of Position 6 has seven connections with Position 1, which is 0.49 per cent of the total inward connections of 1. However, the one outward connection Position 1 has with 6 represents 100 per cent of the total membership of 6 and the seven connections 6 has with 1 comprise only 1.36 per cent of the membership of 1. There is, therefore, an enormous difference in the amount of influence the two positions have on each other.

In the horizontal relations one individual can occupy several statuses; in the vertical order he can hold only one position, for he belongs to but one class in a given moment of his lifetime. The connections in the vertical relations therefore were of a different order and had to be computed by different methods from those just described.

Positions 1 has no positions above or below it, so we shall turn for our example to Position 3, which is connected with Positions 13 and 26. There are 399 members in Position 3; 395 in 13; and 632 in 26. Position 3 has four more members than 13 and therefore has a greater numerical influence on 13 than the latter has on it. On the other hand, 26 has 233 more members than 3, with a similar result. If the total number of members of 3 and 13 is divided into the difference between them, the percentage of difference is obtained; and when this is done for all positions it is possible to compare the amount of numerical influence they have on each other.

These vertical computations are of less significance and are less reliable than are those for the relations of equivalence. But they are useful for rapid calculation of the proportionate amount of relation between two or more positions.

In spite of limitations, the positional method supplies a relevant social framework for the analysis of particular relations and events and allows the investigator to include or exclude all, some, or none of the other types of relations which compose the social system of Yankee City. It also allows a psychologist to examine the behavior of a particular individual by comparing it with that of others in a similar and comparable situation and facing similar problems. The psychiatrist, for instance, can compare the behavior of a particular upper-upper individual not only with that of other upper-uppers (which gives him a first delimitation of the field) but also with other upper-uppers who participate in the same part of the relational system. Such comparisons will provide a far more accurate method of estimating the degree of individual deviance and a much better understanding of the problems which the patient is attempting to solve than present-day psychiatry possesses.

CHAPTER 7

Larger Organizations in the System

The Church in the Class System

THIRTEEN churches of four different faiths cared for the religious needs of the Yankee City community. The majority were of the Protestant faith and comprised eleven congregations; two churches were Catholic, one Greek Orthodox, and one Jewish. The Greek Orthodox and the Jewish religions were not included in this statistical study because our material was incomplete at the time of the church analysis.

The first Catholic church was formed by the Irish immigrants to Yankee City in the middle of the nineteenth century, and is now the largest single church in the community. Commonly referred to as the Irish Catholic church, it was attended by other ethnics of the Catholic faith including most Italians, a very few French Canadians, and a few Poles. Socially ambitious members of these ethnic groups attended it rather than the other Catholic church.

The second Catholic church was founded by the French Canadians who came from the province of Quebec as early as 1880. Many of these people still spoke French and lived in the Riverbrook and Uptown sections of Yankee City, the area of the largest concentrations of ethnics in the community.

The First Church of Yankee City was the oldest Protestant organization in the community. Located in Oldtown (the earliest settled section of Yankee City), many of its members were families descended from first settlers who had attended for several generations. It was one of three Congregationalist churches. This denomination was first to establish itself in the community.

Old South Church, located in Uptown, was Presbyterian. This church was notable because certain upper-upper-class families supported it financially and paid for repairs and up-keep of the building. The building has considerable importance in community symbolism because it is old and is related to the ancestors and ancestral objects. It also drew members from the lower-class Yankees as well as ethnics who were concentrated in the Uptown and Riverbrook sections of Yankee City in which this church was located.

Central Church, the newest of the three Congregational churches, had the most modern building and equipment of any church in Yankee City.

The Homeville Church was the third and last organization of the Congregational denomination and was located in the solidly middle-class residential section of Homeville. It was built and endowed by a wealthy upper-class family who former-ly resided in this section.

The Methodist Church was the only one in the Riverbrook section of the town, and it drew its congregation mostly from the lower classes of this section. Its membership included a large proportion of Yankee Riverbrookers and a few individ-uals from various ethnic groups which resided in its vicinity. The class position of this church was closer to the bottom of the hierarchy than that of any other Protestant church.

The Baptist Church was one of the more recent Protestant churches; it had few upper-class members. It had dropped in membership, probably because some people in the community placed a low status evaluation upon membership in this church.

St. Paul's Church, the only Episcopal church in Yankee City, was composed of more upper-upper and lower-upper class members than any other church of the community. Great emphasis was placed by this group upon the preservation of symbols of antiquity. This was most apparent when their old wooden church building, erected in the early years of Yankee

City's establishment, burned down. In its reconstruction, the plan of the destroyed wooden building was faithfully followed, except that it was made of stone. Certain ornaments saved from the original building have been preserved as relics and placed on exhibit in the new church building in receptacles which guard them from destruction. The importance of ancestry may be seen in this behavior in that the upper class dominated St. Paul's Church and related itself to the past history of the Yankee City community and placed itself above the other churches which existed there.

The Unitarian Church was the only one which could offer competition in any way to St. Paul's Episcopal Church. It was housed in one of the most beautiful buildings of the community, designed by Bulfinch, the architect for many other noteworthy buildings in early New England. Although the Unitarian Church boasted a rather large membership, few people attended its regular Sunday services. It was, however, very well endowed, and many upper-class members of Yankee City held themselves responsible for preserving it as an ancestral object.

The Christian Science Church was the most recently established of all churches in Yankee City. Although it had a small membership, mostly from the upper-middle and lower-middle classes, it was gaining rather than losing in class position.

The two churches with the largest proportion of upper-class individuals in their congregations devised a method of limiting the number of persons from the lower parts of the class hierarchy. St. Paul's Church had a branch in Newtown called Christ's Chapel which functioned as a mission and was composed of many persons from the upper-lower and lower-lower classes. The Unitarian Church also had a mission unit called St. Peter's Chapel which was located in the Riverbrook section and was also composed of many people from the lower classes.

All churches save the Christian Science had a large number of satellite associations connected with them. These organizations offered all kinds of secular activity to the church mem-

bers and helped to bring more people into church affairs.
While the churches restricted themselves to sacred rituals at
their meetings, they were enabled, through these satellite associations, to enter other activities. Such satellite associations not
only held existing members to these various churches, but also
acted as proselytizing agencies in attracting new members from
other churches. The nine Protestant churches had many more
of these organizations than those of the Catholic faith although
satellites of Catholic churches had larger memberships.

Our statistics show that about 53 per cent of the 10,866
Yankee City church attendants were women.[1]

The Catholic and Methodist churches are predominantly
lower class, the latter the lower-lower class only. The First,
Central, and Homeville churches are favored by the middle
classes. St. Paul's and the Unitarian churches are favored by
the upper and middle classes and avoided by the lower ones.
The Christian Science Church is favored by the upper-middle
class.

Upper-upper-class persons who attend the various churches
in Yankee City are significantly predominant in St. Paul's
Episcopal Church and the Unitarian Church. They are significantly absent in the two Catholic churches, the Central
Church, and the Homeville Congregational Church. Lower-
upper-class persons attend St. Paul's, the Unitarian, and the
Central churches in significantly high numbers and are significantly low in the Immaculate Conception and St. Aloysius
Catholic churches.

Upper-middle-class persons have a significantly high attendance at the First Church, the Central, Homeville, Baptist,
Unitarian, and Christian Science churches. Upper-middle-class
individuals are significantly low in attendance at the two Cath-

1. Christ's Chapel, which was connected with St. Paul's Church, and
St. Peter's Chapel, connected with the Unitarian Church, are included
in these fifteen churches. The Greek Orthodox and Jewish churches
have not been included in the above statistical analysis. Christ's Chapel
and St. Peter's Chapel were included in the St. Paul's and Unitarian
totals.

olic churches and at one Protestant church, the Methodist. Lower-middle-class persons have a significantly high membership in St. Paul's, First Church, and the Central and Homeville churches but a significantly low attendance at the two Catholic churches.

Upper-lower-class individuals attend the two Catholic churches in significantly high numbers, but are significantly low in attendance at all Protestant churches with the exception of the Methodist. Lower-lower-class individuals are significantly high in attendance at the two Catholic churches and the four Protestant churches, including the Old South, Homeville, Methodist, and Baptist churches. Lower-lower-class individuals have a significantly low attendance at St. Paul's, the Unitarian, Central, and First churches.

The Schools of Yankee City

The Yankee City High School is located in the approximate center of population in the Business District. It draws its students from three elementary schools located in the Middletown section, the Business District, and the Homeville area. In addition to these city grammar schools, there are two parochial schools, financed and operated by the Catholic churches of the community. There are no parochial high schools in Yankee City and boys and girls who attend the parochial grammar schools pass on to the city high school for advanced education. The latter draws its students from all segments of the society and from all sections of Yankee City.

Few subadult persons from the two upper classes attend the local high school. Most of them go to private schools in Boston or to boarding school for a period covering at least the last two years of the high school course.

The elementary school in the Middletown area is composed mostly of lower-class Yankee and ethnic students from the Riverbrook, Middletown, Downtown, and Uptown sections of the city. It is in these sections that the most recently arrived ethnic groups are concentrated, together with many of the lower-class Yankees. A grammar school located in the Business

District has a cross-section of subadults of different social types in Yankee City, with Yankees of all classes and persons from all ethnic groups. An elementary school located in Homeville is largely attended by middle-class Yankees and Irish who come from Middletown, Centerville, Newtown, and Hill Street.

The parochial school operated by the Immaculate Conception Church is predominantly Irish, while the school operated by the St. Aloysius Church is attended almost entirely by French Canadians.

The Yankee City High School offers four courses in its program of study: Latin, scientific, commercial, and general. The Latin course is concentrated on such subjects as languages, history, and mathematics. Over two-thirds of the upper-middle class youth take this course, and upper-upper and lower-upper girls usually make it their choice. This course is not designed to train students for business careers but to give them a cultural background preparatory for college. More girls than boys are enrolled in this course.

The scientific course offers special technical preparation for college work and includes a maximum of mathematics, physics, and chemistry, with secondary subjects such as languages and English.

A wealthy upper-class resident of the community some generations ago left a sizable amount of money, the interest from which was to be spent in payment of college tuition and other expenses for Protestant students of Yankee City. The Wright Fund, as it is called, was designated entirely for scientific study and, therefore, applied to male rather than female students. Male students take the scientific course, with upper-upper and lower-upper students in the majority. Boys from the three upper classes usually prepare themselves for and attend the Massachusetts Institute of Technology, Harvard, and Yale, while boys of the three lower classes more often go to Northwestern Y.M.C.A. College, where the study programs are scheduled to allow them to alternate work and school attendance at intermittent periods. The Wright Fund seems to be one of the many devices for subordinating people in the lower classes, particularly ethnic groups, and consolidating the control of the upper-class Yankee City persons.

The commercial course includes such subjects as typing, shorthand, bookkeeping, business arithmetic, and allied studies which teach skills suitable to business and office work. The commercial course is aimed to equip students to enter the economy of the society immediately upon completion. Most of the people taking the commercial course are girls who are training for secretarial and other jobs; but such courses are frequently taken in preparation for a year or two years' work at a business college.

The general course is a catchall for those students who attend the Yankee City High School but do not intend to prepare for college and have no particular objective in mind for earning a living.

In the Latin and commercial courses female students predominated, while all students in the scientific course and the larger proportion of those who took the general course were males. Of the 599 students, 290 (48.41 per cent) were male and 309 (51.59 per cent) were female.

The Yankee City High School was attended by students from all ethnic groups.[2] Yankee students composed somewhat over two-fifths of all who attended, and ethnic students had somewhat under three-fifths. Native students had a significantly high representation in the scientific course, while ethnics were significantly low in number.

Of all ethnic groups, the Russians were significantly high and the Irish students were significantly low in representation in the scientific course. The French-Canadian and Jewish students were almost evenly represented. Italians were high in the commercial course and low in the scientific and general courses.

2. Of the 599 students, 263 (43.91 per cent) were native, and 336 (56.09 per cent) were ethnic. In the total enrollment, 181 (30.22 per cent) were Irish; 49 (8.18 per cent) were French Canadian; 31 (5.18 per cent) were Jewish; 8 (1.34 per cent) were Italian; 3 (0.50 per cent) were Armenian; 22 (3.67 per cent) Greek; 29 (4.84 per cent) Polish; 7 (1.17 per cent) Russian; and 6 (1 per cent) were Negro.

The Armenian students were high in the Latin and commercial courses; Greeks were low in the general course.

The Polish students had a low representation in the Latin and scientific courses but were high in the commercial course. The Russians had no members in the Latin course and were heavily represented in the scientific and commercial courses.

The numbers of Italian, Armenian, Russian, and Negro students, however, were too small to be of any significance.

Most of the ethnic groups were affiliated with the Catholic Church and were not eligible for participation in the advantages of the Wright Fund and, therefore, could not be expected to rank high in the scientific course. Natives, however, ranked very high in this course because of the advantage of this fund.

Of all Yankee City High School students, none was found in the upper-upper class; 4 (0.67 per cent) were in the lower-upper class; 57 (9.52 per cent) belonged to the upper-middle; 217 (36.23 per cent) to the lower-middle; 245 (40.91 per cent) to the upper-lower; and 76 (12.69 per cent) belonged to the lower-lower class.

The commercial course attracted almost two-fifths of the students, and the Latin course slightly over one-fifth of all students.

With the exception of the lower-upper-class students, the percentage of each class who took the Latin course declines with lower position in the class hierarchy. Only four lower-upper students in all were represented, and one of the four took the Latin course. More than two-thirds of the upper-middle-class students were in this course. Except for students of the lower-upper class, those of the lower-middle class had the highest proportion of persons who attended the scientific course, and upper-middle-class students were next in number. A larger proportion of persons from the middle classes than from the lower classes took the scientific course. Persons in the lower-upper class, however, were greatly in the majority and had three-fourths of their number within this group. More than half of the lower-class persons who attended the Yankee City High School took the commercial course, and about one-third of the lower-middle-class students were in this course. Upper-middle-class students were not significantly represented in the commercial course, and students of the two upper classes did not appear.

Only students from the two middle and the two lower classes were enrolled in the general course, and those of the upper-middle class had a significantly small representation. Students of the upper part of the class hierarchy attended the Latin and scientific courses more frequently than those of the lower classes, while conversely those of the lower classes more frequently attended the commercial and general courses than did students of superior classes.

Politics and Government

The political structure of Yankee City was composed of a group of officers and a group of voters. The officers were elected by the voters or appointed by other officers who had been elected by the voters. Voters were distinguished from non-voters: the latter were people below twenty-one years of age, citizens who did not have the residence requirements, people of foreign birth who were not citizens, and residents who had failed to register or fulfill other technical requirements.

Although the voters among the three lower classes far out-numbered those in the three higher, they had a dispropor-tionately small percentage of officers in the political hierarchy. In other words, the upper classes held a greater proportion of the higher offices than their numbers in the voting and general population would by mere chance allow them. Indeed, as the importance of the political offices increased, the proportion of upper-class officeholders increased. Class is therefore an impor-tant factor in Yankee City politics.

The political structure of Yankee City helps to articulate the various internal institutions to each other through their common relation to this political structure. The governmental structure is a hierarchy of offices through which the political functions are exercised. At the top of the structure are the mayor and city council. The council has eleven elected members: six representing their respective wards, and five, the city at large. Most of the final powers of control are assigned to the council. Those concerning appropriations and the budget, appointments to office, control over the various departments and over the various boards are all lodged with the city council. The council is not a salaried group and does not give full time to its office. It is an instrument of supervision and direction which represents the community directly and has control over the whole political structure. Besides the mayor and the school board, its members are the only elected officers in the hierarchy. It has its own internal organization. It elects a president who presides as chairman at the meetings and apportions the councilors among the five standing committees which consider specific kinds of business before the council finally passes on them. These committees are public safety (fire and police departments), public service (street and highway department), licenses and recreation, general government (finances), and soldiers' relief.

The council as a whole supervises directly the work of the different departments, which have specific functions to perform. In times of political crises the council may conduct public hearings in order to sound out general community opinion on the issue involved.

In addition to the departments there are the boards, which are immediate supervisory offices whose members are appointed with the approval of the council. The members of these boards are also nonsalaried, although they employ full-time clerks and agents to carry out their business. These boards have the power of final decision within the limits defined by their special function, but the ultimate authority rests with the council. The council has such authority because it allocates the annual funds to each board, each board has to make an annual report to the council, and all appointments of each board have to be approved by the council. The boards are (1) the water board, (2) welfare board, (3) board of registrars, (4) board of health, (5) commons commission, and (6) library board.

The school board, which is elected, has final authority in

appointing the personnel for the schools. The school board prepares its own budgets but its funds must be approved by the city council. The mayor is the chairman ex officio of the school board and is the intermediary between it and the city council.

The final control of the city council lies in its powers to create such departments and boards as are necessary to serve the community. During the field work for this study, the council created a department of public works combining functions which were hitherto uncoordinated among different departments. The mayor stands in relation to the city council somewhat as the corporation president does to his board of directors, inasmuch as the city council represents the community as the board of directors does the stockholders, and like the board of directors, the city council holds the purse and the power of policy making and of supervision.

The mayor, an elected, salaried officer, gives full time to the office. His relations to the city council are well symbolized by the ritual performed at all meetings of the council when he is in attendance. The president of the council, while in the chair, appoints a committee of two to escort the mayor into the chamber. There he is given a place at the foot of the table with the president of the council at the head and the other councilors seated along the sides. The language used by the council and the mayor is also significant to show the relation of each to the other. Thus the mayor "proposes to the city council," or he may "recommend to the city council"; we also hear "on plea of the mayor, the city council considered" and "the mayor hopes the council will not oppose." On the other hand, the council in making its decisions "orders" or "instructs" the mayor as to its will. The mayor makes recommendations to the council which the latter may either accept or reject. He is expected to bring before the council all business which belongs within the functions of the political structure. The mayor has direct and defined relations with all the administrative boards and departments since he is the liaison officer between these and the city council. As the chairman ex officio of most of the boards, he presides at their meetings. He ordinarily appears before the council as a representative of the boards. By reason of his central position in the political structure, which both serves and is identified with the community, he obtains a central position in times of crisis when certain actions beyond the strict functions of the political structure are necessary to organize the community. The activities of the mayor who was in office during World War I and the behavior of the mayor during the early years of the Depression were examples of his functioning as the leader of the community in behavior which was in large part not politically defined.

One more group of offices in the political structure remains to be considered. These are the auxiliaries of the executive function of the mayor and consist of the following: (1) city clerk, (2) city auditor, (3) city solicitor, and (4) treasurer and collector. These offices are all appointive and full-time; they have specialized functions in the political structure as a whole. The officers who fill them are underfunctionaries who keep the political structure running and help provide continuity to the city government.

Let us now examine the structure in terms of the kinds of people in the community who are voters and those who control and operate the political hierarchy.

The voters in the Yankee City political organzation were unequally distributed throughout the several classes. The lower-middle class and the upper-lower class possessed about an equal number of voting citizens: 2,161 (34.34 per cent) in the lower-middle class and 2,151 (34.19 per cent) in the upper-lower class. The lower-lower class had the next largest percentage of voters (14.49 per cent), but far fewer in number (912) than its percentage of the total population. Although the upper-middle class had approximately 10 per cent of the population of Yankee City, it possessed 14.11 per cent (888) of the voters. The lower-upper class had the fifth largest percentage of voters, 1.61 per cent (101); and the upper-upper class had the smallest percentage of voters, 1.26 per cent (79).

In order to clarify our analysis of the political hierarchy, we must distinguish three classes of office in the political structure:

(1) offices of high control where there are final authority and broad supervision, i.e., the city council, the mayor, and the several boards; (2) offices of mediate control, where authority and supervision are limited, i.e., auxiliary executive offices, heads of departments, and agents of the several boards; and (3) administrative subordinates who are the employees of the various departments.

Let us examine the relation of the six classes to these various types of offices. There were 136 persons who held office in the city government during the years 1930-31. They were distributed among the three major classes as follows: upper, 6 per cent; middle, 53.60 per cent; lower, 40.40 per cent. There were 2.30 per cent of the offices held by upper-upper people; 3.70 per cent by lower-upper people; 19.10 per cent by upper-middle individuals; 34.50 per cent by lower-middle-class people; 35.30 per cent by upper-lower people; and 5.10 per cent by lower-lower individuals. The upper class held twice as many political posts in the city as its proportion of the total population. The upper-middle class occupied about twice as many offices as its proportion in the community; the lower-middle class and the upper-lower classes, somewhat more than their proportion of the total population; while the lower-lower class had about one-fourth as many offices as its proportion of the general population.

The disproportions of the several classes in the political hierarchy become more apparent when the three types of control —high, middle, and low—are examined. In the high control group, the class proportions were as follows: 14.30 per cent from the two upper classes; 71.40 per cent came from the two middle classes; and 14.30 per cent from the two lower classes. The upper-upper class held 6.10 per cent of these offices; the lower-upper 8.20 per cent; the upper-middle 34.70 per cent; the lower-middle 36.70 per cent; the upper-lower 14.30 per cent; and there were no lower-lower people in these positions. Over 85 per cent of the high control offices were in the upper and middle classes.

In the mediate control group, the class percentages were as

follows: The two upper classes had 3.20 per cent of the offices; the middle classes had 71.80 per cent; and the lower classes 25 per cent. There were no upper-upper-class people in these positions. Twenty-five per cent of these positions were occupied by upper-middle-class people; 46.80 per cent by lower-middle people; 25 per cent by upper-lower people; and there were no lower-lower-class people in the offices of mediate control. In the mediate control group, the middle class maintains the same high proportions as in the high control group, the upper-class representation falls off sharply, and there is corresponding gain in the upper-lower class.

In the lowest and subordinate group of officers, the class proportions continue to shift. The two upper classes were not represented; the two middle classes held 27.30 per cent of the offices; and the two lower classes, 72.70 per cent. Only 1.80 per cent of the officers in this lowest political stratum were upper-middle; 25.50 per cent were lower middle; 61.80 per cent were upper-lower; and 10.90 per cent were lower-lower. Most of the firemen and policemen belong in this category.

In summary it can be said that the upper classes, together with the upper-middle class, dominate the high control offices. They have a proportion of these offices far out of keeping with their representation in the general population. The mediate control offices tend to be upper-middle and lower-middle class, while the subordinate offices tend to belong in the order named to the upper-lower, lower-middle, and lower-lower classes.

The positions of sixteen members of the city council in office during 1930 and 1931 were examined to determine their place in the class system. Of these, 6.40 per cent were lower-upper; 18.70 per cent were upper-middle; 43.70 per cent, lower-middle; and 31.20 per cent, upper-lower. There were no upper-upper or lower-lower persons in the council.

The personnel of the school board was also examined for the class status of its several members. Because of the high importance of the educational structure in American society, the class position of the members of this board is of obvious importance. One member of the board was upper-upper, one lower-upper, five upper-middle, and one lower-middle. No members of the two low classes served on the school board. It is perhaps significant that the two unsuccessful candidates in the election in which these members took office were both of the lower-middle class. The library board, which had a high symbolic function in the community, was, unlike the school board, an appointive group. But it, too, shows just as strikingly the disproportionate representation of the several classes. There was one upper-upper person on the board, two lower-upper, six upper-middle, and one lower-middle person. The single representative of the lower-middle class was the priest of the Greek church. He was placed there deliberately because of his position as the head of one of the ethnic churches in order that the "foreign interest" might be represented on the library board.

Sixty-one of the 136 persons in the political service of the city were native, and 75 were ethnic. Of the ethnics, 65 were Irish, 5 French, 1 Jewish, and 1 Greek. The Armenians, Italians, Poles, Russians, and Negroes had no representatives. The Irish had a higher proportion of members in the city's political organization than did the natives. Although the Irish outnumbered the natives in the city service, the natives had twice as many representatives in the high control group of offices as the Irish, about the same number in the mediate group, and about half as many in the administrative subordinate group of offices. One of the members of the library board was Jewish, and another was Greek. French Canadians were largely in the subordinate groups.

Crime and Class

Class and ethnic factors are very important in determining liability to, and protection from, arrest by the local police in Yankee City. The person most likely to be arrested in Yankee City is a Polish lower-lower-class male around thirty years of age. If the Pole were in a higher class he would be less liable to arrest. The person least likely to be arrested is an upper-class or upper-middle-class female Yankee below twenty-years of age. It may be argued that the members of the lower classes are more inclined to break the rules of the community, but the interviews demonstrated that the same acts committed in the higher and lower classes resulted in fewer arrests for those who were better placed socially. An upper-class position protects a person from many undesirable experiences in Yankee City, one of them being hailed before a judge and acquiring a police record.

From an analysis of the arrests over seven years, we found that the males had the highest percentage: 89.06 per cent were males and 10.94 per cent were females. The median age for first arrest for males was 29.50 years and that for females was 31.70 years.[3]

The highest percentage of the population of any area that had been arrested came from Middletown and Uptown. Downtown and Riverbrook ranked third and fourth. Newtown, Homeville, and Hill Street were significantly low. In other words, the areas in which the higher classes live tend to have fewer arrests, and those sections where the lower classes reside have higher crime records.

The ethnic groups form a larger percentage of those arrested by the police of Yankee City than do the Yankees: 60 per cent of all those arrested are ethnics, and 40 per cent are natives. It will be remembered that the Yankees comprise 54 per cent and the combined ethnics 46 per cent of the population of Yankee City. It is clear that the members of the ethnic groups are more liable to arrest than are the Yankees.

The newer ethnic groups and the Negroes, both tending to

3. Over 20 per cent (20.26) of the males and 22.08 per cent of the females were first arrested before they were eighteen years old; 9.25 per cent of the males were first arrested between the years of eighteen and twenty and 2.60 per cent of the females; 21.53 per cent of the males were arrested between the ages of twenty-one and twenty-nine years, and 18.18 per cent of the females; 24.24 per cent of the males were arrested at the age level of thirty to thirty-nine years, and 36.36 per cent of the females were first arrested at this time. This last is the only age level in which the proportion of females arrested is higher than the proportion of males. Approximately 25 per cent (24.72 per cent) of the arrested males were forty years and over; and 20.78 per cent of the females were arrested at that age.

be lower-class, are the ones who are most liable to arrest. This is true for all groups except the Armenians who have the lowest percentage of arrested individuals. The full explanation for the low rate of arrests for the Armenians cannot be given; they were, however, slightly higher in class than most other ethnic groups and were a closely organized community. Furthermore, they were better related than the others to the larger Yankee community through their affiliation with Protestant churches.[4]

The two upper classes accounted for less than three-fourths of 1 per cent of those arrested; the two middle classes, for about 10 per cent; and the two lower classes, for approximately 90 per cent of the crime in Yankee City.[5]

All of the causes for arrest in the three upper classes were petty ones. Some of them were driving and parking offenses. One of them developed from a quarrel over a dog, and there were other minor offenses. The crimes in the lower class ranged from the most serious, such as rape and theft, to the least serious, such as drunkenness and improper driving of automobiles.

Eleven per cent of the lower-lower class and 3 per cent of the upper-lower class had records of arrest. One per cent of the lower-middle class had their names on the police records and less than 1 per cent of the lower-upper and the upper-middle were recorded. Only two of the lower-upper class had their names on the police records; three of the upper-upper class had been arrested by the police. All five of these cases were minor

4. There was a higher percentage (13 per cent) of the Polish population arrested than any other ethnic group. The Russians were second with 12.77 per cent. The police had arrested 9.51 per cent of the Italians. The Negroes ranked fourth with 8.75 per cent. There were 6.31 per cent of the Greeks, 5.32 per cent of the French Canadians, and 4.79 per cent of the Jews who had been arrested; 3.91 per cent of the Irish, 3.07 per cent of the Yankees, and 2.85 per cent of the Armenians.

5. Approximately 65 per cent (64.69) of all those arrested were in the lower-lower class; 24.96 per cent were in the upper-lower class; 7.80 per cent were in the lower-middle class; 1.84 per cent in the upper-middle; 0.43 per cent in the upper-upper; and 0.28 per cent in the lower-upper class.

violations. Thirteen of the upper-middle class had been arrested; each was for a minor infraction of the law.

Sixty-three per cent of all the arrests of the lower-lower class were ethnic, and 37 per cent were native. In the upper-lower class, 63 per cent were ethnic and 37 per cent were native. In the lower-middle class, 49 per cent were ethnic and 51 per cent were native. In the upper-middle class, 15 per cent were ethnic and 85 per cent were native.

Since the ethnic population of the lowest class was only 56.57 per cent of the stratum, it holds that being an ethnic in that class (many of them foreign-born) contributed to a man's chance of arrest; this chance became less in the upper-lower class and disappeared in the lower-middle class. The Yankees in this class had a higher rate of arrest, but in the upper-middle class the ethnics again were more liable to arrest. The discrepancy in the lower-middle class is more than likely accounted for by the extreme emphasis placed on being "respectable" and "Yankee" by the ethnics in that class.

In the section which follows we present the rise to political power of a lower-class ethnic. The political events are given status and symbolic analysis.

Biggy Muldoon: The Rise of a Political Hero

Biggy Muldoon, the "Yankee City Bad Boy," is a big-shouldered, two-fisted, red-haired Irishman. He was born down by the river on the wrong side of the tracks, the only child of Irish-Catholic immigrant parents. Once a street-fighter, brawler, and all-round tough guy, he was arrested by the police for shooting dice, using profane and abusive language, fighting, and other rough behavior distasteful to the pious and respectable.

Despite Biggy's background and the traditions of the office and city, he was nominated and elected by the voters of Yankee City to be mayor. They gave him a very substantial majority, until then the largest ever received by any candidate. He was voted into office in preference to a respectable, conservative incumbent whose life conformed to all the better usages of Yan-

kee City, a man who lived on the social heights of Hill Street
and belonged to "the better class" of the town.

Moreover, from shortly before his first election and for
several years after, his political fortunes received intense and
continued treatment in the great metropolitan newspapers,
national magazines, and radio systems. Clearly such an extra-
ordinary reversal of the political traditions of the town and the
strong feelings Biggy aroused among millions of Americans
throughout the country indicate that some of the vital forces in
American life were at work. As research men studying the community where this political drama was played, we asked ourselves what its significance might be to us as scientists and to
Americans generally. We believed that if we were fortunate
enough to learn some of the answers we would acquire a better
understanding of how and why Americans think, talk, and act
the way they do.

Although economic factors, among others, were involved,
economic discontent and distress do not explain his defeat of
the other candidate, for the city at the time was prosperous.
There had been no change in local politics to account for his
unpredicted victory. The political principles for which he stood
—lower taxes, efficient and honest government, and a square
deal for everyone—while commendable, are not of the stuff
that arouses the electorate of a conservative city to political re-
volt or brings representatives of the great mass media of the
nation hurrying to a small community to report to their millions
of readers what a Biggy Muldoon is doing to his home town.
He did not have a formal political organization to help him; the
other candidate did. His opponent, while mayor, had not alien-
ated any large block of voters who could become Biggy's
natural followers. He had voted against prohibition—but Biggy
was an ardent pro-liquor man. His opponent was for Sunday
motion pictures—but so was Biggy. Moreover, he stood for
other, similar activities which were not to the liking of many
respectable people of Yankee City. Yet they elected him mayor.

It might appear that this was the kind of man who could have
been elected earlier had he but tried; that, if given the oppor-

tunity, Yankee City would have favored him as a pleasant escape from the restraints of its middle-class propriety and aristocratic conservatism. But this explanation, too, is wrong, since he had been an unsuccessful candidate in previous elections for minor office. At the time of his first victory in a mayoralty contest he was thirty-one years old. Ten years earlier, at twenty-one, he had run for councilman in a field of six and had come in sixth. He then ran for similar positions several times and was badly defeated, once coming in twelfth in a field of fourteen. A year before his triumph as mayor he had again stood for election as councilman of his ward, receiving an embarrassingly small number of votes, 47 in all. Yet twelve months later, when he was elected mayor with a grand total of 2,852 to his opponent's 2,357, the people of his ward contributed 355 votes to his victory. Something had happened to bring about this change. But what?

The explanation of the triumph of Biggy Muldoon is not to be found among the ordinary reasons given for political victories. The succeeding events of his career, briefly sketched, will help to bring the problem into rounded view. At the end of his first two-year term he ran again. This time a number of prominent men had been informally selected to run against him and thereby divide his vote. One was a powerful and highly respected member of a very old family in Yankee City. Once again Biggy won, but this time by a reduced majority, defeating his nearest opponent by the narrow margin of 40 votes. He next ran for the state senate in the hope of gaining more recognition among the state's electorate, and lost this election. Thereafter he ran again for mayor and was badly defeated, losing by over a thousand votes to one of the Hill-Streeters, a man in the "right" tradition who enjoyed a high position in the community.

When he was first elected mayor Biggy's percentage of the vote was so unprecedentedly large, his backing so strong, and the interest in him as a public man so great among the people of Yankee City, the state, and for that matter the nation, that he publicly announced his intention to run for governor or for the United States Senate and voiced his ultimate ambition to be

President. Given the evidence and the time when we examined it, his hopes and expectations were well within the bounds of any strong man's dreams. But the dreams were not realized.

Biggy is still a major factor in Yankee City politics. He has run in every election for mayor since his first, sixteen in all. Of these contests he has won six and lost ten. By custom in Yankee City, a field of several men try out in the primary to determine which two will be candidates in the final election, which is nonpartisan. In every election save one Biggy has been one of the two finalists. Yet with the exception of 1935 he was not elected mayor again after his first two victories until 1949; in 1959 he was again elected mayor of the city.

From this brief and limited review of his affairs several obvious but fundamental questions emerge about the rise of Biggy Muldoon. The social behavior resulting in his elections and defeats and the kind of role he has played are not wholly unknown in the local, state, or national elections of the United States. The political careers of such men as Al Smith, Huey Long, Fiorello La Guardia, and—for certain purposes—such names as William Jennings Bryan, Andrew Jackson, and even Abraham Lincoln must be considered.

The crucial questions to be answered are: Why did Biggy Muldoon rise to local and national fame? Why did he gain political power? What prevented Biggy from going beyond the political apex he quickly achieved as mayor to the higher positions in state and nation to which he aspired? Men far less talented and much less able than Biggy occupy places in the halls of Congress and our national life. Why did he lose the power and position he had achieved?

Despite his defeats, why, since the first great days of his political career, has he retained the affection and respect of a solid core of voters and the dislike and even hatred of a powerful group in his community? Why do many of the city's voters continue to love a hated Biggy Muldoon? And why have his enemies failed to achieve his ultimate and decisive defeat—failed to destroy him as a political force in Yankee City?

Several kinds of evidence are needed to answer these questions. The social and psychological evidence required is diverse and complex. We must know the essential and immediate facts of his career and the campaigns by which he was first elected and then defeated. Knowledge of the structure and condition of the society at the time is of great importance. The way he conceived of himself in the social world in which he lived—the personality of Biggy Muldoon, who played the principal role in the drama of the bitter elections for mayor—and the continuing development of his personality, as well as the social circumstances largely responsible for what he became, are all relevant.

Above all, the meanings of the symbols of political attack and defense wielded by Biggy and his opponents in their struggle for power and their effect upon Biggy himself, his political foes, and the people of Yankee City and the country at large are crucial and of the highest significance.

Before examining at close range the evidence in these diverse categories, a general hypothesis consisting of several propositions may be offered to keep our attention focused on relevant factors and to guide our investigation.

It goes without saying that a hero always expresses fundamental and important themes of the culture in which he is found; this is no less true in historical or contemporary America than elsewhere. Each theme is a symbolic statement which relates and organizes some of the beliefs and values of a community or a nation to each other and to the group. Rational thought is not the real source of evocative symbols or the themes, values, and beliefs expressed by them. The creation of heroic forms, their crystallization around actual persons, makes these themes and the beliefs and values they represent manifest in a human being. In this way they easily become emotionally and convincingly understandable to everyone, with personal meaning to the young as well as to the mature, to the unlettered and the lowly as well as to the educated few. These social beliefs and values have a universal significance to the members of a culture because the basic emotional structure of each person is largely acquired and formed in childhood from his earliest

intimate experiences as a new member of a society. Each growing individual sees, feels, and hears beliefs and values not as
abstract concepts and principles but as integral, personal parts
of loved or disliked persons whom he experiences through social and personal interaction. The child's strongest feelings are
very often directed to other individuals who are part of his immediate environment, and to his own self as an integral part of
this intimate personal environment. Abstract principles, precepts, and moral judgments are consequently more easily felt
and understood, and more highly valued, when met in a human
being endowed with a symbolic form that expresses them. Obviously the "hero" is ideally suited to this role.

The functions of a hero for the individuals who believe in
him are related to, but different from, his functions for the
society. He functions in at least three significant ways for members of the group. His actual presence stimulates those who believe in him to project their own private feelings and beliefs
directly on him. His presence also serves as a model for their
imitation and learning and for the measurement of their own
moral inadequacies. Further, the hero arouses the hopes and
fears of those who believe in him, and he energizes and gives
social direction to some of their anxieties.

The hero clearly has internal as well as external significance
for individual members of a group. The inner world of each is
forever in danger of sinking into the malaise and disquiet of
personal chaos. It is in constant need of the moral strength, intellectual stability, and hard realities of the social order which
lie both within and beyond each of us. The belief in a hero helps
single members of a group to relate themselves more effectively
to each other and to the general and more universal beliefs and
values of the whole society. Privately, the presence of a hero
organizes the individual's hopes and fears and expresses them
in a meaningful way, both for him and for the society. The belief in a hero can release the individual from anxiety and reward
him with a faith that his hopes are, or are about to be, realized.
Such belief is always exciting and reassuring to the individual
in his private world, but the excitement is greatly increased

when, from the evidence of his senses and the physical presence of his hero, he can publicly validate his faith. Heroes and hero-worship are integral parts of any complex, changing society; which is to say that heroes must always be present in the cultures of nations and civilizations, whether ancient or contemporary.

Let us now return to Biggy Muldoon, the man who became a hero.

We believe that Biggy, through a set of circumstances and a sequence of events presently to be related, was transformed in the minds of many in Yankee City from the mundane referential image they had of him as another tough kid from the wrong side of the tracks into a type of symbolic hero much beloved by Americans. For them he became the champion of the people, the strong man who attacks the proud and powerful and protects the poor and lowly. In their minds he conformed for a while to all the necessary criteria for this heroic role. Then, through other events, for some who had faith in him he lost his hero's stature; they joined those who thought of him as contemptible and a fool or a villain, and came to hate him in large enough numbers to bring about his defeat.

We believe that through it all Biggy, the person, changed very little. Though later facets of his behavior may have gone beyond people's first reckoning, ironically he stayed very much the same live, vibrant man, Biggy Muldoon. What did change were the symbols, and their component beliefs and values, that were attached to him in a political drama in which he played the leading role, symbols that first made him a hero—perhaps even something of a martyr—and then for many, for a time, turned him into a "fool" and even a "traitor" to his town. The distribution of these negative and positive symbols in the electorate and in the national mass media changed as time went by and as the sequence of incidents in his dramatic career had their effect.

Mary Muldoon, Biggy's mother, arrived in Yankee City from Ireland as a seventeen-year-old country girl with ten dollars in her pocket. She was an ambitious and very determined

young woman. She worked for a time as a domestic in the Judge
Sampson house, a "beautiful mansion" in the aristocratic Hill
Street section of town. Judge Sampson, a former mayor, was a
member of the so-called superior class of the city.

Mary Muldoon married and, shortly before her husband
went back to his native land, gave birth to her only child,
Thomas Ignatius Muldoon, who subsequently became known
to all as Biggy. During her early career Mrs. Muldoon worked
as a cook and as an employee of a shoe factory. She saved her
money and in time opened a little store in the front of her small
house. During World War I a tip from a well-placed friend
showed her how she could borrow money and, with the help of
her savings, buy sugar and flour in carload quantities. With
these profits and others arising from war inflation she accumulated considerable capital. She invested in real estate. Among
other buildings, she acquired a jail abandoned by the city—the
jail where she had once served time for refusing to pay for a
license for Biggy's stray dog (a few years after that episode
Biggy had also been incarcerated in the same jail). Somewhat
later, when the Sampson house came on the market, she bor-
rowed money and, with Biggy, purchased it. They made a home
of the sheriff's quarters and lived there together—it gratified
their strong sense of humor and irony. But Mrs. Muldoon's far
from easy life ended in a heart attack not long after.

Biggy, meanwhile, had grown into a hard-muscled, tough-
fibered boy. Although he "ran wild," his mother's moral influence was so strong on his life that he never drank or smoked.
She also taught him to attack his enemies and, being of humble
Irish origin, to define them as those who occupy the seats of
the mighty. Perhaps he would have learned most of this anyway, for the district in which he grew up teaches its children
to be aggressive and prizes physical violence as the means of
solving problems.

Biggy took charge of the family property shortly before his
mother's death and attempted on several occasions to get a
permit from the mayor and the city council to move the Sampson house, destroy its garden and terrace, as well as the wall

about it, and put up a filling station. Viewed purely from the commercial angle it was perhaps a reasonable venture. But each time the authorities refused. He then tried other tactics.

One morning the gentle people of Hill Street awakened to find large, highly colored circus posters, advertising a Wild West show, covering the chaste walls of the Sampson mansion. A few days later Biggy tore down the walls of the terraced garden. Of its stone slabs he fashioned gravestones, placing them at the heads of suitably shaped mounds of earth. The names of the members of the council and of the mayor, many of them Hill-Streeters, were written on the headstones. The garden, in the most prominent place in Yankee City, had been turned into a graveyard to mock the enemies where the rude and the vulgar could laugh at them. The trucks and vehicles that removed the wall and earth from the garden had signs which announced their ownership as "The Biggy Muldoon Destruction Company." While the soil was being removed one of the veterans' organizations, having no members above the lower-middle class, paraded in the town. Biggy gave them permission to place their chapter's American flag over the house, and there it waved.

Obviously indignation was very intense on Hill Street. The circus was persuaded by state officials through indirect channels to take down the posters, but a few days later the indignation of Hill Street swelled to outrage, for hanging from the windows and high gables of the proud old house were several rows of bedroom crockery and, beneath them, a large sign which read: THE SPIRIT OF YANKEE CITY. Lindbergh had recently flown the Atlantic, thrilling all Americans with pride in their scientific progress and in American ability to triumph over the limitations of time and space. It will be recalled that the *Spirit of St. Louis* was the plane that made the historic flight. Everyone in Yankee City knew that certain great families on Hill Street clung so tenaciously to the ways of their forefathers that they had refused to install the amenities of modern plumbing. A few still used outside privies, gas lighting, and tin bathtubs because they disapproved of "all this modern nonsense." Biggy's allusion was clear.

He tried again to get a permit for his filling station, but when he went to the mayor's office he became so angry from the tongue-lashing given him by this official that he struck him, or, as he said, "socked the so-and-so on the jaw." He was arrested, sentenced on several charges, and served two months in jail —the county jail this time.

Previous to this on several occasions, as we have noted, Biggy had run for city councilman and had been defeated. Less than a year from the time of the jail sentence, after some hesitation, he ran for mayor. The announcement of his candidacy drew the attention of a metropolitan paper in Boston. A long front-page story was printed when he became one of the two candidates chosen in the primary for the "run-off" in the final election. The article immediately attracted great interest. It told of Biggy's struggle with Hill Street and referred to him as Yankee City's Bad Boy. The story in general had a favorable and positive, although gently humorous, turn. Immediately other papers in Boston, New York, and other large cities sent their reporters to Yankee City; their shrewd editors knew a good story when they saw it. The dramatic tale of the rebel, the man from the wrong side of the tracks who hated cops, socked mayors, challenged the high and mighty, and thumbed his nose at the rich and powerful, was told repeatedly in news columns throughout the United States and Canada. The stories described how he was running for mayor of Yankee City, then controlled by the Hill-Streeters, by telling his highly placed foes he'd throw them out and run the town in his own fashion. With the realization that here was a dream hero come to life, functionaries of radio, motion pictures, and stage were rushed to Yankee City and Biggy's name was soon known from coast to coast. He was a welcome relief from the usual bad news found on the front pages or in the newsreels. People far and wide who had never heard of his home town loved Biggy and laughed at the discomfort of his high-born enemies, or reacted with indignation and contempt and predicted that he would "get what he deserved."

Soon after his first election Biggy again applied to the city council for a permit to sell gasoline and permission to cut down the ancient elms which blocked the entrance to his proposed filling station. Both requests were immediately refused. The next day Biggy cut down the trees, started the installation of the storage tank, and soon was selling gas to thousands of people who came from everywhere to see and shake hands with the celebrated Biggy Muldoon, then hurried home to tell their friends what the Yankee City Bad Boy had said to them as he filled their gas tanks.

Hill Street quickly retaliated. Biggy was arrested, tried, and convicted. He was sentenced to two months at hard labor and fined over four hundred dollars. He conducted the affairs of the mayor's office from a cell in the county jail. Newsreel cameras took pictures of him there, while the papers carried his jail story to millions of people across the continent.

When he was released—two days before the local election—over forty thousand people gathered around and about the jail to welcome him and a great parade was spontaneously formed to carry him in triumph back to his home. When they arrived in Yankee City Biggy delivered a speech which blasted his enemies, told of his martyrdom, and urged the election of his friends to the city council. The citizens of Yankee City responded: every one of Biggy's candidates was elected and all his opponents defeated. The council soon changed the zoning law. Biggy triumphantly—yet anticlimactically for those emotionally involved in the struggle—sold his gas station for $41,000 to one of the great oil companies. The battle of Hill Street was over.

The normal political behavior of the lower-lower group before Biggy arrived on the scene fitted into the general way they participated in all the life of the community. They were decidedly apathetic to political appeals. The great majority rarely took the trouble to vote. Interviews demonstrated that they were often indifferent to the point of not knowing an election was pending or caring little about the candidate, the issues, or the outcome. Of the few who voted, most felt that it would have little or no consequence to their own existence because the candidates ordinarily did not represent their interests. It may be observed in general that the organizations which stir others into action in voting rarely reach these people. The symbols that will appeal to and energize all other levels, including the hardworking members of the upper-lower class, have only a minimal appeal to the private and public worlds of those who live at the Level below the Common Man. Something more is needed to get to them. Different kinds of organizations and associations must be used, with different symbols and appeals, to pull these people out of their apathy and indifference and bring them to the voting booth.

As regards Biggy's personal life, perhaps the most significant events in his career as a boy and man in Yankee City were his several arrests by the police and his conviction by the courts for crimes of physical violence and other infractions not explicitly violent but still expressive of aggression against the respectability and superiority of the higher social levels of Yankee City. An inspection of the proportion of arrests of members of the six classes, when related to Biggy's own troubles with the police, tells a significant story. It will be recalled that 65 per cent of all the arrests appearing on the police records of Yankee City were from the lowest social level of the community, a class with 25 per cent of the population. Ninety per cent of those arrested were from the two lowest classes, 58 per cent of the population. Less than 3 per cent were in the three upper classes with 13 per cent of the inhabitants. Biggy's arrests and convictions were not those of an aberrant individual. They fit neatly and tightly into the conventional pattern established by the relations of the police and the higher political authority to the lower levels of the ethnic groups at the bottom of the heap in Yankee City.

These percentages obviously sharpen the social drama and status significance of Biggy's arrests. When in his informal speeches to the people of his district he told them he was "going to tell the cops where the hell to get off," he spoke words whose meaning and values they could enjoy with an intensity experienced perhaps by no other level of American. Traditionally and informally most Americans are believed not to like "cops" and are reputed to take satisfaction in seeing these symbols of authority brought low; but no level has as much provocation to take pleasure in seeing "cops shoved around" as those at the bottom who are most vulnerable to them. The long-suffering Biggy, who had a history of arrests himself and whose mother had gone to prison rather than give the cops and the courts five dollars for a dog tag, was a man who "everyone said" would know how to act when he "got to be the man who was boss over the cops." The people at the lower levels of the society, the clammers—particularly those who had registered for the first time and were about to vote in large numbers—were delighted to read in one of the great Boston papers that Biggy had said, "A cop who made a lot of talk about voters who went to register and called them wharf rats, drunkards and bums, is going to be publicly reprimanded," and "A couple of cops who thought they were pretty smart are going to get the cemetery beat where they will have a lot of other dead ones for company." When Biggy was elected mayor and "walked down to the cop station to tell a few flatfeet something for their own good," a multitude of followers in fact, and more in their fantasies, walked beside him and enjoyed the tongue-lashing given the cops as Biggy "put them in their places" and told them "where the hell to get off." The great crowd of his followers who carried the traditional red fire that night, and cheered at his inauguration while Biggy told Yankee City and the world what he was going to do now that he and his kind were "top dogs," took in very clearly the significance of at least one man's behavior: the policeman who had once arrested Biggy now stood obediently holding his hat, ready to provide more service for the "boss man."

Many other social conditions were among the forces that operated in the structure of the community and in Biggy's personality and influenced what happened. But those reviewed provide us with most of the necessary background for understanding what occurred during the conflict on Hill Street and his later political career.

The Symbols and Facts of Political Conflict

The great leaders of the multitude have often used the evocative and dramatic power of the simple parable to arouse the masses; its traditional symbols are deeply rooted in the common core of experience, in precept and example felt by all men. Biggy, in the Hill Street episode and those following it, manipulated far more dramatic and compelling symbols to center favorable attention on himself and his aspirations. This social drama made the difficult abstractions and conflicting values underlying his argument significant to the great body of the people. It is doubtful whether the figurative words of a parable could have equaled its effectiveness.

If we think of the whole series of incidents as centering around the backdrop of the mansion, Biggy can be easily seen as an impresario producing and directing a public spectacle, in which he is also the principal actor, for the entertainment and edification of the masses. He had a story to tell, an argument to win, and a goal to achieve. With masterful instinctive artistry, his choice of symbols and mounting episodes, each topping the other, accomplished his ends, defeated his enemies, and gained the recognition and the economic and political goals at which he aimed.

To what extent Biggy *explicitly* understood the significance of the symbols and anticipated the kind of impact they might have on Yankee City and the United States cannot be established. But it can be said that he felt their significance and, with the skill and insight of the artist, fashioned his burlesque in such a way as to outrage only the superior few and a minority (although a substantial one) of the common people. His pageant delighted a large proportion of ordinary persons. His great skill appears even more remarkable when it is recalled that at this time he made such remarks as "They're dead but they won't lie down," about respected men, some of whose names had also been written on the Hill Street gravestones. Clearly, although humorously put, his hostility carried an unconscious death threat; but most of what he did and said was so well disguised, both to himself and to others, and seemingly "unreal," that it aroused no strong fears or anxiety but, instead, the appropriate laughter. Just as the slang stereotype "drop dead" is often used for amusement, so Biggy's symbolic idioms aroused pleasurable feelings and meanings rather than fear in those who viewed his spectacle. But still the use of these symbols out of their context stretched the bounds of propriety almost beyond the limits of easy permissiveness into areas where anger and disgust dominate the response of the people.

The flamboyant circus posters with which Biggy covered the walls of the Hill Street mansion advertised a well-known Wild West show. Their gaudy colors, rampant lions and tigers, rodeos with cowboys and bucking broncos, trapezes alive with the buxom forms of lady acrobats, all conveyed the young explosive vigor of untamed frontier country. They aroused the youthful free fantasies of all ages. But such posters ordinarily tell their gay and devil-may-care stories on the sides of old barns, abandoned dwellings, outhouses, or billboards and other objects of low status. Their excitement, while suggesting festival, and their gaiety, while appealing to almost everyone, are secular, profane, and beyond the realm of private life. They are for the public; they advertise spectacles not for the exclusive view but for the masses, where payment makes anyone as good as anybody else.

Although appealing to everyone, these shows and posters largely depend on exciting the imagination of the crowd, the hoi polloi, the common man. They tell of fun and reckless excitement, of "death-defying acts" where actors take a chance; they are not concerned with the safety and quiet where people live a life of order, respectability, and tranquil uneventfulness. Risk-taking is something more than an investment which results in a coupon clipped from a bond.

Such posters now were plastered over an elegant structure in an area of the highest status significance. Symbols common, secular, and profane were attached to—and covered—those which were private, superior, and "sacred." Thus a superior, private, in some sense sacred world was symbolically transfigured into a common, public, and inferior secular one.

Moreover the untamed, raucous symbols of the "Wild West" were in stark opposition to the quiet walls of the mansion of conservative old-family class and historically well-disciplined Hill Street. Thus symbols of the vigor of youth, of newness and the future, were dramatically placed in dominating opposition to those of the old, the familiar, and the past—the untamed and the unregulated against tamed domesticity. To state fully what Biggy accomplished by his action would require a very long essay. Yet what he meant was established for the common people in one dramatic moment. The posters disrespectfully said, in the most forceful circumstances, that the past was interfering with the progress of the new technology—of filling stations, of the automobile age, and the pressing demands of the future. Nor was response wanting. The circus advertising man who wrote Biggy to thank him for the use of this point of vantage said, "The cloth banners on your residence caused our show to get a world of publicity." One of the kids who went to the circus did even better: "Those old kill-joys up there always try to stop things. They don't want any of us to have any fun." Biggy's plea for what he claimed as the demands of an advancing technology against the dead hand of proper usage had been positively interrelated in people's feeling with fun, impulse excitement, and desire of almost everyone to have a good time.

The gravestones made from the stone slabs of the terrace wall, the grave mounds fashioned from the lawn, and the likeness of an ancient cemetery formed in the garden, transformed sacred symbols into profane and comic objects. The whole history of Western ceremonial tells of days of festival when sacred symbols are used profanely for the laughter and entertainment of the masses; but it also often speaks of the pain and effort of constituted authorities to reduce or eliminate such outbursts. Attempts to confine such revelry to the narrow, respectable limits of appointed times and places are never completely successful.

The grave and its stone headpiece, marking the end of a life and the dead remains of a once live body, are the visible and permanent signs of a sacred ceremony, the funeral or *rite de passage* which symbolically translates the body from the world of the living to that of the dead and helps to re-establish the relations of living members of the group to each other and to the memory of the dead. The name on the gravestone is more than a mark of respect for a dead person. Seen in the context of the sacred ceremonial, the funeral, and the consecrated ground of the cemetery, the name of the departed becomes the ultimate symbol which helps to relate the secular living to the sacred dead. It is a sign that the dead are eternally related to deity and to the sacred world. Accordingly, gravestones and the cemetery are two of the very few most dramatic and powerful symbols referring to the ideal parts of our past and reaffirming our respect for our traditions.

The grave and the gravestone are of particular significance in a status society. Since the upper-upper-class position is greatly dependent on lineage to validate its claims to superiority and its position at the apex of the class system, the graveyard is often the ultimate demonstration and source of social power. The names of a long line of ancestors composing a superior lineage are "eternally" located on the gravestones within the protection of the cemetery—visible and confirmatory proof to its still living members of old family, birth aristocracy, and their high position in the community. As the Yankee City *Herald* said, Biggy's cemetery bore "a remarkable resemblance to an ancient graveyard." The emphasis upon the very old cemetery related the spectacle he had contrived immediately and directly to the old families and reduced its connection with modern and contemporary graveyards. Thus the mansion with its garden, the cemetery with its graves—two great symbols of membership in the upper class—were combined in a single composition for the vulgar laughter of the crowd. They became a kind of symbolic pantomime or charade. This episode, it will be remembered, immediately followed upon that of the circus posters. It was a fitting and satisfactory answer to the question in the minds of most people in Yankee City: What would Biggy do next to torment his Hill Street enemies?

Moreover—and on the other hand—the grave is an unan-

swerable symbol of the equality of men. As a repository of the
remains of those who have died, it is a reminder that all men
must die and give up their earthly claims to prestige and power.
Funeral sermons and Memorial Day orations are eloquent with
allusion to the fact that "six feet of earth make all men equal."
Christian doctrine declares that all souls are equal in the sight
of God; in the absolute reckoning of supernatural values and
beliefs the cemetery and its graves are equalitarian and democratic, while in the secular reckoning of the living they help to
establish claims of rank and status. In Biggy's graveyard the
headstones, instead of validating high status, were signs that
reduced such claims to a joke for the amusement of the common crowd.

The next sets of symbols displayed, with the emotionally
charged building as a backdrop and timed to the expectations
aroused by the previous scenes, demonstrated that, like any
gifted writer and producer of comic drama. Biggy could make
each act cap the last.

The display of the old-fashioned chamber pots from the
ridgepole and windows of the mansion and the sign referring to
them as the "Spirit of Yankee City" achieved a new peak in
the growing excitement he aroused, and a new extreme in the
use of emotionally powerful symbols whose appeal reached into
the deeper psychological levels, often beyond the limits of social acceptance. Whereas the impact of the gravestone episode
came largely from his attack on the upper class by the trans-
ferral of revered objects from a respected to a comic context,
the next incident's great impact came from the degradation of
an upper-class house, symbolic of superiority, to inferior and
unclean levels. The chamber pots obviously referred to excretory behavior and aroused anal feelings. They mocked the
house and the upper-class world for which it stood with the
whole array of dirty excretory jokes in which men and their
claims to moral and social respectability are made to appear
ridiculous and absurd. The force of tens of thousands of humorous anal stories, told and retold for many millenia in human
culture, was here released by Biggy and directed against his

enemies. The human feelings of animal inferiority and the contempt and distaste everyone learns very early as part of his
cleanliness training now became part of his attack.

No doubt there are symbols other than the chamber pots that
might have derogated the traditional values of the upper class,
but none could so easily and effectively have aroused ribald
laughter. The excretory and anal aspects of the crockery theme
reintroduced another motif into Biggy's struggle with the superior people of Hill Street. Just as all men are equal "in six
feet of earth," so are they equal and reduced to the same unclean and very human level in their need to defecate. That the
feces of each man, whether high or low, are equally repulsive
and unclean and smell equally unpleasant is the point of
many well-known and much appreciated American jokes. The
scatological symbols employed are not for the drawing rooms of
the superior or the gathering places of the respectable, but the
underlying moral statements of the values of democracy and
equality are to be found in some of the more profound declarations of the founding fathers.

Scatological humor plainly styled and openly stated, although
accepted and sometimes appreciated by the higher levels, is
most enjoyed by the levels at the lower extreme of American
life. The superior classes are most likely to respond to subtle
sexual jokes, less to bluntly told sexual ones, and least to anal
ones where the humor largely depends on explicit and conscious
use of fecal symbols.

Death and the corruption of the grave have always been
objects of terror and awe as well as laughter and ridicule in
American, English, and general European tradition. By his
elaborate charade Biggy mobilized the enormous power of
graveyard and barnyard humor against the upper-class symbol
of the mansion. Looked at from a distance, such humor may
be funny to all levels, but *felt* within the context of Yankee
City is was modified by the assertion of class values operating
in the community. Most people of the middle classes may have
laughed momentarily, but they could not officially approve of
his humor or go so far as to vote for him.

But here we must modify our previous remarks, for perhaps the most significant characteristic of Biggy's scatological humor and the art he used generally in his spectacle of the mansion on Hill Street was the style he used to express them. Given his exuberance, the strength of his hostility, and the openness of his aggression (it must be remembered that he "socked the mayor in the jaw" and struck other public officials), it might be assumed that he would overstep the acceptable limits and repel almost everyone. Let us suppose he had forgotten all physical restraint, as with the mayor, and had smeared the walls of the house with feces to express his contempt and hostility. Humor would have been lost and mere disgust resulted. Chamber pots as originally used in the society were not only objects of necessity and utility but also forms of self-respect which surrounded the physical act with propriety and reduced its offensiveness to a minimum. While reducing shame and embarrassment they helped increase the satisfaction and pleasure usually experienced but seldom admitted. The chamber pot increased man's sense of being a person and helped to disguise his animal nature. Although Biggy's joke was excretory and animal, it was, in fact, told with more decorum than is at first realized.

Biggy's style of attack, his symbolic rhetoric, despite its explosive and violent qualities, although offensive to many, was always confined within certain limits of tradition—limits outrageously stretched beyond the boundaries of staid propriety. His chamber pots were old-fashioned, directly comparable to Chick Sales' outhouse humor: household artifacts that could be used as excretory symbols, but still symbols rather than facts. Biggy used them like a great actor, thereby escaping the condemnation of many for telling dirty and offensive jokes. For large numbers of people he kept the theme and its point within the realm of what is considered funny rather than embarrassing and disgusting.

But the degrading excretory theme, although important and reaching depths greater than the others, was not in fact the most powerful and immediately potent one aroused by the episode. The chamber pots were anachronistic relics of a former period. They were "artistic" reminders of a past that technological invention had made obsolete for most people in the town. By the legend under his exhibit Biggy told his more elegant fellow townsfolk, "Some of you people don't want electric lights, gas, airplanes, or any of the twentieth-century improvements and inventions. Just the same way some of you don't want me . . ." The resistance to the inventions of a new technology could not have been better illustrated than by this allusion to the known backwardness of certain members of the ruling group in the matter of household plumbing.

The picture of Lindbergh as the "Lone Eagle" with the athletic Rupert Brooke face hung in the homes and offices of thousands of Americans, and all over the country rhapsodic poetry and editorial prose had poured out in tribute to the "unconquerable youth" whose adventure and daring symbolized man's progress. The flight over the forbidding Atlantic represented man's need for triumph over great obstacles; it also symbolized his freedom from old frustrations and release from past confinements. Thousands of editorials spoke of its promise for the future and evoked feelings of human progress and ability. The plane itself—the *Spirit of St. Louis*—embodied achievement and American technological advance; it became the symbol of the promise of a better world, identified in the optimistic twenties as the "Spirit of America." Lindbergh and his plane were powerful symbols to every citizen of what an American should strive to be. The ancient chamber pots and the traditions of the old families to which they referred in Biggy's derogatory lampoon did not conform to this ideal that surged in the emotions of the people.

Another important American theme emerges from the incident. Lindbergh, the Lone Eagle, who flew high and far, was universally thought of as a once unknown mechanic and small-town aviator who, struggling against great odds, had acquired the skill to fly and finally accumulated enough money to finance his flight to Paris. The American theme of a country where everybody has his chance was embodied in this unknown boy who had succeeded in his inalienable American right to make good, who had landed at the top and received the acclaim of presidents and kings.

Lindbergh had been given his chance. Biggy had been thwarted by the anachronistic spirit of Hill Street. It cannot be proved that Biggy fancied himself another Lindbergh. Yet the pantomime he fashioned symbolically identified him with America's greatest contemporary hero. As he said just before his first election, "I only want my chance to show what I can do." The "dead ones" symbolically portrayed in their graves, who stopped progress and prevented him from having his filling station, personified the values represented by the ancient bed-room crockery. Perhaps it is not too much to say that the contents of these two kinds of symbolic repository were identified as one in the nonlogical world of the unconscious.

It is small wonder that to many people in Yankee City Biggy himself soon embodied the values and beliefs which were intrinsic parts of the several incidents: Riverbrook against Hill Street, the rights of the common against the privileges of the superior, the equality of opportunity and birth against the inequality of inherited wealth and aristocracy. None of these social themes could be felt or mentioned in Yankee City without the figure of Biggy Muldoon entering and increasing the emotional heat of all present. Biggy was no longer just another man from the river flats but "a man of the people," a hero or villain according to the role assigned to him by each member of his audience as part of his new symbolic significance.

If the message of a marching song is a more telling argument than the reasoning of a proposition, then the triumphant acts of a flesh-and-blood champion of the people in a drama of real life carry the final, validating force of a knockout blow. Through Biggy and the drama he created, the common people and lower class of Yankee City told the high and mighty ones living on Hill Street to go to hell and made them like it. Later some of them did this in the comparative safety of voting for Biggy and thus approving his smashing attacks on the political power of the higher classes and the symbols of their great prestige. What he did openly as a hero, common men could do vicariously; when he "socked" authority and respectability on the jaw and knocked the mayor to the floor, or when he tore an ugly wound in the mellow beauty of Hill Street and pulled down an old mansion from its lofty status, they, by identifying with him, could feel a deep satisfaction, a rare one for those who seem helpless and are frustrated because of humble position. They could laugh when Biggy assaulted the dignity of sedate Hill Street. Later, voting for him and his men, they were able to seize the instrument of political power. Biggy's show was something more than buffoonery to entertain the masses.

The first and most obvious targets of his attack were the persons and symbols of political authority, among them the police, the fire chief, the mayor, the city council, the superintendent of schools, and jails and jailers. Lawyers, judges and prosecuting and state's attorneys were part of this list. Almost any role or status of authority and some of the apparatus of local government and law enforcement are involved. The ordinary conventional resistance of Americans to authority was carried to an extreme; yet Biggy placed this dangerous attack within the same framework of comic-strip humor. The laughter of children and grown-ups at the comic mass symbols of an earlier period—the Captain and the Katzenjammer Kids, Buster Brown, Happy Hooligan, the Keystone Cops—and later ones such as Mickey Mouse and Donald Duck, was turned on the people who occupied authoritative positions in real life. Many of the traditional fantasies and the private and unconscious feelings of joy in being able to attack authority were released in some people, while in others the fears of what may happen when authority is attacked aroused them to fight Biggy.

He also attacked the bankers, the trust and loan companies, the Chamber of Commerce and the manufacturers' association, as well as the bosses he had personally worked for. They occupied a position similar to that of the political group, for they wielded powerful authority in the economic world. The attack on these figures was verbal, not physical or visual as in the symbols used on Hill Street. Just as the police and the political authorities, in Biggy's mind, had made him and his mother suffer when he was young, so had the bankers and the economically strong. Yet Biggy and his mother, despite opposition, had done well financially. They owned several important pieces of income property. Biggy's announcement that he was "damn well off" clearly said he was not among the "wage slaves" or economically frustrated. He wanted more money, and as a competent enterpriser he knew how to get it. He was not bucking private enterprise so much as the system and power inherited by the old families.

Other objects he attacked were "foreigners," "hypocrites," "immoral people," and young men who were not drafted and did not enlist. The symbolic pattern is not so clear in this list as in the others, but the theme of not being a good member of the group runs throughout. The "foreigners" he felt ambivalent about; he wanted them to be good Americans and then they were "just as good as anybody else." The others, including the hypocrites, immoral people, and the young men "whose fathers kept them out of uniform," were largely people from the higher levels of Yankee City society. They were attacked for their moral delinquencies, but were particularly reprehensible because most of them belonged to the symbolic cluster he called the "codfish aristocracy." The intense feeling aroused by such attacks, although enhanced by the belief that they were unethical or immoral, sprang more from a sense of inequality and injustice and status frustration among his followers than from moral disapproval.

The elms, old gardens, the Sampson mansion, lace-curtain Irish, Hill Street and the codfish aristocrats, all from the upper levels of the social-class system of Yankee City, form a logically heterogeneous but nonlogically homogeneous group. Since they are at the focal center of his attack we have examined them in the context of the conflict. The significance of trees and mansion as a ramified symbol we will explore separately.

The list of loved objects is important and revealing. Biggy's mother stands in a class by herself. She was loved, admired, and respected by her son in a way perhaps that only the widowed mother of an only child can be. She was feared and at times defied, but was deeply loved and served as a model for much of what he did. In another category were his boyhood friends, hobo comrades, and his Navy pals. All were former members of intimate face-to-face clique groups. All were particularly loved in an atmosphere of youthful defiance of authority and symbolized some of the feelings he had about being young, free, and autonomous.

Another cluster includes the clammers, his cur dog Bo, workers on strike, a prisoner up on charges of murder, prisoners generally, and Al Smith, William Lloyd Garrison, and Andrew Jackson. Biggy identified with all of them either as an underdog himself or as a champion of the underdog. The significance of the list, of course, parallels the previous one. Still another group would include fighters, Julius Caesar, football, the Navy, those who enlisted and fought in World War I, and technological progress generally. Among other common values here expressed are competition, aggression, dominance, and success.

Biggy also had a deep love for Yankee City, particularly for the streets along the river. Perhaps most interesting of all was his identification with the taxpayers and his liking for schoolteachers. Since he was a large taxpayer himself and a man of property, the former feeling is easily understood. It might be supposed that, because of their authoritative role, he would have disliked teachers, but his liking for them seems to be connected with their understanding of his boyhood deviltry. Few of the people, statuses, or symbols he liked belong to the experiences of adult life. Even the taxpayers may reflect his memory of his mother's often reiterated claims of being a large taxpayer in Yankee City. His mother, his native city, his childhood neighborhood, and his friends are at the core of his positive feelings.

To the list of positive objects must be added the jail, once a prison to his mother and himself, now his much beloved and admired home. Since he now owned it, this former symbol of authority was his to do with as he willed.

Biggy Muldoon spent three periods in jail. These experiences embittered him and increased his hostility toward authority, but the several days his mother spent in jail for refusing to pay for a license for his stray dog grieved and angered him far more than his own incarcerations. When the judge sentenced him for cutting down the elm trees he said he'd "run for governor and fire the judge," and when he did time for hitting the mayor, he said that when he got to be mayor he would fire the superintendent of the jail. When he did indeed become mayor he did not forget the time he and his mother spent in the local jail and retaliated by firing certain officials and giving some of the "cops" menial and distasteful tasks.

The purchase of the jail was an economic action, no doubt judged by the criteria of economic risk-taking; yet it was a source of great satisfaction to Biggy and Mrs. Muldoon to control the symbol of their humiliation. The symbolic significance of the act becomes even more apparent when it is remembered that they lived in the sheriff's quarters, where they now had liberty to come and go as they pleased. The people of Yankee City at the time did not miss the point; they were excited by it, many being pleased with the idea of former prisoners owning and controlling the jail that had held them captive. The purchase of the Sampson house where Mrs. Muldoon had once worked as a domestic easily fits into this same symbolic category. Economically it was a good buy, but the social significance of ownership by one who had once served there was not overlooked by the citizens of the town.

Biggy dramatized some of the basic conflicts of our society, perhaps most specifically those around technological change. Symbolically he supported the values of progress and change against those of conservatism, which supports the moral, aesthetic, and intellectual worth of the past. The conflict between the technology and the conservative mores of the past in a democratic society makes the manners and morals of the old-family status vulnerable to attack, particularly by the distortions of satire and burlesque. When matched against the symbols of old family and the past, the symbols of youth and new technology with its discoveries and inventions, intertwined as one in a changing world where "progress" is a highly valued process, are very formidable.

This force is felt particularly by common men who have ambition for higher status. Once the economic barriers have been conquered by mobile men, only acceptance by the aristocracy—that always necessary legitimizing of the personal success of the mobile man and his family—keeps them from being triumphant. Here lies the possibility of conflict. Those who have been at the top for only one or two generations are likely to be the very people who in fact and symbol oppose the social and economic advance of men beneath them. There is a desperate need for such a class to control the processes by which people enter, and become part of, their group. It is also necessary for their security and stability that they exercise a considerable control over the forces (or channels) which produce successfully mobile people. The low birth rate at the top requires continual recruitment to fill their superior ranks. As long as they dominate the tacit agreements which constitute the rules for social and economic success at their own level, they and their forms of behavior are secure. When the principles by which they establish control are threatened, they and their whole way of life face destruction. The basic power of the old-family class is their right to accept a few sheep of peculiar whiteness and reject all others who try for admission. Because of this power, in effect, they control how an ambitious family will spend its money, the social rituals its members will adopt, the charities and philanthropies, arts, and other similar highly regarded behavior they will support; the associations and churches they will join and maintain, and, for many mobile families, the beliefs about the world and themselves that they will accept and make their own.

Biggy Muldoon had challenged all this and invited the little people of Yankee City and the world to join him. The elegant and forbidding presence of the mansion and its walled gardens and the great moral and economic power and prestige of embattled Hill Street had not intimidated him. He behaved socially in character as a man from the wrong side of the tracks: he used a violent style of attack to settle arguments. The metropolitan papers which frequently reprinted (to the delight of their mass audiences) the story he told a reporter, that he did not go in for boxing but only bare-knuckled street fighting, caught one important aspect of Biggy which, among many, identified him with this class. But his faith in money, hard work, saving and investing capital, and taking a risk was something else again. Benjamin Franklin, a charter member of the middle class and phrase-maker for it, would have admired and sponsored the Biggy who believed in enterprise and making money and wanted no "socialist" nonsense about "dividing my money in half." Economically Biggy was a middle-class man and conformed to the central precepts of that part of the success story.

But he did not want, as a reward for such splendid successful enterprise, to marry the boss's daughter—that symbol of acceptance by, and submission to, the social authority of the upper class. Nor did he make any other moves for social acceptance; rather, he regarded all advances he made as attacks on the upper class and everything they and those who emulated them stood for. Biggy was not an economic but a social rebel, who vigorously assaulted the social, not the economic, foundations of superiority. The contradictions between his economic and social ideologies created a seeming paradox which confused both his foes and many of his followers. On the other hand, it protected him from serious charges of being a "goddammed bolshevik" who wanted to overthrow the American way of life. The fact that he was willing to pay the price demanded for economic success, but not for social acceptance, was of fundamental importance in determining his successes and failures.

We have examined some of the meanings of Biggy's treatment of the Hill Street mansion. We must now return to the significance of the house itself.

The Destruction of the Mansion

At the time Biggy and his mother purchased it, the Sampson mansion rested securely within its pleasant and spacious garden, which spread across the highlands marking the summit of Hill Street. Surrounded by a terraced wall of heavy granite slabs, the estate was effectively separated from the public highway below. The wall shut out the world of common people from the superior and well-bred life of the few. The ancient elms growing along the street at the side of the house made a part of the long rows of elms bordering Hill Street to form a great canopy stretching for miles along that broad avenue.

The beauty of the tree-lined street and the common sentiment of its residents for the venerable elms unify the homes of Hill Street in the minds of its people, the fine old trees providing an outward symbol of that superior region's self-regard. The trees themselves are part of a planting that physically and symbolically interrelates the contemporary families and their homes with the larger cultured world of their dwelling area, and this whole world with the values and beliefs of an upper-class style of life through past generations. In the living presence of the elms, the past lives too. Hill Street is the most important public symbol of the upper classes of Yankee City.

Although rows of fine trees are the hallmark of old New England towns and villages, it cannot be denied that in a fair-sized city, in the residential section, they constitute a public expression of the presence of upper-class manners and gentle refinement. Here on Hill Street, their age and the agreeable and historic style of most of the houses give eloquent testimony that good form, good breeding, and a proper ritualistic consumption of wealth have been and are being maintained by the families who have lived there for generations. The historical markers on many of the houses, placed there at the time of the three-hundredth anniversary of the state, tell of their continued claims to superiority, the ultimate mark of old family.

A house with its landscaping and architecture is usually the very heart of the technical and symbolic apparatus necessary for the maintenance of self-regard in upper-class personality, and for the persistence of the culture of the group which occupies this social level. The decor, furnishings, paintings, and their arrangements in the various rooms where the family life is differentiated and defined are all symbolic objects belonging to a subculture which expresses to those who occupy the house, and those who frequent or know about it, the nature of the inner world of each person living there. The symbols not only refer to the manners and morals of the subculture and express the significance of the people and their way of life, but also evoke and maintain in people sentiments about who they are and what they must do to retain their superior images of themselves and keep before them an interesting and gratifying vision of the superiority of their world. The subjects of the paintings on the wall of a living room often directly refer to an ancestor and to his and their superior position. They may evoke sentiments and express values which reinforce the learning of childhood within the private worlds of the family members, or strengthen the present solidarity of the family by indirectly relating its members more closely to each other and tying each more closely to a shared ancestor.

The upper classes in our culture have characteristically taken unto themselves, and have had yielded to them by most of the society, the principal role of fostering the arts and cultivating the taste necessary for their existence. Since these classes are rarely sufficiently creative to supply the artists necessary for the survival of the great arts, they patronize artists and often by social recognition or marriage recruit many of them to be members of their own level. The presence and control of objects of art provide a permanent mirror of superiority into which the upper classes can look and always see what they believe to be their own excellence, thus reinforcing one of their principal claims to superiority, their belief in their own good taste.

Landscaping transforms the surroundings of the house into a superior aesthetic form, functioning for the exterior setting much as the beauty of furnishings and decor for the interior. To have significance for status purposes, a garden must reflect taste and an understanding of beauty; the owner must have suitable knowledge of shrubs and plants—better still, the garden, its trees and flowers, should have their own superior history.

The old-family tradition demands understatement about outward forms, particularly personal possessions. The perfect expression of the "ideal" should be avoided for it is often the mark of the parvenu, driven by his feelings of anxiety that "he won't do it right" while running from his inner sense of inferiority, to have everything perfect about the house and "all the parts fitting in perfect harmony." The presence of such values and fears is also the reason interior decorators are numerous and well-paid in this society. The often expressed hostility and contempt for them is symbolically similar to that generally felt for undertakers—each is felt to be necessary to cover human pain and inadequacy.

Many of the better houses are occupied by lower-upper or new-family people without family lineage. Since they have been able to become the proud owners of houses whose lineage strengthens unspoken claims for recognition the owners feel they themselves deserve, they too belong to a culture founded on inherited achievements.

Despite what the theorists say, conspicuous expenditure *per se* is insufficient to achieve this end. The form and manner in which conspicuous expenditure is made determine its efficacy for advancement in status. It can end all hopes for those who are upward-mobile, simply by the manner in which it is carried out. Only when a house encloses a style of existence that conforms to its outward form, and when its inner way of life has been recognized and accepted through the intimate participation of its owners with the top group, does it cease to be no more than a claim to upper-class status and become a symbol of the actually achieved status of the family.

The social position of the children of upper-class families, as in other classes, is entirely dependent on that of the parents. The economic position of the family is ordinarily, though not always, dependent on the husband and father; but the maintenance of the private life of the family and its status are usually centered in the wife and mother. Family life is planned and organized around her, and as the lady of the house she often becomes the gracious symbol of the family's way of life.

Given its physical form, it is easy to understand why the house has come to be regarded in the study of symbolism as feminine rather than masculine. For other nonlogical reasons, it is also no cause for wonder that a garden is considered a feminine rather than a masculine symbol. The most private and protected part of social life that is shared by two or more people is the family; the most intimate relation, highly protected by secrecy, is the sexual one between husband and wife. The sexuality of the woman is guarded by many restrictions and taboos. They help to make her the most significant person in the continuing life of our culture and the subcultures of the social classes. The enclosed and concealed physical character of her sexual being is further enclosed by convention and, for some Christians, transformed into a sacred mystery. The core of all family life in America, particularly that of the upper-upper class, is the person of the wife and mother. She is usually the most important factor in the formation of the growing child's personality and the transmitter of some of the basic values and attitudes which are the foundations of the learning determining the class to which her children belong. The persistence of the culture of a social class as a way of life is partly founded on her strength as wife and mother within the protective spiritual walls of family and the material ones of the house.

If the enclosed, inner world of a house and garden is feminine and a symbol of aloof superiority, the outer world of a Hill Street is a mixed symbol at once of feminine grace and privacy and of masculine dominance and superiority. This avenue is the present symbolic expression of the past glory of Yankee City when it was one of the great aggressive trading cities of New England, a port which built and sent its sailing ships to fight and trade all over the world. When the ships returned, Hill Street received a major share of their wealth, for the shipowners and wealthy merchants lived in many of its houses.

The separation of the inner and outer worlds of particular homes and the general dwelling area into feminine and masculine symbols is worth exploring. The early period of Hill Street's and Yankee City's glory was more masculine and aggressive, the whole order dominated by the values and virtues our culture commonly ascribes to males. The sailing ships, classed symbolically as female, were part of a larger world dominated and run by men. In the economic life of the time they occupied a symbolic position similar to that held by the houses, then and now, in the life of the town. They were owned by men and, as economic objects, were under their control and protection. Essentially, this parallels the position of most upper-class women in our society; during most of their lives they are economically dependent upon and socially protected by men.

When Biggy attacked the mansion he attacked the most potent symbol of the superior classes of Yankee City; he struck at their very foundations. Not only did he violate the house and threaten the values attached to Hill Street as well as old-family sentiment, but he injured and threatened the deeper unconscious emotions felt for that protected place where wives and mothers live, whose persons are the emotional center of the group and the channel through which social forms and symbols persist, for they train the young in their particular usages.

Biggy's removal of the great house and substitution of a commercial filling station were simple utilitarian acts. The increased use of cars on Constitution Avenue, part of an interstate highway, made the gas station a good business risk. The traditional values protecting Hill Street were breached as part of the social changes resulting from the progress of the automobile and other technological improvement. The mansion on Hill Street served the few and excluded the many; payment could not buy entrance into it. The filling station, a commercial and technological machine, served and included everyone. It was not endowed with "social" prestige. It was frankly for profit rather than for the spending and display of wealth to establish a family's claims to superior status.

Of all these acts which were transposed into the realm of evocative symbols, the cutting of the great trunks of the ancient elms went deepest and pervaded most fully the conscious and unconscious life of the members of Yankee City society. Trees have long been symbols of man's vitality and of his hopes for eternal life. The tree is an evocative symbol, important in legend and religion and in poetry and the art of the theatre; it is an essential part of our cultural context as people. Its significance for all life and its symbolic interdependence with man's existence, enhanced by sentiments of the agricultural societies which were our cultural forebears, are deeply rooted in the very beginnings of man's social existence. Frazer's *Golden Bough* is a literary and scientific monument marking the significance of the tree in man's feelings and beliefs about himself and what he is.

To the author of the *Cherry Orchard* what happened at Hill Street and Constitution Avenue would have been easy to understand. In the Chekhov drama, it will be recalled, the merchant who had risen from serfdom to affluence purchased the orchard from a decaying aristocratic family. A new railway had given the land a new kind of social value. The self-made man who bought the cherry orchard declares that it can be "cut up . . . into building lots" and great profits made. He reminds all who will listen that "my father was your father's serf." For the aristocrats, the orchard is the past living in the present and in each of them. "When I walk through . . . in the evening or at night" one of them says, "the rugged bark on the trees glows with a dim light and the cherry trees seem to see all that happened a hundred and two hundred years ago." Just before the sound of the axe announces the climax and end of the play, the merchant Lopokhin cries, "I have bought the property where my father and my grandfather were slaves."

On the morning Biggy cut down the elms an old man who lived on Hill Street passed by. It was said he cried openly and wiped the tears from his eyes as he continued down the street. One of his friends told us, "For a person like me, born and brought up in Yankee City, walking under the elms on Hill Street is always an experience. Sometimes I'm in another world; I'm back talking to my grandfather and listening to all the fine things he used to say. Those trees are like people, the people I used to know, the kind of people my parents were."

Perhaps such a man as Biggy Muldoon will never again

appear in Yankee City or even in America, but others will come forward to play the role of hero or champion of the downtrodden, or the common man who challenges the select few and slays the dragon. Some of these will rise to national positions, but they will achieve the highest levels only when they learn how to conform to the basic beliefs and values of the group. When they fail, sometimes it will be caused by their inability to adjust their basic beliefs and values to those that govern American society.

CHAPTER 8

Social Class Configurations: An Overview

The Level Above the Common Man

AN upper-upper person in Yankee City belongs to a class having a much larger number of women than men and a larger percentage of females (over 60 per cent) than any other class in the community. In this respect it differs markedly from the lower-lower class, which has the smallest percentage of women, and is most like the upper-middle class, which also has an excess of females. The preponderance of females in the upper-upper class is statistically significant.[1]

The upper-upper class has the smallest percentage of children and the largest proportion of people over sixty years of age. In both respects it stands in strongest contrast to the lower-lower class, containing about 11 per cent of persons under twenty-one, as against 28 per cent, and over 39 per cent of persons sixty years of age or older, as against fewer than 11 per cent. The upper-upper most closely resembles the lower-upper and upper-middle classes in numbers of old people, the upper-middle in percentage of children. The excess of older people in the upper-upper population is accounted for in part by the large number of unmarried females who are the sisters and maiden aunts of other members of the group, in part by the number of "ladies" who have lived on in the old family

1. The measurement used to test significances is that of mean-square contingency. All percentages were figures for two points beyond the decimal. This was done not because such detail is ordinarily necessary for most social data, but to insure statistical accuracy.

houses after their parents' death and after their brothers and
sons have gone elsewhere to marry and rear their families.

Ethnicity All members of the upper-upper class are Yankees, none
belonging to any ethnic group in the community. The lower-
upper class, which contains less than 5 per cent with an ethnic
background, all of them Irish whose families have been in
America for several generations, approximates the upper-upper
class most closely in this. By contrast, 57 per cent of the lower-
lower and 61 per cent of the upper-lower classes belong to
ethnic minorities, with large concentrations of Irish, Poles, Russians, Greeks, French Canadians, Italians, Jews, Armenians,
and Negroes. Upper-upper individuals rarely associate with
persons of other ethnic stocks. Lower-class Yankees try hard
not to do so and sometimes join associations having "racial"
prejudices; physically, however, they are continually in the
company of people with traditions that differ from their own.

Marriage Upper-upper individuals marry later than those of any other
class. Their median age at marriage is almost twenty-eight
years (27.90), which is closest to that of the lower-upper class
(26.60 years) and furthest from that of the lower-lower class
(23.20 years). Very few of the upper-upper marry before
reaching twenty-one (3.70 per cent), whereas over thirty-five
per cent of the lower-lower do; none of the lower-upper class in
our survey was married before twenty-one years of age. Over
half of the upper-upper class married during the ages from
twenty-one to twenty-nine years, while about one-third married
between thirty and thirty-nine. This class has a larger percentage of single people than any other, and a smaller percentage of
married members; about 40 per cent are single, while in all
other classes the range is from 31 to 33 per cent. It has a larger
number of widowed individuals than any other class, being
most similar to the lower-upper in this respect and least like
the lower-lower.

occupation From the viewpoint of occupation, upper-upper-class people
cluster overwhelmingly in professional and proprietary positions, over 83 per cent being thus employed. They are most like

the lower-upper class in this respect and least like the lower-lower, less than 1 per cent of whom are gainfully occupied in these occupations. Upper-upper people are listed in only one other occupational classification: that of clerks and kindred workers (16.67 per cent). Hence they are the least differentiated occupationally, although the lower-upper class follows them in this. The upper-upper class has no gainfully occupied people who are classified as skilled, semiskilled, or unskilled workers, as against 85 per cent of the lower-lower class so designated. No wholesale or retail dealers are members of the topmost class. The lower-upper class likewise lacks any who are listed as "workers." The members of the upper-upper class are but slightly represented in the principal industries of the town —shoe and silverware manufacturing—with only 5 per cent in the former and none in the latter, whereas 40 per cent of the lower-lower class are employed in the shoe industry alone. *employment*

The topmost class has the highest percentage of employable individuals who have never worked, being most like the lower-upper in this respect and least like the lower-middle. When the unemployment census was taken, the community was suffering from the 1930-35 business depression. But the upper class was most favorably placed, since 90 per cent of its employables had jobs, while only 27.57 per cent of the lower-lower were fully employed. No members of either of the two upper classes were on relief, although some of them were penniless. All other classes had a greater or lesser number on relief, topped by the lower-lower among whom one out of three had his name on the relief rolls.

The upper-upper families are inferior only to the lower-upper *Property* in the percentage who own their own homes, being least like the lower-lower class. The median assessed value of their homes is less than that for the lower-upper class but more than that for any other, the median for the lower-lower class being lowest of all. The median assessed value of all real estate owned by the upper-upper class in Yankee City is higher than in any other class ($5,833); it is most like the lower-upper ($5,600) and least like the lower-lower class ($1,606).[2] Few upper-upper people pay rent. All who do, pay by the month instead of the week, and all fall in the higher rent classification. Again this class is most like the lower-upper, least like the lower-lower.

A larger percentage of upper-upper members (67 per cent) live in large houses and a smaller percentage in medium- and small-sized houses than of any other class. The size of the house is important if for no other reason than the fact that it was so considered in Yankee City. Eighty per cent of the upper-upper houses were found in good condition, 19 per cent in medium or ordinary condition, and less than 1 per cent in poor condition. Once again, the two upper classes are most alike. By contrast, 71 per cent of the houses occupied by the lower-lower class were in bad condition, and only 3 per cent in good condition.[3] Fifty-six per cent of the upper-upper class have large and good houses, 10 per cent have large ones in medium condition, and less than 1 per cent have large houses in bad condition. In all these respects the upper-upper class is most like the lower-upper and least like the lower-lower. It is, moreover, the only class which does not occupy small houses in bad condition, none of its members living in medium-sized and small houses in bad condition or in business dwellings. On the basis of the mean square contingency, both the upper-upper and lower-upper classes are significantly high for houses which are large and good, large and medium, and medium-sized and in good condition. The lower-lower class, on the other hand, is the only class significantly high for houses of all sizes in bad condition and for dwellings built primarily for business purposes. As regards the ecological areas, the upper-upper and lower-upper classes are concentrated in significantly high numbers in the Hill Street, Oldtown, and Newtown areas, and they are significantly low elsewhere, with the exception of Centerville. The two classes differ only in the fact that no one in the lower-upper

2. These evaluations are from the assessor's records. They do not represent the actual market value of the properties.
3. Business dwellings comprise the remainder of this total.

class is found in the Newtown area. In living areas the upper-upper is least like the two lower classes. *Associations*

Up to this point in this brief descriptive summary of the upper-upper class, we have concerned ourselves largely with observable characteristics of its members and have not attempted to describe their participation in social institutions of the community. Let us now look at the kinds of voluntary associations to which they belong. Both men and women of the upper-upper class have a significantly high membership in what are ordinarily called social clubs. They also have a significantly high percentage of associations organized for charity, and are significantly low in membership in fraternal organizations (lodges and secret societies), or in associations which are age graded. The upper-upper class, moreover, does not stress membership in associations having auxiliaries. In its associations it is most like the lower-upper class and least like the lower-lower class, the latter being significantly high for male and female fraternities, for auxiliaries, and for age-graded associations, and significantly low for female associations organized for sociable and charitable purposes.

The upper-upper class is also different from the other classes *relig.* in religious affiliations. Its members favor the Unitarian and Episcopal churches in significantly high numbers, Moreover, they neither attend the Catholic churches nor favor other Protestant sects. In these respects, the upper-upper is most like the lower-upper class and least like the lower-lower class, which is significantly high in membership in the two Catholic, the Methodist, Baptist, and Presbyterian churches and significantly low in membership in the Unitarian and Episcopal churches.

Members of the upper-upper and lower-upper classes give *educ.* their children a different formal and informal education. No children of the former attended the local high school at the time of our census, and, as far as we could determine, but few had attended this institution previously. Moreover, only four lower-upper-class children were enrolled in the high school. Most of the children of the two upper classes are sent to private preparatory schools, where they not only prepare for college but also acquire the etiquette and attributes of their group. Because the two upper classes were so sparsely represented in the local school, it is impossible to show how the higher classes select their courses of study, but we know that the subjects chosen are the conventional ones which colleges and universities demand as entrance requirements.

Formal education of adolescents does not always take place in school, since some are employed before they reach twenty-one. There is obviously a relationship between the kind of high school course chosen by the children and the age at which they intend to go to work. If one knew nothing about the American class system, he might suppose that since only a few members of the two upper classes attended the local high schools they would be found in the town's economic life. However, in a study of subadult employment, we found no upper-uppers represented and but eight lower-uppers, as contrasted with a large percentage of lower-lower adolescents who worked.

library Yankee City has one large and well-stocked library. A smaller percentage of the upper-upper than of any other class uses this institution. In this respect it is most like the lower-lower and least like the upper-middle. From interviews we learned that the upper-upper buy their books and belong to discussion clubs where they get the "latest and most current books," while the lower-lower class's failure to use the library is due to the fact that they read less. Of the upper-upper members who use the library, over 85 per cent are adults and slightly over 14 per cent children, whereas of the lower-lower users, over 50 per cent are children.

arrests The frequency with which members of a class are arrested and get their names on the police blotter is a fair index both of the kind of authority exercised by political organization over each class and of the kind of behavior in each class which is sufficiently disapproved by the whole community to warrant the more drastic sanctions of police action. Of the total arrests in the city, the upper-upper class accounts for but one-half of 1 per cent, while the lower-lower accounts for 65 per cent. As regards the figures within the class itself, only a little over 1 per cent have been arrested, a slightly larger percentage than the classes just below it, while 11 per cent of the lower-lower class have had their names placed on the police records. Moreover, none of the upper-upper and lower-upper-class arrests is below twenty-one years of age, while 30 per cent of the lower-lower-class arrests are juveniles. This great disparity is not to be accounted for by the fact that "criminal behavior" is proportionately higher among lower-class juveniles or that there are more ethnic members whose children have been imperfectly adapted to Yankee City life. It must be understood as a product of the amount of protection from outside interference the parents can give the members of their families. Our interviews together with police records demonstrate that the lower-lower adolescent boys are guilty of crimes against property, and that some girls are caught in sexual delinquencies. But these same interviews likewise demonstrate that boys and girls in the higher classes as frequently commit the same acts but do not get on the police records. They are not arrested because social pressure prevents the police from taking action when they make threats to do so or forces them to overlook the behavior at their own volition, or, more important, because the social controls of the class system operate in such a way as to hide successfully all such activities from the authorities.

The security of younger members of upper-upper-class families from outside interference is further demonstrated by the fact that all charitable associations, in which the upper classes are represented in large numbers, serve to subordinate the lower classes and interfere with their ordinary family life. An organization such as the Society for the Prevention of Cruelty to Children, for example, is ostensibly free from class bias; yet all of the cases with which it dealt came from below the two upper classes, and most of them, from below the three uppermost classes. In brief, the social power of the upper classes highly protects their families, while the subordinate position of the lower classes leaves their families more vulnerable to the sanctions of the rest of the community.

The upper-upper is most like the lower-upper and least like

Books the lower-lower class in the type of books its members read. Seven per cent of the upper-upper members read books classified as biography and history. The upper-upper also read more books on science than any other class. They and the lower-upper likewise read fewer, while the lower-lower read more, children's books than the other classes. The members of the upper-upper class also read a smaller, and the lower-lower a larger, percentage of adventure stories, than any other class. The upper-upper people read a larger percentage of detective stories than the members of any other class, but in this respect they are most like the lower-lower and least like the lower-upper and upper-middle classes. They are also most like the lower-lower and least like the upper-middle in the percentage of the reading which falls under the general heading of family and courtship.

For books which accent social climbing, the upper-upper class ranks last, the upper-lower first, in the percentage of its reading members. For those which emphasize patriotism and warlike activities, the upper-upper class is below the lower-upper, which leads all others, and it is least like the lower-lower. The upper-upper is most like the upper-middle class for the percentage of readers of books which emphasize the theme of man's fight against fate, and most like the two middle and least like the lower-upper and lower-lower classes in the interest it shows in reading books about social techniques such as manners. Generally speaking, the upper-upper-class readers show a special interest in detective stories, courtship and the family, and man's fight against fate, and less interest in farce and humor, children's stories, social techniques, and scientific books. But it is not significantly high or low in its preference for any category of book.

Magazines The upper-upper (28.51 per cent) is most like the lower-upper and least like the lower-lower class (3.64 per cent) in the number of its magazine subscribers, in the number of magazines per subscriber (1.87 per cent for the upper-upper class), and in preferences and avoidances in the magazines its members read, these being in most cases almost exactly opposite those of the lower-lower class.

The lower-upper class has already been compared in part with the upper-upper class, but its own special characteristics will now be summarized. The sex ratio of the lower-upper class is slightly over 50 per cent female, 49 per cent male. In this respect, it is most like the lower-middle and least like the upper-upper and lower-lower classes.

In age distribution, the lower-upper class has approximately the same percentage of subadults as the upper-middle class and also approximates the age ranges from twenty-one to thirty-nine, and sixty years or more. It has a somewhat higher percentage of people aged forty to fifty-nine years. The lower-upper is least like the lower-lower class in the percentage of subadults and of those from twenty-one to thirty-nine, and it differs most from the lower-lower class in the age group over sixty.

The lower-upper is most like the upper-upper and least like the lower-lower in the birthplaces of its members. Half of the lower-upper were born in Yankee City and less than 1 per cent outside the United States. The other members of the class were born in contiguous areas (12.39 per cent), in the rest of New England (13.27 per cent), or in the remainder of the United States (23.02 per cent).

As regards ethnic composition, 95.42 per cent of the lower-upper class are Yankee and but 4.58 per cent ethnic, all of whom are Irish. In this respect it is most like the upper-upper class, the members of which are all Yankee, and least like the lower-lower, which contains representatives of all ethnic groups.

Sixty per cent of the lower-upper class are married or widowed. In marital status, the lower-upper members are most like the upper-middle but vary little from all other classes except the upper-upper, which is decidedly different. The lower-upper tend to marry late; only the upper-upper members marry later. The median age for marriage in the lower-upper class is 26.60 years. In this respect it is most like the upper-middle and least like the lower-lower class. The percentage of those who marry under twenty-one years in the lower-upper class is most like that of the upper-upper, but for all other age ranges it is most like that of the upper-middle.

The relative age of the spouse is approximately the same for all classes. Seventy-four per cent of the lower-upper men marry women younger than themselves, 10 per cent have wives of the same age, and 6 per cent wives older than they are.

Eighty-six per cent of the occupations of the lower-upper class are professional or proprietary. There are only two other classifications in which lower-upper members are found: (1) wholesale and retail dealers and (2) clerks and kindred workers. Each of these two types of occupation comprises 7 per cent of those who are or have been gainfully employed in this class. The lower-upper is most like the upper-upper and least like the lower-lower in its occupational distribution.

The industries in which the members of the lower-upper class participate are chiefly shoe and silverware manufacturing— similar to those of the upper-upper and, to a certain extent, to those of the upper-middle—and least like those of the lower-lower. Ninety-four per cent of the employables of the lower-upper class are fully employed, none has a part-time job, and 6 per cent are unemployed (most of these latter not seeking employment). The lower-upper is most like the upper-upper and least like the lower-lower in these respects.

The lower-upper class has a higher percentage of home owners (24.05 per cent) than any other class. In this regard it also closely approximates the upper-upper and is least like the lower-lower class.

The median assessed value of all real estate of the lower-upper class is $5,600. This figure is topped only by that of the upper-upper class and is far above that of the lowest class, which it is least like. All rentals of the lower-upper, like those of the upper-upper class, are paid monthly, while those of the lower-lower class are paid weekly. The median rental for the lower-upper could not be computed exactly because of too few cases, but it seemed to fall between $60 and $50 per month, being least like the median monthly rental of the lower-lower class ($16.23).

The majority of the lower-upper class live in large houses, a high percentage in medium-sized houses, and a small number in small houses. Seventy per cent of the cases live in houses which are in good condition, about 30 per cent in houses ordinarily well cared for, and but a small percentage in houses in bad repair. No houses occupied by members of the lower-upper class which are large or medium in size are in bad repair, and less than 1 per cent are small and in poor repair. None of the lower-upper class lives in dwellings built primarily for business purposes. The lower-upper occupy houses which are significantly high in respect to size and condition (large and good, large and medium, and medium and good). The two upper classes are most alike both as to size and condition of the house and least like the lower-lower class.

As regards ecological distribution, members of the lower-upper class are concentrated in significantly high numbers in areas where the upper-upper persons are also significantly high. The areas with the highest lower-upper concentrations are Hill Street and Oldtown. All other areas are significantly low except Centerville.

The lower-upper members participate in significantly high numbers in "social clubs" which are for men only, for women only, and for both sexes. They are also found in associations organized for charity and in social-economic associations such as the Rotary Club. The lower-upper members, however, are not found in men's or women's fraternal organizations, organizations with auxiliaries, or those which are formally age graded. In all these respects they closely resemble the upper-upper class and are least like the lower-lower class.

The lower-upper are members of the same churches as the upper-upper people and they are not members of those churches in which the lower classes are represented in significantly high numbers.

Only about one-fourth of 1 per cent of all the arrests in Yankee City are from the lower-upper class, and but 0.76

per cent of the class membership has been arrested. Interviews attest the same kind of "delinquent" behavior for the children of this class as that for which the lower-class children are classified as delinquent, but like the upper-upper-class children, they are protected from the police and do not appear on their records.

The lower-upper children, like those of the class above them and unlike those of other classes, tend to avoid the local high school and to attend private preparatory schools. There were only four lower-upper children in the local high school, all of whom subscribed to either the science or Latin curriculum in preparation for college. Moreover, very few of the lower-upper children worked, and these were distributed in a variety of economic activities.

The upper-middle class most resembles the upper-upper in sex ratio, since slightly over 55 per cent of its representatives are female, and least resembles the lower-lower which contains a disproportionate number of men. About 40 per cent of the upper-middle class are below fifty years of age, in which respect this class is most like the lower-upper and least like the upper-upper and lower-lower. For the proportion of young and old people it most closely approximates the lower-upper class, then the upper-upper class, and is least like the lower-lower class.

Eighty-three per cent of the upper-middle are Yankee by birth and tradition, being most like the lower-upper and least like the upper-lower class. This class is also most like the lower-upper class (next like the lower-middle) in the composition of its ethnic population, most of which is Irish, less than 1 per cent of the class membership being from any other ethnic group. About 6 per cent of the Irish, 3 per cent of the Jews, 2 per cent of the Greeks, 1 per cent of the Armenians, and less than 1 per cent of all other ethnic groups in Yankee City belong to the upper-middle class. It contains no Russians, Poles, or Negroes. The total membership of the upper-middle class comprises 10 per cent of the total population of the city.

Over 94 per cent of the upper-middle class were born in the United States. They are most like the lower-upper and lower-middle classes for the percentage of native-born and least like the two lower classes. Approximately 58 per cent were born in Yankee City, the same percentage as the lower-middle class, this being least like that of the lower-lower class. About 13 per cent were born in the region near Yankee City, about 26 per cent in the rest of New England, and only 6 per cent in the rest of the United States. They are most like the lower-middle and least like the two upper classes in the amount of population born in the rest of the New England States.

Almost four times as many members of the upper-upper as members of the upper-middle class were born outside of Yankee City in the rest of the United States. A good part of this difference can be accounted for by the fact that many of those listed as "old family" in the study of Yankee City have been elsewhere and have frequently returned with spouses and children born outside of Yankee City. It is also true that a person who has married into an upper family has a better chance of being classed in that stratum if he was born a sufficient distance away from Yankee City to be unplaceable in class except by marriage and by judgments of present behavior. A New Englander is likely to be identifiable and, if he is not of the "proper" class, less likely to be chosen as a spouse by a member of that class.

The median age for marriage in the upper-middle class is 26.10 years. This figure is slightly lower than that of the lower-upper and somewhat higher than that of the lower-middle class and least resembles that of the lower-lower class. The upper-middle is most like the lower-middle class in the percentage of those who marry before the age of twenty-one. About 50 per cent of the members of this class are married, 21 per cent are single, and 10 per cent are widowed. With the exception of the upper-upper class, it is like all other classes in the percentage of those who were single and married. The comparative age of husbands and wives resembled that of the other five classes.

The occupations of the upper-middle class are, in many respects, most like those of the lower-upper and in others, like those of the lower-middle and least like those of the lower-lower class. The upper-middle is like the higher classes in the percentage of members who are in professions or are proprietors. More of their number are wholesale and retail dealers (the great majority of retail dealers are middle-class) than in the lower-upper and upper-upper classes, and fewer are clerks than in the lower-middle class. A small percentage of skilled and semi-skilled workers appear for the first time in the upper-middle class, but it contains no unskilled workers.

Eighty per cent of the upper-middle class were fully employed, which is smaller than the lower-upper class and higher than the lower-middle class. For this characteristic the upper-middle is least like the lower-lower class. Less than 1 per cent of the upper-middle class were on relief at the very worst point in the 1930-35 depression.

The upper-middle is most like the upper-upper and least like the lower-lower class in percentage of home owners. The median value of upper-middle-class homes is less than that of the lower-upper class. The median value of all property, including houses, owned by this class is most like that of the lower-middle class. The upper-middle has a higher percentage than the lower-upper class of owners of property with an assessed value less than $1,000; whereas, when compared with the lower-middle class, less than half its members belong to this category of ownership. However, it most resembles these two classes in this respect and is least like the lower-lower class.

Over 86 per cent of the upper-middle-class renters pay by the month; the rest, by the week. It is most like the two upper classes in this respect and next like the lower-middle class. The median rental for the upper-middle class is $29.75 a month, while that for the nearest class to it, the lower-middle, is $20.80.

Sixty per cent of the upper-middle-class houses are medium in size, 23 per cent are small, 16 per cent are large, and 1 per cent were built primarily for business purposes. The upper-middle class, having the highest percentage of its members living in medium-sized houses, most resembles the lower-middle (50 per cent) and the lower-upper (43 per cent). Both of the two upper classes have relatively more large houses; and the three lower classes, relatively more small houses.

Fifty per cent of the houses of the upper-middle class are in good repair, 45 per cent in medium, and 5 per cent in bad condition. It has twice the percentage of houses in good repair as the lower-middle class and 30 per cent less than the lower-upper and upper-upper classes. It has about the same percentage of houses in medium repair and about one-sixth the percentage in poor repair as the lower-middle class.

The upper-middle-class members live in significantly high numbers in houses which are medium in size and in ordinary repair and large or medium in size and in good repair. They resemble the lower-middle class for houses which are medium-sized and in good or ordinary repair, and the lower-upper and upper-upper classes for the large houses which are in good or ordinary repair and medium-sized houses which are in good repair. This class is the only one of the upper three which has members living in business buildings. Like the upper classes it has a significantly high participation in female social clubs and a significantly low participation in male and female fraternities, auxiliaries, and female age-graded associations. Like the lower-upper class it is significantly high for charitable and economic associations but unlike this class, significantly low in participation in mixed social clubs.

The upper-middle class favors the Unitarian Church, but it also belongs in significant percentages to the Baptist, Christian Science, and the Congregational Churches. It avoids in significant numbers the Catholic and Methodist churches.

This class accounts for but 2 per cent of all the arrests in Yankee City. Its members are socially powerful enough to prevent their arrests for many crimes such as drunkenness which would ordinarily cause arrest in the lower classes. Less than 1 per cent of the members of the class have been arrested. In this respect they are exactly the same as the lower-upper class.

Approximately 87 per cent of the upper-middle children in the high school were enrolled in the Latin and scientific courses.

The upper-middle most resembles the lower-upper class in the type of education its children choose in the high school, but it is most like the lower-middle in the way it educates them, since most of them go to the public school and but very few attend private preparatory schools. It is like the two upper classes in the small number of its children who work. Our records show but seventeen cases.

About 22 per cent—the highest of all classes—of the upper-middle class use the library; this class is followed by the lower-middle, which is followed by the lower-upper. Over 83 per cent of the users of the library in the upper-middle class are adults. This class is only exceeded by the upper-upper class in the percentage of adults and is followed by the lower-upper and lower-middle classes respectively.

The Common Man Level

The sex ratio of the lower-middle class shows a slight excess of females; it is most similar to the distribution of the sexes in the upper-lower class. About 50 per cent of its members are below forty years of age. It is most like the lower-upper and upper-middle classes in the percentage of its subadults; it has about the same percentage of people in the age range of twenty-one to thirty-one and is very similar to the upper-middle and upper-lower classes.

Sixty-seven per cent of the lower-middle class are Yankee. It is most like the upper-middle class in the number of Yankees in its population and least like the upper-lower and lower-lower classes. The great majority of ethnics in the lower-middle class are Irish, 4 per cent are French Canadian, and 3.50 per cent Jewish. All the other ethnic members have a representation of less than 1 per cent in the lower-middle class. Over 86 per cent of the lower-middle class were born in the United States. In this respect it is most like the upper-middle class and least like the two lower classes. Sixty per cent were born in or near Yankee City. It is similar to the upper-middle class for the per cent of its population born in the community. It also has a distribution of people born in the rest of New England and people born outside of New England but in the United States similar to that of the upper-middle class. It has more than double the amount of foreign-born that the upper-middle has, but about half as many as the upper-lower class.

The median age at marriage for the lower-middle-class members is 25.10 years. This figure falls midway between that of the upper-middle and the upper-lower classes. In the lower-middle class, the professional and proprietary groups are no longer first in occupational affiliation as in the three upper classes. This category of occupation ranks fourth and contains approximately 14 per cent of those employed or employable. Clerks exceed all others in the percentage of occupations in the lower-middle class, semiskilled workers are second, and skilled workers, third. They are followed by wholesale and retail dealers and unskilled workers. The lower-middle class is the highest of the six classes for the percent of skilled workers; such workers are present in significantly high numbers. The lower-middle class is most like the upper-middle for the number of clerks: about three-fifths of the clerks in Yankee City are lower-middle. Most of the wholesale and retail dealers are in the two middle classes. The percentages of skilled and semiskilled workers in the lower-middle class are most like the upper-lower class.

Slightly over 62 per cent of the workers in the lower-middle class are fully employed, and about 15 per cent are unemployed. This class has about twice as many unemployed as the upper-middle and less than one-fifth as many as the upper-lower class. It is the first of the four upper classes which has a sizable amount of the relief population: about 4 per cent, as compared with about 1 per cent of the upper-middle, none of the two upper classes, and over 10 per cent of the upper-lower class.

About 17 per cent of the lower-middle class own their own homes, in this respect being most like the upper-lower class and then the upper-middle class. They are most like the upper-lower class in value of their homes. The median value of all their real estate is $2,477, being, in this respect, most like the upper-middle and upper-lower classes. The upper-middle class owns more and the upper-lower, less.

The lower-middle class pays rent by the month, and its median rental is $20.80. It is the only one of the three lower classes which is significantly high for rent paid by the month. Its median rental is most like that of the upper-lower class and falls in between the median rentals of the upper-middle and upper-lower classes.

Fifty per cent of the lower-middle class live in medium-sized houses, 42 per cent in small houses, and only 7 per cent in large houses. In all but house size it falls between the upper-middle and upper-lower classes, but it is most like the upper-lower for all characteristics. Slightly under 50 per cent of its houses are in ordinary condition, about 25 per cent in good repair, and the same per cent in bad repair. The percentage of its houses in good and bad repair falls between the upper-middle and upper-lower classes. There is a slightly higher percentage of those in ordinary repair in the lower-middle class than in the upper-middle class. The lower-middle-class dwellers live in significantly high numbers in houses which are medium in size and in ordinary repair, small in size and in good repair, and small in size and medium in repair. They are most like the upper-middle class in preferring medium-sized houses but unlike it because they do not have large houses in significantly high numbers. In other respects they are most like the upper-lower class in the types of houses in which they live.

The lower-middle-class houses are located in significantly high numbers in Homeville, Newtown, and Oldtown. This preference for Newtown is shared only with the upper-upper class, but their choice of Oldtown is shared with all three upper classes. They avoid Riverbrook, which is significantly high for the two lower classes, Downtown and Middletown, which are significantly high for the lower-lower class and significantly low for the upper classes. They also avoid the Business Area, which is significantly high for the upper-lower class and low for all the upper classes.

The members of the lower-middle class favor men's fraternal organizations and the semi-auxiliary type of association. But they are represented in significantly low numbers in social clubs for women, for both sexes, and in associations organized for charity. They are like the two lower classes for their small membership in charitable organizations and unlike the three upper classes where membership in such associations is high. They are like the lower classes in the avoidance of social clubs and unlike the upper classes where a preference for them is strong. They are unlike the upper-middle class in their preference for fraternal and semi-auxiliary organizations. In general, the lower-middle class is more like the lower than the upper classes in the types of associations it joins and does not join. The churches which this class favors are the Congregational and Episcopal. It avoids the two Catholic churches in significantly high numbers. It is like the two upper classes in its preference for the Episcopal church and avoidance of the Catholic church.

Eight per cent of all those who were arrested in Yankee City were in the lower-middle class. This comprises 1.17 per cent of the whole membership of the lower-middle class. The lower-middle class is more like the three upper classes than the two lower classes in its rate of arrests. Like the upper-middle class, over three times as many juveniles were arrested than adults.

Less than one half of the lower-middle-class children favor the Latin and scientific courses in the high school. This is the first of the four upper classes where the preference changes from a type of course which prepares for college to one which is designed for immediate use. The lower-middle class falls between the upper-middle, where 87 per cent of the children take Latin and scientific courses, and the upper-lower, where only 27 per cent are enrolled in such courses.

There were 183 subadults in the lower-middle class who had jobs. A high percentage of them were in the chain or locally owned stores and a.low percentage in shoe manufacturing.

Fifty-two per cent of the upper-lower class are female, 48 per cent male. It is most like the lower-middle class and least like the lower-lower class. It falls between the lower-middle and lower-lower classes in percentage of its various age groups.

The upper-lower class has the smallest percentage of Yankees of all six classes (38 per cent) and is followed by the lower-lower class with 43 per cent. About half of the Irish and Armenians, between 40 and 50 per cent of the Jews, French Canadians, and Italians, about one-third of the Greeks, one-fourth of the Russians, and one-tenth of the Poles are in this class.

Seventy per cent of its membership were born in the United States. The upper-lower class falls exactly between the lower-middle and lower-lower classes. About one half of the members were born in or near Yankee City. This compares with 60 per cent of the lower-middle and 45 per cent of the lower-lower.

The upper-lower class has next to the lowest median age for marriage. Only the lower-lower class has a lower one. Their age for marriage falls between the lower-middle and lower-lower classes. Twenty-one per cent of their marriages occur before the individuals are twenty-one years old, being exceeded in this respect only by the lower-lower class. Although their age preference for spouses is in general similar to that of other classes, the upper-lower men lead all others in having wives older than they (20.14 per cent).

The principal industries in which they are employed are shoe manufacturing, retail stores, transportation, and building trades. This class has a significantly high number of workers in shoe factories and a significantly low number in silverware factories. Over 21 per cent of the upper-lower class had no jobs. Only the lower-lower class has a larger percentage of its population unemployed. In all categories of employment, the upper-lower class falls between the lower-middle and lowerlower classes but is nearer the lower-lower group.

The upper-lower class is most like the lower-lower class in percentage of home owners and next resembles the lowermiddle class. It also falls in between these two classes for the median value of its homes, and is most like the lower-lower class in the median value of all real estate owned.

Fifty-two per cent of all houses where upper-lower-class members reside are small dwellings, 41 per cent are medium size, 4 per cent are large, and slightly under 3 per cent are business structures. The several house sizes compare closely with those of the lower-lower and lower-middle classes but in general they most resemble those of the lower-lower class.

Forty-two per cent of the houses in which the upper-lower members live are in poor condition, the same percentage in medium condition, and but 13 per cent in good condition. They live in four times as many good houses, about twice as many ordinary houses, and three-fifths as many poor houses as the lower-lower class. The upper-lower class lives in significantly high numbers in small houses in medium condition. It has double the number of small houses in bad repair as the lower-middle class and slightly less than half as many as the lower-lower class. The upper-lower class has a significantly high percentage of its members living in the Business Area, Centerville, Littletown, and Riverbrook, and a significantly low number living in Hill Street, Middletown, Oldtown, and Across the River. It shares living areas with the lower-lower in Riverbrook, but it is concentrated in Centerville where the lower-lower class is significantly low. Moreover, it is low in Middletown where the lower-lower class has a high concentration of population. It is like the lower-lower class in its avoidance of Hill Street and Oldtown, areas of the upper classes.

The upper-lower class participates in significantly high percentages in male fraternities with auxiliaries, in female fraternities with and without auxiliaries, in semi-auxiliary organizations, and in associations which emphasize formal age grading. They are not found in male and female social groups, charitable associations, and economic associations. The upper-lower resembles the lower-lower and lower-middle classes in participation in associations.

The upper-lower class in pre-eminently the Roman Catholic class of Yankee City. It is significantly high for membership in both Catholic churches and for no others in the community, and it is significantly low for all Protestant churches, except the Methodist. It is most like the lower-lower class insofar as the two classes are the only ones that have such a high percentage of Catholics, but it is different from the lower-lower since the latter is also significantly high for several Protestant churches. In general, this means that a large number of the members of the various ethnic groups were sufficently mobile to get into a higher class than the Protestant Yankees in the lower-lower class. The upper-lower class is least like the two upper classes in its church affiliations.

About one-fourth of all the arrested people of Yankee City are in the upper-lower class. In this respect it is exceeded only by the lower-lower class. Over 3 per cent of the members of the upper-lower class have been arrested. This class resembles the one below it in its relations with the police of the city. Approximately 23 per cent of those arrested were below the age of twenty-one, but it has a smaller percentage of juvenile offenders than either the lower-middle or lower-lower classes.

The Level Below The Common Man

The sex ratio of the lower-lower class is not like that of any other in Yankee City. It is the only class in which men are more numerous than women (52.83 per cent males). It is the exact opposite of the upper-upper class. The lower-lower class has the highest percentage of children in its population of all classes. It also has the smallest percentage of people over sixty years of age. It is most like the two other lower classes in this respect and least like the upper three. The lower-lower class is most like the upper-lower for its large number of people with ethnic affiliations. All the Negroes, about nine-tenths of the Poles, seven-tenths of the Russians, more than half the Greeks and slightly less than half of the French Canadians and the Italians are in the lower-lower class. But only one-third of the Armenians, one-tenth of the Irish, and one-fourteenth of the Jews are in this class.

Approximately 70 per cent of the lower-lower class were born in the United States, in which respect it is most like the upper-lower and least like the upper-upper class. Forty-five per cent of the lower-lower class were born in or near Yankee City. It is most like the upper-lower class for the region of birth of its members.

The members of the lower-lower class marry earlier than those of any other class. They are most like the upper-lower and least like the upper-upper class for age at marriage. Over 35 per cent of lower-lower marriages were under twenty-one years of age. Although in general the lower-lower class is like all other classes for the age differences between spouses, the men of this class show a greater preference for women younger than themselves, and a smaller percentage married older women than any other class. A slightly larger percentage of this class was married than of any other class.

Most of those who work for a living are in semiskilled occupations. This class has a higher percentage of the semiskilled and of the unskilled than any other class. There is a larger percentage of skilled people in the upper-middle, lower-middle, and upper-lower classes than in this one. In its choice of occupations, the lower-lower class is most like the upper-lower class. Members of the lower-lower class are employed in significantly high numbers in the shoe and hat factories and in transport. Two-thirds of all clammers are in the lower-lower class. This class contains a significantly low percentage of workers in retail and business enterprises and in the silverware factory.

The lower-lower class has the largest percentage of unemployed of all six classes. A greater percentage of this class than of any other class has only part-time employment. About one out of every three people in this class is on relief, and the lower-lower class contains over 65 per cent of the total relief population of Yankee City.

Less than 6 per cent of the members of the lower-lower class own their own homes. They diverge from all other classes in this respect but are nearest the upper-lower class. The value of their homes is also less than that of all other classes, in which respect they are most like the upper-lower and least like the lower-upper class. The members of the lower-lower class own less property than those of any other class and are most like those of the upper-lower class in the value of property owned. The lower-lower class pays the smallest rentals in Yankee City, and it is the only class which is significantly low for paying rent by the month.

The lower-lower class has a larger percentage of small houses and a smaller percentage of large houses than any other class. Only the upper-upper class is below it in the occupancy of medium-sized houses. The lower-lower class occupies a larger percentage of bad houses and a smaller percentage of good houses than any other class. In general, the lower-lower class most resembles the upper-lower in condition of house. The lower-lower class lives in significantly high numbers in business buildings, in small houses in bad repair, in medium-sized houses in bad repair, and in large houses in poor condition. The houses in which the lower-lower class reside are located in significantly high numbers in Middletown, Downtown, Riverbrook, and Uptown, and in significantly low numbers in Hill Street, Centerville, Homeville, Newtown, and Oldtown. The lower-lower class is most like the upper-lower in dwelling areas and least like the upper-upper.

The members of the lower-lower class form a high percentage of those who join male fraternities of the nonauxiliary type. They also join female fraternities with auxiliaries and age-graded associations. They avoid, or are prevented from joining, female social clubs, charitable and economic associations. Their associational behavior is most like that of the upper-lower class and least like that of the two upper classes.

The police arrest the members of the lower-lower class more frequently than any others in the community. As we said earlier, 65 per cent of those arrested in Yankee City are from this class, and approximately 11 per cent of its members have been arrested. By way of comparison, about one out of every three people in the lower-lower class, three out of a hundred in the upper-lower class, one out of a hundred in the upper-upper and lower-middle classes, and still fewer in the lower-upper and upper-middle classes have been arrested. About one-fourth of those arrested in the lower-lower class are below eighteen years of age, and about 33 per cent are below twenty-one. The lower-lower class has not sufficient power to protect its young from the police.

The members of the lower-lower class are affiliated in significantly high numbers with the Presbyterian, Methodist, and Baptist churches, one of the Congregational churches, and the two Catholic churches. They avoid the Episcopal, Unitarian, and two Congregational churches located in middle-and upper-class areas.

Approximately three-fourths of the high school children of the lower-lower class are enrolled in commercial and general courses, and of these, 54 per cent are in commercial courses. Only 12 per cent are enrolled in the Latin and 14 per cent in the scientific courses. A larger percentage of the lower-lower children work, and more of them go to work before sixteen than do those of any other class. They are in this respect most like the upper-lower class.

Part II. Transition: The Corporation and the Factory in the Community

Introduction

DURING the field research a great strike broke out. All the workers in the shoe factories quit their jobs, joined a union, and through union intervention defeated management. To find out the meaning and significance of what happened in this crisis, we studied the structure of the factories and corporate enterprise. Research was done on the history of the city's economic life from the early 1600's until the strike. Special attention was given to the development of the great shoe corporations and the loss of local control to the big cities. The breakdown of the skill hierarchy and the effect of this on the workers and the city became apparent. The movement of the city's separate life into the larger American society and the loss of part of its autonomy are reported in the next several chapters. The emergence of what appears to be the great society which includes all of America is indicated.

CHAPTER 9

From Clippers to Textiles to Shoes

The Industrial History of Yankee City

WHEN we explore the social and industrial history of Yankee City, moving back through the years marked by the beginning of industrial capitalism and through the brilliant years of the clipper ship era to the simple folk economy of the earliest community—noticing how an earlier phase of the constantly changing society limits and molds the succeeding ones—it becomes certain that some of the knowledge necessary for explaining the strike can be, and must be, obtained by this scientific process. Furthermore, we see very clearly the times when certain necessary factors which explain the strike appear in the life of the town and how, in conjunction with other causes, their gradual evolution made the strike inevitable. It also becomes abundantly clear that the Yankee City strike was not a unique event but must be treated as representative of a type and that this type is almost certainly worldwide in its importance and significance.

The town began in 1635. The colonial settlers of Yankee City, having been tenant farmers in England, founded an agricultural community. For several generations thereafter the colonists continued to perpetuate social and economic patterns essentially similar to those in which they had participated in the motherland; their rural agricultural life centered around the political institution of the town and the religious institution of the church. As in the case of all societies recently transplanted,

the community was beset with threats to its existence, both
internal and external, and met them by close adherence to
traditional modes of life.

The commercial advantages of a location on the river bank
were recognized, and the present town site was laid out. According to the records, the first wharf in Yankee City was built
in 1655. By 1700, interest in commercial enterprises had
grown to such an extent that the land along the river, hitherto
held in common, was divided into water lots. Maritime commerce was seriously affected by the Revolution, but in the following period, between 1785 and the War of 1812, it revived
and the city prospered greatly as a shipping center. The difficulties between France and England following the French Revolution made it possible for American vessels to take over much
of the European carrying-trade; Yankee City ships cruised the
Atlantic from Baltic ports on the north to the Gold Coast on
the south. The economy of the city remained predominantly
maritime from the War of 1812 down to the decade of the
1870's. Our local historian records that on one day in this
period, a fleet of forty vessels, detained for weeks by easterly
winds, set sail from Yankee City. Shipping and shipbuilding
reached their apex between the years 1820 and 1865; in the
single year of 1854 seventeen new vessels were launched from
local shipyards. The rich mythology centering around the exploits of Yankee City ships refers in large part to this glorious
period.

Fishing, likewise, reached its greatest importance to Yankee
City in the first half of the nineteenth century. Yankee City's
historian tells us: "In 1851 there were ninety vessels, measuring
6090 tons, and carrying 985 men, engaged in fishing on the
banks of Newfoundland and the coast of Labrador." Within
twenty years the number of fishing vessels had declined to thirty
and by the turn of the century only a handful of small fishing
craft remained. Today the only representatives of that calling
are a group of clammers.

The causes of the decline of Yankee City's maritime trade
after the middle of the nineteenth century were technological,

economic, and geographic. Steam engines were gradually replacing sails, and the increasing size and draft of both sail and steam ships necessitated the use of larger and deeper harbors than that of Yankee City. In addition, improvements in inland transportation made coastwise transportation less important.

Industrial developments as early as the eighteenth century had set the stage for the decline in Yankee City's maritime enterprise. Some of the more farsighted merchants, realizing that the heyday of shipping could not continue indefinitely, began to promote industrial ventures. Yankee City, in its early days, had depended upon England for most of its manufactured goods. During the eighteenth century it began to rely in part upon its own craftsmen, and family enterprises were moved into separate shops. The Yankee City shoe industry can be traced to just such an origin.

As a result of the downward spiral of their maritime commerce after 1850, Yankee City's citizens were again forced landward for their livelihoods, even as their ancestors had been before the days of maritime glory. Cities along the upper river furnished the cue for this change. By harnessing waterpower for industrial purposes, they had already surpassed Yankee City in size. Yankee City had no such natural advantages for development; it had no rapids or falls for waterpower, no tradition of organized industry, and was farther away from the denser population centers than the cities up the river. Although Yankee City set out to adapt itself as best it could to the industrial patterns of nearby communities, it met with only limited success.

From a simple and undifferentiated society, there developed in Yankee City the type of economic life with which standard histories of New England have made us familiar. During the era of shipbuilding, shipping, and fishing, a great number of handicrafts also developed. These included such primary industries as wood-carving, cordage-making, carpentering, blacksmithing, and sail-making. During the winter months the fishermen of Yankee City, as of other New England towns, made shoes. The women manufactured wool and cotton garments within the household. During the nineteenth century, numerous other independent crafts appeared, such as silversmithing, comb-making, leather-tanning, and carriage-building. The most important industry in view of its later development, however, was the manufacture of shoes.

Apprenticeship functioned in the handicraft system of the eighteenth and most of the nineteenth centuries as our trade, engineering, art, and professional schools do in our industrial system today. It was society's educational device for transforming its youth from the "green," unproductive stage to the stage of full economic maturity as master craftsmen. From a history of comb-making, an important craft in Yankee City during the last half of the eighteenth and the first half of the nineteenth centuries, we have the following description of the institution of apprenticeship:

> As in most of the handicraft trades the apprentice system was the only entry to comb-making. Its rigorous requirements approached the border line of slavery, for it bound one by legal indenture to serve and obey a master and to be faithful to him in all things. Usually he was allowed two terms of schooling, each three months long. He must not be out after nine, should attend church twice on Sunday and spend Saturday evening preparing for Sunday school. . . . Some of the more generous employers gave their apprentices thirty dollars a year with which to buy clothes. . . . The indenture that bound the apprentice to certain duties also bound the master to certain obligations. He must treat his apprentice kindly, look after his moral character and give him what was known as a freedom suit at his majority.

In the various industries machine methods slowly evolved out of tools and techniques centuries old. Comb-making, in which Yankee City led the country until the middle of the nineteenth century, again offers an example. The first comb establishment in Yankee City and in the country was opened in 1759, using strictly handicraft methods of manufacture. In

1798, the first hand machine to make combs was patented. It was fully forty years later that a comb-making machine run by steam power made its appearance in Yankee City. The first steam-run comb factory was opened in Yankee City in 1842; and in the same year two large "steam mills" for the manufacture of cotton textiles were built. In the next decade there appeared the following establishments: one lace factory, twenty-three comb shops, one woolen yarn factory, one machine shop, one iron foundry, four silver factories, one hosiery factory, and one chair manufactory.

The development of the factory system in Yankee City had three phases, each defined by the dominant industry of the respective periods: comb, textile, and boot and shoe. The comb craft had been founded and developed in Yankee City, and by 1840 there were more than one hundred persons employed in comb manufacturing. During the next five years, seven of the establishments moved to another New England town, which has since become the comb manufacturing center of the country. After 1845 the Yankee City comb industry declined in importance while that of the other town grew. By 1883 only three comb factories remained in Yankee City; by 1893 there were but two; and in 1919, only one—the factory which had been established by the eighteenth-century founder of the craft. Even this succumbed during the depression of 1929-33.

The textile industry was developed during the decade when the comb industry began to decline. This defines the opening of the second phase, which covered roughly the period between 1845 and 1890. The cotton mills never numbered more than five, but in 1853 they employed 1,530 people. The last mill closed in 1930. Two of the remaining mills in this last period moved to the South as part of the general movement of the textile industry out of New England.

As the textile industry lost importance in the economy of Yankee City, shoe manufacturing took its place and employed the major part of the industrial workers. In 1865, there were four shoe shops employing in all about 110 hands. By 1890, about two thousand were employed in the shoe industry, most of them in one factory. This figure of two thousand remained approximately the maximum of employees in the city's shoe industry. During the last seventy years, over forty shoe manufacturing companies have been organized and put into operation in Yankee City, some as reorganizations of units previously operating. In 1945 three shoe factories were in regular operation. These figures indicate both the high mortality rate among the shoe factories and the struggle of the community to maintain its status as an industrial city.

From Cobbler's Bench to Assembly Line

During the first years of the settlement of Yankee City and New England and in the earliest phase of shoemaking, families made their own shoes. The second phase of the first stage was characterized by the itinerant shoemaker who, owning his own tools, made shoes in the kitchen of his customer, using materials supplied by the customer. In the process, the shoemaker was assisted by his customer's family and received his compensation largely in the form of board and lodging. Many families in Yankee City and in the outlying communities, particularly those dwelling on the north bank of the river, became proficient in the art of shoemaking at this stage. They made their own shoes during the winter months, passing down the art in the home from generation to generation. This section of New England has, therefore, a strong tradition of shoemaking.

The next stage began (*circa* 1760) when the shoemaker set up a small shop and made shoes to order for his local customers. These shops were known as "the ten-foot shops," and the customer's order was known as "bespoke." During the first part of this period, the shoemaker still made the complete shoe, but his relation with the market became indirect. The entrepreneur appeared. He was a capitalist shoemaker, hiring workers in their homes to make boots and shoes for him to sell at retail or wholesale. In the second phase of the period the central shop developed where materials were sorted. The parts were cut in the shop, distributed and served in the homes, then collected and the soles joined to the uppers in the shop. Machines were used scarcely at all. The processes of shoemaking were divided, and workmen specialized in one or more operations. Jobs were thus defined within the industry; for the most part, the worker no longer faced his customers.

During this period the market remained local, and the interests of the merchant-master and the journeyman were the same. When improved land and water transportation brought about an expansion of the market, the merchant became an increasingly dominant figure. The bargain became one of price as well as quality, and the interest of the merchant to produce cheaply in order to undersell competitors began to conflict with the maker's desire to earn as much as he could from his labor.

Professor John R. Commons, in an article entitled "American Shoemakers 1648-1895,"[1] traced the evolution of the industry in this country from court records of cases involving conflicting interests both within and without the industry. He reports that the first guild of shoemakers, known as the "Shoomakers of Boston," was granted a charter of incorporation in October 1648. Since the days of the Shoomakers of Boston other formal organizations have come into existence and left concrete evidence of the various conflicts of interests within the industry.

Before 1852, the menaces to the industry and to the groups within it resulted mainly from the expansion of markets. Until this time all shoes were made by hand, and each craftsman owned his own set of tools. But to meet the increasingly exacting demands of an expanding market, as to both price and quality, it was inevitable that the growing technological knowledge would be utilized to mechanize some phases of shoe manufacture. In 1852 a sewing machine for stitching uppers was invented, and the following decade saw the mechanization of many other processes. This development intensified the split in interests between the owner-control group and the operatives; it also established the subordinate position of the latter, which they have occupied ever since. Accelerated mechanization of

1. In *Quarterly Journal of Economics*, XXIV, No. 1 (Nov. 1909), 39-84.

the industry in the decades after the Civil War occasioned changes in the social structure of the shoe factory.

[One of the most important results of the introduction of machinery into shoemaking was the enormous decrease in labor costs.] The cost per one hundred pairs was reduced by the machine to well under one-tenth of the costs of 1850, and the average labor cost in 1932, we were told, had dropped to forty cents per pair. Another result was the great potential increase in production. For example, an expert hand-laster produced fifty pairs a day; a lasting machine, from three hundred to seven hundred a day. A welt machine is fifty-four times as fast as welt sewing by awl and needle. The introduction of machines into shoemaking converted it from a strictly hand trade to one of the most specialized of machine industries. The position of labor was greatly modified by the technical revolution. The product has changed only in detail, but the process of manufacture has changed from a single skilled trade, carried on by a craftsman from start to finish, to one of two to three thousand operations in greater part done by machine.

The security of the workers as craftsmen was threatened by the new developments. The shoe workers did not make the machines they were suddenly forced to operate, and they had no way of predicting what jobs would next be mechanized. The owning group had in the machines an effective weapon to lessen the value of the worker's craftsmanship.

Out of this situation arose the Knights of St. Crispin, active from 1868–72, the most powerful labor organization known up to that time and probably the most important one previous to the modern labor unions. The Knights were organized to protest against the substitution of many "green hands" for the old-time craftsmen, which was made possible by the new use of machines. It was a violent protest, but its life was short.

Since the collapse of the Knights of St. Crispin there have been few effective labor organizations among New England shoe operatives and none in Yankee City until the strike of 1933. Mechanization, however, did not cease, and with it went the subordination of the workers. Several complete processes of shoemaking were standardized in the course of time. One of them was the "turn" process, particularly adapted to the manufacture of high-quality women's shoes. This process, one of the oldest of modern shoe-building techniques, was standard in Yankee City at the time this study was made in 1931–35.

The turn process has given way, in Yankee City as elsewhere, before the inroads of price competition. Cheaper shoes for women are replacing those made by more complicated and costly processes such as the welt, McKay, and turn methods. Cement and lockstitch processes were evolved to produce shoes that could be sold at a lower retail price. These changes also permit great factory flexibility in adjusting to style variations, an important consideration to the modern manufacturer of women's shoes. The rapidity with which styles change has created rush work demands, necessitating speed in manufacturing processes and a quick and ready adaptability to change. When an order is received, the factory must push production so that the order may be completed before the style changes. With the changing styles, there is a decreasing demand for standardized types of shoes. The result is alternation between rush work and lay-offs. This trend in the manufacture of women's shoes induces a greater than average fluctuation in employment and has contributed to the instability of employment in Yankee City shoe factories.

Another factor in the instability of the shoe factories is the practice of leasing machines. The leasing system was first introduced by Gordon McKay in 1861 and was continued by the larger shoe-machinery companies. The machine manufacturers adopted a royalty system in which the rates per unit of output were the same to both large and small manufacturers. This worked to the disadvantage of the former, who preferred a sliding scale. The small entrepreneur who had been attracted by this feature of shoe manufacture seldom had sufficient capital investment to insure success. The relatively small initial cost of establishing shoe factories resulted in a high mortality among these enterprises.

With the development of a large market in the West and

South, the shoe industry has moved many of its production units away from the New England states and closer to the markets. One entire NRA hearing in January 1935 was devoted to a study of the migration of the boot and shoe industry from Massachusetts, and showed that state's share in the national production of shoes to have declined from 47.13 per cent in 1899 to 20.05 per cent in 1934, while its volume of production had diminished—in spite of the increase in national production —from 102 million pairs in 1899 to 71 million in 1934. Some of the important factors contributing to the migration of the shoe industry were the following:

1) labor disturbances;

2) the necessity to reduce manufacturing expenses and obtain lower labor cost, in order to meet severe price competition;

3) the location of manufacturing plants in or near the principal markets;

4) inducements offered to Massachusetts manufacturers by cities and towns located in other states to move to their localities. Such inducements take the form of freedom from taxes, free rent, donations of factory sites and/or property, and, frequently, cash subsidies.

The conditions we have described (national, state, and local) have placed the Yankee City shoe worker in a precarious position. Changing methods of production and the vicissitudes of the trade itself have led to instability among shoe-manufacturing enterprises. Yankee City is in no position to absorb the output of its factories, and the latter have become more and more dependent on the large chain stores for retail distribution. The number of shoe companies operating in Yankee City and the number of employees have varied from year to year. In 1929, sixteen shoe factories were operating in Yankee City— the largest number operating at one time. The peak in actual employment was reached in 1926, when 2,060 individuals were employed in the shoe factories in the city.

The shoe industry, not only in Yankee City but throughout the country, was one of the first to suffer before the general depression of 1929, showing a decline from a 1923 peak in value of product. During the period of high production, the shoe workers were in a position to dictate their own wages, but during the period of decreasing employment the manufacturers held the dominant position in the internal factory organization and gradually forced down the price of labor.

This pressure, deriving ultimately from retail-price competition, stimulated a concentrated effort on the part of the workers to organize in order that they might resist the manufacturers' desire to reduce costs by reducing wages.

The Strike and the Evolving Social and Economic Systems

Before we ask ourselves what this economic history has told us about the causes of the strike, let us re-assess our findings. We have spoken of an economic history. However, we do not have one history but several—at least six histories can be traced. We can conveniently divide the technological history of Yankee City's shoe industry into five phases (see Fig. 9). At least two important stories are to be found here; the tools change from a few basic ones entirely hand-used to machines in an assembly line, and the product from a single pair of shoes to tens of thousands in mass production.

The changes in the form of division of labor are another story of the utmost importance.[2] In the beginning, the family made its own shoes, or a high-skilled artisan, the cobbler, made shoes for the family. In time, several families divided the high-skilled jobs among themselves, and later one man assigned the skilled jobs to a few men and their families. Ultimately, a central factory developed and the jobs were divided into a large number of systematized low-skilled jobs. The history of ownership and control is correlated with the changes in the division of labor. In early days, tools, skills, and materials were possessed by the family; eventually, the materials were supplied by the owner-manager, and soon he also owned the tools and machines. The sequence of development of producer-consumer

2. The sequences in the vertical columns of Figure 9 are exactly ordered; the horizontal interrelations are approximations and indicate basic trends.

Fig. 9 The History of the Differentiation of the Yankee City Shoe Industry

	Technology	Form of Division of Labor	Form of Ownership and Control	Producer - Consumer Relations	Worker Relations	Structure of Economic Relations
IV The Present (1920-1945)	*Machine tools:* mass production, assembly line methods	Nearly all jobs low skilled; a very large number of routinized jobs	*Outside* ownership and control of the f a c t o r y (t o o l s leased)	Very few retail outlets; factory merely one source of supply for a chain of shoe stores	Rise of industrial unions, state supervised. No (or weak) unions	Center of dominance New York. Very complex financial, producer, and retail structure. Local factory not important in it
III Late Intermediate Period (approximately to World War I)	*Machine tools:* machines predominate; beginning of mass production through use of the machine (McKay)	A central factory with machines; still high degree of skill in many jobs	First small and later large *local* men of wealth own or lease the tools and machines	National market and local capitalist; many outlets	Craft and apprenticeship (St. Crispin's Union)	Center of dominance local factory; complex hierarchy in local factory system
II Early Intermediate Period (approximately to the Civil War)	*Machine tools:* few machines, first application (Elias Howe, etc.)	One man assigns highly skilled jobs to few men; highly skilled craftsmen ("letting - out" system)	Small, locally controlled manufacturers; tools still owned by workers, materials controlled by "owner"	Owner and salesmen to the consumer regional market	Informal, apprenticeship and craft relations	Simple economic, no longer kinship; worker subordinate to manager
	Hand tools: increasing specialization and accumulation of hand tools	Specialization among several families; a few highly skilled jobs	*Local control:* not all shoemakers need own all tools; beginning of specialization	*Local* buyer from producer several families sells products (no central factory)	Kinship and neighbors among workers	Semi - economic but also kinship and neighborliness
I The Beginning (early 1600's)	*Hand tools:* few, basic, and simple	All productive skills in the family, including making of shoes; a few cobblers for the local market	*Local control:* skills, tools, and materials owned and controlled by each family; or by the local cobbler	The family produces and consumes shoes and most other products	Largely kinship and family relations among workers	Very simple non-economic; the immediate family

relations tells a similar story. The family produced and consumed its shoes all within the circle of its simple unit. Then, the local community was the consumer-producer unit, and ultimately the market became national and even worldwide. Worker relations changed from those of kinship and family ties to those of occupation where apprenticeship and craftsmanship relations were superseded and the individual unit became dominant in organizing the affairs of the workers. The structure of economic relations changed from the immediate family into a local hierarchy and the locally owned factory into a vast, complex system owned, managed, and dominated by New York City.

With these several histories in mind (and with the help of Fig. 9), let us ask ourselves what would have happened if the strike had taken place in each of the several periods. In period one, with a family-producing and consuming economy, it is obvious that such a conflict would have been impossible. The social system had not evolved to sufficient complexity; the forces had not been born which were to oppose each other in civil strife. In the second phase, several families in a neighborhood might have quarreled, but it is only in one's imagination that one could conceive of civil strife among the shoemakers.

In the third phase, however, there appears a new social personality, and an older one begins to take on a new form and assume a new place in the community. The capitalist is born and during the several periods which follow he develops into full maturity. Meanwhile the worker loses control and management of his time and skills and becomes subordinate in a hierarchy. There are, thus, distinct and opposing forces set up in the shoemaking system. What is good for one is not necessarily good for the other, but the interdependence of the two opposing groups is still very intimate, powerful, and highly necessary. The tools, the skills, and the places of manufacture belong to the worker; but the materials, the place of assembly, and the market are now possessed by the manager. Striking is possible but extremely difficult and unlikely.

In the fourth period, full capitalism has been achieved; the manufacturer is now the owner of the tools, the machines, and the industrial plant; he controls the market. The workers have become sufficiently self-conscious and antagonistic to machines to organize into craft unions. Industrial warfare still might prove difficult to start, although it did occur, because in a small city where most people know each other the owner or manager more often than not knows "his help" and they know him. The close relation between the two often implies greater compatibility and understanding, which cut down the likelihood of conflict. But when strikes do occur the resulting civil strife is likely to be bitter because it is in the confines of the community.

In the last period, the capitalist has become the supercapitalist; the workers have forgotten their pride in their separate jobs, dismissed the small differences among themselves, and united in one industrial union with tens and hundreds of thousands of workers throughout the country combining their strength to assert their interests against management. In such a social setting strikes are inevitable. The remaining chapters will fully demonstrate this proposition about contemporary industrial America.

Technological change and Organizational change.

CHAPTER 10

The Break in the Skill Hierarchy

Skill and Status

SKILL is generally related to control over objects through the use of tools, simple or complex. Its technological import is recognized by application of the term to persons showing technical ability as distinguished from those whose prestige is derived solely from mental ability. For example, we may speak of a *skilled* surgeon or dentist, but we are more apt to refer to an *able* physician or lawyer. This limited application of the term *skill* is confusing since any technique can demand skill in its performance if an operative has some freedom of choice in the manner in which he performs his task.

Skill is an attribute of a person, but by convention the word is also applied to jobs. The use of the term as an attribute of a job may be confusing. Obviously, a job of itself cannot be skilled. The idea of skill involves its accomplishment; the accomplishment involves an individual. It is the individual who possesses the skill. Strictly speaking, a job cannot even be said to demand skill. The job can be done in some fashion, or at least begun, by an unskillful person. The only definite meaning the term can have in an expression such as "a skilled job" is that the job affords an opportunity for the exercise of skill in its performance. A job is skilled if the person who undertakes it can put his skill to use in its accomplishment.

Although skill is a valuable concept, it is not an easy one to use in comparisons; for it is generally associated with a sequence of actions, and different sequences of actions are not easy to compare unless they happen to be of the same type. An observant foreman is able to make a very fair estimate of the expertness that can be shown in any one type of job under him. Only with difficulty, however, can he make comparisons of the expertness that can be shown in different jobs in his own department.[1] If he compares the expertness that can be displayed in the performance of jobs in his department with that permitted by jobs in other departments, he is usually unable to justify his words by sound reasons.

Technological skill can be considered a measure of the control over objects that a job affords an individual. But before endeavoring to locate a hierarchy of jobs, such as those of shoe workers, on the basis of the skill which their efficient performance would require, we must discover some of the common factors in the expertness allowed by jobs involving different techniques. Then, by using these factors as measuring units, a uniform basis of comparison may be set up which is applicable to all such jobs in the factory.

Within limitations, a skillful person chooses what to do, decides how to do it, and then does it dexterously. Selecting and deciding plus dexterity in accomplishment are characteristics of skill. We shall apply the term "high skill" to jobs permitting the exercise of judgment and the making of decisions as well as dexterous accomplishment. A job is high skilled to the extent that it permits freedom of choice to the worker and necessitates, for its efficient performance, reasoned selection from different modes of action. Further, we shall designate as "low skilled" those jobs of a routine nature in which the worker functions according to a set pattern that is definitely prescribed but may be executed with dexterity. Those jobs which are to a large extent prescribed but which still permit some freedom of choice to the worker we will term "medium skilled." No type of skill can be measured satisfactorily in terms of another type.

1. In interviews, a stitching room foreman, a factory executive, and a union official selected from the numerous jobs in the stitching departments the same four jobs as the most skilled; but each person interviewed advocated a different ranking among the four.

In the days when shoemaking was a handicraft there was a highly developed hierarchy of jobs based on skill. The hierarchy, moreover, was functionally arranged so that a raw apprenctice entering upon his training period performed low-skilled jobs and worked at them until he gained some degree of proficiency. In these jobs he began to train his hand and eye so that when he had mastered the low-skilled jobs he was prepared to begin learning the medium-skilled ones. Gaining proficiency in these journeymen jobs, in turn, prepared him to undertake the high-skilled jobs of the master craftsman. When he had attained proficiency in the high-skilled jobs he was a master shoemaker and stood at the top of a technological hierarchy where great prestige was attached and where he was economically secure because the services of master shoemakers were always in demand and the supply was limited because of the long period of training required to attain the position of a proficient master craftsman. Also, when a man achieved high status in the technological hierarchy he acquired supervisory status as well, for master craftsmen were also working bosses, overseeing the work of those lower in the hierarchy.

The situation of the individual technological worker in a modern turn-shoe factory is quite different from all this, we discovered. No longer is it possible for him to start in low-skilled jobs and progressively prepare himself for higher-skilled jobs. The loss of this opportunity to the worker is mainly attributable to two related trends in modern shoe manufacture. One is the tendency toward greater and greater division of labor, which means that individual jobs are broken into two or more components which are thereafter performed by different individuals. The other trend is toward increasing mechanization of the technological processes, which tends more and more to make the workman perform routine operations. These developments are interrelated and reinforce one another.

Watching the shoe operatives working in the techniques of shoemaking, we could not fail to recognize that as new machines were installed in the factory more and more of the tool-using function of the operatives was absorbed by the machine and the job of the operative became more and more routinized. Real craftsmanship lost its usefulness as the operatives who had had much freedom of action in tool-using techniques were forced to conform to a set pattern of behavior attuned to the rhythm and tempo of the machine.

It stood out in clear relief that when a machine is built it becomes a mechanical device which of itself has no social value. The social value of a machine is derived from its use. The inventor of a machine in reality invents a mechanical process in which a machine and an operator interact in a prescribed way. The inventor of the process defines the working behavior of the operative in his relation to the machine. To a large extent, the operative is denied freedom of choice in his actions. The denial of opportunity for the use of any creative initiative by workers, bound so closely to their machines in their daily tasks, has had a marked effect upon the operatives.

The relation between an operative and the machine at which he works may be called a mechanical relation—in essence it is not a social relation at all. But when the operative's working behavior is almost completely controlled by the functioning of the machine he serves his attitudes toward it are likely to change. Instead of regarding the machine as merely a mechanical object, part of the factory equipment, the worker tends to assume a proprietary attitude toward it, to refer to it as "my machine," etc.[2] Not only does the worker develop proprietary attitudes toward the machine, but he tends to personify it and to develop quasi-social attitudes toward it. These various sentiments on the part of the worker tend to integrate him closer and closer to the machine at which he works.

Anything that disrupts his integration with his machine or

---

2. A foreman described an incident illustrating this point. A girl who operated a machine had been sick for a time and had not been able to work. The foreman said: "Of course I put another girl on the machine she used. She came back and said, 'Where is my machine?' I said, 'Your machine? Did you buy it? Maybe you would like to. Maybe you could buy the factory, too. What do you mean, your machine? You were out sick, weren't you? You take the machine I give you.'"

the technique of operating it is likely to be most unwelcome to the worker. Even changes intended to increase his comfort or safety often arouse his indignation. This is probably because, since the worker learns how to operate his machine merely by practicing, and any change in the simple routinized technique requires re-learning on his part, such a change seems to the worker to threaten his security and may, in fact, actually do so. At times, a considerable part of the friction between operatives and management in a modern shoe factory springs from this source. Workers' reactions to innovations are frequently surcharged with emotions that are incomprehensible to management.

The attitude of the worker that he is socially integrated with his machine probably tends to change the character of his social relations with other workers during working hours. We further observed that operatives working on machines had far less opportunity to converse with their co-workers than operatives working alongside each other at benches or tables. Even though the spatial distance between operatives may be small, as in the case of the operatives of sewing machines in the stitching department, the exactitude of the demands of the machine precludes conversation while working. As soon as the bell rings for noon hour or at the end of the working day the stitching room reverberates with voices of machine operatives.

The operatives of the larger machines in other parts of the factory are sufficiently apart from their co-workers to make conversation impossible. All this is in marked contrast to the continual hum of conversation noticeable among all bench or table workers engaged in hand operations.

The work of the latter may be in many cases simple and monotonous, but the freedom to converse may relieve much of the strain from the work and make it less exacting. Thus, the noise many machines make and the spatial isolation of workers that is a frequent result of mechanization both contribute to the social isolation of workers during working hours. The effect of this is to prevent social solidarities from developing between workers or to lessen whatever solidarity has formed prior to mechanization. Mechanization is, for this reason and others we shall mention shortly, valuable to management as a means of control over workers. While machine processes were adopted by shoe factories primarily to reduce costs and to speed the processing, the machine has other great advantages over the human worker from the managerial point of view: its performance (barring breakdowns) can be predicted with certainty, and a machine presents no problems of a disciplinary nature. The forces which govern human behavior are little known, and the maintenance of productive activity is always more or less problematical when management has to deal with socially integrated groups of workers. Control problems are simplified, therefore, on two counts through mechanization: (1) machines are easier to control than human beings and (2) mechanization tends to disrupt the social solidarity of the workers, who thereby become easier to control than they would be if they were able to maintain close social relations during working hours.

One of the specific points at which worker-management relations are most directly affected by mechanization is in the relations between workers and their immediate superiors, the departmental foremen. With the establishment of the set pattern of working behavior which results from mechanization, the foreman does not need to be a working boss interested in improving the technical ability of the shoe worker. In the handicraft days journeymen or master shoemakers directed the activities of apprentices and corrected their errors, instructing them in the craft of shoemaking. The foreman of a mechanized department in today's shoe factory need not have had long training in shoemaking techniques in order to supervise simple mechanized operations. He can be selected by management purely for his ability to enforce a prescribed, set pattern of working behavior. Sometimes men are even taken from other industries to be foremen in the shoe factories. This new relation between workers and their supervisors accentuates the division of interest between the two groups. Workers today tend to feel, with considerable justification, that even their immediate superiors may not understand or care about them. The social situation is quite different from the one that existed when the technological worker's boss was a man who had always followed the same course as his subordinate until, after years of training, he had become a master shoemaker.

Moreover, in the handicraft days every man learning the shoe trade could look forward with justifiable hope to the day when he might be a working boss himself. With the advent of mechanization, however, the changed nature of the relations between worker and foreman has largely destroyed the worker's chances of getting into the supervisory hierarchy. As a machine operator he has little chance to train himself in the techniques necessary to a modern foreman. Even if he were capable of doing a foreman's job, he has no opportunity to demonstrate the fact. The modern operative is virtually condemned to seek his security and his working prestige strictly in the working techniques.

The machine operator's chances of enhancing his prestige or his security through his technological ability are very small in the modern shoe factory. Nearly all the machine jobs entail the set pattern of working behavior which characterizes the low-skilled job. Some individual operatives become surprisingly expert at their low-skilled jobs, spurred on to speed by the piece-work basis of pay. But greater proficiency in one mechanized, low-skilled job does not prepare the modern worker to do any other mechanized job. Even if it did, the fact would be of little value to the operative because the job for which he might prepare himself would be another of low skill, offering no greater security, pay, or prestige than before. There is, in other words, no skill hierarchy in the mechanized processes of the modern shoe factory through which an operative may progress as his abilities develop. In addition, there is the constant threat to the operative's security that the machine process at which he has attained proficiency may be discontinued in favor of some other process; he has no control over such technological changes. Again, even at best, nothing but a few days' or a few weeks' practice protects a proficient operator in one of the simpler machine jobs from the large group of unqualified workers who seek employment. All of these factors tend to increase the subordination of the individual worker to management; from the management viewpoint they are valuable means of social control over workers.

Low-skilled jobs in the factory are not limited to machine jobs. Hand operations, too, through the great division of labor which has taken place in modern shoe manufacturing, have in many cases been split into simple, standardized operations. So far has this division gone that no technological jobs remain, either hand or machine, which by our classification could be rated as higher than medium-skilled; the great bulk of jobs belong definitely in the low-skill category. Fig. 10 graphically

Fig. 10. *The Leveling of Technological Jobs*

Hierarchical arrangement of jobs in the days of handicraft shoemaking. The individual's security and prestige increased as he progressed upward from job A to job D.

The common level of nearly all technological jobs today, showing the breaking up of each old job into several simple ones (division of labor). Modern operatives are nearly all at the same low level of prestige and security because there is little difference in either of these respects between any of the jobs from A^1 to D^4.

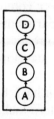

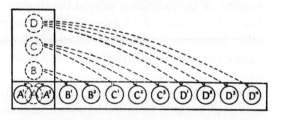

The upward pointing arrows imply the preparation an individual got by working in one job for doing the next higher job in the hierarchy.

The lack of arrows connecting the jobs A^1 to D^4 implies that working in one job does not prepare the modern operative to do any other job.

shows the leveling of jobs that has occurred through the division of labor and mechanization.

Social Effects of the Break

What, then, has become of technological skill in shoemaking? With the constant demand for better shoes at lower prices there would seem to be need for greater creative effort and manufacturing flexibility than ever before. This would, in turn, suggest that there should be more high-skilled jobs in shoe manufacture than ever before. The answer is that these high-skilled jobs do exist—they may even be of a higher order of skill than master-craftsman jobs in the handicraft days—but they are *not* to be found in the shoe factories today. They exist in allied industries—the manufacture of shoe machinery, for example. Designers and engineers invent new and cheaper ways to make shoes and design machines to perform the new processes. Since the shoe-factory workers holding high-skilled jobs are a potential threat to management's control of shoe operatives, inventors apparently are encouraged to break down complex jobs into series of simple, easily standardized operations. An important result of their work, therefore, is to eliminate more and more of the skilled jobs from shoemaking, tending to accelerate the leveling of technological jobs in the shoe factory to a common low order of skill. To a lesser extent, research departments in other industries (chemistry is a case in point) also reduce the number of high-skilled jobs in the shoe factories by developing new substances which simplify shoemaking. Designing departments and the skilled jobs in connection with them have been almost eliminated from modern shoe factories. Pattern makers, whose training is obtained outside the shoe factories, take the place of designers in the factory.

This change in training opportunities offers a clue, of special significance to the social organization of modern shoe factories. All high-skilled jobs require special training of the individuals who hold them: the designers of shoe-manufacturing machinery, for example, are trained in engineering schools; research chemists have special university training; and pattern makers are trained in schools of design. The operative in the shoe factory, on the contrary, has no opportunity to acquire the training that would fit him to hold any one of these high-skilled jobs. Moreover, since the high-skilled jobs connected with the shoe industry are to be found in separate though allied industries, the technological worker in a shoe factory is barred from aspiring to one of them by the interpolation of two managerial hierarchies between his low- or medium-skilled job and the high-skilled job in another company. The management of the shoe-machinery companies directs the making of machines, and the top management of the shoe-manufacturing companies orders the installation of the mechanical process in the shoe factory.

Even the workers in high-skilled jobs, the research men in industries allied to shoemaking, today occupy a position of much greater subordination than that formerly occupied by the master craftsmen in the shoe industry. For, although they have absorbed nearly all of the high technological skill involved in the production of shoes, they have no control over the use of the machines they assist in creating. The machines, new chemical substances, designs for shoes, and all the rest are useless to the inventors until they are sold (or rented) to concerns that manufacture shoes. This transfer from one company to another is carried on between the managerial hierarchies of the two companies; neither the holders of high-skilled jobs in the allied industries nor the holders of low- and medium-skilled jobs in the shoe factories have any control over the agreements made between them.

The gradual elimination of craftsmanship from shoe manufacturing has had far-reaching effects on the type of personnel attracted to technological jobs in the shoe factories, on the type of individuals whom management wants for such jobs, and on the relations between management and worker. The limitations that have been placed on working behavior restrict the worker in making any satisfying use of his individual mental or manual abilities. Workers ambitious for individual betterment are frequently frustrated in the shoe factories of today. This often makes them discontented and critical of superiors. Educated persons particularly are prone to such discontent. Management is aware of this and attempts to overcome the difficulty by discriminating against educated persons who seek technological jobs. Some foremen (who frequently do their own hiring and firing) are quite conscious of their own discrimination. One of them said: "We don't want educated workers. Educated workers are no good." Management wants workers who will do simple unskilled jobs without questioning the authority of superiors.

Nevertheless, an effort is still made by management and workers to rank technological jobs in a status hierarchy. Management feels a need for such ranking in order to justify wage differentials in various technological jobs; and operatives cling to the ideology that theirs is a skilled craft. This traditional view of the latter is flattering to self-respect, giving the workers a sense of pseudo-security and prestige. It is an attitude they find hard to relinquish even though reason shows it to be obsolete. The workers' view of shoemaking as a skilled craft does not require them to regard all factory jobs as skilled. Certain jobs only, the modern equivalents of formerly high-skilled jobs, still wear this aura of high prestige among workers, though often the skill differentials have actually diminished to the vanishing point.

We found a positive correlation between some of the lowest-skilled jobs and the low pay and low prestige of the jobs. All the jobs in the assembling department and most of those in the packing department, for instance, consisted of the simplest sorts of object handling. Most of such jobs are on a time basis of pay. Hourly earnings for men in both departments (excluding the treers in the finishing department) were about 20 cents per hour below the factory average (for men) of 59.5 cents per hour. Jobs in some other departments, such as leather heeling and most of the finishing, were about average for the factory in complexity and skill and also approximated the factory average in pay.

Some jobs, if not actually classifiable as medium-skilled jobs, at least required care on the part of the operative. On them may depend the ultimate fit and wearing qualities of the shoes. One such job was that of the channelers in the sole-leather department who cut the channels for the Goodyear stitching operation. The pay of the channelers averaged 39 cents an hour above the factory average for men. Goodyear stitching was another important job, since a poorly stitched shoe will neither fit well nor give good wear. Goodyear stitchers were the highest paid of all factory workers, earning nearly twice the average pay for men. Edge-setting and edge-trimming of soles in the finishing department were jobs which required careful work because the rotating knives and oscillating hot irons used in these operations on nearly finished shoes could easily mar or ruin them. Workers holding these jobs averaged a little over 67 cents an hour, about 8 cents above the factory average for men. These jobs were regarded by workers as the most skilled, and the better-than-average rates of pay reflected, in part, management's evaluation of the importance of the jobs.

It is a striking fact that some of the least skilled jobs in the factory, by our classification as well as by the consensus of workers and management, were paid well above the factory average. This was true of jobs in the sole-leather department other than those of the channelers. Although these jobs were repetitive and monotonous, they afforded the workers an opportunity for tremendous speed-up. The sole-leather department, exclusive of channelers, averaged 9 cents per hour more than the factory average for men. Other examples occurred in the stitching department where some of the girls working at extremely simple jobs, such as stamping, earned more than anyone else in the department. Again these were jobs which were capable of great speed-up. Earnings of many of the stitchers, on the other hand, especially fancy stitchers, were low even for women operatives, who averaged in general 20 cents an hour below the average for men. The explanation given for the low pay of stitchers was that styles change so rapidly that the girls could not work up much speed at any one style. Another factor entered here: the speed of stitchers was limited by the tempo of their machines whereas the simpler, higher-paid jobs, like stamping, were often hand operations without mechanical limit on speed-up. Then, too, the stitching operations were so varied that management admitted great difficulty in determining proper basic piece-rates. As a result, there tended to be in this department an inverse relation between complexity of jobs and rates of pay. Some of the lowest-skilled jobs paid the most, and some of the most complex jobs paid the least.

According to community and worker traditions, cutters are the aristocrats of the shoe trade. Actually, cutting is not a particularly skilled job in the factory today because skins are well sorted before they are delivered to the cutting room; therefore, the operatives no longer need the thorough knowledge of leather they once had. Nevertheless, cutting is definitely a higher-skilled job than most sole-leather operations and compares favorably with such highly paid jobs as channeling, Goodyear stitching, and edge-setting and trimming. Despite this fact, cutters averaged in earnings over a cent an hour below the male average. Bases of evaluation other than skill entered into the rate of pay for cutters.

The two remaining jobs in a turn-shoe factory which still require some craftsmanship on the part of operatives are "making" and wood-heeling. Makers, particularly, must be proficient with a greater variety of hand tools and techniques than any other workers in a turn-shoe factory. Moreover, these blacksmiths of the trade perform exceedingly arduous work, and the making operation must be done more carefully now than ever before. Makers formerly could turn out eighty-pairs of shoes a day; but, to match the quality of machine-lasted shoes, their output has been reduced to only about thirty pairs. In spite of all these considerations, the makers earned only 57.8 cents per hour, 1.7 cents less than the factory average for men. The principal explanation for this lay in the disparity between the supply of qualified makers and the demand for their services.

Wood-heeling is a somewhat less skilled job than making; but, except for the makers, wood-heelers had to master more hand techniques and use a greater variety of tools than any

workers in the factory. Wood-heelers' earnings averaged 12.8
cents per hour over the factory average for men and thus correlated with the skill characteristics of their jobs much better
than did makers' earnings. The special explanation for this fact
lay in the solidarity of the workers in this department.

As we have shown, there has been a break in the skill hierarchy in modern shoemaking; shoe factory operatives are
limited to low-, or, at most, medium-skilled jobs in the technological end of shoe manufacturing. This break has come about
through the great division of labor and extensive mechanization
in the shoe industry and through the removal of all high-skilled
jobs connected with shoemaking to the research departments of
allied industries. These same factors have brought about a fundamental change in the social relations between workers and
management. Instead of a working boss (foreman), trained in
a complex technology of shoemaking, and a managerial hierarchy with a similar background, the workers' supervisors are
becoming mere enforcement officers and disciplinarians, forcing set patterns of working behavior on the operatives. This
new relationship accentuates the split in interests between
workers and management. It also tends strongly to prevent
workers from leaving the technological end of shoe manufacturing to enter the supervisory field. Finally, there is confusion
in the value systems of the workers and management for there
is no consistent correlation between skill of job and rate of pay
in the technological jobs of the modern shoe factory.

The Strike and the Break in the Skill Hierarchy

We believe that the break in the skill hierarchy contributed
importantly to the outbreak of the strike, to the course it took,
and, in particular, to the coming of the union. The hierarchy
of crafts which once organized the relations of the workers and
provided a way of life for the shoe workers was really an age-
grade system. Youngsters served their hard apprenticeship and,
as neophytes, learned their task; even more importantly, they
were taught to respect the skills they had learned and those they
looked forward to learning. Above all, they acquired respect

Age-grading and mobility

and admiration for the older men above them who had acquired the skills and who occupied the proud positions of journeymen and master craftsmen. These youngsters aspired to achieve for themselves a similar high position and respect. Each young man, in direct face-to-face interaction with those above him, imitated and learned a way of life while being highly motivated by the strong desire to escape the irksome limitations of his present low position and to attain the higher place where he would have the satisfaction of making his own decisions and possess the prestige and pay consequent to such great eminence. By the time he had learned how to do the things needed to equip himself for advancement, enough time had passed to mature him sufficiently to act the part of a man. There can be little doubt that age factors as well as those of skill determined the time for advancement.

Socialization

During this preliminary period he learned that he was a craftsman, with a particular place in the whole system, and that there were responsibilities and obligations he had to learn which would give him certain rights and privileges. Thus, while he internalized this behavior and all its values and their many subtleties and learned what he was as a man, he became an inextricable member of the honorable fraternity of those who made, and who knew how to make, shoes. In this system, workers and managers were indissolubly interwoven into a common enterprise, with a common set of values. In this system the internal personal structure of workers and managers was made up of very much the same apparatus, and their personalities were reinforced by the social system of shoemaking.

In learning to respect the skill of the master craftsman, the apprentice learned to respect himself. He had security in his job, but he had even greater personal security because he had learned how to respect his job. And because he was a member of an age-graded male fraternity made up of other men like himself who had the knowledge and necessary skills to make shoes, he possessed that feeling of absolute freedom and independence and of being autonomous that comes from being in a discipline. He spent his life acquiring virtue, prestige, and respect, learning as he aged and climbed upward, and at the same time teaching those who were younger than he and who aspired to be like him.

Slowly this way of life degenerated and the machine took the virtue and respect from the worker, at the same time breaking the skill hierarchy which dominated his occupation. There was no longer a period for young men to learn to respect those in the age grade above them and in so doing to become self-respecting workers. The "ladder to the stars" was gone and with it much of the structure of the "American Dream."

When the age-grade structure which organized the male aborigines of Melanesia and North America into a hierarchy of prestige and achievement was broken under the impact of white civilization in many of these societies, the frustrations suffered by those who had once known respect for themselves and others crystallized into aggressive movements or into attempts to abolish the new ways and to retreat into the old and cherished ways of the past. There are many resemblances between what happened to these simple, non-European societies and what happened to the craft hierarchy of Yankee City.

The parallel between Yankee City's age-grade structure and theirs cannot be pushed too far, but certainly the two share obvious characteristics. In the earlier days of the machine, the Knights of St. Crispin was organized and attempted to stop the further introduction of machinery. Most of the members longed for the good old days when there were no machines—when a trained hand and eye did the whole job. These attempts failed and the organization collapsed because it was not adaptive and could not stop the inevitable advance of industrial technology.

When the whole age-grade structure of craftsmanship had almost entirely collapsed and the American shoe worker was thereby denied his share of the American Dream, he and his kind were ready for any mass movement which would strike at those they charged, in their own minds, with the responsibility for their present unhappy condition. Much of this behavior was not conscious. Much of it was feeling rather than thought, as indeed it had been in the mass movements of the aboriginal

Melanesians and North American Indians. In seems certain, however, that American workers, taught from childhood that those who apply themselves to their craft and practice the ethics of the middle class would be rewarded by achievement and success, would rebel and strike back out of sheer frustration when they found out that the American Dream no longer was attainable for them and that the hard facts belied the beautiful words they had been taught. It seems even more likely that the effects of the break in the skill hierarchy were potent forces which contributed their full share to the workers' striking and the union's becoming their champion.

CHAPTER 11

Yankee City Loses Control of its Factories

The Big-City Men Take Control

Two fundamental changes have been occurring concomitantly, in these years, in the social organization of Yankee City shoe factories. The first is the expansion of the hierarchy upward, out of Yankee City, through the expansion of individual enterprises and the establishment by them of central offices in distant large cities. The second is the expansion of the structure outward from Yankee City through the growth of manufacturers' associations and labor unions, also with headquarters outside Yankee City and with units in many other shoemaking communities in New England and elsewhere. Both the vertical and horizontal extensions (of these developments) have gone on concurrently, each reacting upon the other. And both decrease Yankee City's control over its shoe factories by subjecting the factories, or segments of them, to more and more control exerted from outside Yankee City.

In the early days of the shoe industry, the owners and managerial staffs of the factories, as well as the operatives, were residents of Yankee City; there was no extension of the factory social structure outside the local community. The factories were then entirely under the control of the community—not only the formal control of city ordinances and laws, but also the more pervasive informal controls of community traditions and attitudes. There were feelings of neighborliness and friendship to each other and the community that went beyond the formal employer-employee agreement.

With the vertical extension of the managerial hierarchy the social distance between the top executives, on the one hand, and the workers and community, on the other, has increased to the point where these bonds of mutual friendship have virtually disappeared. Absentee ownership, which usually accompanies absentee control, accentuates this condition. The conflicts of interest between the two groups of owner-manager and worker-community thus become more pronounced because they lack the bonds of mutuality. Factory policies are established in the distant offices of large concerns; neither worker nor community now has any voice in them.

The participants—manufacturers and operatives—realizing the increasing potency of these conflicts, have formed horizontal associations, aimed to protect the interests of their members from the encroachments of the opposed group. Headquarters of these associations are also outside Yankee City and their policies are determined independently of the local community. This institutionalizing of the manufacturer-operative conflicts has thus further infringed on Yankee City's control of its shoe factories and in some degree has set worker interests in opposition to community interests.

Yankee City shoe factories are no longer owned exclusively by local citizens. More and more of them are being absorbed by larger enterprises whose executive offices are in New York City. At the time of our study, the largest shoe factory in Yankee City was owned by a company which operated several other factories in New England and also owned the nation-wide ABC chain of retail shoe stores, all of which were controlled from a central office in New York. Even some of the smaller Yankee City shoe factories, although still locally owned and managed, sold most of their shoes to chain-store organizations. But before we examine in detail the organization of shoe manufacturing in Yankee City, let us see what has been happening to shoe manufacturing in general, in terms of the vertical extension of

managerial hierarchies resulting from the increase in size of
individual enterprises.

As a shoe manufacturing enterprise expands, either through
combination with other manufacturing or distributing organizations or by self-segmentation, the business structure becomes
more complex and new grades appear in the hierarchy of jobs.
The division of labor in both supervisory and technological jobs
is extended, and new administrative positions are created. In
the lowest grades of the manufacturing hierarchy the division
of labor is carried to such an extent, as we have observed in
Yankee City shoe factories, that many of the technological jobs
become simple enough to be performed with very little practice
by almost anyone.

The job of the factory manager is also simplified with the
expansion of the enterprise. Whereas the manager of a small
independent shoe factory performs two quite distinct jobs, the
manager of a factory which is one of several production units in
a larger enterprise has only one job. The former must concern
himself not only with the internal organization and operation of
the plant, but also with the whole manifold of relations between
the factory and the outside world: he must be in touch with
producers of materials and equipment used by his factory, with
buyers of shoes, and with investors and bankers who finance the
company. The manager of the local production unit of a larger
enterprise, on the other hand, need concern himself only with
production; the broader administrative duties are performed by
a higher executive, or group of executives, at the main office of
the company.

These higher executive jobs which are created when the enterprise expands are, neverthless, concerned with broader problems than any faced by the manager of a small independent
shoe factory. The larger concern must buy materials in greater
quantities, frequently in greater variety, and from a larger
number of different sources. It has more shoes to sell, perhaps
of several grades, each of which must be sold to a different segment of the public. Its problems of financing are larger, re-
quiring wider contacts with sources of financial aid. The higher

executive of the large enterprise, therefore, must relate the enterprise to a much larger segment of the total society than does the manager of a small independent shoe factory. For this reason he must have very great freedom of action in performing his job.

The combination of shoe factories into larger enterprises, the creation of new superordinate jobs, the increasing freedom of action required by jobs in the higher levels of the hierarchy, and the increase in social distance between operatives and the higher executives are represented diagrammatically in Figure 11.

Fig. 11. *Vertical Extension of the Managerial Hierarchy*

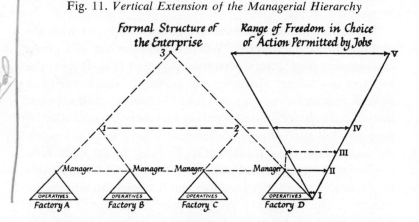

The four small triangles represent the total personnel of four shoe factories.[1] The technological workers in each factory are

1. We are purposely refraining from mentioning the important divisions of a manufacturing enterprise which handle the purchase of materials and equipment, the sales of the product, the finances, and the legal division through which the rights and privileges of the enterprise are protected. These have been eliminated from our description because the typical Yankee City shoe factory of today is absentee-controlled. Almost all the activities, other than those directly concerned with production and those auxiliary activities necessary to regulate and order the production processes, such as accounting and the necessary maintenance of the building and equipment, are organized and directed from the head office in New York.

at the base of the triangle, the bottom of the hierarchy. Each factory manager is at the apex of the factory hierarchy.

The large inverted triangle at the right symbolizes the range of social relations of individuals who occupy jobs at different levels in the hierarchy, with the corresponding freedom of action which must be allowed these individuals. The exceedingly small range of choice allowed operatives in their working behavior is shown in line I of the diagram. Line II represents the freedom of action allowed the factory manager to insure adequate internal organization of the production activities of the factory. Line III symbolizes the additional freedom of action needed by the manager of a small independent shoe factory to enable him to organize the external relations of his factory, the relations with suppliers, buyers, sources of finance, the community, etc.

Now suppose shoe factory A merges with factory B, and C with D. Each plant continues operations but there are now two concerns of intermediate size where formerly there were four small ones. Two new administrative jobs are created at 1 and 2. These administrators coordinate the activities of factories AB and CB respectively, but each of the four factory managers is still responsible for the internal organization of his own plant. The factory managers, however, are not responsible for the external relations of the factory; hence their range of action is cut from line III to line II. The new executives at 1 and 2 take over the jobs of relating the enlarged enterprises to the total society. The external relations they must organize are more complex than those which had to be organized by the individual shoe-factory managers because of the increases in range and quantity of supplies needed, the size of the market that must be tapped to sell the manufactured shoes, the need for increased financing, and the growth of legal problems that accompanies growth in the size of an enterprise. Therefore, the new administrators at 1 and 2 need greater freedom of action to perform their jobs adequately than was needed by any one of the four factory managers when each took care of the external as well as the internal relations of the individual factories. This is symbolized by line IV.

If these two intermediate-sized concerns merge into one large company, still another superordinate job is created at point 3. Now the general policies of the entire large concern are dictated from 3, as are the major organizational features and production activities of all four shoe factories. The relations among the four factories, and between them and the new apex at 3, are now parts of the internal organization of the large enterprise, controlled by the administrator or administrators at 3 through the delegation of authority to individuals subordinate to them in the managerial hierarchy. Managers of individual factories are more closely than ever restricted to the job of organizing the internal relations of the factory and maintaining production. All the external relations of the enterprise, which by its increased size have now become still more complex, are ordered from 3. The executive, or group of executives, who occupies this apex of the enlarged hierarchy must therefore be allowed even greater freedom of action—as symbolized by line V—than that characteristic of jobs 1 and 2.

Theoretically, such a process of combination could continue until one huge enterprise monopolized a whole industry, or combinations of various industries. With each enlargement of an enterprise would come an expansion of the managerial hierarchy and concomitant widening of freedom of action for those at the top to enable them to cope with problems of ever-increasing complexity. Actually, however, the difficulties of internal organization usually check the growth of individual enterprises well short of complete monopoly. If these internal difficulties do not do so, the leaders of the larger society invoke anti-monopoly laws so that the growth of the enterprise is stopped by outside pressure.

The ultimate limitation on the growth of the enterprise, then, shows the top executives of the enterprise to be subordinate to other leaders of the society. Even short of that point, however, the executives of large enterprises must gauge broad public opinion in setting the courses of their concerns. The head of a large shoe-manufacturing concern must predict fashion preferences, for instance, in order to make shoes the public will buy. This becomes a very large problem when a concern is so big that it must depend on nation-wide and even export sales. In many other ways, too, the top executive must understand what society demands of his enterprise and must adapt his organization to satisfy those wants. The very large manufacturing company is subject to the informal sanctions of a large part of the American public in a way that is somewhat comparable to the informal control exerted by a community on a small locally owned and managed factory.

Although the large enterprise remains, in the last analysis, subject to the control of the larger society, it tends to escape the control of individual communities in which the individual manufacturing units are located. With the expansion of the enterprise to the point where it operates several factories in different communities and has its main office and chief executives in some large city at a distance from any of the factory towns, the social distance between the top executives and the factory community becomes very great. This is true, too, of the relations between the operatives and the top executives. Every level in the managerial hierarchy above the factory manager increases the social distance between the operatives and the chief executives of the enterprise. This is symbolized in Figure 11 by the vertical distance from operatives to top executive which increases with every expansion. In large companies, therefore, the individuals at the two extremes of the hierarchy are strangers rather than friends; the top executives may issue orders in conformity with business logic which injure the interests of the workers—and not even be aware of the fact. Workers, on the other hand, do not know their ultimate boss; and, because he is a stranger, they are liable to suspect his motives and to blame him for untoward events for which he is not responsible.

Along with absentee management usually goes absentee ownership. In the case of a small factory, the owners as well as the manager are local residents; they belong to the community, subscribe to its beliefs and ideals, and are subject to its social control. When the local factory is but part of a large enterprise, however, the owners as well as the top executives are strangers. Frequently, ownership rests with a large number of stockholders who have no personal interest in the social structure or operations of the enterprise. In such cases the workers and the factory community suffer further loss of control over the factory through their complete loss of social control over the owners.

Yankee City at the time of our study had partly lost control of its shoe factories through the development of absentee management and absentee ownership such as we have described. During the early part of 1933 there were nine shoe factories operating in Yankee City, one of which was absentee-owned and managed. At one time during the progress of the study only the absentee-owned factory was in operation, and at the close of our investigations it dominated shoe manufacturing in Yankee City. The organization of shoe manufacturing in Yankee City is represented in Figure 12.

Fig. 12. *Shoe Corporations in Yankee City*

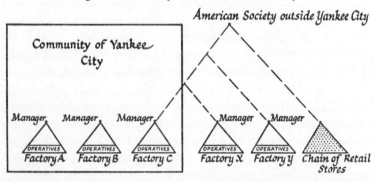

The shoe factories A, B, and C in this chart are all located in Yankee City. A and B are locally owned and independent, but factory C is owned by outside interests which also own shoe factories X and Y, located in other communities, and a chain of retail shoe stores also located outside Yankee City. Factories C, X, and Y and the chain of retail stores are all managed from one main office in New York City.

Similar manufacturing processes are used in the three Yankee City factories, and the operatives in all three factories occupy similar low levels in the business hierarchy. The managers' function as organizers of production is likewise similar in the three factories.[2] In formal internal organizations the three Yankee City shoe factories are, therefore, essentially similar. The differences between the locally owned and managed factories (A and B) and the absentee-owned and managed factory (C) are to be sought in the manner in which they are related to the community and the outside world.

The managers of the locally owned, independent shoe factories A and B direct the external relations of their factories from their offices in the local community. Besides their concern with the internal organization of their factories, they must procure supplies of material and equipment, secure a market for their shoes, and obtain whatever financial aid the factory needs in the form of either capital or credit. The manager of the absentee-controlled and owned factory C, however, is concerned only with the internal organization of the factory he controls; all the external relations of this shoe factory are ordered from the New York office of the large enterprise of which it is but one production unit.

This arrangement gives shoe factory C a distinct business advantage over the locally owned factories A and B, because vertical extensions comparable to those we have described for the shoe industry have occured also in the case of many of the organizations with which the head of a shoe manufacturing enterprise must maintain close relations. Many of the producers of the materials and equipment needed in the manufacture of shoes have expanded like the shoe business into large enter-

2. For the sake of simplicity we are omitting discussion of the intermediate jobs of supervisory control between the managers and the operatives, as these jobs need not be considered in dealing with the relations between the factories, with the community, and with the larger society; these jobs, however, are also similar in the three factories.

prises within main offices in New York City. New York is like-wise the center of banking and finance. Many chains of retail shoe stores also maintain head offices in New York.

Thus the top executives in the New York office of the large enterprise that controls factory C are able to establish and maintain close social relations with the heads of many of the outside organizations on which a shoe factory must depend for maintenance of its production. Moreover, the large enterprise of which factory C is a part has its own chain of retail stores, which insures an outlet for the shoes made in this factory. The managers of the locally owned shoe factories A and B, on the contrary, cannot establish these close social relations with out-side organizations. They must spend most of their time in the factory office and establish outside contacts by mail or wire; only occasionally can they go to New York or elsewhere to establish personal relations with organizations whose coopera-tion is essential to the business welfare of their factories. In comparison with factory C, the locally owned factories also are greatly handicapped because, having no retail chains of their own, they do not command the certain market for their prod-ucts that factory C does. All of these advantages enable shoe factory C to maintain more continuous production closer to its capacity, making it a more efficient production unit than either of the locally owned and managed factories A and B.

The factor of vertical extension and absentee control which is so advantageous to factory C in a business way puts it at a disadvantage, compared with factories A and B, in insuring smooth functioning of the internal organization of the factory. In locally owned factories A and B, an operative knows his ultimate boss. In many cases operatives and managers have been acquaintances, perhaps even friends, all their lives. This induces close social relations between workers and manage-ment, mutual trust, and some recognition by each of the point of view and problems of the other. When situations arise wherein the interests of the two groups diverge, some compromise is likely to be effected after essentially friendly discussions between workers and management. In the case of factory C, however, the social distance between the operatives and the top executives who live and work in New York City is tremendously increased. Neither knows nor understands the other. Operatives' relations with the owners—stockholders, in this case—are even more distant.

A result of all this is that operatives are suspicious of the motives of strangers, and the higher executives and owners fail to appreciate the social needs of operatives. Small dissatisfactions of operatives are thus likely to be greatly magnified. They have, moreover, a sense of insecurity in their jobs which is not overcome by the greater regularity of employment offered by factory C as compared with factories A and B. Workers in factory C cannot feel as sure as those in A and B that the factory is an integral part of the community of Yankee City. Operations of factory C might be removed to another community at the whim of the unknown persons in ultimate control of it. This is not an idle fear. Shoe-manufacturing operations can easily be moved from one community to another because factory buildings and much of the machinery are rented rather than owned by the manufacturer. And many communities in New England offer inducements, besides an adequate supply of labor, equal to or even superior to those advertised by Yankee City. There have been numerous instances in recent years of such movements of shoe-manufacturing operations from one New England community to another or even outside New England altogether. Thus the maintenance of a smoothly functioning internal organization is more difficult for the manager of factory C than it is for either factory A or B because of the great social distance between the top and bottom of the hierarchy of which this shoe factory is a part. This social distance, in turn, is the result of the vertical extension of the managerial hierarchy through the growth of the enterprise of which factory C is a part.

The vertical extension of its managerial hierarchy and the absentee control of factory C also made its relations with the community of Yankee City much different from those of factories A and B. Typically, the managers and supervisory staffs of the locally owned, independent factories are native Yankees; frequently, they were born and grew up in Yankee City. They are thus involved in the general social life of the community, belonging to various associations, clubs, and other organizations. They subscribe to many general community attitudes which impinge upon their working relations, frequently causing them to modify working behavior away from that which would follow the single-minded dictates of the profit-making logic. Their business status and, especially, their general social status depend upon the opinions of their fellow townsmen. Their life in the factory is not divorced from life in the community outside working hours. Part of the motivation that determines their business behavior is the desire that fellow townsmen regard them as upright and fair businessmen who treat their employees properly. Such desires frequently militate against their acting strictly in accordance with the profit-making logic; business advantages are sometimes sacrificed because the manager (or owner) places greater value on community prestige than he does on increasing factory earnings by some means which would endanger that prestige.

In the case of absentee-controlled shoe factory C, however, there is little business need for the manager to participate in community activities. He can operate the factory in strict accordance with the orders of the main office more easily, in fact, if he does not take part, either as an individual or as a representative of the factory, in local associational activities. If he does involve the factory in community activities, he involves it and the larger enterprise of which it is a part in community responsibilities and subjects it to community pressure and control. This is precisely what the top officials of the large enterprise do not want. They want the factory to be as free as possible of community pressures so that its operations can be dictated in strict accordance with the profit-making logic. This would even allow them, if it seemed desirable, to move their factory to another community.

In view of the advantages that accrue to the total enterprise if factory C is kept free of informal community pressure and control, there appears to be special significance in certain differences between the persons who hold similar jobs in locally owned factories A and B. In factory C the manager and many of the subordinate members of the supervisory staff reside outside Yankee City. Many of them are also members of ethnic groups that have comparatively low prestige in Yankee City. This may be merely a coincidence, but it seems more likely that it is explicit company policy to hire supervisors who are not firmly entrenched in the community life of Yankee City.

However this situation came to be, its effect on the community and workers of Yankee City has been to increase the social distance between them and the local managers of factory C. It has also contributed, along with the division of labor and mechanization, to lower the prestige of shoemaking as an occupation in Yankee City; for people do not like to take orders from those they regard as social inferiors—and many of the native Yankees, Irish, and French who are the traditional craftsmen of the shoe trade in Yankee City do regard members of the present supervisory staff of factory C as social inferiors. This attitude tends to precipitate the withdrawal of such persons from the industry; and they are replaced largely by members of the newer ethnic groups, again lowering the prestige of shoe manufacturing. Loss of prestige of the industry means some further loss of effective control of its shoe factories by the community since societies protect more diligently the forms of institutions having high social value than those whose value is considered low.

As far as Yankee City shoe factory C is concerned, the manufacturing processes have become so standardized, and personal relations and community control so minimized, that the production of shoes requires little time or attention from the higher executives. These men can thus concentrate on the problems of integrating the enterprise into the larger society. The problem of merchandising, for example, has absorbed much of the working time of these higher executives, but this essential operation is coming to be standardized, too: witness the development of the chain-store method of selling. With both production and merchandising largely routinized, top executives devote most of their attention to other problems of widening the extent of the enterprise's relations with the total society. The financing of the large and expanding enterprise, for instance, assumes major importance.

Other even broader problems loom on the business horizon. Institutional advertising, for instance, which has increased greatly in recent years, consists of efforts to "sell" the American public on the virtues of an individual company or even of a whole industry rather than merely on its products. Such attempts to expand the base of integration of business enterprises in the total society were hardly considered to be business problems at all a few years ago. It is to be expected that, as individual businesses grow larger and affect the lives of ever-increasing segments of the American public, these very generalized problems of establishing satisfactory relations between the businesses and the total public will occupy more and more of the time and effort of the top executives.

Small, locally owned and managed factories, like Yankee City's shoe factories A and B, face powerful competition today from factories, like C, which are production units of large enterprises. We have mentioned some of the reasons why this is so, but even before the development of such large enterprises there was a high rate of mortality for Yankee City shoe factories. Over forty factories have failed in Yankee City in the past seventy years. Today the difficulties of these small independent shoe factories are greater than ever before. They find it increasingly difficult to so organize their external relations that they can insure sufficient volume and continuity of production to meet the price competition of the larger and more efficient enterprises. It seems reasonable to expect that large enterprises, like that with which factory C is associated, will become increasingly dominant in New England shoe manufacturing.

This trend, together with the type of integration of external relations characteristic of these large enterprises, indicates the sort of role towns like Yankee City must prepare themselves to play in American industrial life. Yankee City needs shoe factories to absorb its plentiful supply of efficient labor, for it is highly important to the well-being of any community that its labor be gainfully employed. Factories like C, absentee-controlled, can best assure local labor of continuous employment because they operate more constantly than small independent plants and also because the large concerns do not suffer as high a rate of mortality.

Such factories, as we have shown, resist many forms of social control by the local community, particularly the informal controls. If the community seeks to impose control, the absentee directors are likely to remove operations from the community. In order to keep such factories, Yankee City must accept a subordinate position and cater to their needs rather than try to control them as the community once controlled the small locally owned factories. Local pride resists the acceptance of this subordinate role as it decries absentee control and ownership. But in the end, if Yankee City is to prosper under the present system of industrial organization, it must learn to play the part it is equipped to play in the development of the industry, even though, for the advantages it will gain thereby, it must relinquish some of its cherished independence.

The full significance of this elaboration of the vertical hierarchy and its powerful effect on the instigation and outcome of the strike will be treated later in this chapter.

Horizontal Extensions of the Factories

Along with the vertical extension of the shoe factories has gone another type of extension outside the factory community, which we are calling the horizontal extension. It consists of the organization of grades in the manufacturing hierarchy across factory and community lines into huge associations, the scope of some of which is industry-wide. Such associations are organized primarily to protect the interests of one grade in the manufacturing hierarchy against the encroachments of other grades. The rapid development in recent years of associations of owners and managers, on the one hand, and of workers, on the other, has gone on concomitantly with the growth of extreme vertical extensions in the shoe business. Manufacturers' associations have been formed without public resistance, but labor unions have been resisted both by management and by some sectors of the general public. This dual development reflects the increasing seriousness of the conflict of interests between the different grades which has accompanied the increasing social distance between them. As far as communities like Yankee City are concerned, these associations further decrease the community control over the shoe factories because the headquarters of the groups controlling the Yankee City units are outside the community and independent of it. These horizontal associations, like the vertical extension of managerial hierarchies, represent integrations of the shoe industry into the larger society, automatically decreasing their integration with the local community.

Horizontal organizations consist of associations formed to protect the working statuses of their individual members. The latter are bound together by reason of their mutuality of interests within the broad industrial hierarchy. Recognition of this mutuality of interests creates a solidarity which, when organized, results in a greater bargaining power for the members of any of these associations within a given factory or a whole industry. Implicit in the logic of such organizations is recognition of the fact that the interrelations in an industry are not comprised solely of the vertical relations of subordination and superordination.

Protective associations are motivated by a logic more abstract than the profit-making logic, and they do not function at all times with the same intensity. The intensity varies with the imminence of the menace which they are organized to resist; in times of crisis it becomes very great. The purpose of any one of these associations is the protection of the interests of the totality of its own membership, irrespective of factory boundaries. Nevertheless, in specific instances of localized antagonisms and tensions, the functioning of these associations focuses on intra-factory relations.

Just as the structure of a business enterprise is subdivided for efficient functioning, so each of these organizations has a hierarchical structure. The national headquarters is usually found at the center of the shoe industry's operations; the suborganizations are situated at various points throughout the area in which shoes are manufactured.

There are few organizations representing any one grade which function universally throughout the shoe industry. Conflicts arise among different organizations formed to protect the interests of a certain grade. This is particularly noticeable in the conflict between the American Federation of Labor and the Congress of Industrial Organization. We shall have more to say about this a little later. *[handwritten: Now united in AFL-CIO]*

Inasmuch as employers' associations are generally organized on a smaller scale than the other two types and are more or less localized, this section will consider only two classes of protective associations: manufacturers' associations and labor unions.

Manufacturers' associations are established to further the interests of the superordinate executives of the various enterprises in the shoe industry. They are simpler to organize than labor unions because, compared to the workers, the number of individuals functioning in the role of merchant-manufacturer is small. Their specific purpose is to enable the executives thus organized (1) to deal more adequately with the problems involved in relating the factories to the larger world, e.g., problems of vertical extension; and (2) to protect themselves as a group against other horizontal associations organized in the interests of other groups.

The current national organization of shoe manufacturers is known as the National Boot and Shoe Manufacturers' Association.[3] Some indication of the aims of this organization to control policies in the shoe industry can be seen from the aggressive role it played in the formation of the NIRA code for the industry. The initiative for the development of a code for the shoe industry was taken by the National Boot and Shoe

3. There are also a number of more or less local manufacturers' organizations which need not be discussed here.

Manufacturers' Association. It foresaw the enactment of some form of legislation prior to the passage of the National Industrial Recovery Act, and accordingly attempted to bring the shoe manufacturers together to obtain consensus on what should go into a code for the industry.

After the code was formulated, the N.B.S.M.A., in conjunction with the Administrator of the NIRA, became the agency for administering its provisions. The Code was presented to the President on October 3, 1933. Between that date and the date of the adverse Supreme Court decision, May 27, 1935, a series of hearings and conferences was held. The NIRA marked a new development in dealing with the problem of competition. Its creation was a recognition that all industry required cooperation within and among manufacturing groups.

We have mentioned previously the apparent lack of divergence of interests between merchant-master and journeyman in the earlier days of the industry. It appeared openly for the first time about 1868 with the short-lived Knights of St. Crispin, and was followed, roughly a generation later, by the National Boot and Shoe Workers' Union. The union was highly centralized, and, in order to create a more democratic form of organization, the Shoe Workers' Protective Union was formed a few years later. Both these organizations still exist. The latter, in fact, called the shoe strike of 1933 in Yankee City, but it decreased in power thereafter. The National Boot and Shoe Workers' Union, as its name implies, is a national organization and has continued to be an important force in many centers of shoe manufacture.

Early in 1934, the United Shoe and Leather Workers' Union absorbed the two locals of the Yankee City Shoe Workers' Protective Union and started to organize the workers under a broader and more extensive national program. In 1936 the U.S.L.W.U. was the dominant union in Yankee City. It is an industrial union to which all shoe operatives—regardless of sex, race, creed—belong. The Shoe Workers' Protective Union has retained a small and relatively unimportant foothold in Yankee City among certain specialized groups of workers.

The aims and purposes of the industrial union are highly significant if considered in conjunction with the division of labor and mechanization which have occurred in the shoe industry. The early unions in the shoe industry were craft unions with a hierarchical relation to one another similar to the hierarchical relations of the various technological levels of the workers they organized. The U.S.L.W.U., with its emphasis on the quality and common interests of all shoe workers, overtly recognizes that the former technological hierarchy has indeed broken down in the shoe industry. The fact that the union grew so rapidly in size and importance during the early thirties shows that shoe workers themselves were aware of the breakdown.

Labor's great internecine struggle, which we have witnessed in the struggle between the A.F. of L. and the C.I.O., can be understood in terms of our analysis of the break in the skill hierarchy if that analysis is given wider application than we have thus far attempted. The A.F. of L. strives to maintain the ideal of hierarchies in technological jobs, arguing that the workers at different levels in such hierarchies have different interests from other workers. The C.I.O. argues that technological jobs in a large segment of modern industry have been reduced to a common low level of skill and that the A.F. of L.'s doctrine is antiquated and nonfunctional in situations like that of the Yankee City shoe industry today. C.I.O. thus wants to organize all the technological workers in a given industry on a basis of equality in order to fight management and owners in the common interests of labor. It appears that each kind of organization fills a need in various realms of American industrial life. The technological jobs in many highly mechanized industries are probably all, or nearly all, on a common low level of skill comparable to that required in the modern shoe industry. In these enterprises, the industrial type of union is functionally consistent with both the actual interests of the workers and their relations with management. There is no doubt, on the other hand, that in some industries there is still a definite hierarchy of technological jobs. In such industries the traditional craft unions probably are more consistent, functionally, with the working relations and interests of workers than the industrial type of union.[4]

The local unions of the U.S.L.W.U. in Yankee City have a central executive board to which the union members annually elect individuals from the various production departments of the factories. The officers of a local include a president, vice-president, secretary-treasurer, business agent, and members of the executive board. The business agent is the officer who represents the local in major negotiations with the factory. Minor union problems within the factory are in the hands of "stewards," elected by shop crews in the production departments. The funds of a local are under the control of trustees who are responsible to the executive board.

The locals are closely affiliated but have separate organizations with separate agents. Workers in the cutting and stitching departments of the factories are organized in one of the locals, and workers in all other departments in the other. This division of union activities under two locals reflects merely an expedient organization device; cutting and stitching rooms are always adjacent and the operatives of these departments, who form a large group including both sexes, all work on the same sorts of materials. The division in union activities does not represent any differential in prestige between cutters and stitchers and other operatives.

Both locals of the U.S.L.W.U. in Yankee City have the same headquarters in a building near the center of the town. This building has a central room for union meetings and two small rooms which are the offices of the two locals. From time to time, lectures on subjects interesting to the workers are given in the main room or union hall. The headquarters is a type of workers'

4. The very terminology of unionism, although it is confusing, betrays the conflicting ideologies of the two types. Craft unions are called "horizontal" unions, the implication being that they organize separately the workers at various levels in a technological hierarchy. Industrial unions are called "vertical" unions, implying that they organize in one union workers at all levels of a technological hierarchy. The hierarchy is so taken for granted that it is implied in describing the type of unionism that developed because of the breakdown of the hierarchy.

club; it functions as a social meeting place according to the amount of, and interest in, union activities.

The executive boards of both locals of the U.S.L.W.U. at the date of this study (1935) consisted exclusively of native Yankees, Irish, and French. These boards, representing the important departments of the productive division of the factory, were elected by the total membership. The members of the executive board served without pay. The choice of members reflects the prestige which was enjoyed by Yankees, Irish, and French over those ethnic groups which had more recently arrived in Yankee City. Thus we see the phenomenon of an association which is founded on the technological logic that all workers are equal denying that logic because of the existence of social classes and a system of sentiments associated with these classes in the community.

The establishment of the United Shoe and Leather Workers' Union reflected a demand for the organization of workers in the shoe trade under a logic which had as its base the common interest of all workers in the industry. This union made a strong appeal because of its extremely democratic organization, in which the ultimate control lay in the hands of the members. The officers were elected for comparatively short periods and were subject to recall at any time.

Although the original appeal of the U.S.L.W.U was effective in expanding its influence, it failed to hold the workers' interest. It grew rapidly: by September 1935, its executive secretary estimated its total membership at 60,000, claiming that it then represented the largest union membership in the shoe industry. As conditions improved in the industry, however, the antagonisms between workers and those in supervisory jobs were reduced to minor grievances, comparatively easy to arbitrate by the executive board of a local, if not by the business agent or stewards. As a result, the influence of the controlling ideology of the union over the members lessened, and attendance at meetings of the locals was reduced.

By the end of 1935, only one large factory in Yankee City— whose operatives were organized under the U.S.L.W.U.—was functioning steadily. Soon after that time, however, one of the formerly important factories was reorganized and started production on a small scale. The union was not strong enough to demand recognition in this smaller establishment. Consequently, by the spring of 1936 the latter was operating as an open shop, leaving only the workers of the one large absentee-controlled factory affiliated with the union. This shows that the workers are apparently unable to maintain an effective organization to protect their interests in the employer-employee conflict of interests in a slack period.

Even while the interest of the workers in the activities of the U.S.L.W.U. was waning by reason of the improving employment conditions in the industry, the union did perform an important function in demanding adherence to regular working hours, the maintenance of established rates of pay, and an equalization of the pay of different workers in the slacker periods. The union has rectified several long-standing complaints of the workers. An interviewer asked a shoemaker what the factory did when work ran low. He answered: "The night before they put out the stock to be worked on the next day, so you know how much work you have to do the next day—that way you know there's only enough for a half day's work, and you come, and when you get through, you go home. You don't have to wait around when you're not working, and if there is no work for the next day you know it the night before, so you don't go to the factory at all." The interviewer remarked that formerly there had been complaints to the effect that the men spent a day at the factory and worked for only two or three hours. The operative said: "Yes, that was before the union, but now the union won't let them do that. Before the union came, some factories would work this same way. They would let you know the night before, but a lot of them didn't; you had to come every morning and stay all day whether you worked or not. But now it's different, and it's much better this way."

The evolution of manufacturers' associations and labor unions gives evidence of the extreme complexity of the relations in the shoe industry which transcend the limited set of relations formed within any single enterprise. Their formation further evidences the basic conflict of interests between those in positions of control and the shoe operatives. Because the superordinate executives have many problems of a highly individualized nature to solve, it is somewhat difficult for them to effect a closely knit protective organization. This difficulty is to some extent offset, however, by the fact that the common menaces and problems which such organizations are established to combat are sufficiently pressing at all times to keep the associations active. Thus the problem of bridging the gap between crises is not so great as that which faces the labor unions.

By reason of the character of the relations organized by manufacturers' associations, their appeal is based upon a more concrete need than that of the labor unions. The former are established primarily to protect the business interests of the owners, whereas the latter are established to protect something less definite, the rights of the workers. The shoe strike illustrated this point. Most of the formal demands of the strikers concerned wages and the recognition of the union, but interviews with workers during and before the strike clearly showed that many of the basic grounds for dissension had little to do with the amount of wages received. The workers believed that these basic grounds for dissension among different individuals could be gradually adjusted if the unions were recognized. The union served as a composite symbol of protection for all those social values which were in themselves unexpressible as well as for the protection of reasonable wages. To the worker, the union represented a medium through which his work within the factory would be better integrated with his life outside the factory.

Since manufacturers' associations purport to protect business rights of the industry as a whole, it is comparatively simple to keep them well financed by contributions from the enterprises represented. Labor unions, on the other hand, comprising a large number of individuals with little personal wealth, find it difficult to maintain the interest of the workers while the latter are reasonably satisfied with working conditions. The manu-

facturers' associations are usually supported by annual dues
whose amount is not burdensome or constantly noticeable.
The weekly dues of the labor unions are a continual drain on
the pocketbooks of individual workers with little money to
spare.

When the sentiments of opposition or antagonism between
operatives and organized leadership in the shoe industry become intense, the feeling of solidarity among operatives in
various factories is greatly strengthened. During these times,
the operatives have an active interest in their collective welfare;
and it is then that the labor unions become the instrument by
which this solidarity is made an effective force in negotiation
with employers. When the factory work progresses in an orderly
fashion, the operatives are apathetic about collective representation. During such times, the labor unions carry on a variety
of minor activities in the interest of the workers which require
the maintenance of local union headquarters near the factories.
But in the periods between employer-employee crises the
interest of the workers flags, collection of dues falls off, and the
union has difficulty maintaining its organization.

With reference to Yankee City, the significance of the development of national manufacturers' associations lies in their
connecting local industrial problems with those of the greater
industry. Many of Yankee City's industrial problems are not
considered in Yankee City but elsewhere at associational headquarters. This same dependence on organizations located in
larger cities is evident in the administration of labor unions.
Labor unions, considered as another example of the horizontal
extension, are organized primarily to protect the welfare of
the shoe operatives as individuals and to regulate the interrelations of the workers as a class with both manufacturers and
employers. Thus, to the Yankee City community, a very important result of both the horizontal and vertical extension
of industry is to lessen its independence and freedom of choice
in meeting problems having to do with the livelihood of its
citizens. Thousands of other small industrial cities are also
involved in the process of wider integration occurring through-

out American industry. They, too, must come to accept the roles in this development that are assigned them by the larger society.

Before discussing the full meaning of the vertical and horizontal extensions of the shoe business, we will examine what these extensions mean in terms of personalities by comparing present and past owners of Yankee City shoe factories.

The Managers of Men Were Gods

Three dead men played powerful, important, and, at times, decisive roles in the outcome of the strike. Paradoxically, although they were former owners and managers of the factories, their influence materially aided the strikers and helped defeat management. Throughout the struggle, the owners, workers, and most of Yankee City continued to recognize the great wisdom of these dead owners and managers and always bowed to their judgments. The authority of these men accordingly was constantly quoted by each side to gain approval for what it said and did and to stigmatize the words and actions of its antagonists. The peacemakers quoted the deeds and sayings of the three as parables and precepts to force the warring parties to come to agreement. It is unlikely that the actual behavior of these men corresponded to the symbols into which they had been fabricated by those who remembered them after their deaths. But it is certain that the values inherent in them as collective representations ordered and controlled much of the thinking of everyone and greatly contributed to the workers' winning the strike.

The three—Caleb Choate, Godfrey Weatherby, and William Pierce—were constantly quoted; episodes from their exploits, as brilliant Yankee City industrialists and wise and generous employers of Yankee City men, were frequently spoken of and applied to present conditions in the shoe industry to the detriment of the contemporary managers and owners. Since the sagacity of the three verged on the supernatural, no flesh and blood owner living in Yankee City at the time of the strike could hope to measure up to the standards of these demigods.

It is small wonder that managers felt weak and inadequate when they compared themselves with the great men of the past, and it is certain from their utterances and deeds that they shared feelings of guilt in the presence of their accusing employees. Their private knowledge of themselves and faith in the great managers of the past made them weak, for now that myth-making had done its work and mortals were translated into gods, the prosaic men of the present could never hope to compete with these heroes and demigods who plagued them from the past.

We will examine the evidence to see what these men were in real life but only briefly since it was what the men and women of the strike believed them to have been that made them important for this study. In the section which follows we will discuss the social personalities of the contemporary managers; then we will compare the evidence from the past and present to learn why the three dead owners were still powerful when their successors, with all the recognized glory of modern technology to support them, were considered weak and inadequate.

Caleb Choate was a pioneer in large-scale shoe manufacturing in Yankee City; both Godfrey Weatherby and William Pierce received their training under him.

Mr. Choate's success is indicated by the fact that from a capital of $100 (in 1866) he had built up a business with annual gross sales of a million dollars. By 1877, at the age of thirty, a local document informs us, he was the "head of a large and successful manufacturing business and was one of the solid and respected citizens of Yankee City. . . . A large factor in the early success of the business was the prompt adoption of the McKay stitching machine while other shoe manufacturers were considering whether it would pay. Mr. Choate was one of the first to combine the many parts of shoe manufacturing under one roof and to successfully operate a large establishment where from the raw materials shoes were made up complete from start to finish under the management and care of one man. By 1892 annual sales totalled $1,440,350."

Before Godfrey Weatherby died he said: "There was almost

entire absence of bitter feeling between Mr. Choate and his employees. . . . There were no strikes by reason of dissatisfaction with wages. He commanded respect rather than won popularity. He was a kindly man and just, intolerant of inefficiency and dishonesty, always master in his own sphere, a good judge of men. Leaders among the workmen were satisfied that they were justly and fairly treated."

Another decided factor in Caleb Choate's business success was the financial help given him by Mr. Davis Cole, a member of an "old Yankee City family." Mr. Cole was in business in Boston and retired at the age of forty-four with a fortune. He owned a home in Yankee City and planned to live on the income from his savings, placed in the bank at 5 per cent interest. Mr. Choate with much ambition and very little money, started his shoe concern and asked Mr. Cole to endorse some notes. Mr. Cole agreed to this several times, so the story goes, without paying much attention to the amounts. Three years later, Mr. Cole was called over to the bank and learned that he had endorsed $100,000 worth of paper. Caleb Choate said "if Cole put him into bankruptcy he wouldn't get ten cents on a dollar but if he was allowed to continue he would get one hundred cents." Mr. Cole, who had complete confidence in Mr. Choate, was put in active charge by the bank and the business was successful.

Reference is made to this venture in Mr. Choate's memorial volume: "To Mr. Cole he [Caleb Choate] always expressed a grateful sense of obligation for the courage which he manifested and confidence he placed in the ability and integrity of the managing partner."

According to an elderly Yankee City businessman (upper-upper), who at one time was in partnership with him, Caleb Choate employed ten salesmen who visited the "whole of the United States from the Atlantic to the Pacific. Up to 1900 he manufactured many times more than all the other Yankee City manufacturers put together."

"His business methods were exceptionally fair and praiseworthy," another said. "The fact that he was in any way connected with an enterprise was all that was needed to inspire complete confidence. His name stood for quality, honest value, fair treatment, and good service in almost every city in the United States."

Caleb Choate started Godfrey Weatherby in business. According to Godfrey Weatherby's friends, they were very different. Mr. Choate was decided and abrupt, while Godfrey was more gentle and kindly. "He wouldn't be taken in by anyone," an old lady from Hill Street said, "but if a man showed he wanted to do what was right Godfrey always stood ready to help him. He became very successful and always showed a great interest in community affairs. Everyone trusted him and he never had any labor troubles of any kind. He had been to the local school with a good many of his employees and they knew his word was as good as his bond."

According to the most important and respected opinion-maker in the city, "if he [Weatherby] had been in business today he wouldn't have had any strike because his employees believed in him and he would have put all his cards on the table."

One of the partners of a large firm which still bore the name of Weatherby said: "Mr. Weatherby has been dead a good many years but we kept his name because he was such a fine man and his name meant so much. He did more for Yankee City than anyone else. If it hadn't been for Mr. Weatherby many big Yankee City companies would have been on the rocks."

At the time of the strike another upper-class informant said: "Mr. Weatherby was highly revered and respected and there's scarcely a meeting during this strike where his name isn't mentioned. He was a real leader."

Both Caleb Choate and Godfrey Weatherby died in their early fifties, Mr. Choate at fifty-one and Mr. Weatherby at fifty-three. The same remark was applied to the lives of both men—"sad that it should be cut off ere it was fully rounded out." Godfrey Weatherby made this comment at the memorial service for Caleb Choate, and Frederick Choate, son of Caleb Choate, repeated it in his address at the memorial service for

Godfrey Weatherby eighteen years later. A close friend, in commenting on his early death, said: "If Godfrey had lived he undoubtedly would have trained one of his sons to succeed him in company with William Pierce's son. But the children were so young when he died that his brother felt he would not have wanted his sons trained by the sort of managers that are in the shoe factories today. So he placed them in banks or bond houses where they would come under the influences of worthy, upright men, the type of men who used to be in the shoe business."

William Pierce started in the shoe business selling shoe laces for Caleb Choate and later became a shoe salesman. Following Mr. Choate's death, Mr. Pierce and Mr. Weatherby went into partnership and continued business under the firm name of Weatherby and Pierce for over thirty years, Mr. Weatherby responsible for the manufacturing end and Mr. Pierce for selling. Following the death of Mr. Weatherby, the firm liquidated.

Fred Jackson, of Jones and Jackson, in speaking about Mr. Pierce, said "what a good man he was. The firm liquidated because one partner [Weatherby] died and another had a bad heart. Mr. Pierce always felt responsible, for all his employees thought he was perfect, and he was worth half a million when he died."

A Greek shoe worker said: "I used to work for his father [Cabot Pierce] before he died. His father was a fine man. He was always a gentleman and would treat you right. He always paid more than anyone else."

The firm of Weatherby and Pierce shared this reputation, too. Among the items appearing in the *Herald* during the shoe strike and signed by the shoe workers, one observed: "The factory under William Pierce and Godfrey Weatherby's management was known the country over as a factory with ideal conditions between employer and employee. They (the employees) were always met more than half way and it was a privilege to work for them."

"The shoe business has changed considerably now," said a member of the upper-upper class. "Weatherby and Pierce was a fine concern. They made a very high-grade shoe, had the best workers in Yankee City, and paid high wages. Both Godfrey and William were born and raised in Yankee City, and a lot of the shoe workers had been to school with them. Consequently they never treated the workers as employees but as friends."

This last statement was embodied in a story told over and over again during the strike: "Once Mr. Pierce met a shoe cutter named Sam Taylor on the stairs. Taylor said, 'Good morning, Mr. Pierce,' Mr. Pierce said, 'Good Morning.' After he got back to his office he sent for Taylor and said, 'Sam, you went to school with me,' and Taylor said, 'Yes, Mr. Pierce.' 'Well,' said Mr. Pierce, 'you called me Mr. Pierce on the stairs just now. You always used to call me William, and I want you to continue to call me William just as you always did.' That was just a little thing, but subsequently whenever there was any dissatisfaction in the cutting room Sam would come down to the office and he and William would sit down at the table and settle the thing, each side giving in a little, and everyone would be satisfied. So there never was even the slightest hint of any labor trouble."

This parable was frequently told during the strike when all relationships between the owners and workers had been severed, the conclusion of the story serving as an eloquent moral lesson which the workers used to attack management.

"Every year they would shut down the plant," our interviewers were often told, in another story, "and the company would pay all the expenses of the employees for a day at the shore or in the country and everyone would have a share of chicken dinner costing two or three thousand dollars. The company had insurance for its employees, a benefit association, a hospital and trained nurse. . . . Of course all this cost a lot of money and added to the expense of making shoes."

In brief, the old owners were gods and not men. They had become heroes to labor as well as management. Where truth ends and idealization begins cannot be learned, but, fact or fiction, these memories stalked through the events of the strike like the ghost of Hamlet's father and motivated their sociological sons, their successors in the shoe business, to make decisions which were disastrous to them.

Before attempting to find out why the old owners became legendary heroes, let us look at the living managers who participated in the strike to discover further clues to this enigmatic situation where dead men often exerted more influence than did the powerful living.

Little Men and Aliens Run Things Now

There were an even dozen of them. John ("The Ram") Land, uterine nephew of the great Caleb Choate, leader of the shoe owners and partner of Cabot Pierce, son of the much beloved William Pierce, was the outstanding man on the side of the owners. His firm, Weatherby and Pierce, sold most of its shoes to Abraham Cohen and David Shulberg of the ABC Company. Cohen and Shulberg were "those New York Jews who are trying to run Yankee City." And then there were the Luntskis and Bronsteins, Jewish manufacturers from the suburbs of Boston.

Tim Jones and Fred Jackson were the local men of the firm of Jones and Jackson, but everyone knew that they took their orders from Abraham Cohen in New York. Finally, there was Biggy Muldoon, who must be thought of as more of a politician than an owner. He had been mayor of the town and was to be mayor again. These several managers divided into the "Yankee City men" and the "outsiders," and, when words grew hot, they were the "white men" and the "Kikes." As we said earlier, all of Yankee City was acutely aware of the powerful control the "outsiders" exerted over their lives, and everyone knew how little control the city had over the "outsiders."

"The men who run the shoe factories now don't even live in town," said a lady from an old family. "They drive down in the morning and spend the day making criticisms, then drive back at night, and no one knows how they live, how many automobiles or what kind of houses or how many children they have. They [the owners] don't know who their employees are or anything about them." Or, again: "At a time like this [during the

shoe strike] psychology is very important. Obviously a workman has just as much right to live as a big fat manufacturer; but
the manufacturers seem to think that their employees are way
beneath them and don't require a living wage. This is a buyers'
market, of course, and the manufacturer should have called his
people together long ago and put his cards on the table. . . .
But instead of anticipating any of these grievances the manufacturers went right on cutting and cutting and then they were
surprised when the employees went out. Anyone could have
known they were up for trouble."

"The Jews don't care a thing about people they employ or
their families," said an upper-middle-class Irishman. "They
think of people only as a means of making money."

"The manufacturers aren't real Americans," said a lower-
middle-class woman. "They have the idea that the more they
get out of us the better."

The several quotations above refer, of course, to the Jewish
manufacturers who did not live in Yankee City and who had
factories in other places. They were accused of "considering
Yankee City only as a shoe town where they could obtain good
quality of workmanship at a low labor cost." They were said
to feel no responsibility or interest in the welfare of their workers. It was said the ABC Company was seeking a monopoly
through price cutting of the turn-shoe trade and, therefore,
"has every incentive to lower labor costs as well as disinclination
through lack of personal interest to consider the welfare of the
shoe workers—and they control 70 per cent of the shoe business."

When the "outside" manufacturers claimed to have a personal interest in their employees, the chairman of the Strikers'
Emergency Committee, sarcastically reporting on a meeting
where such claims were made, said: "The manufacturers explained to us workers what good fellows we were and how
much they liked us shoemakers and how we had been one happy
family for all these years and they just couldn't see why us shoe
workers went out." When this story was told, as it often was, all
the workers laughed knowingly and remarks of the following

character were frequently made: "Yeah, we're all just one big happy family where all of us work for nothing," and "Picture that goddam New York Kike, he and his stooge, 'The Ram,' trying to get away with that kind of stuff. Why those bastards wouldn't give you the sweat off their balls!"

John ("The Ram") Land was the logical leader of the manufacturers' group, for he was the nephew of Caleb Choate. He had lived in Yankee City all his life and had always been associated with the shoe business there. His father and uncle started in the shoe business in 1866, Mr. Land's father putting in $2,000 and Caleb Choate, $100. Mr. Land's father soon went into partnership with a local man while Caleb went on salary as a cutter with the expressed desire of learning the business "from the ground up." In the next year, Caleb Choate went into business for himself and forged ahead. Later Mr. Land was in business with his son, John, and within a few years before the strike John had entered into partnership with Cabot Pierce, son of William Pierce, who had invested a large sum of money in the firm in return for which his son was offered a partnership. So by tradition and experience Land should have been the leader of the manufacturers' group. And yet let us see what the various shoe workers had to say of him:

"Land is an awful hard man to work for," said one. "He doesn't care how little money he pays."

"Land has a hard reputation," said a Riverbrooker. "He won't pay. He doesn't like to pay his help but spends money on himself freely."

"They brought out a new-style shoe, paying eighty-nine cents a case," said an Armenian worker. "I worked six hours on the first case. Had to do it over four times so that I worked two days for eighty-nine cents and I quit. The boss [Land] came around and finally said to pay time instead of piece. You work and slave and can't do a thing. A man with a family can't quit; they say if you don't like it, get out, there are plenty more. Land is the worst of them all, paying eighty-nine cents and others ninety- two cents to a dollar twenty-five for the same work. Sometimes shoes look just alike but have different prices. The boss said, "I can't help it, the buyer makes the prices.' We can't go on that way. I'd rather go out and starve."

"Land couldn't get in more workers," said a Greek worker, "because he has the reputation of only looking out for himself. People say no use working there."

An old and very much respected prominent Yankee City citizen (upper-middle) said: "He is a smart young man but the kind of person who whistles when he is on top and when he's beaten doesn't have much to say. He used to have meetings of his employees and I heard that he came in one afternoon to a meeting and said in a loud voice, 'If anyone wants to know who is boss around here just start something.'"

Shortly after the shoe strike, Mr. Land expressed his opinions about the strike and the reaction of the public to it and to him. He said: "The strike was illegal anyway. My workers were all under contract with me—perfectly legal and binding and they had no right to walk out the way they did. I believe in organized labor; in fact, I signed an agreement with the shoemakers just two months before to work through a shop committee. I always tried to be fair to them; when times were good I paid them very good money, but what would you do in times like this?

"I was surprised that merchants and townspeople sided with strikers right from the start when they knew the odds the manufacturers were working under just to give people work. It would be cheaper for me to go out of business, but I feel I owed the working people something and I didn't like to fail them out of a job. I felt like getting someone to organize store clerks and see how the merchants would like that. The shoe would be on the other foot.

"I realize conditions are bad sometimes but usually they're unintentional and due to some foreman. The people up at the top just didn't learn the facts about it. I thought I had been helpful and fair. I don't think I'm God Almighty so I was perfectly willing to leave the decision to a third party. I didn't get any credit for it, I know. Everybody in town thinks I am awfully hard-boiled."

During the strike, Land defended himself in a letter to the

strikers by likening his own behavior to that of Godfrey Weatherby. He said:

> Godfrey Weatherby, highly regarded in this community and considered a fair man, taught me that the correct division or breakdown of the hundred-per-cent selling prices was as follows: fifty per cent material, twenty-five per cent labor, ten per cent overhead, five per cent selling, five per cent discount, five per cent profit. I have checked up on this several times in all prices of shoes and with the National Shoe Manufacturers' Association and it is a fact that the breakdown of the sales dollar averages in these proportions, varying in some instances slightly where the selling is particularly low-cost because of connections, association, or some other condition permitting better materials to be used or higher paid labor.
>
> This last condition has prevailed in Yankee City and because of a fortunate position with respect to marketing they have paid their labor in excess of thirty-five per cent of their selling price. I don't believe there is a single factory in Yankee City whose labor cost is not thirty per cent of their selling price.

Even the president of the union gave us evidence which belied Land's "confession" that maybe he was "hard-boiled." The union president said: "Land started out determined not to recognize the union. He said he had always dealt with his employees individually and intended to continue doing so. I said to him that I didn't blame him for his attitude but I'd like to have him think a little bit. I said I understood he had had trouble with his employees two or three times before and that he had won, but it must have cost somebody a lot of money. Maybe he'd win this time, too, but who would guarantee that next year he wouldn't have trouble again. Land said he supposed everyone in town was calling him The Ram, and I said, 'Well, you go along the street and people say, "Good morning, Mr. Land," but you know very well they are calling you something else behind your back. Maybe you enjoy that.' After a while I won Land over and he was very helpful.

"I doubt if we could have settled the strike without Land. I had heard that in Yankee City Land had the reputation of being a pretty tough customer but he certainly hasn't shown up in that light this time."

Thus, we have a picture of the reputation of the man who, by tradition and experience, seemed destined as leader of the shoe manufacturers' group. He was characterized as selfish and grasping, hard-boiled, and lacking in personal dignity. He was disliked and distrusted by a good many of his employees. His very nickname, The Ram, suggested toughness and obstinacy. Contrary to his own words, he was believed to feel little or no responsibility for the welfare of his employees. His employees in town felt little or no loyalty toward him. And yet he must have had many qualities of leadership, judging by the labor arbitrators' comments concerning him and by the letters which appeared in the *Herald* over his signature during the strike.

As to Land's partner, Cabot Pierce, he seemed to take no very active part in the management of the shoe business. "Cabot Pierce is all right but hasn't any say," said a shoe worker. "Cabot Pierce has no brains. He has been to about six schools, but he didn't learn anything. His father took him in, but he couldn't seem to amount to much. He used to take the men away from their work to play cards with them. When his father discovered it he scolded the men and didn't say anything to Cabot. . . . I think he won't last very long on this job."

And from an interview with Pierce himself: "I feel badly about the small money people are making but what can we do? We have to make shoes just as cheaply as possible and there isn't any profit now in the shoe business."

During the shoe strike, Pierce appeared at the various conferences as a member of the manufacturers' group but did not participate actively in discussions; at least no mention is made of any contribution on his part. Cabot Pierce, resigned to defeat before management had lost the strike, sat on the sidelines frustrated and unhappy. The loss of thousands of dollars was on his mind, but the losses of the workers and his inability to think of anything he might do also pained him deeply.

Fred Jackson, of the firm of Jones and Jackson, on the other hand, over-participated in the strike with disastrous results to himself and interruptions to the negotiations in progress between the manufacturers and striking employees. Here is the story as John Nixon, president of the union, told it to an interviewer (later verified from interviews with management):

"One of the manufacturers, Fred Jackson, a snappy young fellow, came into a meeting and slapped a piece of paper down in front of me with a list of things Jones and Jackson proposed as an independent settlement. Jackson said, 'I'm going to make you eat that, Nixon.' And I said, 'Well, I don't happen to like paper, Mr. Jackson.' Jackson got very red and pulled a fifty dollar bill out of his pocket and slammed it down on the desk and said, 'You cover that, Nixon, and we'll go downstairs in the Mayor's office and whoever comes out first wins.' I said, 'Don't be so childish, Mr. Jackson.' I only had about forty cents in my pocket at the time. The story got to New York and Jackson was called down the next day and fired."

According to Fred Carter, the labor representative of the State Board of Arbitration, "the strike would have ended two weeks before if it hadn't been for Jackson. The manufacturers had all agreed to accept the union. Then someone started a rumor that the union intended to drive ABC out of Yankee City. Jackson heard it and, instead of investigating it or taking a trip to New York and discussing the matter, he got scared about his own job and wired ABC, who refused to sign up with the union. After ABC heard about Jackson's fuss with Nixon, Jackson got a long vacation. He was just a hot-headed young man with little experience or judgment."

The upper-class Mayor said: "Jackson was a hot-headed young fellow with no experience of this sort. It was just crazy, and flourishing the fifty dollar bill was crazier, of course. Nixon handled him beautifully."

From another we learn that "the Mayor followed Nixon almost to Boston to apologize for Jackson's action."

And a member of the Citizens' Committee observed: "Only a young man. He lost his head and tried to start a fight with Nixon. It shows pretty clearly he is not the type of man to win the confidence of his employees."

Jackson is the son of a small shoe retailer. He is said to have come from a Riverbrook family. His father set him up in business. He married a local girl who had formerly worked in a jewelry shop. According to one informant, "She flaunted her spending money, Pierce Arrow, chauffeur, and speedboat in a local beauty shop to the resentment of the other customers and staff who said that not so long ago she had been working for very little money herself." From behavior such as Mrs. Jackson's came the local opinion: "The manufacturers lowered wages but still get the same amount of profit, although they claim they are not making any money."

Of Timothy Jones, Jackson's partner in Jones and Jackson, we learn the following: "Jones and Jackson is a big plant. When they started, Jones had the experience and Jackson the money, or his father did. Jones lives across the river, and he has a lot of shoe workers for friends."

"Jones," said a shoe worker, "is a good man to work for. He came up from the bench himself, and he understands the shoe game. When they organized the workers and Jones encouraged them to walk out, he did it publicly. No secret about it."

A foreman of Land's said: "I know Tim Jones had been stirring up trouble. I think it's pretty poor for a man in his position to try to agitate the workers even though he is in sympathy with them. And I think it is terrible the way he talked about Mr. Land. . . . Jones told his employees that the last [pay] cut was due to Land, when, as a matter of fact, Land hadn't cut at that time."

"ABC owns a controlling interest—fifty-two per cent—in Jones and Jackson," said Cabot Pierce. "Jones and Jackson are only salaried managers. They have no power."

Jones often went to Polock Lizzie's (a speakeasy frequented by workers) with his Riverbrook cronies. He had lived in Yankee city all his life and claimed to know everyone.

A significant extract from an open letter from the shoemakers in the *Herald* during the strike tells the same story about Jones: "There is one man in the shoe business who has been very fair. We are sorry to have to cause him any trouble. We are all for him and know that conditions are beyond his control."

This item seems to prove conclusively that, in the minds of the shoe workers, Jones was identified with them in spite of his position as part-owner and manager. In his own mind, Jones was a paid employee rather than an owner. He said that in spite of owning stock he was just a paid manager and had to take orders from New York without any say as to what should be done.

The president of the Moses Bronstein firm lived in Boston and had a factory there as well as in Yankee City. The shoe workers said his attitude toward his workers could be judged by the story of the water cooler, reported by three different informants, apparently with some foundation. Bronstein installed a water-cooling system so that the employees could have cold water to drink in the summer. He bought it second-hand but ever since has been taking ten cents a week out of each employee's pay envelope to pay for it. The employees say they have paid for the cooler ten times over.

Bronstein's was called the "Penny Arcade" by the shoe workers because wage rates had been lowered so much.

A prominent Yankee City citizen said of Bronstein: "They say his sister comes into the factory and sells fruit and ice cream. Employees have to buy their food there, and she charges plenty high prices. Now you know Yankee City workers can't like that sort of thing . . . and the weekly ten cents out of each employee's pay envelope. That doesn't inspire a workman with confidence in his employer."

"At Bronstein's," said an Armenian worker, "the foreman doesn't like Yankee City men. They won't take them. They

want somebody from Boston or Lynn. The union will prevent
all that. We've been just like slaves."

The other Jewish concern in the city was Luntski's. One
worker said, "Luntski is a pretty good Jew. An item in the
Herald early in the strike said that the owners at Luntski's
promised to give five hundred dollars to the Shoe Workers'
Protective Union 'to carry on its work when an agreement is
made.' Nixon reported that Luntski's wanted to sign up with
the union without the 10 per cent increase. The strikers were
willing, but Nixon said he had given his word that all would be
treated alike."

Biggy Muldoon reported in his paper: "Luntski's say they
will give the union a five-hundred dollar gift when it starts.
Believe it or not. What big-hearted boys these birds are! When
they first came to Yankee City they came in a Ford. Next they
had a Packard, and now they are driving a big LaSalle. No
wonder they can offer five hundred dollars as a gift. The union
officials are hoping to be able to call their bluff."

Whatever the motive, Luntski's seem to have been perfectly
sincere in their desire to sign up with the union. They were the
first to sign the final agreement and the first, by several weeks,
to reach an agreement with the union on wage-rate adjustments.

Biggy Muldoon, president of the Muldoon Shoe Company, a
very small enterprise, showed significant contradiction in his
attitude toward the strike. A former mayor of Yankee City and
a local resident, Muldoon was the publisher of *Hard Facts,* a
weekly filled with personal material about the reputable citizens
of the city. People feared him because he was fearless and because his news items sometimes contained more than a grain of
truth about matters which citizens might prefer not to have
published.

During the strike Biggy came out repeatedly for the strikers
and against the manufacturers. Yet he complained in an issue
of *Hard Facts* that the Muldoon Shoe Company, of which Biggy
himself is the president, treasurer, and largest stockholder,
was not invited to the Saturday conference which the local

paper says was called by the Mayor. I think I should have been
at least invited, but then you know our Mayor is such a gentleman. He wouldn't want a roughneck like me in his company.

"Perhaps the Mayor was afraid Biggy might let out some of
the secrets. You know, folks, our Mayor was formerly in the
shoe business and posed as a shoe manufacturer, but in reality
he supplied about $80,000 in three years to let his brother-in-
law play around with a shoe system."

At a later meeting of the manufacturers and strikers which
Biggy did attend, he seems to have comported himself with
some dignity. According to an observer, he was quite reserved
and said very little compared to what he usually said.

Carter, of the State Board, reported that at a meeting of the
Board Muldoon sat alone on one side of the room. He sat quietly
for half an hour, then got up and went over and pointed his
finger at the other manufacturers who were sitting together and
said, "Why, if I knew as much about shoe manufacturing as you
fellows are supposed to I'd be ashamed not to pay employees
more money."

Muldoon asked why "you shoe manufacturers who make
your money in Yankee City don't sleep here, too?" He also
charged that the ABC firm was trying to monopolize the shoe
industry. He asked why "if the union could be recognized in
Boston it couldn't be recognized in Yankee City?"

His last question made a strong impression on everyone. According to the Mayor, "there was one thing the ABC people
couldn't explain and that was the reason they finally agreed to
the union, I think." He said, "They controlled the women's shoe
part of the ABC shoe factory in Boston. They are under contract with a union there, affiliated with the American Federation of Labor, to be sure. But in Boston the ABC factory is
under contract with this same union, the Shoe Workers' Protective Union, that the workers are striking for in Yankee
City." The Mayor said, "Cohen tried to get around it by talking
about greater speed in Boston but that didn't explain it."

Biggy's remarks in *Hard Facts* were most emphatic regarding
his stand on the strike situation. In an item headed "Labor

Rebels!" he said: "The greatest labor demonstration in the history of Yankee City has been witnessed during the present week with the outpouring of workers from every shoe factory in rebellion against starvation wages and in many factories against unsatisfactory conditions. It is evident that the workers have the public with them and they should keep a united front so as to be able to demand a just and living wage as a reward for their labor. Pull together and *Hard Facts* will stand by you one hundred per cent. We don't sit on the fence."

Yet, after the strike was settled the Muldoon Shoe Company was the next to the last to sign the contract with the union, a week after most of the other factories had signed.

Structural Analysis of the Status of the Old and New Managers

Shortly after Caleb Choate's death, a number of prominent Yankee City men published a memorial volume which contained the usual words of high praise for a great man. Since these same words, unlike those of many memorial volumes, were said about him by ordinary men of the street, and, as we have said earlier, were used during the strike, it is important to examine them. Mr. Perkins Cantridge of Hill Street, a member of one of the oldest families of Yankee City, wrote: "Caleb Choate was one of the most remarkable men ever connected with Yankee City; a businessman of liberal culture, of fine literary taste, gifted as an orator, in music and theatricals, . . . he was an acquisition to any society. He honored any public station, however high. . . . He achieved more in his fifty years of life than most men can point to after marking a very old age. . . .

"He was identified with the public health of this city and was a conspicuous figure in all its great social functions as long as his health permitted. He was a leading financier and a man who at once took and ever afterwards occupied a prominent position in this community. For years, by common consent, he was the leading man of the city. . . . Forcefulness of character made him the commanding spirit in every undertaking in which he shared and in every circle in which he moved."

Our analysis of Mr. Choate's participation in the community provides the crucial evidence on why Mr. Choate became the powerful symbol and collective representation which were used against the contemporary managers during the strike. We will briefly review some of the memberships that he had in the more powerful institutions of Yankee City.

In the business and financial sphere he was:

owner and head of his million-dollar shoe company;

president of one of the most powerful banks in the city;

member of the Board of Trustees of the Financial Institute, a firm of the utmost prestige and power in the community;

director of the Security Trust Company, another powerful financial institution;

director of the Yankee City Gas and Electric Company.

He was involved in a large number of civic enterprises and was a member of many civic institutions:

director and one of the founders of the city's most important hospital;

director of the Public Library;

member of the School Committee;

trustee of the Revere Free School;

president of the City Improvement Society.

He also took an important part in politics. He was:

chairman of the Republican City Committee;

member of the City Council;

delegate to the National Republican Convention;

mayor of the city.

Mr. Choate was also prominent in church and religious affairs. He was:

president of the Yankee County Unitarian Club;

president of the Yankee County Unitarian Conference.

He was a leader in fraternal affairs and was:

Past Master of St. John's lodge;

member of several important fraternal orders.

Mr. Choate was an active member of some of the most exclusive clubs of the city including:

the Drama Club;

the Thursday Night Club;
the January Club;
the February Club;
the Lowell Club;
the Country Club.

The evidence demonstrates that in all these organizations he was active and powerful. This brief survey of some of his participation in the community demonstrates that his activities ramified throughout the city and that much of the life of the city was centered in him. It also demonstrates that he accepted responsibility for the larger affairs of the community and helped integrate its activities, for he provided responsible leadership for the whole life of the community. "He was a man you could depend on."

Very much the same could be said about William Pierce and Godfrey Weatherby. They, too, were responsible elders of the city. Their factories provided jobs and wages. They were citizens of the town and men who felt obligated to it. Their membership in local institutions compares very favorably with that of Mr. Choate.

The essential point to remember about all three of these men is that they were subject to local control, because, first, they were dominated by local sentiments which motivated them "to take care of their own people"; second, they were under the powerful influence of the numerous organizations to which they belonged; and, third, their personal contacts with the local citizens directly related them to influences from every part of the city.

Mr. Cohen, Mr. Shulberg, Mr. Bronstein, and Mr. Luntski did not even live in the city. The workers knew or felt that the forces which controlled the local men did not control these outsiders. The vast network of relations and memberships which made Choate, Weatherby, and Pierce local leaders, as well as local manufacturers, was reduced to a purely economic relation of employer and employee. It was that and nothing more. It is small wonder that the workers "gave the horse laugh when the managers talked about being good fellows."

Mr. Cohen and his group belonged to the last period in the economic evolution of Yankee City we spoke of earlier, that of big-city capitalism, which had superseded the small-town capitalism in the vertical structure of corporate enterprise and had extended on beyond Yankee City to the great metropolises. At the time of the strike the local men, although born and reared in Yankee City, were little more than the factory managers for big-city capitalists since they occupied inferior positions in this vastly extended vertical structure.[5] They were not in a position to take leadership; they were not in a position of great power where they were free to make the decisions which always characterized the lives of Choate, Weatherby, and Pierce.

Each of these local men felt what had happened very deeply, and some of them were explicit enough about it to say so. We knew some of them well. They were not weak men or unscrupulous persons as their opponents made them out to be. They had good personal reputations in the business world. Some of them had been trained by their own fathers to be community leaders, but their place in the new socio-economic structure of Yankee City prevented them from playing this role, and each in his own way contributed directly to the defeat of the managerial group. Part of their ineptness was due to their inability to measure up in their own minds to the great men of the past. This was a dead past, glorious and safe, when men knew themselves to be free men and Yankee City was "the hub of the universe." Clinging to the traditions of Choate, Weatherby, and Pierce, both workers and management longed to return to those days when it was possible for William Pierce, with all his power and prestige, to stop and gently chide Sam Taylor, the cutter, and he and Sam could talk about "the trouble in the cutting room." Power was under control and security was present then; manager and worker were part of a self-contained system in which each knew his part.

5. In 1945 all the local men who had been managers during the strike were no longer connected with the shoe industry in Yankee City, but one of them was employed in the shoe business elsewhere. Shoe manufacturing in Yankee City is still dominated by outsiders and ethnics.

In these days of big-city capitalism, when Yankee City has lost control of its own destinies, few workers go up to the "big boss" to tell him about "what's wrong in the cutting room," and those who do are not considered respected friends at court of the workers but "stool pigeons who are getting theirs from management."

During the strike the local men cut poor figures as fighters for management's side. Tim Jones and Biggy Muldoon openly lined up with the strikers. Local sentiment and the feeling against "the foreigners" were too much for them. They materially contributed to the workers' victory.

Jackson damaged the cause of management when he tried to fight the head of the union. Everyone said he blustered, and everyone said he acted badly when he challenged union leadership. Jackson was under the control of higher management and occupied an inferior managerial position where he had little freedom to assume command and take leadership. Yet he had learned from William Pierce when he worked for him how his kind of man should act, and he knew that an owner and manager should assume control. It seems a reasonable hypothesis that the conflict between his beliefs about how a man should act (how Mr. Pierce would do it) and what he was permitted to do by his status greatly contributed to causing his unfortunate act, an act which materially aided the union. He tried to take command in a situation where it was impossible, and he could only "bluster."

His antagonist, on the other hand, was "top manager" of the union. He did have power and he could make decisions. His beliefs about what should be done and his status were commensurate, and he used them to the greatest effect for the cause of the union.

To the workers, Mr. Land was everything that an owner should not be. His letters to the workers only embittered them. His "high and mighty attitude" was ridiculed because they believed he wasn't free and that he had to take orders even as an owner from his one big customer, Mr. Cohen. Cabot Pierce refused to take any action. He felt defeated before the strike began and acted accordingly, and thus gave no strength to the managers' side.

All of these local men knew somehow they were "not the men their fathers were," and the three dead men, symbolizing the glorious past, overawed and helped defeat them.

In the days before big-city capitalism took control, the local enterpriser was financed by Yankee City banks. These banks and other investment houses possessed more autonomy and prestige than they do now. In the development of Mr. Choate's shoe empire, local financiers played important and necessary roles and, at least part of the time, were silent partners in the business. Much of the wealth they derived from their investments was reinvested in Yankee City. The money was put into new enterprises, their own living, or in civic activities. Their white Georgian houses on Hill Street, whose gardens bordered those of the manufacturers, were majestic symbols of their power and prestige and forever reminded, and often reassured, everyone of the visible presence of these powerful and protecting men in Yankee City.

The Yankee City financiers, too, were men of responsibility, dominated by sentiments of local pride. They did well for themselves, but they also did well for the city. Perhaps the price was high, but the product bought by the rest of the community was substantial and of high quality. Their philanthropies, combined with their power and leadership, contributed enormously to the city's development and provided a firm foundation for the larger civic life of the community. Parks, libraries, hospitals, societies to help the unfortunate and aged, foundations to send young men to college, endowments of schools, churches, and many other worthy civic and public enterprises were granted and maintained by the money and leadership of the local financiers and manager-owners.

The ABC chain store with all its satellite factories, scattered through many cities and financed by several New York investment houses, is but one of many enterprises that these New York financial houses control. Their body of investment included Yankee City because it is one of the tens of thousands of living areas which make up the world. The flow of wealth from Yankee City's banks and factories, once a great local arterial system giving life and strength to the town, now has shrunk to an infinitesimal part of big-city, world-wide capitalism, where it has no vital significance.

The following account about the finances of the ABC Company, taken verbatim from a June 1945 issue of a large New York newspaper, supplies clear evidence for every statement which has been made here about the extension of the vertical hierarchy and the submergence of Yankee City into a very minor role in a world-wide financial-industrial structure:

> A group headed by Oppenheimer and Co. and Brandeis and Son, and including the Stultz Co., has concluded an agreement for purchase of the majority of Lion Shoe Corp. stock, it was announced today.
>
> Lion Shoe will be merged into its wholly-owned retail subsidiary, the A.B.C. Shoe Corp., with subsequent public issue of securities of the latter company.
>
> Abraham Cohen, associated with the companies in an executive capacity for more than 20 years, will be elected president and general manager. Frederick Stultz, president of the Stultz Co., will be made chairman of the board.
>
> The A.B.C. Shoe Corp. owns a number of factories equipped to manufacture 20,000 pairs of shoes daily and operates a chain of 110 stores in 56 cities.

Decisions which vitally influence Yankee City and its chances of survival can be, and are being, made at the high levels of national and international finance which totally disregard all Yankee City's needs and vital interests. It is certain that decisions charged with ruin or success for the economy of Yankee City and the stability of the lives of its people are made by men at the policy level of such international financial houses who do not so much as know the name of Yankee City and who, beyond all doubt, do not care what happens to the town or its people.

The men of yesterday are dead; but their "souls go marching on" in the memories of the living, and Mr. Choate, Mr. Weath-

erby, and Mr. Pierce are collective symbols of that lost age
when the prestige and power of local financiers and producers
"took care of our own people." Admittedly, these men did it for
a high price, but at least the workers and ordinary town people
were more highly rewarded by Mr. Choate than by the banking
houses of New York and London. Today even the name of Yankee City is not known to those whose financial power often controls decisions of the utmost importance for the town. It is not
difficult to understand why the symbols of Mr. Choate, Mr.
Weatherby, and Mr. Pierce collectively represented small-city
finance and its lost rewards and satisfactions, as well as the one-
time security of local ownership of the factories. Given the significance of the symbols, it is obvious why they became allies
of the strikers and helped force management into submission.

From this analysis, several important propositions can be
offered which contribute to our understanding of why the strike
happened and why it took the course it did. The vertical extension of the corporate structure of the shoe manufacturing
enterprises had pushed the top of the hierarchy into the great
metropolises and, in so doing, had brought in outsiders who
were "foreigners' 'in culture and lacking in understanding, feeling, and prestige for the local workers and for the town itself.

This extension of the industrial hierarchy reduced the local
men to inferior positions where they were incapable of making
decisions and could not initiate actions which would give them
the power of leadership for the workers and for the rest of the
town. Reducing the local managers to inferior statuses in the
factory contributed to their lower social-class ranking in the
community and thereby greatly reduced their strength as leaders
and men who could form community opinion in times of crisis
when the position of management was threatened. They could
no longer lead the workers or the community. Because of the
inferior position of the managers, those men in the community
who would have once been their natural allies and who enjoyed
top social-class position were now above them and shared none
of their interests, were hostile to them and friendly to the workers. The vertical extension of the corporate structure of the shoe

business introduced owners into the community who had only economic memberships, whereas in the previous period of local control an owner had power and leadership in all of the important institutions.

The longing for the idealized past when men had self-respect and security was symbolized in the three dead owners; and these symbols materially aided the workers in defeating management, since the workers and management felt that the present men could not match the "gods" of the past. The workers and managers in the shoe industry had lost their sense of worth and mutual loyalty. No longer were they men who had a common way of life in which each did what he had to do and, in so doing, worked for himself and for the well-being of all.

Rationality, Nonrationality, and the Expansion of the Social System

This brings us to what is called the "human factor" in industry and other highly rationalized institutional systems. A human social maze may be so constituted that the planned society can train its citizenry from infancy to learn to act as rational men in a rational social universe. But these same men and women are composed of muscle and bone, viscera and nerves, and animal impulses. As members of their species they possess a subcultural interactive system of behavior that is species behavior, which existed before culture and still lives within it. This basic species behavior must forever be expressed through cultural forms and seep into the rational and logical world of men; thus the world of human feelings and of deep sentiment must forever establish its place in men's actions and their social systems.

Risk-taking has been decreased enormously in man's relations to nature. The margin of safety has steadily increased, and some small advance has been made in understanding and controlling the human factors to reduce risk in human interaction; but no people can impose logical and rational action on its social order too far without experiencing serious and possibly disastrous results. All too often in the minds of the planners, planning means the reduction of the impulse and nonrational

life of the people and the increase of logical behavior. Successful planning must necessarily be fashioned around the basic
needs of our human kind as members of an animal species. The
family in large part provides the institutional control which men
have fashioned for this purpose. Behind its walls impulse life is
permitted. It can be argued that our present and past efforts to
reduce economic risks and to rationalize social relations have
reduced the role of the family and enormously decreased its
effectiveness as a place where the two sexes and the two generations can satisfy the deep basic needs of their species and dis-
charge their animal energy in a form suitable to them and their
society. When built on the fragile and explosive foundations of
family and community systems in which the basic human needs
of the people are not satisfied and often frustrated, such well
meant schemes will always be failures unless those who fashion
these logically planned orders take account of the species whose
culture needs must be cared for. No social order extending itself
vertically and horizontally, while systematizing and rational-
izing the actions and relations of its members, can ever achieve
any kind of permanent equilibrium.

While our corporate hierarchies have heightened and expanded into more powerful enterprises and spread throughout
the nation and the world, the unions have developed from weak,
ephemeral, and loosely organized local units into vast systems
with their own powerful hierarchies whose higher officials deal
at a coordinate level with top management. The effects of these
developments cannot be overemphasized. Not only the executives of local factories and unions lose the power to deal with
each other as they did in Yankee City, but the executive heads of
great companies are now relinquishing their right to make decisions in favor of the representatives of the whole industry who
meet and deal with the union representatives of workers from
that same industry. Although their common industrial interests
are basic, the status interests of the top levels of management
and the workers are in opposition. This conflict necessarily results in the employment of a third party to act as a referee. Since
the church has lost its great power as a regulator, the only ref-

eree now available to the high representatives of these great opposing forces is the government. As the other hierarchies have elaborated larger and more diverse units into new structures, the government has reduced the power of its local and secondary offices and placed power in the upper brackets of the federal state. The referee between the two great conflicting forces of workers and management must necessarily be endowed with great social power and be able to apply sanctions with sufficient force to maintain moderate collaboration between the two for the good of all the people.

As long as the governmental, labor, and management systems remain separate, the partial or full integration of American society can only be maintained by the subjugation of one of the contestants by the other, by the destruction of the power of one of them by the government, or by the government's treating the whole matter as a combat between two equal forces where each side can score a little but not too much. This latter condition will probably remain with us in America until a time when our country's social system re-integrates itself and the opposing forces now focused in the conflict of capital and labor are controlled or express themselves in some other form.

There are increasing evidences that, if catastrophe does not overtake us, the power to compose labor difficulties will move beyond national governments to an international governmental locus. The present chaotic condition of world affairs is not so much due to ideological differences, great as they may be, as to the failure of human beings to evolve a substantial social organization which will encourage and reward cooperation and collaboration around the common enterprise of making the world socially inhabitable. The failure to fashion such a system should not necessarily be made a moral score against us, for it is possible that the processes to which we have referred earlier may be operative but not apparent to us because we are too close to what is happening. It may be that the dual and interdependent processes of specialization and greater division of labor, on the one hand, and increasing social complexity, development of larger groupings, involvement of a greater number of people, and lengthening of the social hierarchy, on the other, are occurring with almost revolutionary speed. Until now these processes and the social movements which ideologically express them have been centered in the great world powers. The British Empire has built one system, Soviet Russia another, and the United States a third, while China is desperately attempting to construct another. Japan and Germany—temporarily, at least —have failed in their attempts. Elaborate economic, political, associational, and ecclesiastical hierarchies have been established in each of these areas to form the scaffolding of cultural activities. Meanwhile the differentiating processes taking place in each of these countries have made the citizens more alive, while forcing the citizens of each to be aware of the fact that they are members of different systems.

The structural hierarchies of the separate world areas interact outside their own orbits with those of other regions, but each areal system possesses strong autonomy, and the locus of power is centered within it. Great international capitalistic enterprises, often monopolistic in character, have succeeded in effectively crossing national boundaries and have developed methods of organizing some of the diverse economic units of the world. Opponents of such systems continue to fight what the authors believe to be no more than rearguard battles which only delay the advance. Such capitalistic enterprises are the enemies of nationalism, and, as citadels of capitalistic power, they are the foes of labor and of the remnant forces of nineteenth-century liberalism. The cartel, one of the most powerful forms of international capitalism, must be recognized as a new social structure, developed by us in our desperate efforts to reorganize human behavior to function on an international basis. At the present time such economic institutions may or may not be evil in their effect, but international economic institutions of some kind are absolutely necessary if the world is to evolve a reliable international order.

Technological processes which are already in existence— such as instant world-wide communication, rapid transportation, and international exchange of goods and services—and the social process inherent in the increasing divisions of labor in each of the larger social areas make people everywhere increasingly alike and interdependent. Therefore, it seems probable that, unless disaster forces us to retreat to barbarism, the present international economic systems must, after adjusting to new social controls, ultimately triumph.

The extension of institutions over more diverse peoples and activities (horizontally) must be accompanied by vertical extensions which increase the social distance from the bottom to the top of institutional hierarchies. The extension both horizontally and vertically of the international economic institutions over more men and a greater variety of their activities will only be secure when the economic institutions are complemented by church, associational, and political hierarchies. The development of these other institutions will permit them to act internationally as counterforces to achieve a balance of power between them and the economic order, much as our society once enjoyed on a national level when there was equilibrium between the social and economic institutions in Western Europe and in the United States. It is impossible to predict what the new social order which is now evolving will be. Once the society is formed it is doubtful if such labels as "fascist," "communist," or "capitalist" could be realistically applied to it. We can say with certainty, however, that if such a system is formed the social principles characteristic of hierarchies will be stressed more than at present, since the peoples who compose it will be more diverse and more difficult to organize, and the need for lines of authority and responsibility will be greater than in any other time in the history of man.

Part III. Transition: The Movement of Ethnic Groups into the Life of the Community

Introduction

THE SOCIAL HISTORY of the ethnic groups of Yankee City was studied from the time of their arrival in the town until the time of the research to discover what residential, economic, class, and institutional developments had taken place and ascertain if there were common tendencies and determinants in the life of each group. The chapters which follow examine residential, economic, and class developments.

The term *ethnic* refers to any individual who considers himself, or is considered to be, a member of a group with a foreign culture and who participates in the activities of the group. Ethnics may be either of foreign or of native birth. For example, a Greek born in the United States who regularly attended the Greek coffee houses, participated in the Greek associations, and served on the school and church committees of the Greek community was classified as a member of the Greek group. In the present chapters greater emphasis is placed on descent (by use of genealogical materials) than in Part I. Because of this there are occasional minor differences in count.

The ethnic groups entered Yankee City in this order:

	Decade of Arrival	Population 1933
Irish	1840-1850	3,943
French Canadians	1880-1890	1,466
Jews	1890-1900	397
Italians	1890-1900	284
Armenians	1900-1910	246
Greeks	1900-1910	412
Poles	1910-1920	677
Russians	1910-1920	141

The ethnic groups of Yankee City, with the exception of the

Jews, originated in a European rural-village type of social economy. They lived in scattered households, each identified for
generations with its own small holding of farm and pasture land
and joined by a network of dirt roads which converged on the
village center. This center generally consisted of the parish
church and cemetery, the village mill, smithy, tavern-clubhouse,
and open marketplace. Near the village were the estate and
grand manor of the aristocrat landowner to whom the peasant
villagers were related as servant tenants. The villages generally
comprised from twenty-five to one hundred families.

Typically this was an unchanging and undifferentiated folk
society in which an event affecting the individual was also the
affair of the entire group, and an event affecting the group was
at once the affair of every individual. Attachments to the land,
locale, and group and family tradition had strong holds upon
the sentiments. These sentiments were at times reinforced by the
solidarities of a larger area such as the county in Ireland, the
province in Poland and Russia, and the section in Italy. These
solidarities often were so strong as to be directed antagonisti-
cally against comparable neighboring areas in the same country.

This pattern is in contrast to the urban type of residential
system represented in Yankee City. The ecological base of the
city is only secondarily and remotely the land as such. Identifi-
cations with place, strong in the peasant village, are shallow and
weak in large American cities, although they are reorganized in
a diluted form around the unit of the neighborhood. Yankee
City, however, is unusual in its preservation of a strong sense of
locale, attributable unquestionably to the part its geography
played in the period of its maritime importance. But even in
Yankee City neighbor relations are much compressed compared
to those in the folk communities of Europe. As a consequence
of spatial crowding and competition for place, impersonal,
somewhat formal relations among neighbors in Yankee City
replace the intimate give-and-take of relations in the peasant
village.

The ethnic in his native village was identified with a plot of
land which had been tilled for generations, often centuries, by

his forebears. Moreover, his relations with the more distant members of the community were almost as close as with his immediate neighbors. In a relatively homogeneous ecological order, he could visit about freely. In Yankee City, however, in spite of relative instability of residence in the areas originally open to ethnic settlement, the ecological system provides barriers limiting the range of residential movement and the range of possible social relations as well. One is a relative stranger in most areas other than the one in which he lives.

The ethnic group, soon after settling in Yankee City and achieving adequate population numbers, is segregated in the most accessible, i.e., in the lowest-grade, areas of the city and remains identified with those areas, often for decades. However, once the group has adapted itself to the new order, it breaks from its isolation and begins moving into the large community.

CHAPTER 12

Living Space and the Advancement of the Ethnic Generations

Methods for the Study of the Generations

THE ethnic generation born abroad and migrant to this country is the one attached most strongly to the ancestral social system and its derivative, the ethnic community in Yankee City, and least to the Yankee City social system. In this study this will be called the "parental" or the "P" generation.

The offspring of these immigrants, the "filial first" or the "F^1" generation, having been born, reared, and schooled in the United States, know nothing of the ancestral society of their parents except as it is partially represented in the ethnic group's community organization. The members of the F^1 generation acquire wider external relations with the Yankee City society than their parents and bring more elements of American culture into their internal group relations. The children of the F^1 generation, whom we label F^2, and the children of the F^2 generaton, whom we label F^3, exhibit similar progressive shifts in social personality.

A final differentiation is made by dividing the immigrants into two distinct generations, the P^1 and the P^2, on the basis of a marked difference in social-personality reorientation which is observed between those who migrated as mature, crystallized personalities and those who migrated as immature, "unfinished" personalities.[1] The latter, quite aside from the fact of their American schooling, are able to shift their social orientation more quickly and easily than can the older immigrants, as is suggested by the fact that in social-personality type the P^2 generation is intermediate in orientation between the P^1 and F^1 generations. We have set the migrational age of eighteen as the line distinguishing the P^1 from the P^2 generation.

The whole classificatory scale of ethnic generations takes the following form:

P^1. The immigrant generation which entered the United States at an age over 18.

P^2. The immigrant generation which entered the United States at an age of 18 or under.

F^1. The native-born offspring of P^1 and P^2.

F^2. The native-born offspring of F^1.

F^3. The native-born offspring of F^2.

F^4. The native-born offspring of F^3.

This generation scale makes possible a more refined analysis of status mobility and progress of assimilation than is permitted by the analysis of historical source materials alone. We were able to follow the rise of each group through the community as a unit and also to isolate variations in mobility among successive generations within the group. Further, we were able to compare corresponding generations among the various ethnic groups for variations and associated factors in status movements and processes. We could also follow the internal changes of the ethnic communities in the order of the successive generations.

We shall attempt to place in a measured time perspective the changes in the internal and external organization of each ethnic

1. In at least one American ethnic group, the Japanese, the generation we have distinguished as the P^2 is explicitly named "Hansei," i.e., "half immigrant." Likewise, the P^1 generation is called "Issei," i.e., "immigrant"; the F^1 generation group labeled "Nisei," i.e., "first native-born generation"; and "Sansei" is applied to the generation we have designated F^2.

group and also to compare the original contexts of the ancestral societies from which these groups were derived. Characterizations of the major aspects of these societies are presented in the chapters which follow. Of course, the complete context of Yankee City must be kept in view. General aspects of the society will be referred to whenever they are related specifically to developments in the ethnic groups.

All the ethnic groups in Yankee City except the Jews stem from a rural-peasant type of social system. Are there cultural differences which have had special effects on the course of group interaction in Yankee City? What effect, if any, has a variant social background of a group on its Yankee City development?

If age of the group in the city is a critical variable, what is the influence of the particular order of appearance in the city upon the eight ethnic groups? That is, will an earlier group have more difficulties, or less, and experience slower advance, or faster, than the group which follows it? Further, what weight must be assigned to changes in the Yankee City social system itself which may present the earliest group with conditions not faced by the group last to enter the city?

In summary, this study is an attempt to accomplish the following:

1. To describe in detail, through two time scales and in terms of the relevant contexts, the steps and processes by which eight ethnic groups have

    a. progressively advanced in the major status hierarchies of Yankee City and

    b. progressively adapted the internal organization of their community systems.

2. To analyze the factors, constant and variable, attending these processes, including the interactive role of Yankee City itself.

3. To abstract wider generalizations concerning the nature of social assimilation and acculturation.

The underlying problem of this study is an examination of

the validity of America's conception of itself as the "great melting pot."

Residential Zones

For purposes of analysis and definition, we have constructed a schematized version of the city's residential areas based on four zones, as represented in Figure 13. Zone I is at the foot of the city's slope directly fronting the river. Here are concentrated most of the factories, coal yards, storage tanks, warehouses, and smaller retail establishments. The houses are usually small, frame, somewhat flimsy, often abutting on the sidewalk. Some are of the box-tenement type. Many are from one hundred to one hundred and fifty years old, often in disrepair. The streets are narrow and some are still unpaved. In population, this is the largest of the zones and also the most dense. The zone has been divided into two sections along Commonwealth Street. Section I-E (East End) is somewhat older than Section I-W (West End), has fewer retail stores, and is more crowded. Houses in I-W are one degree better in quality and upkeep. Section I-E is associated primarily with the lower-lower class and secondarily with the upper-upper class, whereas in Section I-W the order is reversed. Wharf Square, a point of concentration for several ethnic groups, is at the intersection of Commonwealth and River Streets, where Sections I-E and I-W join.

Zone III runs the full length of Hill Street and includes the residences immediately adjoining on the side streets. In contrast to Zone I, the finest and largest houses in the city are found here —those which in an earlier period were known as "princely mansions." Many are set far back from the street with well-kept gardens and shaded by old trees. Hill Street itself is forty feet wide and covered by an arch of ancient elms. There are no business establishments, with the exception of an ice-cream parlor beside the high school and a garage and small store where railroad tracks cross the street at the only low-evaluation spots in the zone. This is the smallest of the four zones, both in area and population, and the lowest, except for Zone IV, in population density. We have already indicated that this zone is primarily

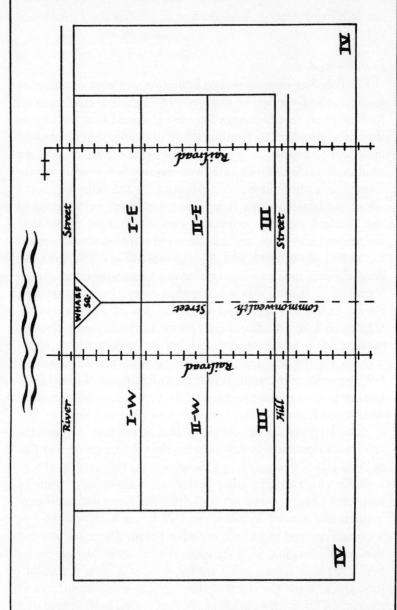

Fig. 13. Residential Configuration of Yankee City

identified with the upper classes, although it is now also occupied by an important part of the upper-middle class.

Zone II, between Zones I and II, has few factories but contains all the better retail shops, including the central business section with its stores, offices, theaters, banks, clubrooms, and public buildings. The houses are midway in quality between those of Zones I and III and in better condition than those of the former. Generally they are set back from the walks, which like the streets are uniformly well paved. In area covered and in the size and density of population, Zone II is second only to Zone I. As in the case of Zone I, we have divided Zone II into two sections, one on each side of Commonwealth Street. The important differences between the two sections are that II-W is newer than II-E and its houses, on the whole, are one grade better and not quite so crowded. The zone is primarily associated with the middle classes. However, by far the largest part of the upper-middle class not in Zone III is collected in the western section of Zone II.

Zone IV is a thinly settled peripheral area. House types range from medium grade to lowest. Many houses, particularly on the southern side, are on unpaved streets, in small groups separated by considerable expanses of field. Gardening and a little light farming are still carried on here. There are no business places. It is the largest of the four zones and, Zone III excepted, the lowest in population density. In class composition Zone IV is the most mixed, ranging from the lower-lower class through the lower-middle.[2]

The zones can be arranged in a graded scale according to status value:

  1. Section I-E: lower-lower and upper-lower classes.
  2. Section I-W: upper-lower and lower-lower classes.
  3. Zone IV: lower-middle, upper-lower, and lower-lower classes.

2. The regions called zones here correspond only roughly to the "areas" in Part I. The "residential zones and sections" were fashioned to meet the needs of the ethnic analysis and are based on the more general evaluation of the territory of Yankee City made by its citizens.

4. Section II-E: lower-middle and upper-lower classes.

5. Section II-W: lower-middle and upper-middle classes.

6. Zone III: upper-upper, lower-upper, and upper-middle classes.

The various residential areas of Yankee City appear in a continuously graded series according to their status value. To determine the average residential status of a group in any one year, we shall utilize a status index. Such an index is computed, first, by assigning consecutive numbers in a series from one to six to each successively higher level (residential areas) in the hierarchy. The group's population by household in any given year is multiplied by the number value allocated to the area of residence. The sum of these products is then divided by the total number of household units in the group for the given year. The quotient is an index number between one and six expressing the status of the group as a whole in terms of an average.

The distribution of the Irish in 1850 is an illustration:

Area	Value	Number of Households	Product
I-E	1	48	48
I-W	2	41	82
IV	2.5	0	0
II-E	3	13	39
II-W	4	2	8
III	6	0	0
		104	177

The correspondence between the sections and zones and the "areas" of Part I is: Section I-E includes all of Riverbrook and those parts of Oldtown, Uptown, Business District (up to the railroad tracks), Downtown, and Middletown which are nearest the river; II-E includes the remainder of the six areas up to Hill Street; I-W includes all of Littletown and the river sections of the Business District beyond the railroad tracks, Homeville, and Newtown; Zone III includes all of Hill Street, the central section of Newtown and Oldtown, and the territory of Middletown, Uptown, Business District, Centerville, and Hometown contiguous to Hill Street; and Zone IV includes the extremities of all the areas which extend beyond Hill Street.

The summation of the products (177) divided by the total number of households (104) give a quotient of 1.70, the residential status index. Were the entire Irish group in 1850 in Area I-E, the index of course would be 1; and were the group entirely concentrated in I-W, the index would be 2. Hence, if we suppose that the Irish index in 1840 had been 1, the 1850 index of 1.7 expresses the fact that for every ten households in the group there has been an average upward mobility of seven steps (in terms of the series of graded areas) during the decade. Had there been an average advance of ten steps, then of course the index would have been 2.[3]

Table 5 presents the status indices of each ethnic group by

Table 5. *Residential Status Indices, 1850–1933*

	1850	1864	1873	1883	1893	1903	1913	1923	1933
Irish	1.70	1.95	2.11	2.11	2.12	2.22	2.37	2.57	2.85
Fr. Canadian					1.67	1.78	1.77	2.13	2.43
Jewish							1.93	2.14	2.77
Italian								2.21	2.38
Armenian								2.39	2.57
Greek								2.40	2.54
Polish								1.25	1.40
Russian									1.32

3. It must be emphasized that the values attached to the several areas are arbitrary and have principally a serial value. The fact that Area I-W is given a numerical value of 2 and Area I-E is given a value of 1 does not imply that the former has twice as much status value as the latter. It means only that Area I-W is one level higher in the residential scale than is Area I-E. Our purpose is to measure the average advance of a group in terms of such levels.

We have allowed two exceptions to our assignment of values in a series of 1. Given the residential and social-class characteristics of Area IV, it is felt that movement to this area, let us say, from Area I-W cannot be considered equivalent to an advance of a full level, such as, for example, would be represented by movement from Area I-E to I-W. Hence, we have considered Area IV as being a half-step between Areas I-W and II-E. On the same grounds, movement from II-W to Area III, covering Hill Street, is by no means equivalent to movement from II-E to II-W. For that reason movement to Area III has been considered the equivalent of two steps upward from II-W.

decades through its occupation of Yankee City in significantly large family numbers. Manifestations of accelerating mobility in successive ethnic groups may be pointed out.

Four of these groups appear in their first important decade year with a higher index than did the group preceding; three—the French Canadians, Poles, and Russians—are lower. The concentration of the French Canadians in the city's East End has tended to depress their index. However, these three groups excepted, the first decade-year indices increase as follows: Irish, 1.70: Jews, 1.98; Italians, 2.21; Armenians, 2.39; and Greeks, 2.40.

A second instance of accelerating mobility is seen especially in the case of the three oldest groups. On the basis of the indices above, the average mobility each decade by the Irish is .14; by the French Canadians, .19; and by the Jews, .42. The most striking advance made by the Irish is in the last three decades, by the French Canadians in the last two decades, and by the Jews in the last decade—each progressing about .66. That is, in these periods fully two families in every three, on the average, moved upward one whole level in residential status.

What conclusions and generalizations of significance may we draw from this evidence of the movements through the years of the ethnic groups?

Ethnic External Pattern in the Residential System

First and most important is the fact that all ethnic groups, in relation to the Yankee City residential system, behave with a varying degree of uniformity in a definite pattern. The elements in this ethnic pattern are as follows:

1. All groups concentrate first in Zone I and within Zone I on River Street. However, Zone IV represents a secondary gate of ingress.

2. Mobility upward into Zone I from River Street begins early and progresses continuously through the zone and out of it into Zone II.

3. Within Zone I every group, except the Irish, confines it-

self predominantly either to the East or to the West End Section and remains fixed.

4. In corresponding periods for successive groups the trend of mobility seems to be accelerated.

The question arises as to the conditions which influenced the first settlement of all ethnic groups without exception in Zone I. Many ethnics give as their answer that industry was concentrated in the zone, and they established residence convenient to their place of work. Of the early Irish, one Irishman said: "They took a job where they could and settled nearby." A Polish informant said of his own group: "The Poles are concentrated on River Street because that is where the cotton mills were and where now are the shoe factories."

But it is clear that convenience to the city's workshop area was only an apparent factor in the ethnics' first residential selection. The Jews, who have never had more than a negligible representation in the factories, were no less concentrated in Zone I.

Three factors seem pertinent, two of which are suggested in the remarks of a Greek informant: "The Greeks, coming like this to America, live in with the lowest classes of Americans. It is because of poverty that they have to go into the poor district to live. But actually it isn't so much different from the way they lived in Greece."

First, then, is the fact that the standard of housing, even on River Street, is no lower and probably considerably higher than that which the ethnics were accustomed to in their native villages, and hence sufficient, at least in the beginning, for their level of need and taste.

Second, even had their demands been higher, the ethnics, on the whole, arrived in Yankee City in a poverty-stricken condition. With rentals continuously graduated upward on the city's incline, the lowest rents were in Zone I on River Street.

The third factor, related to the second, is that upward from the waterfront the proportion of homeowners increases regularly. Zone I, with the lowest proportion of homeowners, is the most accessible to an ethnic group since there are more places to occupy by tenancy and a greater degree of residential movement.

In all these respects, except in the number of rentable houses, the sparsely settled peripheral Zone IV, at certain points, closely approximates the conditions in Zone I, accounting for the fact that as a threshold to the city for the ethnics it was second in importance to Zone I.

The second element in the pattern is that, once established on River Street, the ethnic group begins to advance, slowly but certainly, in one direction predominantly, southward and upward toward Hill Street. We shall undertake an analysis of the force which impels the undeviating ethnic drift up the city's incline and of the factors which have influenced the rate of progress.

Such movement on the part of all eight ethnic groups in Yankee City may be attributed to what we shall call "hierarchical attraction," a force which disposes those resident in any one area to aspire to a home in the area next higher in the scale. The act of translating that aspiration into movement into the higher area is what has been constantly referred to here as residential mobility. This force operates in the three status hierarchies of Yankee City.

It is true, of course, that conditions both in his background and in the Yankee City system compel the ethnic to settle first in River Street. Influenced early, however, by the attractions of the Yankee City hierarchy, the ethnic takes his first step upward by moving from his original River Street house to a residence somewhat higher in Zone I. But each step upward immediately defines and presents the next higher step. Hence the ethnic at intervals continues his ascent, pausing only as long as his income or other considerations preclude his paying the added cost and until a dwelling place for him in the higher area is available. The latter is no minor condition, as we shall soon see. Residential mobility, partially at least, is contingent upon economic mobility and is almost an indispensable condition for social-class mobility.

Insight into the process of residential mobility is afforded by the remarks of an elderly Irishman: "The Irish were laborers, but they were thrifty and saved their money. Just the minute they had enough, they took it to buy property in a better section. The same thing is true of the French, and the rest of the new workers. So there was considerable movement." The key to the thinking here lies in the "but" which implies the tentativeness of the status value identified with "laborers"; and the "but" hinges this tentativeness of status upon the acquisition of a home "just the minute they had enough money" in a section, which we know from evidence already reviewed, was upward from River Street.

Similarly, a Jewish informant told us: "First the Jews were all around Wharf Square and River Street. When they made money they bought up property gradually more and more outside the Square."

As in the physical realm, where attractions are partially counteracted by resistive frictions, mobility in social hierarchies does not proceed free of resistance. In fact, at each successive level the resistance tends to become more active. Such resistance is an aspect reciprocal to attraction and takes different forms in different hierarchies.

If a given area is attributed a relatively high value, and if persons of lower status attempt to move into that area, the area is threatened with a reduction, to some degree at least, of its current values. The work of the Chicago sociologists attests to the "decline" or "disintegration" of areas in American cities through shifts in the population. To protect an area's status value, its residents will resist the incursion of a lower-status group. This resistance appears in a number of different forms, both systemic and individual. In the first place, the higher the value of the area, the higher is the level of the rent demanded. There is money sacrifice involved in residential mobility which operates as a highly selective factor to reduce mobility. Second is the fact that the proportion of family-owned homes increases up the the residential scale, so that progressively fewer houses are available for rent. Hence mobile families are confronted with a contracting supply of places open to tenancy and the increasing necessity of purchasing a house. The latter, together

with the rise of property values in successively higher areas, acts
as an even more rigorous resistive force. Third is the pressure
applied to counteract mobility by property owners who, in defense of the area's status and property values, refuse to sell or
rent to "undesirables." A fourth form of resistance is the social
ostracism practiced by residents of the area on those who have
succeeded in "crashing." One Jewish woman, after ten years
of residence in Zone III, complained bitterly of her neighbors
that "they are not friendly at all."

Finally, when all else fails, more drastic steps may be taken.
For example, one upper-class woman, in discussing the house
occupied by her daughter, added: "The landlord has just rented
the next house to some terrible Jewish family, so my daughter
must move." It is significant that the imperative "must" is used
here. Similarly, one Irish informant related that immediately
after he had purchased a house on the edge of Zone III, the
owner-occupant of the next house "came to us and offered to
pay us a thousand dollars more than we had paid, because he
didn't want to have us living next to him." The offer was turned
down, and the discriminating gentleman who had made it soon
after sold his place and moved to Hill Street.

Another incident was reported by a Jewish informant: "Mr.
Cohen was the first one on Apple Street [Section II-E]. And the
people around objected to his horse and wagon and the junk in
the barn. So right away houses on both sides and across from
him went on sale, and other Jews came in and bought these.
So now there are six Jewish families on Apple Street where
there used to be none. That's the way it went." Today these six
families form a closely knit nucleus on Apple Street, such nuclei
having been found from time to time among other ethnic groups
who were beginning to penetrate Zone II. In fact, of the fifteen
Irish families who were in Section II-E in 1850, ten are arranged in exactly such a nucleus along a single street.

Still another instance of resistance exerted not against an
ethnic family but against the ethnic group at large was described
by an old Irish gentleman: "When the Irish built their church
here they had to have someone else buy the land for them be-

cause no Protestant would have sold them the land in that place (Zone III). And when the people found out about it they were very sore." Some eighty years later, when the Jewish community came to buy a vacated church building in upper Section II-W for use as a synagogue, the families in the area again "were very sore," and a petition was circulated to influence the mayor "to keep the purchase from being made."

At certain points in the city this type of resistance has operated successfully to bar entrance of ethnics, as in the case of one special area in Section I-E, almost completely devoid of Irish or other ethnics. An Irishman said of the area: "There is plenty of room in it, but the Irish never made much headway in it. They all hate the Irish."

Certainly, resistance has not stopped ethnic mobility in other areas, Zone III not excluded, but it has greatly impeded the rate of advance. How else can one explain the phenomenon that a group as socially aggressive as the Irish went through almost eighty years of slow "inching along" before its members reached representation on Hill Street?

Furthermore, but for the regular emigration of natives from Yankee City, such resistance would have been even more effective; the emigration opened houses for rent and sale, especially in Zone II, that would not otherwise have been available. Partially counteracting this condition were the facts, first, that natives from the lower areas were competing with the ethnics at an advantage for the openings on Zone II; and second, that the ethnic population grew faster than the native population declined, and hence increasing numbers of ethnics were competing among themselves for a relatively fixed number of places in the "better" areas.

A clear-cut manifestation of increasing resistance among areas consecutively higher in the residential scale is found in the higher rates of ethnic advance in Section I-E as against I-W, and in II-E as against II-W. In fact, this has been a condition which determined the original choice of each group between Sections I-E and I-W.

It will be remembered that the Irish in 1850 were living along most of the length of River Street through Sections I-E and I-W and that by 1873 they were beginning to move upward from River Street. While this progress was relatively slow in Section I-E, the pace was even more retarded in Section I-W. Hence, when the French Canadians first came to Yankee City in some numbers in the middle eighties, they found the Irish almost clear of the Section I-E strip of River Street and well up into the section, while in Section I-W the Irish were still at the bottom of the area and still well represented on River Street, which they were not to leave until 1903. Thus, River Street in the former section was open to the French Canadians, whereas in the adjoining section it was effectively blocked off by the Irish. As a result, the French Canadians settled en masse in Section I-E, especially on River Street, exhibiting here a far higher concentration in the section in proportion to the group's total households than did the Irish in a corresponding phase.

The French Canadians were followed by the Jews and the Italians who, small in numbers relative to either of the older groups, found space immediately around the Wharf Square sector of River Street, the city's old market place, where neither the Irish nor the French Canadians had settled to any great degree. The Jews selected the eastern side (I-E) of the Square, and the Italians the western (I-W). The Jewish advance, thereafter, was directly upward, whereas the Italian was first westward into Section I-W proper. Hence these two small groups found homes in the very center of River Street and Zone I. They were followed in a decade by the Armenians and the Greeks in quick succession, who would have been expected to select Section I-E as their place of residence. However, they settled on River Street in Section I-W because the Jews and the French Canadians were still well represented along the waterfront in Section I-E. Although the Italians were still on River Street in Section I-W, the Irish had succeeded in pushing into the interior of the section proper. With Section I-E relatively blocked off, the Armenians and the Greeks settled on River Street in Section I-W, on either side of the Italians.

The Poles and the Russians were the next to arrive. But the

resistance in Section I-W was still confining Italians, Armenians, and Greeks to the foot of the section, whereas in the brief interim both the Jews and the French Canadians had been able to move forward in Section I-E. The Poles and Russians, therefore, had no choice but to settle Section I-E.

Thus the differential resistance exerted by Sections I-E and I-W has largely determined the shuttling selection made by succeeding ethnic groups as between settlement in one or other of these sections. There are, therefore, both a primary continuous stratification of ethnic groups between River and Hill Streets and a secondary alternating stratification between the East and West End.

The third element in the ethnic residential pattern is the tendency of each group to remain fixed in either the East or West End, depending upon where it first settled. In other words, movement has occurred from any given area to the one next higher on the city's incline, rather than to the one next higher in the residential scale. Zone IV is an exception.

It has been established that each successively higher residential area exerts greater attraction and greater resistance, explaining both the fact of continuous ethnic advance and the fact that such advance is very slow through the extremely narrow north-south dimension of Yankee City.

The phenomenon of differential or accelerating mobility, observed among successive ethnic groups, is the fourth element in the ethnic residential pattern. Numerous factors are involved in this accelerating mobility among consecutive groups. The most important is that the pioneer ethnic group, the Irish, encountered resistance throughout its advance, especially since it was the vanguard in areas hitherto not entered by ethnics. However, while resistance stiffens in the path of the first ethnic column, in the "rear" it tends to collapse. Property values tend to decline, but the relative position of the area in the residential hierarchy does not change. Those residents of the area who can do so move to another area as yet unavailable to ethnics, thereby opening new places for ethnics. And those who are unable to leave give up active resistance and become reconciled. An

illustration of such resignation was given by a native living in
Section II-E: "Some Jews have gotten in here, and they don't
belong. But they have money and can't be kept out." As the
ethnics push farther ahead, they leave vacancies immediately
behind them. Thus the second group to arrive in the city remains on River Street only a relatively short time before it can
move into these vacancies left by the vanguard group. In the
wake of one ethnic group's advance, the area of exodus is left
open for the following group.

The second factor in differential ethnic mobility is related to
the size of the group in terms of household units. The smaller
the number of such units in an ethnic group, the less resistance
it encounters and the greater is its possible mobility. The reaction of a society to a social deviant such as the "foreigner" and
the "alien" is generally sharp, but the intensity of the reaction
is in direct proportion to the number of such deviants who in-
vade the society. For example, in their amorphous phase, the
French Canadians, consisting of about a dozen families, settled
as freely in Zone II as in Zone I, at a time when the Irish, num-
bering hundreds of households, were fighting every step of their
way into Zone II. It is obvious that with a relatively fixed supply
of housing facilities, a group of a thousand households will succeed in entering a new area in far smaller proportions than will
a group of a hundred household units. The fact that the French
Canadians since 1903 have never exceeded one-third the size of
the Irish group in family numbers has contributed without question to their greater rapidity of residential mobility as compared
with the Irish. Similarly, the more rapid advance of the Jews in
comparison with the French Canadians may be attributed in
part at least to the fact that their household numbers have consistently been about one-fourth those of the latter group. An
added factor in this case is that the urban background of the
Jews, as against the rural-village background of all other ethnic
groups, has helped them to make a relatively quick adjustment
to the urban conditions of Yankee City.

Ethnic residential mobility is conditioned by both attraction
and resistance. But, whereas the force of attraction is fairly con-

stant as a result of the unusually clear-cut configuration of Yankee City's residential system, the force of resistance varies with
the order of the ethnic group's residential antecedents. Whatever the variation in resistance and consequently in the rate of
mobility, the response and orientation of the ethnics to the attractions of Yankee City have been unvarying. The push of the
ethnics toward Hill Street, through their entire ninety years in
the city, has never ceased.

Pattern of Ethnic Internal Residential Relations

There are four elements in the pattern of ethnic internal residential relations:

1. From an original amorphous scatter, as the group grows
in numbers within Zone I, families increasingly congregate in
residential formations.

2. With entrance into Zone II, large residential coagulations
dissolve, but in some cases much smaller nuclei are re-formed.

3. There is a definite relation between the rate of a group's
mobility and the duration of its residential formations.

4. Developments in an ethnic group's community system are
related to changes in its residential formations.

Except for the Irish and the Armenians, families in an ethnic
group in its earliest years and while it was small in numbers did
not live near to one another in a nucleus of residences. However, with increasing numbers residences of an ethnic group
congregated in progressively larger formations, expanding from
small nuclei to large nuclei, minor clusters, and finally major
clusters.

The increase in the group's population not only strengthens
the pressures exerted against its mobility but also brings into
play the internal centripetal forces which draw the group together in a community in successively larger residential formations. Mobility through Zone I is carried out largely by families
gathered in these residential formations moving en masse. As
the ethnic wedge approaches the Zone II line, the resistance increases to the point where the group can no longer proceed as a
unit; individual families break off from the formation and push

into whatever openings can be found in the higher zone. Hence there are no clusters and few nuclei formed by the ethnic groups ine Zone II. Such nuclei generally appear late and only when, as in Section II-W and in the case of the Jews on Apple Street, small groups of natives protestingly move out in a body.

As crossing into Zone II proceeds, the residential formations in Zone I are depleted and contract successively in size and density from major clusters to minor clusters, large nuclei, small nuclei, and finally to a condition of dispersion.

We may conclude, therefore, that an ethnic group maintains important residential relations among its member families only so long as it remains in Zone I. Thus there is a correlation between the rate of a group's mobility and the duration of its own residential cohesion. The more rapid the advance, the shorter lived are the group's residential formations in Zone I. Up to a point, resistance tends to induce consolidation in a group's residential formations, as was observed in the greater persistence of Irish nuclei and clusters in Section I-W, as compared with those in Section I-E. But once transit is made into Zone II, the group must disperse its residences or cease its movement forward. Mobility, therefore, is the single factor in the dissolution of an ethnic group's residential base.

The three oldest of the ethnic groups have no residential base. The Irish and the Jews, their former residential coherence having disappeared, are no longer identified with a certain area but are scattered through the entire city. The French Canadians are identified with a strip in the city's East End at the center of which is their church, but with the exception of several nuclei little residential juxtaposition remains among their households. These three groups in their internal residential relations are in disintegrative stages.

The other five groups, however, in 1933 appear to be in a phase of consolidation since all are in process of expanding their large nuclei and clusters. That each of these groups has a residential base is manifest in the fact that certain parts of Zone I are identified by natives and ethnics alike as the "center" or "section" of one or other of the five groups.

The three major residential stages of an ethnic group are correlated with its own community organization. In the first and amorphous stage there is no community organization. With residential consolidation of the family structures appear ethnic stores and informal associations such as the Greek coffee shop, then formal church and school structures, and finally the first men's association. In the disintegrating phases new association structures are formed to maintain the community system in spite of the loss of the group's residential base. Therefore, there is a relation between the rate of residential mobility of an ethnic group, the degree and duration of cohesiveness of its residential relations, and the structural crystallizations of its community organization.

With the spread upward of more recent ethnics, there has been an increasing degree of residential "mixing" of groups. A Greek informant's remark is typical: "I have as neighbors two Greek families, an Italian family, an Armenian family, and a French-Canadian family." A spot map for 1933 shows about one hundred cases through all four zones in which Irish and French Canadians occupy adjoining houses, thirty-five cases in which French-Canadian and Jewish families adjoin, and fifteen of Italian and Irish families. There are also scattered cases of residential juxtaposition of other ethnics in all the various combinations.

In moving out of their own residential formations, the ethnics are brought into immediate or "neighbor" relations with native and other ethnic families.

CHAPTER 13

The Ethnic Generations Climb the Occupational and Class Ladders

IN one aspect the economic system of Yankee City appears as a system of occupations and occupational classes which constitute highly important criteria for wider social classifications. The position of the eight ethnic groups in the occupational system of the city was studied as well as the economic and occupational antecedents of these groups.

Ethnic Economic Backgrounds

Ireland in 1841 had a population of 6.5 million. In 1926 it had only 2.9 million, the loss of 55 per cent due in large part to migration. Seventy-eight per cent of the emigrants were from the villages and towns and were almost exclusively farm laborers.[1] That most, if not all, of the Irish immigrants to Yankee City came from a rural-agricultural type of economy is confirmed by a septuagenarian Irish informant: "The Irish who settled here had all been farmers, that is, those who were from Counties Cork and Kerry. The only ones who were not adapted to tilling the soil were those from Waterford. They were seafaring, but weren't so many."

1. W. F. Adams, *Ireland and Irish Emigration to the New World* (New Haven, Yale University Press, 1932), p. 6. Conrad M. Arensberg, *The Irish Countryman* (New York, The Macmillan Co., 1937). C. M. Arensberg and S. T. Kimball, *Family and Community in Ireland* (Cambridge, Harvard University Press, 1940).

A French historian reports of the French Canadians: "The mass of the population was absorbed by agriculture and but few were common labourers. . . . In the rural parts trades and professions were and still are few."[2]

An American student of Italian emigration ascribes a similar background to the Italians:

> Working upon his data of 1870, Carpi classified the emigrants according to their origin in country or town. The rural he deemed to be about five-sixths of all. When statistics of occupation were first officially collected, in 1878, they indicated, just as their successors have done, that the great mass of emigrants came from the agricultural districts.[3]

Similar citations from the literature could be presented for the Greeks, but more precise figures have been made available by an occupational census of the Yankee City Greek immigrants and their fathers who remained in Greece. The occupations of these fathers were distributed as follows: agriculture, 50 per cent; handicrafts, 39; merchants, 8; and professions, 2.

A Yankee City Pole came close to our census figures when he said: "In the old country, 85 per cent live on farms." In the United States Census Report for the fiscal year 1912–13, of 142,000 Polish immigrants with professed occupations, 72 per cent were farm or "day" laborers, 20 per cent were classed as "servants," less than 1 per cent as merchants, and about 6 per cent as craftsmen.[4]

An Armenian writer,[5] from the figures of the United States Bureau of Immigration, reports the following distribution of

2. J. C. Bracq, *The Evolution of French Canada* (New York, The Macmillan Co., 1924), p. 243.
3. R. Foerster, *Italian Emigration of Our Times* (Cambridge, Harvard University Press, 1932), pp. 39-40.
4. Quoted by J. Korski Grove in "The Polish Group in the United States," *Annals of the American Academy of Political and Social Science,* 93 (1921), 154-155.
5. M. V. Malcom, *The Armenians in America* (Boston, Pilgrim Press, 1918), p. 81.

adult male Armenians who entered the United States from
1899 to 1917: farm laborers, 53.5 per cent; handicrafts, 31.9;
domestics, 7.9; merchants, 3.7; professions, 1.8; and miscellaneous, 1.0.

The Jews are the only ethnic group to deviate from this predominantly agricultural-handicraft type of economy. They have
been commonly accepted as traders par excellence, but the figures of the first Russian census of 1897 show that only about
one-third of the Russian Jews gainfully employed were actually
tradesmen.[6] Another third fell under the official classification
of "manufacturing and mechanical pursuits." These artisans
were for the most part independent manual workers who carried
on their handicrafts in their own homes. They included tailors,
cobblers, carpenters, blacksmiths, etc. A fourth of the Jewish
employed were divided among the unskilled forms of labor,
such as domestics, carters, and drayers. About 5 per cent were
classified under "professional service," which included teachers
of Hebrew, doctors, and lawyers. The Jews, therefore, are derived from a town trade-crafts economy, rather than from a
village-agrarian economy. Important consequences of this fact
appear in the marked deviation of their economic behavior in
Yankee City.

The Jews excepted, then, the ethnics have their source in a
simple economic system which is predominantly agricultural,
organized around the productive and self-sufficient family unit,
and marked by only a slight specialization of occupations and
relatively little circulation of labor, money, and goods. This is
in sharp contrast to the highly geared economic system of Yankee City, with its narrowly specialized economic structures and
occupations, lack of family self-sufficiency, complex circulation
of values, and relatively impersonal, contractual types of exchange relations.

Another important aspect of the economic background of the
ethnics is that in the complex of factors which contributed to the

6. I. Rubinow, *The Economic Conditions of the Jews in Russia,* Bul-
letin, Bureau of Labor, Department of Commerce (Washington, Government Printing Office, 1908).

mass emigrations of the nineteenth century, the economic factor was predominant in all cases except that of the Armenians. An Irish observer visiting the United States after the Civil War writes: "The mass came because they had no option but to come, because hunger and want were at their heels, and flight was their only chance of safety."[7]

With the Irish the economic factors compelling them to leave Ireland outweighed the attraction of American economic forces. With the Jews and the Armenians the expulsive forces were even more important, the economic being aggravated by the violent antagonisms to these groups on the part of the Russian and Turkish societies. For the other ethnic groups there was a more even balance between the economic forces of expulsion in the homeland and the economic forces of attraction exerted by the United States. Had not the American economic system offered its prizes, they would not have come. On the other hand, had not serious economic dislocations occurred in their own societies they probably could not have been easily lured away from home. This has been succinctly summarized by a Greek informant: "The majority of the Greek men here came as a result of the poverty of the land in Greece, in search of the wealth they thought they would find easily in America." Poverty in Greece and the expectation of wealth in America were the related factors which induced migration.

How powerful the economic forces have been is suggested by Foerster with respect to the Italians:

> . . . there is in all agricultural folk, or at least in those that possess even a bit of land, so great an inertia, such an identification of the whole content of existence with home and habitat, that the decision to flee can only come slowly: and with the mass it has been as with the individual. That is why, as late as half a century ago, men were led . . . to regard the Italians as a people not given to emigrate—a

7. J. F. Maguire, *The Irish in America* (London, Longmans, Green & Co., 1868), p. 4.

people as attached to the soil, some one has said, as an oyster to its rock.[8]

These economic forces, apparent in the motives for migration, have had a profound effect on the relations of the ethnics to the American economic system as they have been observed in Yankee City.

The Occupational System as a Hierarchy

In the Yankee City economy, characterized by a highly developed division of labor, each specialized type of "productive" function, carried out by a defined set of techniques, is designated as an "occupation." Each occupation is ascribed a status value relative to all other occupations, according to criteria of the importance of its function to the operations of the economic and social systems. Among such criteria are the following:

1. Range of relational controls in an economic structure, e.g., in a large corporation, foremen are "higher" than the machine operators, factory managers are "higher" than foremen, corporation executives are "higher" than factory managers, etc.

2. Degree of freedom in applying occupational techniques, e.g., the custom tailor producing made-to-order suits in a shop has higher status than has the machine operating tailor in a factory producing ready-to-wear suits.

3. Skill, training, and special knowledge required to execute the occupational techniques, e.g., the surgeon tends to have a status higher than the general medical practitioner, the physician has a status higher than the dentist, the dentist tends to have a status higher than the chiropodist, etc.

4. Relative economic value of the occupation's product or function, e.g., the designer of machines is above the machinist who builds them, and the latter is higher than the operator.

These criteria, among others, in combination determine the relative status values of the occupations in an economic system. The values are translated, often incompletely, in the variable money rewards attached to the different occupations.

It must be clear, therefore, that the occupational system in a

8. Op. cit., p. 416.

Hierarchy

complex economy appears as a graded series of positions, resembling in pattern a hierarchical organization. For purposes of tracing the occupational evolution of the eight ethnic groups, we shall arrange the occupations appearing in the Yankee City economic system into three broad, widely recognized, hierarchical categories and six classes, according to types of techniques, in the following ascending order[9]:

1. Manual techniques:
   a. Unskilled labor—involving simple, loosely organized techniques with few, if any, tools.
   b. Skilled-factory operations—involving highly specialized productive techniques in relation to complex machines and a factory organization.
   c. Skilled-craft operations—involving less specialized and wider range of techniques, with or without relations to machines, set within a relatively simple "shop" type of economic structure, e.g., tailoring and barbering.
2. Exchange-control techniques, i.e., the "white-collar" occupations:
   a. Management-aid operations—involving techniques facilitating management operations, e.g., foremen, supervisors, secretaries, bookkeepers, salesmen, clerks, etc.
   b. Management operations—involving techniques of administering and controlling market and factory structures.
3. Professional techniques—involving advanced knowledge directed toward highly important group functions, e.g., crisis stabilization—the law, medicine, social work, the priesthood; technological or symbolic creation—engi-

9. The category of professional occupations can be divided, of course, into subsidiary classes; since the number of individuals found in the professions in Yankee City is comparatively small, this division was not made. Depending upon the context, the professional occupations will be treated as comparable with either the other two occupational categories or the occupational classes.

neers, scientists, and artists; socialization—teachers; etc.

The correlations of these occupational strata with the six levels of the Yankee City social-class system are broad and general rather than narrow and specific. With only one exception, no occupational class in Yankee City is identified exclusively with any one social class. Rather, in describing the social-class aspects of the occupational hierarchy, it is necessary to speak in terms of the range of social classes covered by each of the six occupational levels, as in the following:

1-a. Unskilled-labor occupations—almost complete identification with the lower-lower class. (The exception cited.)

1-b. Skilled-factory occupations—range from the lower-lower through the lower-middle class, although most strongly represented in the upper-lower class.

1-c. Skilled-craft occupations—range and principal class identification are the same as for 1-b, with a greater secondary representation in the lower-middle class.

2-a. Management-aid occupations—range from upper-lower through the upper-middle class, although falling predominantly in the lower-middle class.

2-b. Management-operation occupations—range from the upper-lower through the upper-upper class, but primary identification with the lower-middle and upper-middle classes.

3. Professional occupations—range from the lower-middle class through the upper-upper class, but predominant representation in the upper-middle class.

Upward from the bottom occupational stratum the social-class range tends to widen. Relative position in the occupational hierarchy is but one among a number of elements which in combination define the individual's place in the social hierarchy. The Yankee City data offer no support for the hypothesis of simple economic determinism of social class.

The Occupational Status Index

Before an account was undertaken of the distribution or "scatter" of each ethnic group among the six designated levels of the occupational hierarchy,[10] the average occupational status of each group was worked out in the form of a convenient index number comparable to the residential status index applied in the previous chapter. The occupational status index here used is computed first by assigning each occupational class a differential numerical value in terms of its distance in class levels from the value arbitrarily assigned to the class lowest in the occupational system. The weights allocated are as follows[11]:

Occupational Class	Weight
1-a. (Unskilled labor)	1
1-b. (Skilled factory)	2
1-c. (Skilled craft)	2.5
2-a. (Management-aid)	3
2-b. (Management)	4
3. (Professions)	6

For a given group in a given year, the absolute number in each of these classes is multiplied by the assigned value of the class, and the summation of these products is then divided by the total employed population of the group. This quotient is a number between one and six, representing the relative position of the group in terms of its average advance from the base occupational level.

Comparing the indices of each ethnic group through the decades indicates the trend of its mobility in the occupational hierarchy, and these trends among the various ethnic groups may then be compared. Table 6 presents the occupational indices of all Yankee City ethnic groups in the period from 1850 through 1933.

The Irish in 1850 have an occupational index of 1.62, which means that for every hundred of employed population an aggregate of sixty-two steps above the lowest occupational level has

10. Distribution of ethnic groups in the occupations, through time, is treated comprehensively in Leo Srole's doctoral dissertation.
11. In the above values, Class 1-c (the skilled-craft occupations) is judged to be insufficiently higher than Class 1-b (the skilled-factory occupations), at least in Yankee City, to warrant being weighted a full added unit. Likewise, Class 3 (the professionals) is felt to involve a considerably longer step from Class 2-b than does 2-b, for example, from 2-a, and, accordingly, has been assigned a value of 6.

Table 6. *Occupational Status Indices of Eight Ethnic Groups by Decades*

	1850	1864	1873	1883	1893	1903	1913	1923	1933
Irish	.62	1.76	1.74	1.76	1.84	1.94	2.14	2.31	2.52
Fr. Canadians					1.95	2.10	2.14	2.23	2.24
Jews							3.10	3.22	3.32
Italians							2.32	2.29	2.28
Armenians							2.46	2.51	2.56
Greeks								2.53	2.34
Poles								1.88	1.97
Russians									1.95
Total ethnics									2.42
Total natives									2.56

been taken. An alternative statement is that the Irish, as a group, have a status in the hierarchy about three-fifths above that equivalent to exclusive identification with Class 1-a, and about two-fifths below that equivalent to exclusive identification with Class 1-b.

By 1864 the Irish index is 1.76, indicating that in the interim the Irish have advanced an average of fourteen occupational steps for every hundred of their employed, or that about one individual in every seven employed, on the average has moved one level upward in the occupational hierarchy. Between 1864 and 1883, there is almost no change whatever in the indices, and between 1883 and 1903 the Irish index is increased by only .18. The period 1864–1903, therefore, is one of relative stability in Irish occupational mobility, paralleling the stability of the Irish in the residential system between 1873 and 1903.

In the two decades after 1913, the Irish index grows by about .20 each decade. These are the three phases in the occupational development of the Irish: (1) 1850–64—mobility moderate; (2) 1864–1903—mobility slight; and (3) 1903–33—mobility rapid.

The native group of Yankee City in 1933 has an occupational index of 2.55. Hence the Irish, with an index of 2.52 in that year, have reached a group occupational status almost identical with that of the city's indigenous population.

The French Canadians appear first in 1893 with an index of 1.95, an occupational status almost equivalent to having their entire employed population in the skilled-factory class (1-b). Between 1893 and 1933 the French-Canadian index increases a total of .29 steps or slightly more than the total increment to the index of the Irish in their first four decades. Although the French Canadians start their Yankee City careers at a much higher point in the occupational scale than do the Irish, their rate of mobility is no greater than that of the Irish.

The Jews, first significantly measurable in 1913, appear with an index of 3.10 in that year, indicating an occupational status equivalent to exclusive identification with the lower (2-a) of the two classes in the exchange-control occupational category. In the two decades following, the Jewish index increases .12 and .10, or a total of .22, which is exactly the increment to the index of the Irish between 1850 and 1893. Therefore, in their first decade year the Jews reach a much higher occupational status than do either the Irish or the French Canadians and are more mobile occupationally, on the average, than are the latter groups. In the period 1913–33, however, the Irish are very nearly twice as mobile as are the Jews. But it should be added that in the last decade, 1923–33, about one-third of the mature members of the younger generation (F^1) Jews have left Yankee City for the greater occupational opportunities of the larger metropolitan centers. Were these to be taken into consideration, which we cannot do legitimately since we are concerned here with group status within the Yankee City occupational hierarchy, the Jewish index for 1933 would probably be above 3.75. As it is, with a 1933 index of 3.32, the Jews have a far higher occupational status index than any other ethnic group, and one considerably higher than that of the Yankee City natives themselves.

Although a handful of Italians were in Yankee City as early as the nineties, the number of their employed was not large enough until 1923 to be meaningful. With an index of 2.32 in the latter year, the Italians as a group are thirty-two out of a possible hundred steps beyond the status associated with the skilled-factory occupational class (1-b). After reaching this status, the Italians exhibit no further occupational mobility, although, as we shall see below, there are actually important occupational shifts among the Italians in the period. In terms of total group status, however, these tend to cancel each other.

The Armenian employed were likewise not measurable until 1913. Their occupational index for that year is 2.46, a group status equivalent to exclusive concentration in the occupational class highest (1-c) in the manual-techniques category. In the two decades following, the Armenian index grows only .10, matching the index accessions in the first twenty years of the Irish development. The Armenian occupational index in 1933 is almost exactly that of the natives (2.55) in the same year.

The Greeks were slightly later than the Armenians in their first Yankee City settlement, but their employed population was not sufficiently extensive for significant analysis until 1923, when they present an index of 2.53—the highest in that year of any group except the Jews. Then between 1923 and 1933 the Greek index falls sharply to 2.34, in the only instance of a marked downward trend among the ethnics. We shall see below that this recession was effected by a concerted movement into the Yankee City factories (1-b), while all higher classes remain very nearly constant in number.

Up to this point each consecutive group reviewed, with the exception of the Jews, exhibits a higher occupational index in its first decade year than that of the group immediately preceding it in chronological appearance in Yankee City, indicating that the occupational hierarchy had become increasingly receptive to the entrance of new ethnics.

The Poles appear to be an exception to this trend since in their first decade year, 1923, they have an occupational index of 1.88, the lowest initial index for any group except the Irish. The elements involved will be considered presently. In 1933 the Polish index rises to 1.97, approximately an occupational status equivalent to exclusive concentration in the skilled-factory class (1-b).

The Russians cannot be treated significantly until 1933 when they present an occupational index almost exactly that of the Poles in 1933, although somewhat higher than that of the latter in 1923.

By 1933 the eight ethnic groups are arranged along the Yankee City occupational scale, by index number, in the following ascending order: Russians, 1.95; Poles, 1.97; French Canadians, 2.24; Italians, 2.28; Greeks, 2.34; Irish, 2.52; Armenians, 2.56; and Jews, 3.32. The index for total ethnics is 2.42; for total natives, 2.56.

The occupational status index applied above is nothing more than a device for stating in a convenient form the *average* rating of the occupational status of a group in terms of its aggregate advance from the base of the lowest occupational class. But, as in the case of all statements of central tendency, it is necessary to indicate the degree of scatter. This will be undertaken in the simple form of an account of the distributions of each ethnic group, per one hundred of its employed population, among the three major categories and the six classes of the Yankee City occupational hierarchy.

Occupational Distribution of Ethnics

The occupational history of the ethnic groups in Yankee City follows a course which is very similar to their residential history. The workers of the newly arrived groups started at the very bottom of the occupational hierarchy and, through the generations, climbed out of it and moved up to jobs with higher pay and increased prestige. Each new ethnic group tended to repeat the occupational history of the preceding ones. By 1933 most of the ethnic groups had attained positions in the industrial life of the community which approximated that of the original native group.

Although the ethnics did not have an industrial background or the skilled-factory techniques, they made the most of the openings presented by the Yankee City economic system and adapted themselves to the special occupational demands. The extent of the ethnic adaptation to industrial conditions of work may be judged by their reaction to a situation of industrial displacement. With the exception of the Jews and the Armenians (who directly upon arrival were absorbed by the shoe factories) all ethnic groups were first drawn into the textile mills. After the local textile industry collapsed, the ethnics made a successful adjustment by widening their industrial representation, although moving predominantly into the shoe factories.

Ethnic mobility, apparent from both decade and generation materials, has been continuous and has effected the diffusion of the ethnics as a totality through the six levels of the occupational hierarchy. In 1933 the distribution of the ethnics closely approximates that of the natives themselves, the difference between natives and ethnics in each occupational stratum not exceeding 14.2 per cent except in the professional occupations, in which the natives outnumber the ethnics two to one. Given that the ethnics started their Yankee City course with heavy concentration in the three occupational classes lowest in the hierarchy, we may conclude that to reach a distribution among all levels approximating that of the natives, the ethnics must have exercised occupational mobility to a degree at least as great as have the natives themselves.

The point was made earlier that the ethnic infiltration of all levels of the local economic system is directly connected with two important developments: industrialization in the 1830's, which drew middle-class natives into the factories, lower-class natives into the occupations abandoned by the middle-class natives, and Irish into the unskilled-labor occupations abandoned by the lower-class natives; and progressive emigration of natives from the factories and the city itself, after the 1880's, which opened the factories to increasing numbers of ethnics.

If we were to accept the thesis often held in the extensive literature on American immigration, we would have to hold that the natives left the city *because* the ethnics, with their lower wage demands, have forced them out. The matter is less simple than such an interpretation implies. Our evidence shows that the early Irish did not force the natives out of the unskilled occupations. Nor did the Irish or the subsequent ethnics *displace* the natives in the factories. Rather, the situation may be described as one in which the ethnics *replaced* the natives. For example, infiltration by the Irish into the textile mills was laboriously slow—rising between 1850 and 1883 from 3 to only 7 per cent of the total Irish employed. In 1893 only 60 of the 2000 employed in the local shoe factories were Irish. At the height of development of the city's textile and shoe industries in 1903, the Irish had less than 250 of their employed number in the factories, only about 5 per cent of the total factory employed in the city. The total Irish employed numbered about 850 in that year, with 38 per cent in the unskilled-labor class. After sixty years of residence in Yankee City, the Irish had less than one in three of their employed number in the factories.

The attractions presented in the Yankee City occupational hierarchy have worked to induce ethnic mobility, but native control of the hierarchy has served to resist and to retard the rate of such mobility. The ethnics are well distributed today through the Yankee City occupational strata because of the departure of natives for larger economic opportunities as well as the driving aspirations of the ethnics themselves.

The attractions of the occupational hierarchy have been exerted not only through the offer of higher occupational status in itself but also through the prize attached to such higher status—expanded money income, implying the opportunity to gather further income at an accelerating rate, bringing greater economic security with acquisition of the material status symbols to aid advancement in social class.

Some ethnics, especially among the Jewish F^1 generation, have begun to leave the city for higher economic attractions in larger places. The same forces have operated here as among the natives who migrated: aspirations for higher occupational status; recognition that within the city's occupational system, given a contracting industrial economy, the opportunities for the acquisition of sufficient value symbols are limited. Not only is the city's economic system contracting, but the ethnic F generation's estimation of what they demand of it has expanded. The city is beginning to be too small for them. In a manner analogous to that of their immigrant parents, they have begun to seek "new worlds."

Social Class of the Ethnic Generations

Upon first establishing himself in Yankee City, the ethnic finds himself in the anomalous position of "belonging" to no local social class and having the identification only of "foreigner." He has brought with him little or no property; he has little familiarity, unless he is Jewish, with the type of economic system represented in Yankee City; he conforms hardly at all to the American behavioral modes—in short, the deviations in his social personality are so marked as to preclude relations with the natives except those of an impersonal economic type. Even in the religious aspect, all ethnic groups, with the exception of the Armenians, are variants from Yankee City's solid, native Protestantism.

At first settlement, therefore, the ethnic is an alien in terms of American law, his social personality, and social-class affiliation. An ethnic informant asserted that he felt himself looked upon as "some kind of a strange animal." The Irish relate, probably symbolically, that before their first pastor arrived the natives had pictured Catholic priests as having "cloven hoofs."

In a sense the ethnic is originally outside the Yankee City class system, but he has a minimum of status by reason of his positions in both the city's residential and occupational hierarchies. Later he appears in a partially differentiated subclass within the lower-lower class but is still not accorded complete equivalence of status with the natives of that class level.

When he has consolidated his position in the lowest class level, the P^1 generation ethnic does not always stay there. As we have observed, he is drawn by the attractions of the Yankee City residential and occupational hierarchies and begins his upward climb in both. Positions in both these hierarchies are highly important criteria determining status in the class system. By means of these two forms of mobility; by great emphasis on the expansion of capital; by further extension of relations, formal and informal, with the natives; and by rapidly becoming more American in outlook and conduct (more slowly in matters which touch the family and the ethnic group), a substantial proportion of the P^1 generation within about twenty years after arrival compelled inclusion in the upper-lower class. On this level, the ethnics again appear as a subclass in differentiation from the natives. Within about thirty years the more successful of the ethnics (in a comparatively small proportion from the P^1 generation) managed to enter the lower-middle class, where they are too few in number at first to be differentiated from the natives. And, after about forty years of residence in Yankee City, a mere handful of ethnics in the P^1 generation succeeded in penetrating the lower border of the upper-middle class. The P^2 and successive F generations, progressively more American in the orientation of their social personalities, continue the movement of their elders in the class hierarchy, although encountering increasing resistance and using, as we shall see, somewhat different techniques of mobility.

In documenting the ascent of each ethnic group in the Yankee City class system, we are not able to utilize decade data comparable to those used for the residential and occupational hierarchies. Old documents offer little material by which to judge the relative class stratifications of all individuals in a group—with the exception, perhaps, of those at the extreme levels of the system. We are necessarily confined, therefore, in rendering account of the class distributions of eight ethnic groups, to the exhaustive social personality data gathered during the course of the present investigation in the period centering on 1933. However, we are able to assess the time factor in the processes of social mobility by supplementing group distributions with the class distributions of each defined ethnic generation, as of 1933.

All of the ethnic groups have advanced themselves in the class system. Some of them have made very great headway; others show little change from the time of their entry. Despite their upward movement, none of them has advanced into the upper-upper (old-family) level. The Irish, the oldest group, are the only people who have entered the lower-upper class. The

French Canadians, Jews, Italians, Armenians, and Greeks have
risen to the upper-middle; and a few Poles and Russians have
climbed to the lower-middle class.

The class indices of the ethnic groups in 1933 are: Poles, 1.1;
Russians, 1.35; Greeks, 1.55; French Canadians and Italians,
1.7; Armenians, 1.9; Irish, 2.3; and Jews, 2.4. The index for
total ethnics is 1.98 and for total natives, 2.5.

Since a progressively larger proportion of individuals in each
successive native-born (F) generation are not socially mature
and therefore incapable as yet of rising in the social scale, any
comparative measure of social mobility of different generations
should be based only on those numbers eligible for class advancement. Hence the distributions presented below are in
terms of that part of each generation which is above the age of
eighteen in 1933. The F^1 generation, by definition, includes the
offspring of both the P^1 and P^2 generations. In the analysis of
generation trends, therefore, it is necessary that the class distributions of the F^1 generation be compared with the distributions
of the combined P^1 and P^2 generations. In Table 7 are presented

Table 7. *Class Distribution of Irish by Generations** 1933
(in per cent)

	LL	UL	LM	UM
P^1	27.6	62.7	8.9	0.7
P^2	12.3	60.2	22.0	5.4
P (Total)	25.7	62.4	10.4	1.3
F^1	13.2	55.7	26.1	4.8
F^2	11.5	40.7	38.3	9.4
F^3	2.3	39.2	41.9	16.6

* Some Irish F^3 members are in the lower-upper class but too few to make
a clear presentation.

proportions for the two P generations both separately and together.

Among almost all groups each successive generation (the F^1,
of course, being considered in terms of the combined P generations) has fewer of its numbers in the lower-lower class than has
the generation before it. Except for the Poles, in those groups
whose modal class is still the lower-lower (i.e., Italians, Greeks,

Russians) the P^2 has a larger representation in the upper-lower class than has the P^1 generation. Among all the other groups, that is, those in which the upper-lower class is modal, the P^2 generation has fewer of its numbers in this modal class than has the P^1. (Among the French Canadians the P^2 proportion in the upper-lower class is very slightly larger than the P^1.) In other words, among both sets of ethnic groups the P^2 generation, in upward movement, exceeds the P^1. In the former set of groups, however, the P^2 generation leads the way into the upper-lower class from the lower-lower; whereas in the latter set, constituting the groups older in the city, the P^2 generation is now leading the way out of the upper-lower class into the levels above. Among all groups, the F^1 generation tends to exhibit an upper-lower class proportion smaller than that of the combined P generations; and succeeding F generations among the Irish and the French Canadians continue this trend of movement out of the upper-lower class.

Every successive generation among all groups is found to have a progressively larger portion of its membership in both the lower-middle and upper-middle classes (the French-Canadian F^1 generation in the upper-middle class is an exception). This means that each consecutive ethnic generation pushes progressively farther out of the bottom level and into each of the successive levels above. That the class index of an ethnic group is related to the length of its settlement in the city is a manifestation of the continuous advance achieved in the hierarchy by each new generation.

By the way of summary of the above generation distributions among the class levels, we have calculated the class index for each generation in every group and have plotted them in Figure 14. As in the case of all our generation statistics, there is a wide disparity in the size of the populations, both among generations within the same group and among corresponding generations of different groups; therefore computations on such varying populations are necessarily of uneven value. Nevertheless, the indices represented in Figure 14 demonstrate that each generation within a group consistently attains a higher average class status

Fig. 14. *Scale of Social-Class Indices of All Generations in Each Ethnic Group*

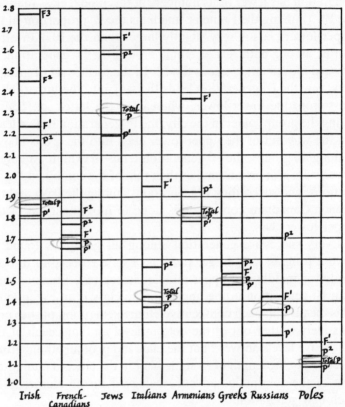

than does the generation preceding. No significant exception is the fact that in certain instances the P^2 index exceeds that of the F^1 generation, since the latter must be compared with the index of its parents—who, by our classification, are the combined P^1 and P^2 generations. And in all cases the F^1 index is uniformly greater than the "total P." What is an apparent anomaly, namely, that among four groups the P^2 index surpasses that of the F^1 generation, may be explained by the fact that among the Greeks,

Russians, and Poles the F^1 generation has emerged to maturity in too recent years to have exhibited the class advance normal for this generation among the other ethnic groups. That the P^2 index is greater than the F^1 among the French Canadians, however, cannot be attributed to this age condition, and the only source to which it can be traced is, probably, the difference in the numbers within each of the two generations (77 in the P^2 and 414 in the F^1).

The factor of differential age has a more general bearing upon the ascending social status of successive generations within a group. Progression in the class scale is a process that may begin when the individual reaches a degree of economic independence from his family through entrance into the occupational system, and may continue through his lifetime, although the greatest efforts seem to be made in the age period, roughly, of twenty-five to fifty. Since each consecutive generation in a group is twenty years younger, on the average, than the generation preceding, it is apparent that each has had that many years fewer to promote its advancement in the class scale. Hence the higher-class index of each successive generation is achieved in spite of its twenty-year handicap. By the time the age of the filial generation approximates the present age of the parental generation, the filial group would normally exhibit an even higher index than it does at present. In other words, the increasingly greater index of the generations in their order must be taken as an incomplete manifestation of status advance, for each consecutive generation in the series has progressively greater potentialities for further class mobility.

This condition is directly involved in the fact that the P^1 generation, which started on its course with an index of 1, has made a greater advance, among most groups, than has any of the following generations, each of which began its social career on the level of the parental generation. Another important factor in differential generation mobility is that the mobile individual encounters increasing resistance at each higher level in the class scale. Yet each new generation has continued its upward push, even the Irish F^3 and the Jewish P^2 and F^1 generations which now have status indices substantially higher than the status norm of the natives.

In both the total-group and the generation class indices, it is apparent that there are differences among the eight ethnic groups which are primarily related to the group's comparative age in Yankee City. The younger the group, in general, the lower is its total-population index, the smaller is its P^1 generation index, and the narrower is the margin of progressive enlargement in the indices of subsequent generations. Accompanying this general correlation, however, are certain marked secondary differences between groups which appeared in Yankee City at approximately the same time. Thus, for example, among the Jews all indices are notably higher than those of the Italians, who were their contemporaries as immigrants, and of the French Canadians, who preceded them into the city by about twenty years. The same type of differences exists between the Armenians and the Greeks, and between the Russians and the Poles, the groups in each pair being of about the same arrival date in Yankee City. Such differences where the time factor is relatively constant will be analyzed later, when an attempt is made to correlate residential, occupational, and class indices.

Social Mobility and Ethnic Solidarity

Social status depends upon the combination of interdependent status-value attributes exhibited by the individual. If he fails to advance in any one of the basic value scales, it is likely that his advance will be retarded in the others as well. For example, if the individual is kept from moving up in the occupational hierarchy, he will be kept from enhancing his money wealth and, in turn, his stock of material status symbols. Unable to provide himself with the "better" kind of residence, clothes, car, recreations, etc., he will continue to bear the external marks of his original class association. He is thereby cut off from acceptance as an equal by those on the class level just above, and he will have little chance of extending his relations in that direction. On the other hand, even if he does rise occupationally and expands his store of material status symbols, qualitatively and quantitatively, he may still be unable to improve his relations if he does not present the behavior demanded by the members of the superior class. In other words, the resistance to occupational mobility, and in a lesser degree to residential mobility, as well as the increasing difficulty in measuring up to the progressively more precise and rigorous behavioral expectations of each higher class, have an indirect, but highly important, effect in retarding and suppressing social mobility.

The superior class group cannot directly prevent an individual from lifting himself in the occupational scale, or from expanding his wealth, but it does make the effort to bar "pretenders" to its status by keeping them from extending their relations in the group. The attempt is made by means of the group's reassertion of the "social distance" which separates them from those of the class below—this through unwillingness to admit the parvenus to equality of status or to accept them in clique or "friend" relations.

An excellent example of the enforcement of class distance is found in the following remarks of an upper-middle-class native who is principal of one of the Yankee City public schools:

"We have the children of the upper class coming from Hill Street, middle class from the East End, and all the lower classes. There are quite a few children from Hill Street here. They mix with the others during school hours and at the playground but not very much after school. Occasionally a boy who came from a very good family would start going around with a Polish boy after school hours. His mother came to me and asked whether I could break it up. All I did was to keep the boys after school separately and keep them in from the playground, one or the other or both all the time, so they did not mix. Another boy was mixing with someone the family didn't want him to, so I went right up to him and said, 'Well, now do you want to mix with a good sort of a fellow?' and I tried to steer him off."

Children, of course, are not so rigid in keeping class distances as are adults. If there is a lapse, the parents are quick to separate them.

Class distance is likewise expressed by people of immediately
contiguous strata, as in the case of an upper-upper-class girl
who, when asked about the girls of a neighboring lower-upper-
class Irish family, said: "I don't know anything about them,
although they are of my own generation and went to school with
me." Similarly, one native woman of the lower-upper class had
as immediate neighbors an Irish family of the upper-middle class
and admitted never having met them. She added: "Neither I nor
my mother have ever called on them. I don't know quite why we
haven't, but we never have." Explicit is the remark of one of the
upper-middle-class Jews with reference to those of the upper
classes: "Socially, we are as far apart from them as the North
and South Poles."

Class distance is generally expressed with passive concur-
rence on the part of both those of the superior and those of the
inferior classes except in cases where certain of the latter become mobile. Then the activity of the mobile individual often
stimulates those of the superior class to active resistance. Certain native associations, especially those composed of members
of the two upper classes, function formally to exclude such in-
truders. An upper-class men's association with a long history is
of such a type. An F² generation, mobile, upper-middle-class
Irishman commented on this organization: "It is too bad they
don't allow any Catholics in the Washington Club so that I
could get in. . . . But it is impossible to get in." Similarly, a
Jewish woman only recently of the upper-middle class complained of the Yankee City Women's Club, which is predominantly upper-middle class in its membership: "I once went to
a meeting, but the women were not at all cordial, so I've never
gone again."

Pressures to restrain or at least to brake the pace of social
advance take an early and specialized form when the mobile
individual begins to assume material status symbols which are
associated with a level higher than his own. For example, an
upper-middle-class native was wrought up about a prominent
lower-middle-class Jewish merchant: "When I purchased my
red Hudson car the only other car like it was owned by Mr.

Sacks. I can't stand him because in the days when cars were more rare he owned a great shiny Marmon and there was a great feeling against the Jew owning such a fine car because it was really a great car, especially as he had started as a junk dealer on Wharf Square." Here is evident a very active resentment against the Jew for acquiring a class symbol, in the form of a fine car, out of context with his class status. A strong point, also, is made of his class origins and mobility by reference to his original residence in Zone I and to his earlier occupation as a junk dealer.

A similar situation was related by the Greek priest in speaking of one of the upper-lower-class Greeks: "Varkas recently bought a second-hand Lincoln and it nearly drove him to the poorhouse. He found it cutting into his business. It was too much for him, so he consulted me about it, and on my advice he gave it up. The trouble was that it was entirely too conspicuous for Yankee City." What is meant here, apparently, is that the car was conspicuous by reason of its owner's class context, and it is significant that pressures were exerted in the direct form of a boycott of Varkas' business.

Of course, resistance notwithstanding, the ethnics have conspicuously succeeded in "getting ahead" in the Yankee City social hierarchy. Where they have advanced without appearing to "push," have slowly consolidated their new positions, and have conformed in their behavior, they have been able to overcome resistance, and have been accepted on the progressively higher-class levels. Thus, an elderly upper-middle-class native, after relating that as a boy "we looked down on the Irish," concluded with the assertion: "Then, somehow, something happened, change came along, and I guess they got *strong,* because all this seemed to disappear, and now we are sort of taking the Irish in as one of our kind."

One significant effect of ethnic mobility, apparent in complete form in the Irish group, is that the scatter of the Irish through all but the topmost level of the class hierarchy has produced a split in the group along class lines. Internally, the Irish group is now differentiated according to position in the city's class system. The growing identification with class level and the usual manifestations of extreme class distance have served to break up the Irish group's inner cohesion. The result is seen in the sharp antagonisms which exist between the Irish of the two lowest classes (lower-lower and upper-lower) and of the two higher classes (upper-middle and lower-upper). The former refer to the latter as "lace-curtain Irish," a term with reproachful connotations, and associate them with the Hill Street "codfish aristocracy." The higher-class Irish, when aroused, will apply to the Irish of the lower classes the familiar epithet, "shanty Irish." The lower-middle-class Irish seem to keep to the fence in this conflict between the two class factions in the group.

Between the Irish and the natives of the two lowest classes today, and between the Irish and natives of the three highest classes, there is a class solidarity greater than the group solidarity between the Irish of the lowest and highest classes or between the natives of the lowest and highest classes. In none of the other ethnic groups have sufficient numbers progressed into the upper-middle class to create the sharp class dichotomy which appears in the Irish group. But among those who have crossed into that stratum from the lower-middle class there is evident in most cases a weakening of the individual's relations with his group's community system.

Comparison of Mobility by Ethnic Groups among Hierarchies

Graphically, all groups except native appear to describe a status line approximating the shape of an "L," either in the normal or inverted position. Specifically, two facts appear: (1) All groups, with two exceptions, show an occupational index higher than the residential—the deviation being relatively small for the Armenians, Greeks, and Italians, and very large for the Jews, Poles, and Russians. The two exceptions are the French Canadians, with whom the two indices are identical, and the Irish, whose residential index is somewhat the higher of the two. (2) All groups, except the Russian, have a class index lower than either of the other two indices—the total deviation being very large for all groups except the Irish. However, among the

Russians the class index is slightly higher and among the Jews and Poles slightly lower than the residential index; but for all three of these groups the former is still far below the occupational index.

Do these facts mean that in general ethnic mobility is more rapid in the residential than in the class hierarchy, and in the occupational than in the residential hierarchy? There is a sequential pattern among the ethnic movements in the three hierarchies which precludes quite so simple a conclusion. Two further facts may be recalled: (1) All ethnic groups (except the Irish), in their first important decade year, achieve higher positions in the occupational than in the residential hierarchy. (2) While mobility through the subsequent decades proceeds in the occupational hierarchy at a more-or-less uniform rate for most groups, in the residential hierarchy it develops at an accelerating rate.

While an ethnic group generally begins with the residential status lower than the occupational, acceleration of mobility in the former in time brings the two indices close together. Among the two newest groups in Yankee City, i.e., the Russian and the Polish, residential mobility has not had time to acquire sufficient momentum to cut down the considerable gap between the residential and the occupational indices. With the next older groups —the Italian, Armenian, and Greek—residential status has advanced until the index is little below the occupational index. With the French Canadians the two indices have reached a point of coincidence. And with the oldest group of all, the Irish, the residential index actually exceeds the occupational. The Jews are exceptional in that they are one of the oldest ethnic groups and yet show a deviation between their occupational and residential indices as wide as those of the two youngest groups. The special factor present in this case is that the Jewish group entered at such a high occupational position and moved so rapidly in the hierarchy that its residential mobility, rapid as it has been, could only narrow the gap by 1933. With the exception of the Jews, therefore, if the ethnic groups are seen in the order of their age in Yankee City, the trend is one in which the occupational and residential indices progressively approach each other.

It is to be expected, of course, that the far more severe and complex standards and demands which govern status in the class hierarchy would retard mobility as compared with the other two hierarchies. The class index also lags far behind the others because all groups enter the hierarchy at the very lowest possible point. However, it tends to approach the two other indices. For example, the smallest deviation (7 per cent) between class and occupational indices is with the oldest group, the Irish; the next (20 per cent) with the French Canadians; and the largest deviation (the Jews excepted) is among two of the youngest groups, the Greeks (34 per cent) and the Poles (33 per cent).

The definite trend toward correspondence of an ethnic group's statuses among the three hierarchies, after the model of the native group, appears to be in three stages. At arrival, a group's occupational status is higher than its residential status; and the latter, in turn, is far higher than its class status. Advances are made in all hierarchies, but most rapidly in the residential and most slowly in class. The P generation, after thirty years in Yankee City, reaches equivalence in the occupational and residential hierarchies, with class status still lagging. The F^1 generation advances (over the P generation) farthest in the class hierarchy, but not sfficiently far to close the gap between the class index and the other two indices. In the case of the Irish, the gap is not closed until the F^3 generation, but it appears that the newer groups, to judge from the Armenians and the Italians, may achieve equivalence in all three statuses by the F^2 generation.

Among successive generations there are different rates of mobility in the three hierarchies—differences which carry the ethnic group in a single direction, from a condition of great disparity among the three statuses toward an ultimate condition of identity among the statuses. The latter is one more native norm which the ethnic group is progressively approaching; and it may therefore be considered as another aspect of the acculturation and assimilation of the ethnic groups within the Yankee City society.

The generalization that the degree of ethnic approximation to the status of the natives is correlated with the length of a group's settlement in Yankee City has been documented in this and preceding discussions. However, an arrangement of the group lines on a vertical scale would by no means be in the exact order of group age in the city. For example, certain pairs of groups arrived in Yankee City during the same decade, yet have status lines at varying distances from each other. The Jews and Italians compose such a pair, the combined status indices of the former being an aggregate 83 per cent greater than those of the latter. The Armenians and the Greeks form another contemporaneous pair; the total indices of the Armenians are an aggregate 21 per cent greater than the total for the Greeks. Three-fourths of this deviation is accounted for by the difference in the indices of the two groups. The difference between the last pair of contemporary groups, the Russian and the Polish, is almost wholly in their class indices. In other words, for each of these pairs of groups the time factor is more or less constant, yet there are significant status differences between the members of each pair.

Second, the status lines of the two oldest ethnic groups, the Irish and the French Canadians, are not as high as might be expected from their age in the city and the status positions of certain younger groups. All three status indices of the French Canadians are almost identical with those of the Italians and much below those of the Armenians. In one index the Irish are below the Armenians and in two below the Jews. It is apparent, then, that although there is a broad correlation between the position of a group's status line and the length of its settlement in Yankee City, this correlation is by no means perfect.

One of the important conditions affecting the mobility rates of the three pairs of contemporary groups, especially that of the P generations in the class hierarchy, is the type of motivation which induced migration to the United States. The Jews, Armenians, and Russians, in act of migration, "burned their bridges

behind them." Arriving with the design of establishing themselves in this country permanently, they were anxious from the
first to strike roots to adapt themselves to the basic demands of
the American society.

On the other hand, substantial portions of the Italian (those
from South Italy and Sicily), Greek, and Polish groups migrated with the original plan to settle only temporarily. Generally, their aspiration was not to rise in status in this country
but to secure sufficient funds with which to increase their land-
holdings and therefore their economic status in the homeland.
The number of those among these three groups who have actually repatriated themselves according to this original plan is
comparatively small, but the decision to remain was reached
only after about a decade or more of residence; until the
decision was made, there was little impetus to meet any but
the minimum terms of the society. Therefore, although many P
generation members of these groups were as quick as any in
accepting better jobs, they were somewhat late in selecting better places of residence, and they were especially slow in adapt-
ing to the opportunities and demands of class ascent. The Poles
and Russians, for example, in 1933 have almost identical occupational as well as residential indices, but the class index of the
latter is 9 per cent larger.

The purchase of a house implies the acquisition of a share in
the property system and a special status, through the function
of paying taxes, in the political system of a society. It involves
driving permanent stakes and, in the case of ethnic groups, may
be interpreted as an indication of the degree to which roots have
been struck in the society. The classification of six Yankee City
ethnic groups into originally permanent migrants (1) and temporary migrants (2) is substantiated in the difference between
the two groups of each pair, as late as 1933, in the proportions
of families owning their homes and other real property:

1.	Jews	63.4%
2.	South Italians	29.0
1.	Armenians	52.7
2.	Greeks	32.4
1.	Russians	55.5
2.	Poles	32.0

In the case of the Armenians and the Jews, additional elements appear to increase mobility. Similarities between the Jewish background and the Yankee City society have been cited. The similarity in background of the Armenians lies only in a religious affinity between the Armenian Apostolic Church and the Episcopal Church, which led to affiliation between the two and more rapid acculturation of the Armenian group.

The French Canadians present a peculiar case in that all three indices of this group are relatively low as compared even with such groups as the Italians and the Greeks. The factors in this situation are multiple and interrelated in a complex manner.[12] Many French Canadians settled in Yankee City with the intention of returning ultimately to Quebec. The fact that they are only a few hundred miles from Quebec, which they can revisit easily, has unquestionably acted to slow the pace of the group's adaptation to the Yankee City social system, especially by perpetuating the traditional lines of the French-Canadian family structure, which is strongly patriarchal. The father decides which son is to inherit the farm (for the family landhold must remain intact and undivided), which is to enter the priesthood, and which are to go to the industrial towns of Quebec and New England. A boy's future occupational status is the choice of the father, and the nature of the schooling he receives determines that status by restricting more or less the range of occupational mobility. Where a boy does rise, as into the priesthood, he does so not through his own efforts alone but through the combined efforts of his family. Therefore, such mobility raises not his prestige alone, which would place him above the family, but that of the entire family unit. Individuals do not advance in prestige; families do—and this only in certain narrow and prescribed

12. The writers have had the benefit of conversations with Everett C. Hughes and Horace E. Miner, both of whom have made extensive studies in the rural and town areas of Quebec. They have either confirmed or themselves suggested, in both conversation and print, the factors incorporated in the interpretation. Cf. E. C. Hughes, "Position and Status in a Quebec Industrial Town," *American Sociological Review, 3*, No. 5 (1938), 709-17; and Horace M. Miner, *St. Denis: A French Canadian Parish* (Chicago, University of Chicago Press, 1939).

channels. Initiative for mobility is not the individual's but that of the family as personified by the father. In short, the basic motif in the pattern of the rural social organization of French Canada is the family unit, and the basic "drive" is to retain unimpaired the family's identification with its land and its customary way of life, which means its customary economic status.

It was stated above that relative to its age in Yankee City and compared with other younger groups, the Irish group's status line is not as high as might have been expected. Two special factors appear to be involved: first, the general rate of Irish status mobility has been retarded as penalty for the fact that the group was the first, among ethnic groups, in order of appearance, arriving in a period of a fixed native population and relatively limited opportunities for advance within the Yankee City social system; and second, as we have shown elsewhere, the larger the ethnic group, the smaller will be the proportion of those able to climb into progressively higher status levels. It is not possible to assert anything more than the fact that the size of the Irish population, which is almost three times as large as the French Canadian and many times as large as that of any other ethnic group, has directly reduced the mobility rates and status positions of the group in all three hierarchies. This likewise would seem to hold, although to a lesser extent of course, for the French-Canadian group in relation to the other and smaller ethnic groups.

To summarize, the degree of ethnic approximation to the statuses of the natives is correlated primarily with the length of the group's establishment in Yankee City. That is, all groups have progressively climbed toward higher positions in the three hierarchies. However, certain secondary factors have produced differences in the rates of mobility among the various groups.

Factors for retardation of status mobility:

1. Original migrational intention of temporary settlement (South Italians, Greeks, Poles).

2. Family structure with patterns of maintaining customary status and of parental determination of status (French Canadians).

3. Order of a group's appearance in the city, both because the earliest group encounters local conditions which no longer operate when later groups arrive and because, to a certain extent, the earliest group reduced resistance to and cleared the way for the advance of later groups (Irish).

4. Large group population, a condition increasing the resistance to mobility (Irish and French Canadians).

5. Proximity to the homeland, a factor for the slowing of the acculturative processes and therefore for the curbing of status advance (French Canadians).

Factors for acceleration of status mobility:

1. Similarities between the ethnic ancestral society and Yankee City in general social-organization type (Jews).

2. Similarities between the ethnic ancestral society and Yankee City in the religious aspect of culture (Armenians).

CHAPTER 14

The Future of American Ethnic and Racial Groups

Ethnic and Racial Persistence and Assimilation

To UNDERSTAND the place of the ethnic group in the American social system it is necessary to see it in the larger framework of all the subordinate groups. A survey of the several types of subordinated groups in this country reveals that, excluding the subordination of lower-class old Americans, there are three basic types which are ranked as inferior. They are (1) the ethnic group, (2) the racial group, and (3) the ethno-racial group. The ethnic group carries a divergent set of cultural traits which are evaluated by the host society as inferior. We have seen in the Yankee City study how these cultural groups are identified with being different and given an inferior rating and how they form their own social world to nurse their members through a period of transition until these members "unlearn" what they have been taught and successfully learn the new way of life necessary for full acceptance in the host society.

The racial groups are divergent biologically rather than culturally. They possess physical traits inherited from their fathers and mothers which are divergent from those of the old-American white population. These traits have been evaluated as inferior. Such physical attributes as dark skin, the epicanthic fold, or kinky hair become symbols of status and automatically consign their possessors to inferior status. The Chinese, Japanese, and Filipinos of California, the Spanish Americans and Mexicans of the American Southwest, and American Negroes suffer from such evaluations of their racial differences. The cultural traits of the ethnic group, which have become symbols of inferior status, can be and are changed in time; but the physical traits which have become symbols of inferior status are permanent. Unless the host society changes its methods of evaluation, these racial groups are doomed to a permanent inferior ranking.

From the researches done in Yankee City and on the Negro groups of the South and the North, and from the recent investigations made on the Spanish Americans and the Orientals of California, all of which are based on the body of knowledge that social scientists have collected on ethnic and racial groups, it now seems possible to present a conceptual scheme which places a subordinate group in its relative rank within our social hierarchy. It permits us to predict with some degree of success the probable degree of subordination each group will suffer, the strength of the subsystem likely to be developed by it, the kind of rank order it will be assigned, and the approximate period necessary for its assimilation into American life.

The conceptual scheme about to be described is based on the following propositions: First, the greater the difference between the host and the immigrant cultures, the greater will be the subordination, the greater the strength of the ethnic social systems, and the longer the period necessary for the assimilation of the ethnic group. On the other hand, those ethnic groups with small differences are quickly assimilated. Second, the greater the racial difference between the populations of the immigrant and the host societies the greater the subordination of the immigrant group, the greater the strength of the social subsystem, and the longer the period necessary for assimilation. Finally, when the combined cultural and biological traits are highly divergent from those of the host society the subordination of the group will be very great, their subsystem strong, the period of assimilation long, and the processes slow and usually painful. With these propositions in mind it is possible to construct a rough scale by which hypotheses may be developed about the relative ranking of each racial and cultural group in American life, the strength of its subsystem, and the period necessary for ultimate assimilation.

The people racially most like white "old Americans," the dominant people in America, are other Caucasians. Those least like them are the Mongoloid peoples, Negroes, and racially mixed, dark-skinned groups such as the peoples of India. The Caucasoid group lies at one extreme, and the Mongoloid and Negroid peoples at the other extreme of the range. To bring out the significant points about assimilation and to point up further questions on the subordination of subgroups, the Caucasoid immigrant population has been divided into those who are largely like the present old-American stock and those who are least like them. For convenience we can refer to the first as light Caucasoids and to the latter as dark Caucasoids. Those people with a mixture of Caucasoid and Mongoloid blood, in particular mixtures from Latin America, occupy the next place in the range. The mixed bloods of Mongoloid and Caucasoid stock who resemble Mediterranean Caucasoids are followed by Mongoloids and Negroes. These considerations provide us with five categories: race type I, the light Caucasoids; race type II, the dark Caucasoids; race type III, Mongoloid and Caucasoid mixtures with a Mediterranean appearance; race type IV, Mongoloids and mixed peoples with a predominantly Mongoloid appearance; and finally race type V, Negroes and all Negroid mixtures.

A similar scale can be constructed for deviation from the dominant American culture. For purposes of the present analysis, the immigrant cultures may be divided into differences of language and religion. (Other customary behavior is associated with language and religion.[1]) In the light of this study, and from

1. A finer cultural screening necessary for making sharper discriminations would divide the culture into more categories, but for general placement of the several groups, language and religion are significant; this is in part true because large bodies of customary behavior are associated with these two basic cultural phenomena. The racial scale must follow the classifications of contemporary texts of physical anthropology, but these classifications may be simplified to fit the needs of the above racial categories.

the results of others, it is clear that emphasis must be placed on religious differences. The dominant old-American religion is Protestant, and much of our customary behavior is closely integrated with a Protestant outlook on life. Our customary way of life is most like the English, and our language is but one of the several English dialects. The ethnic people most like us are English-speaking Protestants with a body of customary behavior no more deviant from our way of life than their language and religion. This cultural type is followed by Protestants who do not speak English and whose way of life is slightly more divergent from ours. The third type includes English-speaking Catholics and other non-Protestant groups. The fourth cultural type includes Catholics and other non-Protestants who do not speak English. The types least like us are the non-Christians, some of whom speak English and others who do not.

When these two scales, the cultural and the racial, are combined into a table, thirty possible categories logically result since there are six cultural types for each of five racial types. However, several of these categories do not exist in actual fact. For example, there are no English-speaking, Protestant, dark Caucasoids.

Table 8 succinctly presents the ethno-racial scale of differences between the dominant white American host society and the present ethnic and racial groups as well as the entering immigrant groups. In the left-hand column are the five racial types in the order of their similarity to the old-American white stock. In the right-hand column are the six cultural types serially arranged according to their similarity with old-American culture. The repetition of the six cultural categories for each racial type reveals that the racial evaluations made by the American host society are far more potent and lasting in the ranking of divergent peoples than those applied to cultural groups. For example, English-speaking Protestant Negroes possessing the same culture as the rest of the American group cannot be ranked as a subvariety of other English-speaking peoples; and it is obvious that they must be placed in a position inferior to all Caucasoid peoples, regardless of the cultural deviation of all the white-skinned peoples. The peoples most like dominant white Ameri-

Table 8. *Scale of Subordination and Assimilation*

Racial type	*Cultural type*
Racial Type I Light Caucasoids	Cultural Type 1 English-speaking Protestants
	Cultural Type 2 Protestants who do not speak English
	Cultural Type 3 English-speaking Catholics and other non-Protestants
	Cultural Type 4 Catholics and other non-Protestants, most of whom speak allied Indo-European languages
	Cultural Type 5 English-speaking non-Christians
	Cultural Type 6 Non-Christians who do not speak English
Racial Type II Dark Caucasoids	Cultural typing the same as for Racial Type I
Racial Type III Mongoloid and Caucasoid mixtures with Caucasoid appearance dominant (appearance of "dark" Mediterranean)	Cultural typing the same as for Racial Type I
Racial Type IV Mongoloid and Caucasoid mixtures that appear Mongoloid	Cultural typing the same as for Racial Type I
Racial Type V Negroes and all Negroid mixtures	Cultural typing the same as for Racial Type I

cans, and therefore ranked highest, are the light Caucasoids who are Protestant and speak English. Those least like them are the non-Christian Negroes.

We will now turn to the second part of our analysis, presenting a way of ranking (1) the degree of subordination and social distance, (2) the strength of the racial and ethnic subsystems, and (3) the forms of American rank. A timetable predicts the approximate period necessary for the assimilation of each racial and ethnic group. For convenience a five-point scale has been set up for each. The degrees of subordination run from "very slight" through "slight," "moderate," "great," to "very great." The criteria for rating a particular group's degree of subordination are (1) freedom of residential choice, (2) freedom to marry out of one's own group, (3) amount of occupational restriction, (4) strength of attitudes in the host society which prevent social participation in such institutions as associations and cliques, and (5) the amount of vertical mobility permitted in the host society for members of the ethnic or racial group.[2]

The presentation here is designed to give no more than a resume of the operations and present only those necessary to understand the whole schema of ethnic and social subordination and assimilation. Any one group may be slightly out of place as, for example, the Catholic French or the Hungarians, but the relative place of most of the groups is accurate. The importance of this system of analysis is that each group's place is established in a total configuration of American society as the result of applying scientific propositions about subordination and assimilation which appear to be laws governing the relations of ethno-racial groups in the larger American society.

The criteria for the strength of the cultural or racial subsystem are (1) the power of the "church" over its members and degree of divergence of the "church" from the Protestant norms; (2) the presence of separate schools and the amount of control they exercise; (3) and (4) the political as well as the economic unity of the group; and (5) the number and power of ethnic or

2. If each of these criteria is re-scaled from one to five and the results added and the sum divided by five, the quotient given provides a rough but fairly satisfactory index of the degree of subordination of each group. The light Caucasoids who are Protestant and speak English get an index of one, and the non-Christian Negroes an index of five, giving the first a rating of "very slight" and the latter "very great" subordination.

racial associations.[3] Our hypothesis is that the light Caucasoids who are English-speaking and Protestant develop the least powerful systems while the Negroes have the strongest.

Criteria for a timetable of assimilation are (1) the time taken for an entire group to disappear, (2) the proportionate number of people who drop out of a group in each generation, and (3) the amount and kind of participation permitted members of the group by the host society. The same procedure as described for the other categories produces a rough index for a group's assimilation: "very short" means that the group is assimilated in a period of not more than one generation; "short" means more than one but less than six generations; "moderate," more than six; "slow," a very long time in the future which is not yet discernible; and "very slow" means that the group will not be totally assimilated until the present American social order changes gradually or by revolution.

To test these hypotheses about subordination and predicted assimilation, let us examine Table 9, in which many of the ethnic and social groups now in America are placed appropriately in the ethno-social scale. The people listed may also be regarded as referring to populations now outside America who in the future might be migrants should our present immigration laws be modified.

Most of the peoples of the British Isles, including the North Irish but not the Catholic Irish, as well as the English-speaking Canadians and the other English-speaking peoples of the Dominions, belong to Cultural Type 1 of Racial Type I. According to our hypotheses, their subordination should be very slight, the subsystems they build very weak, and their period of assimilation usually less than a generation. In Yankee City there were numerous Canadians, and a fair representation of Scotch, English, and North Irish, but they had not formed ethnic groups and were considered as members of the total population.

3. Each of the five characteristics of the strength of a subsystem can be redivided into a five-point scale and the same procedure can be used for determining the strength of the subsystem as that described for the degree of subordination.

Table 9. *Ethnic and Racial Assimilation*

Cultural and Racial Type	Degree of Subordi- nation	Strength of Ethnic and Racial Subsystems	Time for Assimi- lation	Form of American Rank
RACIAL TYPE I—LIGHT CAUCASOID				
Cultural Type 1 English-speaking Protestants. Tests: English, Scotch, North Irish, Australians, Canadians	very slight	very weak	very short	ethnic group to class
Cultural Type 2 Protestants not speaking English. Tests: Scandinavians, Germans, Dutch, French	slight	weak	short	ethnic group to class
Cultural Type 3 English-speaking Catholics and other non-Protestants Test: South Irish	slight	moderate	short to moderate	ethnic group to class
Cultural Type 4 Catholics and other non-Protest- ants who do not speak English Tests: ("fair-skinned") French Canadians, French, Germans, Belgians	slight	moderate	short to moderate	ethnic group to class
Cultural Type 5 English-speaking non-Christians Test: English Jews	moderate	moderate	short to moderate	ethnic group to class
Cultural Type 6 Non-Christians who do not speak English Tests: ("fair-skinned") Europe- an Jews and Mohammedans from Middle East	moderate	moderate	short to moderate	ethnic group to class
RACIAL TYPE II—DARK CAUCASOIDS				
Cultural Type 1	—	—	—	—
Cultural Type 2 Test: Protestant Armenians (oth- er "dark-skinned" Protestants)	slight to moderate	weak	moderate	ethnic group to class

Table 9. *(Continued)*

Cultural and Racial Type	Degree of Subordination	Strength of Ethnic and Racial Subsystems	Time for Assimilation	Form of American Rank
RACIAL TYPE II—DARK CAUCASOIDS				
Cultural Type 3	—	—	—	—
Cultural Type 4 Tests: "dark skins" of Racial Type I, Cultural Type 4; also Sicilians, Portuguese, Near Eastern Christians	moderate	moderate to strong	moderate	ethnic group to class
Cultural Type 5	—	—	—	—
Cultural Type 6 Tests: ("dark-skinned") Jews and Mohammedans of Europe and the Near East	moderate to great	strong	slow	ethnic group to class
RACIAL TYPE III—CAUCASOID MIXTURES				
Cultural Type 1	—	—	—	—
Cultural Type 2 Tests: Small groups of Spanish Americans in the Southwest	great	strong	slow	ethno-racial to class or color caste
Cultural Type 3	—	—	—	—
Cultural Type 4 Test: Most of the mixed bloods of Latin America	great	strong	slow	ethno-racial to class or color caste
Cultural Type 5	—	—	—	—
Cultural Type 6	—	—	—	—
RACIAL TYPE IV—MONGOLOIDS				
Cultural Type 1 Tests: Most American Chinese and Japanese	great to very great	very strong	slow	racial to semi-caste

Table 9. *(Continued)*

Cultural and Racial Type	Degree of Subordi- nation	Strength of Ethnic and Racial Subsystems	Time for Assimi- lation	Form of American Rank
Cultural Type 2	—	—	—	—
Cultural Type 3	—	—	—	—
Cultural Type 4 Test: Filipinos	great to very great	very strong	very slow	racial to semi-caste
Cultural Type 5	—	—	—	—
Cultural Type 6 Tests: East Indians, Chinese, Japanese	great to very great	very strong	very slow	racial to semi-caste
RACIAL TYPE V—NEGROIDS				
Cultural Type 1 Test: Most American Negroes	very great	very strong	very slow	racial to color caste
Cultural Type 2	—	—	—	—
Cultural Type 3 Test: Some American Negroes	very great	very strong	very slow	racial to color caste
Cultural Type 4 Tests: Negroid Puerto Ricans, etc.	very great	very strong	very slow	racial to color caste
Cultural Type 5	—	—	—	—
Cultural Type 6 Tests: Bantu Negroes and West African Negroes	very great	very strong	very slow	racial to color caste

The Protestant Germans, Dutch, and Scandinavians of Cultural Type 2 and Racial Type I, according to our hypothesis, are quickly assimilated into American life. The facts in general support this theory. Some of the Scandinavians and Germans, however, have formed sects that do not conform to the general rule we have laid down and present special problems which demand added dimensions to place them accurately in a timetable of assimilation.

The non-Protestant Christian groups who do not speak English are in Cultural Type 4. The great strength of the Catholic

Church in organizing and maintaining separate ethnic groups is clearly illustrated here. The French, German, Belgian, and Dutch Protestants, it seems likely, assimilate very rapidly, develop less powerful subsystems, and are less subordinated than those of the same nationality and language who are Catholic. The Catholic Irish of Cultural Type 3 assimilate more slowly than the Protestant Irish despite the fact that in all other respects the two cannot be distinguished by most Americans. Whereas the Catholic Irish develop moderately strong subsystems and take many generations to assimilate, the Protestant Irish form very weak ones and almost immediately become assimilated.

Cultural Types 5 and 6 of Racial Type I include the light Caucasoid Jews, particularly those of Western Europe. We can best understand the place of the Jew and of the other peoples in this category if we glance down Table 7 to the same cultural types of Racial Type II (see "dark-skinned" Jews). A comparison of these categories of Jews tells us much about the place and problems of the Jew in American life. Jews and other non-Christians are likely to assimilate less easily than Christians, but the light-skinned Jew, who is not physically different and thereby not burdened with negatively evaluated racial traits as is his dark-skinned co-religionist, assimilates more rapidly than those who belong to Racial Type II. In the first case five or six generations may see most of the group disappearing; in the latter the members of the group assimilate very slowly.

This general hypothesis on assimilation was developed after the field work had been completed in Yankee City, but the evidence points to the fact that the German, English, and other less racially visible Jews disappeared into the total population more rapidly than those who were racially variant.

The Catholics and non-Protestants of Cultural Type 4 and Racial Type II include a large number of nationalities such as Italians, Greeks, and French who are also found in Cultural Type 4 of Racial Type I. The subordination of the former group is likely to be greater and their period of assimilation much longer than those of the latter despite the fact that they are often co-religionists, speak the same language, and have the same body of customary behavior. The factor of race, or rather the strong negative evaluation of it by American society, is sufficient to explain most if not all the differences in ranking of the two groups.

The power of the evaluation of the racial factor becomes even clearer when Cultural Type 4, the Catholics and other non-Protestant Christians of Racial Type III (the Mongoloid and Caucasoid mixture), are compared with those of the dark Caucasoids. These Catholics, most of them dark-skinned Latin Americans, are heavily subordinated as compared with moderate and light subordination for the same type in the other two racial categories. The prediction for their assimilation is slow, which is to say there is no predictable time when they will disappear into the total population, whereas that of their coreligionists of lighter skin is predicted to be short and moderate. We see plainly that while the Catholic Church is a powerful instrument for the conservation of the ethnic tradition, it is much less powerful than the force of American organized "prejudice" against the dark-skinned peoples. The Negroid Puerto Ricans, Cubans, and West Indians who are of the same cultural type as the lighter-skinned peoples of these islands provide final and conclusive evidence that it is the degree of racial difference from the white American norms that counts most heavily in the placement of the group and in the determination of its assimilation.

The place of the English-speaking Protestant American Negro in our life yields the most eloquent testimony for this proposition. The Negro is culturally more like the white "old American" than the English and Scotch of Cultural Type 1, yet he occupies a very subordinate position where there is little likelihood of his ultimate assimilation unless our social order changes. Although the American Negro belongs to the same cultural type as the English and the Scotch, his racial ranking is near the bottom of the rank order.

These considerations of the relative rating of the cultural and social traits of American society bring us to consideration of the last column in Table 9, the form of American ranking ultimately given each of these groups. All of the six cultural types in Racial Types I and II we predict will change from ethnic groups and become wholly a part of the American class order. The members of each group, our Yankee City evidence shows, are permitted to be upward-mobile in the general class order. But all of the six cultural types in each of the Racial Types IV and V are likely to develop into castes or semi-castes like that of the American Negro. When the racial deviation reaches the Mongoloid and Negroid extremes the cultural factors are of little importance in the ranking of a particular group, and race is all-important.

Racial Type III provides an interesting difference from the others. These ethno-racial groups are likely to divide into two parts: If and when the Spanish Americans and Mexicans lose their cultural identity, those of the more Caucasoid type will become a part of our class order and be capable of rising in our social hierarchy. The darker ones will probably become semi-caste. There is some evidence that it may be possible that this latter group will merge with the Mongoloid or Negroid groups. There is also fragmentary evidence which indicates that some of the Mongoloid groups may merge into the other dark-skinned castes.

The future of American ethnic groups seems to be limited; it is likely that they will be quickly absorbed. When this happens one of the great epochs of American history will have ended and another, that of race, will begin.

Paradoxically, the force of American equalitarianism, which attempts to make all men American and alike, and the force of our class order, which creates differences among ethnic peoples, have combined to dissolve our ethnic groups. Until now these same forces have not been successful in solving the problem of race. The Negro and other dark-skinned groups are still ranked as color castes.

How we will solve the problem of race in the future is problematical. The major areas of the earth, including the United States, are now closely interconnected into an interdependent totality. The effects of important racial and social movements in Europe, Asia, and South America are felt in the United

States; our color-caste structure is an ever-present reality in the thoughts of the leaders of China, India, and Latin America. The dark-skinned races' struggle with the dominant whites for social equality is rapidly being organized on an international basis. To calculate the future we must interpret what happens in the United States in this larger setting. Whether we try forcibly to subordinate dark-skinned people, and thereby face certain failure, or use democratic methods, and thereby increase our chances of success, may depend more upon how this decision is made in the rest of the world than upon what happens in this country.

Index